# Implementing Biometric Security

John Chirillo, CISSP and Scott Blaul, CISSP

WILEY

Wiley Publishing, Inc.

**Implementing Biometric Security**
Published by
**Wiley Publishing, Inc.**
10475 Crosspoint Boulevard
Indianapolis, IN 46256
www.wiley.com

Library of Congress Control Number: 2003104778

ISBN: 0-7645-2502-6

Manufactured in the United States of America.

10 9 8 7 6 5 4 3 2 1

1B/SS/QU/QT/IN

# Implementing Biometric Security

# About the Authors

**John Chirillo** began his computer career at the age of 12, when he spent a year teaching himself the basics of computers and then wrote several software pieces that were published. He went on to become certified in numerous programming languages, including QuickBasic, VB, C++, Pascal, Assembler, and Java. John later developed the PC Optimization Kit, which increased speeds up to 200 percent of standard Intel 486 chips. After running two businesses, Software Now and Geniusware, John became a consultant (specializing in security and analysis) to prestigious companies where he performed security analyses, sniffer analyses, LAN/WAN design, implementation, and troubleshooting. During this period, John acquired numerous internetworking certifications, including Cisco's CCNA, CCDA, CCNP, Intel Certified Solutions Consultant, Compaq ASE Enterprise Storage, UNIX, CISSP, and CCIE (pending). He is currently a Senior Internetworking Engineer at a technology management company. John is the author of several security and networking books, including the *Hack Attacks* series from John Wiley & Sons.

**Scott Blaul** has been in the electronics industry since 1981 when he started as an electronics repair technician in the United States Marine Corps. As an instructor in the USMC, Scott taught electronics for five years. After leaving the Marines in 1989, Scott went to work for Inacomp Computer Corporation, which was ultimately acquired by ValCom. During his time at the company, Scott has worked in and been in charge of many facets of the computer service industry including field services (desktop-related technology and services) and professional services (server, infrastructure, storage, and security-related services). His involvement has included support for many Fortune 1000 companies. During these 14 years, Scott has acquired internetworking experience and has obtained several certifications, including CNE, ASE, CCNA, CCNP, CISSP, and CCIE (pending).

# Credits

**EXECUTIVE EDITOR**
Carol Long

**ACQUISITIONS EDITOR**
Katie Feltman

**PROJECT EDITOR**
Marcia Ellett

**COPY EDITOR**
Richard H. Adin

**TECHNICAL EDITOR**
Tom Brays

**EDITORIAL MANAGER**
Mary Beth Wakefield

**VICE PRESIDENT AND
EXECUTIVE GROUP PUBLISHER**
Richard Swadley

**VICE PRESIDENT AND EXECUTIVE PUBLISHER**
Bob Ipsen

**VICE PRESIDENT AND PUBLISHER**
Joseph B. Wikert

**EXECUTIVE EDITORIAL DIRECTOR**
Mary Bednarek

**PROJECT COORDINATOR**
Bill Ramsey

**SUPERVISOR OF GRAPHICS
AND DESIGN**
Shelley Lea

**GRAPHICS AND PRODUCTION SPECIALISTS**
Beth Brooks
LeAndra Johnson

**PROOFREADING**
D&G Ltd.

**INDEXING**
Virginia Bess Monroe
Julie Bess

**SPECIAL HELP**
William A. Barton
Gabrielle Chosney

# Preface

As unfortunate as it may be, the events of September 11, 2001, forever changed our lives. Among these changes is much heightened security at many of our high-profile landmarks, airports, bus and train stations, and among the general workplace. Some of these changes become readily apparent when you take the following into consideration:

✓ If you've visited the Statue of Liberty, you've likely been checked against a database of known terrorists.

✓ Many airports are scanning faces and comparing the results.

✓ Many corporate buildings are ensuring that they capture video of everyone who enters and leaves the building.

✓ More employees have been issued token devices than in the past.

✓ More companies are implementing hand scans, keycard, and face-recognition technologies together to create a more comprehensive identification process.

✓ Security has been stepped up to the extent that in many offices every visitor must produce, at minimum, a photo ID.

Although these security methods each have strengths and weaknesses, the fact remains that security overall is being strengthened daily. It's only a matter of time before biometric solutions become much more common in the workplace; evidence of this is beginning to surface as biometric solution providers rev their engines and fine-tune their offerings.

Many publications discuss biometric technologies and how they've been used for physical access, law enforcement, crime forensics, and data networks. As biometrics become more viable for data networks, however, a gap emerges in regard to how biometric solutions can essentially be used for data security.

The primary goal of *Implementing Biometric Solutions* is to provide you with the basics, as well as real-world uses for biometric technologies. To accomplish this, the book describes the various biometric technologies to create a baseline from which to build a solution. Throughout the chapters, this book helps create a mental illustration of different methodologies, provides custom code for proprietary development, and demonstrates product deployment. This combination, in conjunction with a proven method of selecting product solutions via Biometric Selection Criteria, provides the reader with the information and tools necessary to make sound biometric decisions.

Finally, this book provides a solid building block from which a biometric selection and implementation strategy can be designed, allowing the reader to create custom selection criteria, design a solution, and prepare a plan to make the migration to data network biometric security practical.

# Who Should Read This Book

There are many facets to consider when determining if/when biometric security is the right choice for a given environment. This book covers the various biometric technologies, and the strengths and weaknesses of each are outlined. Real-world examples are used throughout to show how given biometric technologies can be used on data networks. Therefore, this book is for anyone interested in biometric security or in creating a more secure data network environment. It contains valuable information for IT personnel, consultants, CIO's, and technical sales personnel and provides hundreds of biometric links, code, evaluation criteria, and actual installation examples.

The "pre" phases—planning and testing—are vitally important to the selection and successful implementation of a biometric solution. Therefore, this book covers not only the information you need to know, but it also provides samples and documents (in the text and on a companion Web site) that you can use as a baseline for your biometric security needs.

# What the Icons Mean

Icons appear in the text throughout the book to indicate important or especially helpful items. Here's a list of the icons and their functions:

This icon warns you about side effects you should watch out for or precautions you should take before doing something that may have a negative impact on your network or systems.

This icon provides additional or critical information and technical data on the current topic.

This icon points out useful techniques and helpful hints.

This handy icon points you to some place where you can find more information about a particular topic.

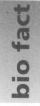

These are important biometric truths that warrant special emphasis.

*To be successful, one must surround oneself with the finest people.
With that in mind, I would like to thank my wife, Kristi, first and foremost,
for her continued support and patience during this book's development.
Next, I thank my family and friends for their encouragement and confidence.*
*—John Chirillo*

*I would like to dedicate this book to my wife, Cherrie, my daughter, Kyra,
and my mother and father—Loretta and Raymond, without whose support, understanding,
and encouragement this project would not have been possible. I would also like to thank
all my family and friends for their support, encouragement, patience, and understanding
during the development of this book.*

*I would also like to thank everyone at ValCom for their support and encouragement
throughout the production of this book, specifically Bob Green and Chuck Birmingham
for their support, backing, and commitment.*
*—Scott Blaul*

# Acknowledgments

We would like to thank all the folks at Wiley who worked in support of this project. We would especially like to thank Carol Long, Katie Feltman, and Marcia Ellett.

We would also like to thank the many folks from the different vendors, software manufacturers, and consultants who contributed information that helped in the production of this material. Specifically, we want to thank Tom Brays, Valyd Inc., and VeriVoice Inc. for their support of this project.

In addition, we would like to thank The Center for Laryngeal and Voice Disorders at Johns Hopkins, The National Center for Voice and Speech, John T. Yung, PC World, Digital Persona Inc., saflink Corporation, BioNet Systems, LLC, Matsushita Electric Corporation of America, Iridian Technologies, Topaz Systems Inc., Symtron Technology Inc., and the International Biometric Group.

# Contents at a Glance

# Contents

# Chapter 1

# Biometrics

IN THE REALM OF computer security, *biometrics* refers to authentication techniques that rely on measurable physiological and individual characteristics that can be automatically verified. In other words, we all have unique personal attributes that can be used for distinctive identification purposes, including a fingerprint, the pattern of a retina, and voice characteristics.

Although the field of biometrics is still in its infancy, it's inevitable that biometric systems will play a critical role in the future of security. Strong or two-factor authentication—identifying oneself by two of the three methods of something you **know** (for example, a password), **have** (for example, a swipe card), or **is** (for example, a fingerprint)—is becoming more of a de facto standard in secure computing environments. Some personal computers today can include a fingerprint scanner where you place your index finger to provide authentication. The computer analyzes your fingerprint to determine who you are and, based on your identity followed by a passcode or passphrase, allows you different levels of access. Access levels can include the ability to open sensitive files, to use credit card information to make electronic purchases, and so on.

If you've ever watched hi-tech spy movies, you've most likely seen biometric technology. Several movies have depicted biometric technologies based on one or more of the following unique identifiers:

- ✓ Face
- ✓ Fingerprint
- ✓ Handprint
- ✓ Iris
- ✓ Retina
- ✓ Signature
- ✓ Voice
- ✓ Watermarking

But how realistic are they in today's computing world, and how can they help you? This text answers these questions and provides templates for biometric applications.

# Introduction

Biometrics refers to the automatic identification of a person based on his or her physiological or behavioral characteristics. This identification method is preferred over traditional methods involving passwords and PINs (personal identification numbers) for several reasons, including the person to be identified is required to be physically present at the point of identification and/or identification based on biometric techniques obviates the need to remember a password or carry a token. With the increased use of computers as vehicles of information technology, restricting access to sensitive/personal data is necessary. By replacing PINs, biometric techniques can potentially prevent unauthorized access to or fraudulent use of the following:

- ✓ ATMs
- ✓ Cellular phones
- ✓ Smart cards
- ✓ Desktop PCs
- ✓ Workstations
- ✓ Computer networks

PINs and passwords may be forgotten, and token-based identification methods such as passports and driver's licenses may be forged, stolen, or lost. Thus, biometric systems of identification are enjoying a new interest. Various types of biometric systems are being used for real-time identification. The most popular are based on face recognition and fingerprint matching; however, other biometric systems use iris and retinal scans, speech, facial feature comparisons and facial thermograms, and hand geometry.

## In History

The term *biometrics* is derived from the Greek words *bio* (life) and *metric* (to measure). Among the first known examples of practiced biometrics was a form of member-printing used in China in the fourteenth century, as reported by the Portuguese historian Joao de Barros. The Chinese merchants were stamping children's palm and footprints on paper with ink to distinguish the babies from one another.

In the 1890s, an anthropologist and police desk clerk in Paris named Alphonse Bertillon sought to fix the problem of identifying convicted criminals and turned biometrics into a distinct field of study. He developed a method of multiple body measurements that was named after him (the Bertillonage technique — measuring body lengths). Police throughout the world used this system until it proved to be exceedingly prone to error as many people shared the same measurements. After this failure, the police started using fingerprinting — developed by Richard Edward Henry of Scotland Yard — after the methods used by the Chinese centuries before.

A biometric system is essentially a pattern-recognition system that makes a personal identification by determining the authenticity of a specific physiological or behavioral characteristic possessed by the user. An important issue in designing a practical system is to determine how an individual is identified. Depending on the context, a biometric system can be either a verification (authentication) or an identification system.

# Verification versus Identification

Today, we have the technology and processing power to employ advanced, cost-effective, and much more accurate biometric identification systems. There are two different ways to resolve a person's identity: verification and identification. Verification (am I whom I claim to be?) involves confirming or denying a person's claimed identity. In identification, one has to establish a person's identity (who am I?). Each approach has its own complexities and could probably be solved best by a specific biometric system, including the following:

- ✓ Physical biometrics:

    - Fingerprint—Analyzing fingertip patterns (see Figure 1-1)

    - Facial recognition/face location—Measuring facial characteristics

    - Hand geometry—Measuring the shape of the hand

    - Iris scan—Analyzing features of colored ring of the eye (see Figure 1-2)

    - Retinal scan—Analyzing blood vessels in the eye

    - Vascular patterns—Analyzing vein patterns

**Figure 1-1:** Fingerprint biometric system for logon identification and authentication

- DNA — Analyzing genetic makeup
- Biometric data watermarking (which is really a method rather than a physical attribute) is used to store/hide biometric information.

✓ Behavioral biometrics:

- Speaker/voice recognition — Analyzing vocal behavior
- Signature/handwriting — Analyzing signature dynamics
- Keystroke/patterning — Measuring the time spacing of typed words

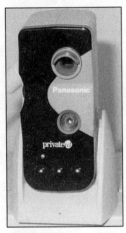

**Figure 1-2:** Iris recognition biometric system

Fingerprint recognition is one of the oldest biometric technologies, and its application in criminal identification, using eyesight, has been in use for more than 100 years. Today, computer software and hardware can perform the identification significantly more accurately and rapidly. Fingerprint technology is among the most developed biometric technologies, and its price is cost-effective enough to make its way into public use.

Facial recognition is among the newer technologies for commercial applications. Two-dimensional face recognition systems impose a high misidentification rate; however, newer three-dimensional facial recognition is showing significant improvements and much better accuracy.

Iris scanning is among the most accurate of all biometric technologies with very little overlap between acceptance and rejection curves. This system type is expensive and is recommended for very high security requirements.

Signature recognition is becoming increasingly popular, and the dynamic recognition of relative pen speeds and pressures has significantly improved the accuracy of this system. This technology is also cost-effective for smaller budgets.

Table 1-1 illustrates the most common biometric systems in use today and their characteristics with regard to accuracy, user-friendliness, and user acceptance.

**TABLE 1-1: Common Biometric Report by the University of Athens**

| Biometric System | Accuracy | Ease of Use |
|---|---|---|
| Fingerprint | High | Medium |
| Hand Geometry | Medium | High |
| Voice | Medium | High |
| Retina | High | Low |
| Iris | Medium | Medium |
| Signature | Medium | Medium |
| Face | Low | High |

User acceptance is also an important issue to consider when selecting a biometric system for employees to use on a regular basis. The following is a general user acceptance list in descending order, from the most accepted to the least accepted:

1. Iris scan
2. Keystroke/patterning
3. Signature/handwriting
4. Speaker/voice recognition
5. Facial recognition/face location
6. Fingerprint
7. Hand geometry
8. Retinal scan

You should consider three factors when designing a biometric solution: *Type I errors, Type II errors,* and *crossover error rate (CER)*. When an authorized individual is rejected by a biometric system — termed *false reject* — this is a Type I error. When an intruder is falsely accepted by a biometric system — termed *false accept* — this is a Type II error. The CER is a percentage rating of Type I versus Type II errors. A lower CER rate means better accuracy.

The following is a general CER list in descending order of accuracy, from the most effective to the least effective:

1. Hand geometry
2. Iris scan
3. Retinal scan
4. Fingerprint
5. Speaker/voice recognition
6. Facial recognition/face location
7. Signature/handwriting
8. Keystroke/patterning

# Applications

Biometrics is a rapidly evolving technology that is being widely used in forensics, such as criminal identification and prison security, and that has the potential to be used in a large range of civilian application areas. Biometrics can be used to prevent unauthorized access to ATMs, cellular phones, smart cards, desktop PCs, workstations, and computer networks. It can be used during transactions conducted by telephone and Internet (electronic commerce and electronic banking). In automobiles, biometrics can replace keys with keyless entry devices.

## APPLIED BIOMETRICS

This book covers the hottest topics in biometrics development for applications, including the following in regards to applied methodology and program development:

- ✓ Fingerprint identification
- ✓ Hand geometry
- ✓ DNA analysis
- ✓ Speaker recognition
- ✓ Face location
- ✓ Retina scanning
- ✓ Iris scanning
- ✓ Keyboard recognition
- ✓ Multibiometrics
- ✓ Data hiding
- ✓ Sample solutions

It also provides a sample installation and usage of each biometric technology in the data arena where it's most practical. During the sample installation and usage specific features of the product being used are noted. This becomes an important factor in determining which product is right for you. For example, one product may provide good protection and make accessing Web sites easier, while another product may allow access to specific applications to be controlled.

The text also shows how the biometric technology is used to control logon access and, where possible, how it can be used for items such as e-mail and file encryption. For executive and information technology (IT) managers, the following biometric concerns are also covered:

- ✓ What form of device is most appropriate for your use?
- ✓ Should the devices be shared or used individually?
- ✓ How large and how skilled a support staff is needed?
- ✓ Should users be coming in from multiple places? Over multiple channels, such as a *local area network (LAN)*, Web, wireless, or *virtual private network (VPN)*?
- ✓ What other forms of IT security should be in place (*Public Key Infrastructure [PKI]*, security portal, firewall, and so on)? How will they interact?
- ✓ Will users be switching access modes?
- ✓ Will different users and groups require different security policies for different applications and transactions?
- ✓ How should all this be administered?
- ✓ Is this for inside the firewall, outside the firewall, or mixed use?

If you have decided to invest in biometrics, you'll find some tips to help you leverage your investment. Can the biometric product(s) be used for multiple purposes, such as the following?

- ✓ Site identification/access
- ✓ Building identification/access
- ✓ Secured location identification/access
- ✓ Equipment identification/access
- ✓ Mobile device protection

## PRACTICAL USAGES

Throughout this book, you'll find example scenarios in which biometrics is both a sound practice and a solid investment that can ultimately help ensure security while reducing cost. Additionally, you'll find some futuristic examples of how biometrics may be used to provide new services while maintaining high security.

According to Charles Lynch, Jr. (Vice President of Sales and Marketing for Datastrip, Inc.), vertical markets using biometrics include the following:

- ✓ Government—Passports, national identification (ID) cards, voter cards, driver's licenses, social services, and so on

- ✓ Transportation—Airport security, boarding passes, and commercial driver's licenses

- ✓ Healthcare—Medical insurance cards, patient/employee identity cards

- ✓ Financial—Bankcards, ATM cards, credit cards, and debit cards

- ✓ Retail and gaming—Retail programs, such as check cashing, loyalty rewards and promotional cards, and gaming systems for access management and VIP programs

- ✓ Security—Access control and identity verifications, including time and attendance

- ✓ Public justice and safety—Prison IDs, county probation offices' use for identification of parolees, county courthouses' use for ID systems

- ✓ Education—Student/teacher identity verification and access control. Biometrics are now being implemented in large-scale ID systems around the globe. Many new passport and national ID card systems use some type of biometric encoded in a bar code or smart chip.

- ✓ Driver's licenses—Technologies being recommended by American Association of Motor Vehicle Administrators (AAMVA), the organization that oversees DMV standards, include biometrics and two-dimensional bar codes. Georgia, North Carolina, Kentucky, and others already utilize biometrics on their respective state driver's licenses.

Outside of the government and military arena, corporate America is stepping up to biometrics for applications ranging from employee IDs to time and attendance. The bulk of the biometrics marketplace still consists of traditional systems used to compare fingerprints to vast, centralized databases of criminals' fingerprints.

Where possible, this text also depicts some potential future developments for the technologies discussed.

# Facts, Characteristics, and How Biometrics Can Work for You

The most popular use of biometrics for network security is for secure workstation logons. Each workstation requires software support for biometric identification of the user, as well as a hardware device, depending on the biometric being used. The cost of hardware devices is one factor that may lead to the widespread use of voice biometric security identification that can leverage common sound cards and microphones, especially among companies and organizations on a low budget. Hardware devices such as computer mice with built-in thumbprint readers will be the next step. These devices will be more expensive to implement on several computers, because each machine would require its own hardware device. A biometric mouse, with the software to support it, is available in the United States for approximately $120. The advantage of voice recognition software is that it can be centralized, reducing the cost of implementation per machine. At the top of the price range, a centralized voice biometric package can cost up to $50,000 but may be able to manage the secure logon of up to 5000 machines.

According to the International Biometric Industry Association (IBIA), the following are important details about current biometrics and the industry:

✓ **The public, opinion leaders, regulators, and legislators need the facts about biometric technology.** During the past decade, the science of biometrics has matured into an industry that offers real-world solutions to serious problems faced by businesses, schools, and government agencies. Hardware and software produced by biometric manufacturers offer a safe and reliable means to ensure privacy, protect assets, confirm identity, and guard against unauthorized access. Clearly, the marketplace has begun to accept biometrics as a better alternative to less-secure screening and identity verification processes. This success has not yet led to broad public awareness about what biometrics do and how they work. At best, this means that consumers might resist using the technologies in place of more antiquated, but familiar, processes. At worst, regulators and legislators will make ill-informed decisions that will stifle the use of biometrics on identity documents, in banking, and in benefits administration. The lack of common and clearly articulated industry positions on issues such as safety, privacy, and standards further increase the odds that governments might react rashly to unfounded accusations about the functions and uses of biometric technology.

✓ **Biometric technology serves as the gatekeeper of confidential personal information.** Biometric technology is used to erect a barrier between personal data and unauthorized access. Technically speaking, the devices create electronic digital templates that are stored and compared to "live" images when there is a need to verify the identity of an individual. The templates use proprietary and carefully guarded algorithms to secure the record and protect it from disclosure. Standing alone, these templates are of no use; they cannot be reconstructed, decrypted, or otherwise manipulated to reveal a person's identity to someone else. Used this way, biometrics can be thought of as a very secure key, but one that cannot be passed on to someone else. Unless this biometric gate is unlocked by the proper key bearer, no one can gain access to that person's information. Compared to other methods of proving identity — producing a driver's license, showing a birth certificate, or revealing one's family history — biometrics are the only currently known tools that can enhance personal privacy and still deliver effective solutions in situations that require confirmation of identity

✓ **Biometric technology is a major defense against identity theft.** Identity theft — using stolen credit cards, phony checks, benefits fraud, network hacking, and other impostor scams to defraud businesses, government agencies, and consumers — costs billions of dollars per year. It is a problem that drives up prices of goods, increases taxes, complicates routine transactions, and strains law enforcement resources. Until recently, the only way to attack the problem has been to add expensive screening and administration procedures; however, steps such as hiring security guards, maintaining accurate databases, reviewing identity documents, administering password systems, and asking personal questions have proven to be costly, stopgap measures that can be defeated by enterprising crooks. Biometric technologies offer effective, low-cost solutions that streamline these traditional, labor-intensive processes. Biometric devices are an effective substitute because they create highly accurate digital records of a person's physiological features. These records can be safely stored for later comparison against a live image that is captured from the user at the time the service or benefit is demanded. All of the devices are nonintrusive, user-friendly units that recognize features such as an iris, a voice, a signature, a fingerprint, a hand, or a face. This gives end users such as banks, merchants, government agencies, and employers extraordinary control over transactions without inconveniencing or embarrassing the customer.

✓ **Biometrics are safe.** Biometric devices and software are nonintrusive technologies that are designed to work effectively under variable and demanding conditions. These products do not present health or safety risks to either users or operators. They don't leave marks, don't take physical samples, and require minimal or no contact by the user.

✓ **Biometrics are reliable technologies that deliver effective solutions.** Although biometric technologies are relatively new to the marketplace, they have already earned a reputation for effectiveness in a variety of demanding environments that require high levels of accuracy, robust security, and solid customer service. The results produced by these solutions have been well documented. For example, several banks in Texas report that check fraud plummeted by more than 50 percent when biometrics were used; employers cite savings of millions of dollars by using the devices to eliminate time and attendance abuse; and a state government agency says that fraudulent welfare claims declined more than 25 percent when a biometric verification process was introduced. On the customer service side, users have repeatedly expressed complete satisfaction with biometric solutions that expedite border clearance formalities, replace network passwords, and authorize financial transactions.

✓ **Biometric manufacturers and developers deliver what they promise.** The devices on the market offer refined, durable, and accurate solutions that have undergone rigorous evaluations and been put through exhaustive trials by end users. As further assurance that the devices work as promised, each member adheres to a strict International Biometric Industry Association (IBIA) code of ethics and attests that any stated product performance claims are accurate and can be independently verified by a competent authority.

✓ **Biometric technology is user friendly.** Biometric devices are engineered and developed with the user in mind. The convenient designs have intuitive interfaces that make them easy to operate whether they are used every day, or just now and then. In most cases, biometric processes are quicker and simpler than those that they replace, and can be set up to function reliably even if the user has forgotten a personal identification number.

In a recent trial in the United Kingdom, a bank reported that 91 percent of all users preferred biometrics to PINs and signatures as a means of identification at ATMs and teller windows.

✓ **Biometric solutions mean lower costs.** The savings from converting manual processes to those driven by biometric devices can be significant. This is especially true in circumstances where safety and security is important, and customer service and accessibility are essential. In the past, maintaining security and controlling transactions meant using labor-intensive screening methods or administering password/PIN systems — often both. Biometrics offers an effective alternative by automating these processes for a fraction of what the other approaches cost. Businesses, schools, and government agencies have found that the return on investment from biometric solutions is high when they are used to deter identity theft and preserve resources at the same time. There are many examples of how biometrics can improve efficiency. Until recently, network security could only be protected by passwords; now, biometric peripherals can be used to automatically identify the user. Financial transactions, particularly those conducted at ATMs, are protected by PINs; biometric technology can replace this vulnerable system with a process that gets high marks from consumers. Going through border controls has always meant waiting in lines, but where biometric devices are in use, travelers are able to move seamlessly through inspection processes. Biometrics can be used in similar ways to stop losses due to payroll fraud and save time in trying to resolve questions of eligibility for benefits.

# Other Common Biometric Characteristics

In general terms, biometric technologies do not actually compare the physical traits that they are designed to use as a unique identifier; rather, they create templates for comparison. The initial comparison templates are created during an enrollment process. This enrollment process may require the individual to provide multiple instances of the biometric trait. For example, a fingerprint enrollment process may require the individual to place a given finger on the fingerprint scanner four times. Depending on the device and the comparison technology, four actual comparison templates may be stored, or the four copies may be used to create a composite comparison template.

Template creation and comparison processes are described throughout this text. However, each manufacturer of biometric technologies often incorporates its own unique method of accomplishing the comparison, and, in most cases, the method is patented.

Finally, the book discusses both the general strengths and weaknesses of biometric technologies. There are many rumors, myths, and misconceptions concerning biometric technology when compared to its much more widely accepted "password protection" counterpart. You will see how biometric technology can provide the next level of security protection when selected and used appropriately.

# Summary

Many forms of biometric systems exist for identification and verification purposes; each has a different price range with associated crossover error rates and user-acceptance levels. This book dissects these systems and formulates a cookbook-style template for your own applications. In addition, it formulates methodologies and examines object-oriented source code for strong authentication solutions. Finally, it looks at the weaknesses of each solution and how to mitigate those weaknesses to enhance security and risk acceptance in your environment—whether it is a small home office, a medium-sized infrastructure, or a vast enterprise.

# Chapter 2

# Fingerprint Technology

FINGERPRINTS HAVE BEEN USED for identification for several centuries. Law enforcement has used fingerprints for many years as a core tool for determining identity. Because of the vast amount of data available, fingerprint technology is probably the best-poised biometric technology for use in the data and cyber world. What is it that makes fingerprints, their use for identification, and fingerprint technology devices so appealing?

Interest in fingerprints dates back as far as the prehistoric era. In prehistoric times, pictures were sometimes used as a method of communication. This communication method has been referred to as picture writing. Picture writing was discovered in Nova Scotia, where a hand was depicted with ridge patterns.

The earliest known hand or foot impression was found in ancient Egypt. The print is a portion of a palm print made in mud that dates back 10,000 years. Hand and foot print impressions in ancient Egypt dating back 4,000 years have also been found. Fingerprint impressions were also made in ancient times using clay tablets, much like a signature is used today.

Thumbprints made in clay seals were used in ancient China as proof that the contents of a message had not been compromised, much like wax seals bearing royal impressions. It is also known that the Chinese routinely used ink fingerprints on documents, and these fingerprints were used in courts to establish identity.

Dr. Henry Faulds, a British surgeon, created a fingerprint classification method between the years 1870 and 1880. Dr. Faulds' classification system would later be used by Sir Francis Galton (cousin to Sir Charles Darwin) in his published book, *Fingerprints*. Dr. Faulds' classification system described fingerprint patterns in terms of loops and whorls. From his research, one of Dr. Faulds' most important conclusions was that fingerprints left on objects might be used as a means of identification. Dr. Henry Faulds is also credited with the first fingerprint identification from an alcohol bottle containing a greasy fingerprint.

Sir Edward Henry published a book called *Classifications and Uses of Fingerprints* in 1900. On May 31, 1901, Sir Edward Richard Henry was appointed Assistant Commissioner at Scotland Yard. In July of 1901, Scotland Yard's fingerprint bureau was established. 1902 marked the first conviction using fingerprints by a British court. The Henry classification system is still in use today.

Throughout history, many additional counts of fingerprint use can be cited. Suffice it to say that there is quite a rich history of information available on fingerprints and fingerprint usage pertaining to identity verification, making it one of the most mature forms of identification. This is one of the main reasons for its popularity within biometric applications.

# Technical Description

Each and every fingerprint is considered to be unique. The probability of duplication has been estimated by many and varies greatly depending on the method used to compare fingerprints. To the best of our knowledge, no two fingerprints have been found to be identical. This does not, however, mean that no two fingerprints can match closely enough to create a false positive.

A false-positive condition occurs when the comparison of a biometric trait from a different individual than the actual owner of a registered (enrolled) biometric trait is identified (incorrectly) as the owner of the registered (enrolled) trait.

Additionally, it is possible for a given biometric technology to produce a false negative, where even though the rightful owner of the biometric trait is the one seeking identification, the identifying device does not recognize the trait.

A false-negative condition occurs when the comparison of a biometric trait from the actual owner of the registered (enrolled) biometric trait is unidentified (incorrectly) as not owning the trait.

To understand how this occurs, it is important to understand the makeup of a fingerprint and how fingerprint devices are used to identify an individual.

## Classification

Fingerprints are made up of ridges and furrows. The ridges are the raised portions of the fingerprint, whereas the furrows are the lower portions. The difference (spaces) between the ridges and furrows creates enough friction so we can grab and hold objects without having them slip out of our grasp. It is not the ridges and furrows that make a fingerprint unique but rather the differences in each ridge and furrow (the patterns created and the uniqueness of how ridges end, split, split and join, or appear simply as a dot). This is called the *minutiae*.

Minutiae are primarily made up of ridge endings, bifurcations, ridge dots, and enclosures. Figure 2-1 illustrates minutiae.

In addition to the above primary minutiae, fingerprint minutiae are often broken down even further in an effort to ensure uniqueness. This can include such minutiae as pores, crossovers, and deltas as well as other subminutiae.

For example, pores are tiny depressions within a ridge on a fingerprint. Crossovers are similar to bifurcations, but create a kind of X pattern (effectively two bifurcations connected end to end). And finally, a delta creates a pattern that looks like a triangle.

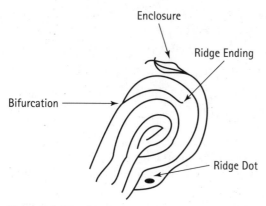

**Figure 2-1:** Minutiae

Fingerprints also fall into one of three major classifications — loop, whorl, and arc. Figure 2-2 illustrates the difference between each type of fingerprint category.

**Figure 2-2:** Loop, whorl, and arch categories

Fingerprints can also be further classified into subcategories. These subcategories include single or double whorl, plain or tented arch, ulnar or radial loops, and even associated subsubcategories for each of these.

The loop is by far the most common type of fingerprint. Type of fingerprint and the approximate percentage of the population containing each are as follows:

- ✓ Loop — 65 percent
- ✓ Whorl — 30 percent
- ✓ Arch — 5 percent

# Identity versus Identification

Before you can identify someone using a fingerprint, you must understand the difference between identity and identification. A person can have multiple identities. A user who has multiple e-mail accounts is a good example. This user is known by each of these e-mail accounts, allowing the person to have multiple identities.

For our purposes, identification occurs when user is uniquely identified using some form of biometric trait. In the case of fingerprint technology, identification occurs when a comparison of fingerprint templates yields a match that is within tolerances (tolerances will be further discussed later in this chapter). Therefore, for identification to take place, a known source (fingerprint template) to compare against must exist.

In support of nonbiometric uses of fingerprint technology for example, police have been using fingerprints for centuries to assist in identification of criminals from crime scene fingerprint information collected by various means. However, unless there is a known fingerprint to match against those fingerprints collected from a crime scene, the collected data is often of little use. Therefore, when a suspect is arrested (even for unrelated incidents), his or her fingerprints are taken—typically using an inkblot system. This information is marked and stored for possible future use.

The fingerprint information taken from such suspects is compared to the evidence collected to help determine whether there is a match. This becomes more difficult when only partial fingerprint information exists. In modern times, fingerprint-matching technologies have been implemented on a broad scale to allow existing and newly collected, known fingerprint information to be compared against unknown crime scene fingerprint information.

So, how then does simply capturing a fingerprint or a portion of their fingerprint uniquely identify individuals?

## Recognition

Relating to data environments, biometric fingerprint analysis and comparison functions similarly to the police scenario described above. However, it is important to understand that most biometric devices do not directly compare the fingerprints; rather, they create templates that are electronic representations of a fingerprint based on minutiae and compare the known templates against the newly acquired template(s). The method in which these electronic representations are created, stored, and used for comparison is often patented for each biometric technology device and is most often manufacturer-specific. However, in general terms, templates can be used individually or as aggregate information.

note

Fingerprint templates are algorithmic representations of a fingerprint but cannot be used in reverse fashion to re-create the pattern of a fingerprint.

To create the templates, the subject/individual must undergo an enrollment process. This enrollment process typically requires that the individual submit their fingerprint(s) multiple times. Each time, a template is created. Once the enrollment process has been completed, subsequent comparisons can be performed against multiple individual templates, aggregate templates, or a combination thereof.

For individual templates, a newly captured fingerprint would be converted to a template and its template compared to each individual template captured during the enrollment process until a match is found, or until all have been compared and no match has been found. If a match is found, identification has occurred. In the case of a non-match, no identification occurs.

When an aggregate fingerprint template is used, the newly captured fingerprint would be converted to a template and the template would be compared to the aggregate template created from the enrollment process. If the comparison is within tolerances, a match would occur and the individual would be identified. If the comparison fell outside of tolerances, a non-match condition occurs.

As stated previously, the captured biometric (in this case, the fingerprint) is not directly compared to another fingerprint. Because biometric technologies create and compare templates using biometric qualities rather than the biometric itself, manufacturers have had to devise proprietary algorithms capable of comparing the templates to determine whether they are a match. Because several factors can affect the actual creation of the comparison template (the template created when trying to authenticate for example), including finger condition, injury, condition of the fingerprint capture device, positioning, pressure and others, it is unlikely that two templates (even from the same individual/finger) would be created 100 percent alike. Therefore, the algorithm must account for a percentage of difference, commonly referred to as *tolerance*.

As with most biometric technologies, outside influences can affect the match/non-match comparisons. Each biometric technology can contain the following conditions.

## FAILURE TO ENROLL

Relating to fingerprint technology, a Failure to Enroll (FTE) occurs when a given individual lacks sufficient unique fingerprint data to uniquely identify him or her based on the required minutiae. Suppose, for example, that the fingerprint technology requires 500 minutiae to enroll, yet a given fingerprint only produces 450 minutiae. The result would be an FTE. An example of a failure to enroll with biometric fingerprint technology is possible for individuals with very faint or worn fingerprints. Construction workers, carpenters, and other individuals that use their hands in abrasive work environments often have worn fingerprint information. In addition, some newer systems also detect temperature alongside fingerprints. Having said that, as you may have deduced, an FTE may result from users with circulation problems or cold fingers.

## FALSE MATCH OR FALSE ACCEPT (TYPE 2)

Conversely, an example of a false match in fingerprint biometrics could be when only 100 minutiae were required to create a fingerprint template, and two fingerprint templates contained the same 100 minutiae points (even though there are other minutiae point differences). It would be possible for the algorithm to falsely accept one fingerprint template as valid when in fact it belonged to a different individual.

## FALSE NONMATCH OR FALSE REJECT (TYPE 1)

Within fingerprint technology, a false non-match can occur when a biometric template generated by a previously enrolled/valid individual does not create a match with the enrollment template information. This can occur when fingerprint information falls out of the acceptable tolerances due to the condition of the finger, placement, pressure, and so on.

# Crossover Error Rate

Crossover Error Rate (CER) is generally stated as a percentage at which the false rejection rate and the false acceptance rate are equal to each other (sometimes also referred to as Equal Error Rate, or EER). In relationship to accuracy, CER is among the most important measures of biometric system accuracy. Because most every biometric system contains the ability to adjust biometric sensitivity levels, the CER can also be adjusted. A biometric fingerprint solution that produces a CER of 1 percent is more accurate than one that produces a CER of 5 percent.

Before determining which sensitivity settings are right for the application, a solid understanding of the purpose for the biometric technology must be achieved. If, for example, the primary purpose of the biometric technology is security, and false matches or false accepts are unacceptable, the sensitivity should be increased to its highest levels to reduce the possibility of false match or false acceptance occurrences.

On the other hand, if the primary purpose of the biometric technology is for ease of use and to accommodate as many users as possible while reducing false rejects, then the sensitivity levels can be reduced or decreased.

For example, if fingerprint biometric technology is to be used to reduce the need for remembering multiple passwords (display later in this chapter) and not as much to increase security, the sensitivity level might be set to either a low or medium setting. However, if the purpose of the fingerprint biometric technology were to as accurately identify an individual from fingerprint information, while reducing the probability that someone could impersonate the fingerprint data, the sensitivity level should be set to its highest level(s).

## ABILITY TO VERIFY RATE

Another very important actor relating to biometric technologies is the Ability to Verify (ATV) rate. The ATV is typically a numerical representation expressed in the form of a percentage of individuals that will not be able to use the biometric technology for authentication and will therefore have to be handled in an exception process. The lower the ATV rating, the better the overall ability to authenticate a greater majority of users. This can be depicted using our previous example, where a fingerprint does not contain enough minutiae to achieve the minimum requirements of the fingerprint authentication system. If this was expected to happen in 10 percent of the population, and the system was required to handle 1,000 users, 100 users would need to be treated as exceptions. These exceptions might need to use another biometric technology or passwords only.

This is an important factor because the fewer exceptions, the better the overall security of the system. However, having a high ATV can also lead to higher levels of false matches or false accepts.

# Fact/Fiction

One of the most important security factors to remember is that no data can be considered 100 percent secure. Even if very stringent security processes, procedures and protection measures are put into place, compromise due to many factors (including system failures) can occur. However, it is very important to ensure that proper and adequate security measures are taken based on the classification of the data. So, now might be a good time to discuss some of the common facts and misconceptions about biometric fingerprint technology and security.

Because biometrics technologies are often discussed in terms of False Match Rates (FMRs), False Non-Match Rates (FNMRs), Crossover Error Rates (CERs) and Ability to Verify rates (ATVs), many people have the misconception that biometric technologies are less secure, or more easily breached, than password-only technology. This is absolutely not the case.

The fact is that fingerprint (and other) biometric technologies have a much higher degree of individual identification accuracy than any password-only technology could hope to achieve. This is predominately due to the fact that a password can be easily compromised either by social engineering, guessing, or simply by the password owner sharing it with others for any number of reasons. Even if hard-to-guess, long passwords are used, the end result is often that the password owner writes the information down in an effort to remember it and places the password somewhere within the work area (often under the keyboard). On the other hand, although a biometric trait like a fingerprint can be relatively easy to obtain using well-known methods, re-creating and actually using it in a properly set-up environment can be much more difficult. Look at why this holds true by examining how a fingerprint template might be built and by listing the security characteristics as well as the strengths and weaknesses of fingerprint technology.

# Fingerprint Security Characteristics

The components used to determine uniqueness of a fingerprint can differ greatly depending on the primary and subminutiae that are used. However, to get a general sense of how a biometric template can be built using fingerprint technology in a digital world, let's look at a fingerprint and a very simplified digital representation of that print, as depicted in Figure 2-3.

 Remember, biometric information is not stored in the form acquired, but rather converted into a digital representation. This conversion can take place even before the data is sent from the acquisition device to the receiving device. The digital representation is most often created using complex algorithms in an effort to ensure high security and uniqueness.

Using our earlier Figure 2-1 combined with a purely speculative template, a template representation might look something like what you see in Figure 2-3. The sample area is outlined depicted by the circle over both the fingerprint and the template.

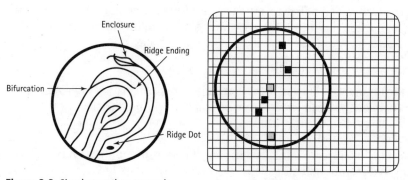

**Figure 2-3:** Simple template example

If, for example, each square in our template could contain multiple values and each value could cross boundaries, the fingerprint characteristics could be mapped based on its type and location. In our example, we show only six minutiae being mapped, but in reality the more minutiae used, the higher the degree of individuality that can be achieved. However, it is not a good idea to build a fingerprint template based only on type of minutiae and physical location (without some form of encryption/algorithm) because such a template could be very easily re-created from a latent print.

A latent print is an impression of a fingerprint left behind when a finger has contacted some other material. The latent print may or may not be visible to the naked eye but is considered to be suppressed.

Table 2-1 indicates some of the additional characteristics of fingerprint technology.

## TABLE 2-1: Additional Fingerprint Characteristics

| Characteristic | Ease of use | Error incidence | Accuracy | Acceptance | Security Level | Stability | Cost |
| --- | --- | --- | --- | --- | --- | --- | --- |
| | High | Low | High | Medium | High | High | Low |

# Strengths

Biometric fingerprint technology has several strengths that allow it to be one of the most popular and quite possibly the best-positioned biometric technology for data security.

- ✓ Among biometric technologies, fingerprinting is one of the oldest, most well-known and researched technologies. This means there is a wide array of information available on how to use it. However, as you will see, this also poses a weakness.

- ✓ Fingerprints are easy to use; simply place a finger on a scanner.

- ✓ Because fingerprints are well-known, many companies are participating in fingerprint technologies. Therefore, you can choose from several different products.

- ✓ A wide variety of application uses exist, depending on the manufacturer.

- ✓ Many fingerprint technologies are designed not only for security, but make multiple authentications to disparate systems easier.

- ✓ Identification on some systems might be set up to only occur from a specific fingerprint scanner.

- ✓ Fingerprint scanning devices differ from manufacturer to manufacturer and are therefore not likely to work on another manufacturer's biometric fingerprint product.

- ✓ Fingerprinting is considered stronger than password protection alone.

- ✓ It allows almost immediate identification for speedy authentication.

# Weaknesses

Because fingerprint technology is one of the oldest and most well-known technologies, a good amount of information is publicly available on how to defeat it.

- ✓ Fingerprints are easily copied/reproduced using publicly available documentation and easy-to-acquire, inexpensive materials (latex, for example). A reproduction of a fingerprint is called a *fake*, or *dummy*. If a user allows an impression to be taken of their fingerprint, it is much easier to create a fake or dummy than from a latent print.

- ✓ Using a fingerprint scanner leaves a latent print on the scanner device, which can also be used to create a fake using publicly available documentation and easy-to-acquire materials. However, this takes more skill than if a user is willing to provide an impression.

- ✓ As gruesome as it might sound, even an actual finger that is no longer attached to the owner can be used to gain access.

- ✓ Fingerprint scanning is not considered as secure as retinal or iris biometric technologies.

- ✓ Should a fingerprint or a fingerprint comparison template be compromised, it is not as easy to fix as if a password becomes compromised.

- ✓ The screens on fingerprint scanners tend to retain an obstruction buildup of oil and residue from user fingertips.

Even with the weaknesses listed, fingerprint identification/protection is considered more secure than password-only protection.

# Countermeasures

As with most technologies, the method in which fingerprint biometric technology is implemented can go a long way toward addressing the weaknesses listed previously.

- ✓ To reduce the possibility that a dummy or fake finger/fingerprint can be used to falsely accept an identification, a few precautionary/countermeasures can be taken:

- Enroll and use multiple fingers for single authentication.

- When using multiple fingerprints for authentication, use a specific pattern. You can occasionally change this pattern, much like occasionally changing a password.

- Use a device that can sense a live finger versus a fake or dummy.

✓ You can occasionally un-enroll and re-enroll to create different enrollment templates, although this has a minimal effect.

✓ Use multiple means of identification and authentication (for example, fingerprint and password) for two-factor or strong authentication.

✓ Allow identification to occur only from a certain fingerprint scanner or specific fingerprint scanners.

✓ Control physical access to fingerprint scanning devices where possible.

✓ Increase sensitivity to reduce the possibility of a false positive.

✓ Regularly scheduled maintenance is required for heavy usage environments to prevent a buildup of oil residue.

The preceding countermeasure tips can greatly reduce the probability that someone could use an obtained fingerprint to breach security.

# Technology Uses and Applications

Inevitably, one of the first questions asked when trying to decide which fingerprint technology to use is "What type of fingerprint sensor is the best?"

Unfortunately, there's no standard answer to this question. Manufacturers may choose to use a different type of sensor, and often provide different features and functionality. However, some general criteria can be used to help narrow the selections.

✓ Cost is often among the top considerations when choosing many technologies.

✓ Maturity of the fingerprint technology within the marketplace is another consideration when choosing a fingerprint technology.

✓ The fingerprint technology should implement strong tamper-security measures. How vulnerable is a system to tampering, sabotage, or deliberate and/or accidental damage?

✓ Environmental conditions should have as minimal an effect on the device as possible. Therefore, the device should perform well in many environments (within reason). For example, it is reasonable to expect that a fingerprint sensor will perform well in an office environment but not as well in an automotive shop unless other measures are taken, such as ensuring that the scanned fingerprint is clean, using some form of protective coating over the device, and so on.

✓ The sensor should be minimally affected by humidity and temperature within reasonable expectations. Again, if the sensor is located near a metal melting pot, it will likely be affected by heat, whereas if it is located in a greenhouse, it might be affected by humidity and moisture.

✓ One of the key selection criteria should be the ability of the fingerprint scanner to reduce the possibility of a forgery. In the case of fingerprint scanners, many methods can assist toward this end.

- The sensor has the ability to sense the temperature of the finger being presented.

- The sensor has the ability to check for a pulse in the presented finger.

- The sensor can check the skin for conductivity (generally not present in latex, which is often used to fake a fingerprint).

✓ The sensor should, at a bare minimum, function in the area of intended use, but ideally should also be able to function under a wide range of conditions and in a wide range of areas without adversely affecting the image quality.

- Dry and/or moist fingers should still be able to be identified.

- Indoor and/or outdoor use.

- Personal and/or public use.

- Should function with normal and/or abnormal fingers.

- The sensor should accommodate varying finger sizes.

- Varying presentations should not cause false accepts and should limit false rejects.

- Varying pressure during presentations should not adversely affect identification.

- Worn fingerprints (as might be the case for construction workers) should be able to be identified.

✓ System performance is also a concern for any biometric system and should be tested, preferably in a live environment.

✓ Who else is using the technology?

✓ Scalability is also a concern. What might work well in a hundred-user implementation might be unusable in a thousand-user implementation.

✓ Are certain fingerprint devices easier to maintain and keep up than others? What maintenance is required, and how frequently should it occur?

✓ What is the backup/backout plan if the fingerprint technology fails?

## Implementation Criteria

One of the reasons why biometric fingerprint technology is so appealing is that it is very easy to use. Simply place the finger (or fingers) on a scanner, and that's it. This means it can be used virtually anywhere a quality fingerprint can be obtained. For this reason, biometric fingerprint technology can be used in many of the following data applications as well as others.

- ✓ Network logon/authentication
- ✓ Individual workstation logon/authentication
- ✓ Application control
- ✓ Encryption control
- ✓ Activity logging
- ✓ Public access protection

However, a biometric fingerprint solution can only be effective if the following criteria is considered.

## Public Acceptance

Fingerprint technology is pretty much in the middle of the scale (or low) as far as its acceptance to the general public is concerned. Because acceptance is based on ease of enrollment and must not appear a threat to an individual's confidentiality or privacy, biometric fingerprint technology tends to cause a threat to users' fingerprint privacy.

Another reason fingerprint technology is not highly accepted is that it may require individuals to share or touch the same device that others touch. This may seem like a trivial issue, but for many, it is not. One of the best ways to overcome this objection is to remind users that they often touch the same household objects that others touch — doorknobs, faucets, towel dispensers, for example — and that the health risks associated with touching a fingerprint device are no greater than with any of these objects.

Because much of this lukewarm acceptance is due more to perception than reality, educating users on how biometric technologies use templates rather than the actual biometric trait, and how the fingerprint scanner can simplify the task, can go a long way toward creating better acceptance.

## Level of Intrusiveness

The level of intrusiveness experienced by individuals is relative, and ties in heavily with acceptance (explained in the previous section). For example, having a user place a finger on a fingerprint scanner is generally less cumbersome than remembering and typing an eight-character password containing upper and lowercase letters, numbers, and special characters. However, many users feel that the first action is more intrusive than the latter because they feel that their privacy is being invaded. In most cases, acceptance and perceived intrusiveness go hand in hand.

Again, the key to reducing the perception that a given biometric technology is intrusive is to educate each individual user.

## Benefits

One of the best ways to overcome many of the roadblocks to acceptance is to create a benefit, or multiple benefits, for the individual. For example, one of the key benefits of biometric fingerprint devices is ease of use. Each manufacturer's fingerprint device and its associated software and implementation differ from one another. Choosing the one that meets the criteria listed earlier in this chapter, and matching it with features that appeal to the user, is one of the best ways to achieve greater acceptance.

Another benefit to the company is that users can be required to authenticate several times throughout a session of multiple sessions easily. Each time identification/authentication is required, the user can simply place his or her finger on the fingerprint-scanning device. This provides an extra level of security without requiring a user to remember many passwords.

Once acceptance and intrusion obstacles are overcome, many users actually become more security-conscious. Because they are using a biometric trait to identify themselves, they often start to use the password-protected screen saver, close their e-mail, or lock their workstation before leaving the work area. This situation is definitely desirable where security is concerned.

# Increased or Decreased Costs?

Fortunately, biometric fingerprint technology has come down dramatically in price over the last few years. This reduced pricing makes it even easier to overcome pricing hurdles. In fact, using biometric fingerprint technologies can truly produce a measurable ROI, unlike many other technologies that can only show soft returns or at best a break-even point. Here's a real-world example.

## Password Cost Example

It is estimated that 40 percent of most help desk calls are related to password issues. This means that in a 200 user environment where 400 help desk calls are placed over a given period of time, 160 would be password-related (most likely password resets). When biometric fingerprint technology is used, the user cannot forget the password, as it is attached to them. So, password resets become virtually a thing of the past (we'll discuss why they do not completely go away). Fewer help desk calls, fewer help desk resources used up, less productive time lost — you get the picture. If you examine the potential cost reductions due to reduced password resets in a large environment, it becomes clear that biometric technology can save quite a bit of money in the long run.

Suppose you worked for a company that had 10,000 users and a help desk that operated from 8:00 a.m. to 5:00 p.m. In the best-case scenario, the help desk would be centralized. More realistically, there is probably more than one help desk. Some studies indicate that the call volume per month is approximately twice the number of users within the organization. If you have 10,000 users, the monthly call volume would be around 20,000 calls per month. If, as stated earlier, 40 percent of these calls were for password problems, 8,000 of the total calls per month would be for password issues. If a help desk person could consistently average one call every 10 minutes, approximately 21 help desk personnel would be needed for the total number of calls (approximately 1,000 calls per day/48 calls per person, given an eight-hour work day with six calls per hour = 20.833 personnel needed). Although six calls per hour might not seem like much, remember that although many of the calls might be shorter, several are also longer, sometimes taking seven or eight times the normal call time.

Many factors affect salaries, including geographic location, experience, and demand. Each environment must determine its average help desk salary information. In this case, use an average help desk salary of $35,000.

So, if you have 1,000 calls per day, 400 of those calls would be password-related. Using the same formula, (400/48), 8.3333 of your help desk personnel are required to accommodate password resets. If there are 230 work days in a year, this equates to $8.333 \times 35,000 = \$291,655$ per year.

A given biometric technology will not work for a certain percentage of users, so alternate provisions must be made, and one of the major factors determining the choice of the biometric technology should be the FTE rate.

If the FTE rate is .5 percent of the total population of 10,000 or 50 people, provisions would need to be made for those 50, but their password reset numbers would be 20 per day rather than 400. If you subtract one from our help desk personnel number due to the FTE factor, the hard cost per year for not using biometric technology is $7.333 \times 35,000 = \$256,655$. In addition to the salary, company perks, benefits, vacations, and so on must be included, which can easily make the cost $375,000 or more.

In addition to the hard cost of help desk support, there are also the very real lost productivity costs due to forgotten passwords. If the average salary throughout the company is $50,000, lost productivity costs can be calculated using a similar logic to that shown above. If 8,000 users per month are not productive for ten minutes due to password issues, and the average salary is $50,000, the lost productivity is 1333.333 hours per month. Multiply this by twelve for 16,000 lost productivity hours per year. At $50,000 per year, the hourly rate is approximately $24 per hour multiplied by the 16,000 lost hours, for a total of $384,000 plus perks, benefits, and so on, and this cost can be $560,640 or more. This means that the estimated total cost of password-related issues is $375,000 + $560,640 = $935,640, a lot of money by any standards.

## Biometric Savings Example

As you have seen, password resets cost a great deal of money. So, what's the solution?

As is often the case, there is more than one possible solution. As it relates to biometrics, and more specifically to fingerprint technology, savings can be realized. Let's take a look at why this is true.

As stated earlier in this chapter, fingerprint technology is very mature and well understood. This translates to several biometric fingerprint offerings available today, each with similarities and differences. Because of this, biometric fingerprint technology can be implemented in an organization for as little as $150 per user. Using the information from the "Password Cost Example," significant long-term savings can be achieved.

In our previous example, password reset costs were estimated at $935,640 per year. If your cost to implement biometric fingerprint technology was $150 per user minus the .5 percent FTE rate, you would need to implement the technology for 9,550 users; therefore, the cost would be $9550 \times 150 = \$1,432,500$. Assuming a 10 percent maintenance fee per year, the cost over a three-year

period would be $1,719,000. Using the previous pass[...]
$935,640 per year and over the course of three years[...]
three years, the overall savings would be $2,806,920 [...]
ment and support biometric fingerprint technology) [...]

As you can see, one of the nice things about biom[...]
help reduce password resets and ultimately the cost a[...]

> **note**
>
> Oftentimes, a biometric technology like fingerp[...]
> scanner in a specific sequence to reduce the [...]
> prints. When this is the case, it is still possible f[...]
> situation to a password reset. However, the o[...]
> passwords.

# How Biometrics Is Used for This Book

An example of one method in which biometric technologies were used can be seen from the creation of the text you are currently reading. Like many industries, the publishing industry is very competitive. Publishers seek out high-quality individuals (authors, technical editors, content editors, and so on) and to help in the writing of books and other materials. The individuals on a team may therefore be physically remote from the publishing facility, as well as geographically dispersed. In this dispersed environment, mechanisms must be created to allow secure transmission of data, very often over public media. To protect the data, several means are employed.

E-mail is very commonly used to communicate and collaborate in this environment, but there are messages that should not be sent in clear text. Such messages must be encrypted by each team member using high levels of encryption that would take hundreds or more years to break with currently available technology.

The nonfiction book-building process generally calls for written material to be submitted individually as it is created (for example, one chapter at a time). These submissions often take place in standard word processing document file format. The files to be submitted must be protected. Therefore, the files are separately encrypted using the same (or an even higher) level of encryption as e-mail.

Other communications might need to take place that allow video streaming, voice, or other such transmissions between team members. Sensitive transmissions must also be secured. This is commonly done by creating on-demand virtual private networks between team members.

Each of these technologies has at least one common factor — the need for highly diverse, long character strings to be used in the encryption process. In some cases, these strings can be "remembered" by software, but this may pose a security risk. Therefore, it is generally accepted that entering this information only as needed, and not "caching or remembering" such information, is more secure. Still, imagine having to type a 32- or greater character string composed of upper and lowercase letters, numbers, special characters, non-printable characters and spaces each time you want to encrypt a file that changes frequently. This string would almost definitely be written down somewhere that is easily accessible, causing yet another potential security risk.

e problems on this project, biometric technology was used to over-
ngerprint technology was used to address many of the above security
to remember or write down long pre-shared keys, encryption strings and
this chapter, you'll see how this fingerprint technology was installed, and its
ality.

# oduct Variations

Because biometric fingerprint technology is mature, different fingerprint scanning options are available. Fingerprint scanners are offered in different forms.

- ✓ **Optical** — Optical fingerprint scanners somewhat resemble common scanner devices. A user places a finger on a platen (glass, plastic or coated glass/plastic) and the device scans the finger. The scan captures the fingerprint image. This may be accomplished very much like a typical scanner, or other methods (such as infrared scanning) can be used.

- ✓ **Silicon** — Most silicon fingerprint scanners use a silicon chip to read the capacitance value of a fingerprint. The two primary types are active and passive capacitance values. Active capacitance measures the finger up to the live layer, whereas passive capacitance measures up to the point of contact. However, some silicon devices can be susceptible to electrostatic discharges.

- ✓ **Ultrasound** — This technology is the least accepted of the three, primarily because ultrasound technology still requires a larger scanning device. It is, however, appealing in some applications because it can better penetrate dirt and other factors that may limit the ability of other devices to adequately capture the fingerprint.

One of the most important factors to consider when choosing a biometric fingerprint technology is its intended use. If the fingerprint device is to be used solely for identification/authentication, the environment, operating system, number of users, distribution/location of users (local/remote), authentication structure, and so on must be considered to ensure that the chosen fingerprint technology will function. In addition, any special features should be evaluated. Most network-based fingerprint technologies have some things in common.

## Network Product Commonalities

One of the more common uses for biometric fingerprint technology in today's network environment is network authentication. Keep in mind, however, that the method used can vary greatly from manufacturer to manufacturer.

- ✓ **Authentication** — Most biometric fingerprint manufacturers have, or are in the process of creating, network identification/authentication products. This allows an individual to use his or her fingerprint information for network authentication.

✓ **Acquisition method** — The acquisition method commonly used comes in some form of fingerprint scanning device. Among the most common are optical and silicon.

## Network Product Differences

One of the major differences between biometric fingerprint products is the method in which they create and manage fingerprint template information. This is often patented per manufacturer.

✓ **Patent** — Most manufacturers have unique algorithms to create and validate templates. Additionally, the method in which they perform validations may differ. For example, one manufacturer might require a finger to be enrolled many times. Each time the finger is placed on the platen, a different template is created. After completion of the enrollment process, when a user places the finger on the scanner, the newly created template is individually compared to each enrollment template. Other manufacturers might use multiple enrollments to create a composite template. When a user subsequently places a finger on the platen, the newly created template is only compared to the composite. Additionally, depending on the manufacturer's implementation, the template might be created at the acquisition device and sent as a template, or it might be sent as a digital signal that is converted to a template by the computer.

✓ **Authentication** — With some manufacturers' fingerprint implementations, authentication is accomplished by replacing the password with the fingerprint template. This would be the preferred method, as it eliminates the password itself. Other manufacturers use a successful identification to send the original password to the authentication device.

✓ **Typed password replacement** — Fingerprint technology can also be used to eliminate the need to type passwords. This can be accomplished by allowing a user to "register" a password with his or her fingerprint.

✓ **Application control** — Another common use of biometric technology is to control access to specific applications. When a user tries to execute an application, he or she is required to place the finger on the fingerprint scanner an additional time to ensure that the person accessing the machine is also the person running the application. This is an excellent feature for applications that must track access and changes (in banking institutions, for example, where multiple users have access to account, general ledger, or other such sensitive information).

# Sample Product

This sample product demonstration, installation, authentication and applications/utilities usage will use the U.are.U Pro Workstation product from Digital Persona. The product will be installed on a Windows XP Professional workstation connected to a peer-to-peer network for the purpose of sharing hard drive and printing resources, and for encrypting e-mail messages and attachments.

# U.are.U Installation Example

Before you begin the installation of U.are.U Pro, ensure that your system meets the minimum requirements based on the version you intend to install. This example installation will use version 1.2.0 of the U.are.U Pro Workstation software, and the minimum system requirements are as follows:

✓ Auto Logon disabled (if applicable)

✓ Pentium-class processor

✓ USB port

✓ Windows 2000, Windows NT with Service Pack 4 or later, Windows 98, or Windows 95 with USB support (also serial with a USB-to-Serial cable)

✓ 24MB RAM (64MB recommended for use with Windows NT or Windows 2000)

✓ Internet Explorer 4.0

Although those are the minimum requirements, make sure your system has been updated with the latest service and security patches, and that you are running the current version of IE with the appropriate patch levels.

It is also recommended that you close all applications and log on as Administrator before beginning the installation. When you insert the U.are.U pro installation CD, the first screen you should see is the Windows Installer, as shown in Figure 2-4.

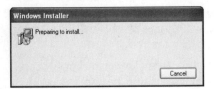

**Figure 2-4:** Windows Installer

If you do not see this screen, you will have to go to MyComputer, select the appropriate CD-ROM drive, use the Open command, and select the SETUP.EXE file to start the installation.

1. After the installation begins, the U.are.U Pro Workstation setup screen should appear, as shown in Figure 2-5.

2. After you have verified that all programs have been exited, click Next. You are presented with the license agreement, as shown in Figure 2-6.

3. In order to continue, you must read and accept the license agreement (as is the case with most installations). Click the "I accept the license agreement" radio button and then click Next. You are presented with the Destination Folder screen, as shown in Figure 2-7.

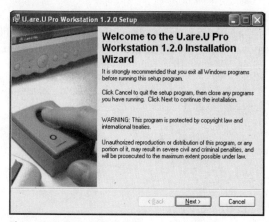

**Figure 2-5:** U.are.U Workstation setup screen

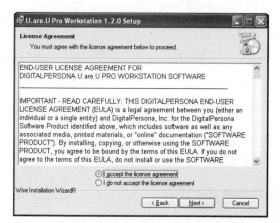

**Figure 2-6:** License agreement

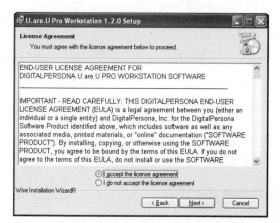

**Figure 2-7:** Destination Folder

4. In this example, the destination folder is F:\Program Files\DigitalPersona\. Your destination folder might be different, or you can click on browse here and select a different installation directory. For the purposes of this example, accept the default directory and click Next. This brings you to the Select Installation Type screen shown in Figure 2-8.

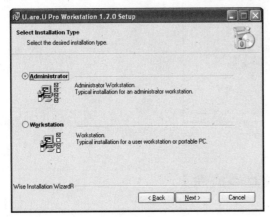

**Figure 2-8:** Select Installation Type

5. The default is Workstation, and because you want to ensure that you have the dPersona Administrator Console, select the Administrator radio button and click Next. The installation program should begin the process of copying the U.are.U program and files necessary for operation, as seen in Figure 2-9.

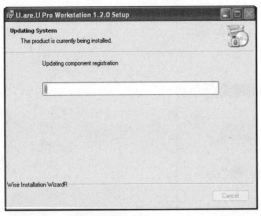

**Figure 2-9:** Updating System

6. If this is the first time you are installing U.are.U Pro and the sensor is disconnected, a window will pop up during the Updating System portion of the install that asks you to connect the sensor. After you connect the sensor, the installation process will continue.

**7.** After the copy process is complete, you are presented with a screen that asks you to register the program via the Internet, as shown in Figure 2-10.

**Figure 2-10:** Internet registration

**8.** Select No because you do not want to register at this time. This brings up the Finish screen, as shown in Figure 2-11.

**Figure 2-11:** Finish

**9.** After clicking Finish, you will be prompted to reboot the system, as shown in Figure 2-12.

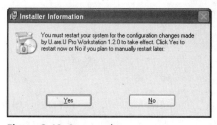

**Figure 2-12:** System reboot

**10.** After the system has rebooted, you are presented with a different logon screen than Windows XP normally uses. This screen is referred to as the One Touch Logon screen, and should look like that shown in Figure 2-13.

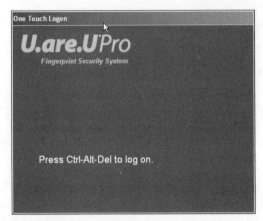

**Figure 2-13:** One Touch Logon

**11.** Press the Ctrl+Alt+Del keys simultaneously to be presented with the Log on to Windows screen. The default should be Administrator, as shown in Figure 2-14.

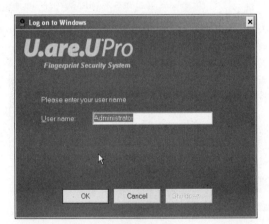

**Figure 2-14:** Log on to Windows

**12.** Click OK. You are now asked to enter the appropriate password. In this case, enter the original Administrator password, as shown in Figure 2-15, and press Enter.

**13.** The program begins to load and you see yet another screen that is somewhat different than the normal Windows XP screen. This loading screen is shown in Figure 2-16.

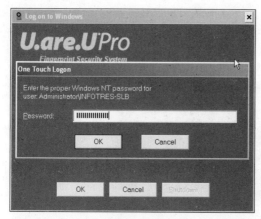

**Figure 2-15:** One Touch Logon password

**Figure 2-16:** Loading screen

**14.** After loading has completed, U.are.U begins with the Administration screen, as shown in Figure 2-17.

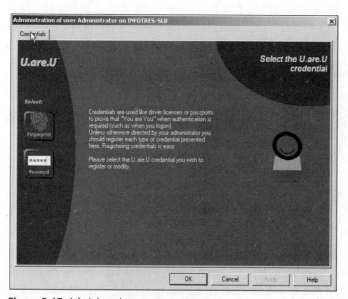

**Figure 2-17:** Administration screen

**15.** To begin the process of registering fingerprints, click the Fingerprint button under "Select:". Once selected, the screen illustrated by Figure 2-18 appears, and you can begin to register fingers.

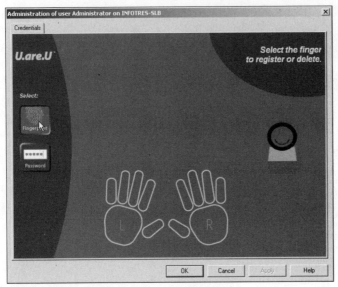

**Figure 2-18:** Administration of user Administrator

**16.** Clicking on one of the finger outlines begins the actual enrollment process. After clicking on the right index finger, the screen changes, as shown in Figure 2-19.

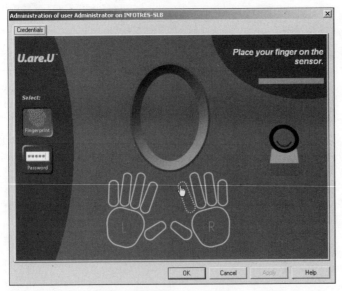

**Figure 2-19:** Index finger enrollment

**17.** Placing the right index finger on the sensor allows the sensor to acquire the fingerprint. Initially, U.are.U asks you to place each finger on the sensor four times. Progress is indicated as shown in Figure 2-20.

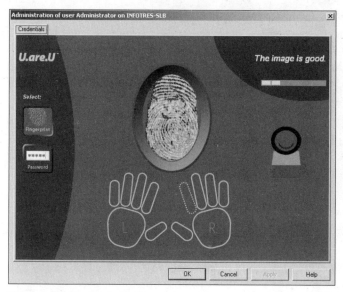

**Figure 2-20:** Progress indication

**18.** Notice that a visual representation of the fingerprint appears on the screen and that having three bars under the Image is a good indicator. This means that this was the third time (out of four) that the right index fingerprint was successfully scanned during the enrollment process. After four successful acquisitions, the representation of the enrolled finger turns green, as seen in Figure 2-21.

Additional fingers could (and should) be registered in the same fashion. It is recommended that at least one finger from each hand be registered. This helps reduce the possibility that a hard-to-read print on one hand will keep a user from being identified and, subsequently, authenticated. However, for the purposes of this demonstration, accept the single finger enrollment and continue on.

After the initial registration process, the installation proceeds by allowing access to the workstation, as shown in Figure 2-22.

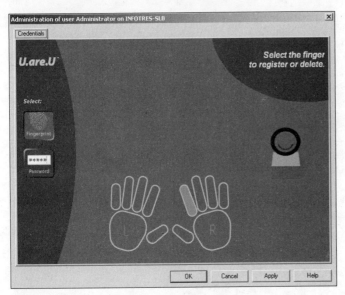

**Figure 2-21:** Successful index finger enrollment

**Figure 2-22:** Authenticated user

# Sample Network Authentication Using Fingerprint Biometrics

The U.are.U product is designed to work in standalone and network environments. The method used is very similar, although different products are required. In both network and standalone implementations, however, login is accomplished simply by placing a finger on the scanner.

Notice from Figure 2-22 that the user is Administrator, and that the authentication is local. If the machine were rebooted, the following logon screen would appear. This screen differs from the normal Windows logon screen.

From this point forward, each time the administrator attempts to log on to the computer at initial boot or after a logoff, the network logon screen shown in Figure 2-23 appears.

From this screen, two options are possible. The first is to simply place a finger on the sensor to log on. The second is to press the Ctrl+Alt+Del keys simultaneously to bring up the screen shown in Figure 2-24.

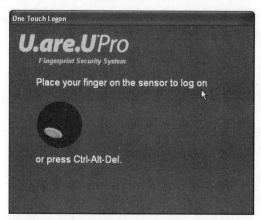

**Figure 2-23:** Fingerprint logon

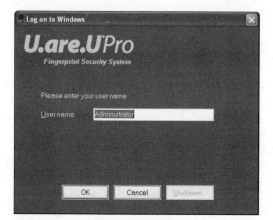

**Figure 2-24:** Manual password logon

Here, you can enter another user to be logged in and then click OK. You will see a screen similar to the one shown in Figure 2-21, and you can use the user's fingerprint for authentication (if the user has been previously created and enrolled, or you can click the Password button and you'll be prompted to enter the password).

## User Administration

The Administrator is the only user that has enrolled a fingerprint for identification/authentication use up to this point. If only fingerprint identification/authentication is to be used, each user must enroll and the password option must be removed from each user authentication profile. Therefore, other users of this workstation must also enroll if they are to use their fingerprint(s) for authentication. This process is completed in much the same way as the initial enrollment. However, the dPersona Administrator Console must be run by a user with the appropriate rights.

In this example, open the dPersona Administrator Console by selecting it from the Start menu →
All Programs → Digital Persona → U.are.U Pro → Administrator Console. The console is illustrated
in Figure 2-25.

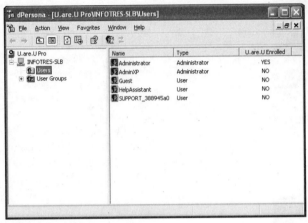

**Figure 2-25:** dPersona Administrator Console

Two Administrators exist on this workstation—Administrator and AdminXP. The Administrator
has been enrolled, as indicated by the YES under the U.are.U Enrolled heading. However, the
AdminXP administrator is not enrolled. To enroll the AdminXP administrator, double-click on the
AdminXP name. Before you can continue, you must authenticate to allow access to the credentials page. The authentication page shown in Figure 2-26 also shows which fingers can be used to
authenticate (currently only the right index finger), or the option to use a password exists by
clicking the Password button. Because Administrator is the current user, simply placing the right
index finger on the sensor provides the necessary identification.

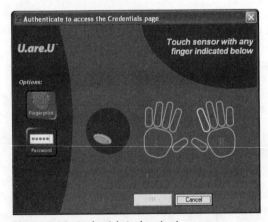

**Figure 2-26:** Credentials Authentication page

After confirmation has been achieved, the registration process for AdminXP can continue in much the same way as the original enrollment process. Click on the finger to be enrolled and have the user place his or her finger on the sensor. After four successful enrollments of the finger, you can continue on to the next finger until all necessary fingers are enrolled.

An unsuccessful acquisition is denoted by a red X, shown on the screen in the area depicted for the sensor.

## Modifying Authentication Steps

Before additional users can be registered, they must be created. You can accomplish this by going to the WindowsXP control panel, selecting User Accounts, and clicking Create New User.

See the WindowsXP documentation or help features for user creation.

After the user has been created, the user will have to go through the enrollment process described earlier in this chapter.

One way U.are.U addresses the issue of fingerprint dummies and fakes is by allowing customizable authentication steps. During user setup, additional steps can be added to provide greater security. For example, a user might be required to submit a specific finger for scanning, then a password. This two-factor authentication makes it more difficult to breach the security in place. Let's look at how two-factor authentication can be accomplished using the U.are.U product. First, open the dPersona Administrator Console by clicking Start → All Programs → DigitalPersona → U.are.U Pro → Administrator Console. This executes the administrator console shown in Figure 2-25. Next, select the AdminXP user by double-clicking the AdminXP user. U.are.U prompts for identification. This is accomplished by using the administrator's (your) fingerprint. Next, click the Policies tab. This allows you to access the authentication steps for the user AdminXP. Next, click on the + symbols for both Main System Logon and User Console, as well as for each Authentication Step 1. This should expand them. The screen should look like that shown in Figure 2-27.

Notice that the user AdminXP only has the ability to use any registered fingerprint to authenticate. To change this, click the Main System Logon object. Notice that the Properties selection at the bottom now becomes available (is no longer grayed out). Again, you are asked by U.are.U to supply your authentication credentials (fingerprint). Clicking on Properties brings up the Policy Properties screen. Policy Properties default to Domain policy. To create a custom policy, select the Custom policy for user AdminXP radio button and click always ask for authentication, as shown in Figure 2-28.

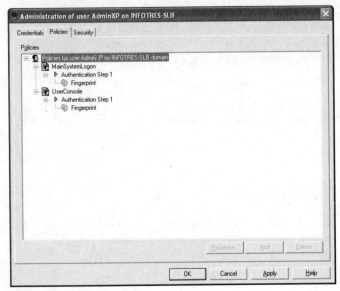

**Figure 2-27:** AdminXP policies

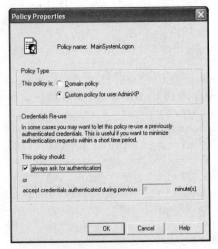

**Figure 2-28** Policy properties

Click OK. You are taken back to the Policies screen. Repeat the same process for User Console. You now have the ability to add authentication steps by right clicking on the associated login (Main System Logon or User Console) and selecting Add Authentication Step. Repeat this process for User Console.

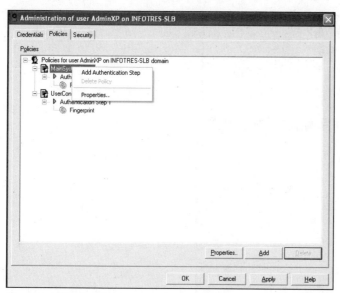

**Figure 2-29:** Add Authentication Step

Notice that there are now two authentication steps for both Main System Logon and User Console. However, the second step has either fingerprint or password credentials listed, as shown in Figure 2-30.

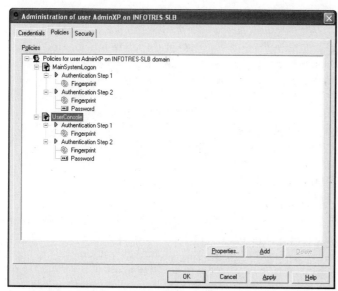

**Figure 2-30:** Multiple credential authentication

Because you want to require both fingerprint and password authentication (for identity and greater security), remove the fingerprint option for the second step under each policy by right-clicking the fingerprint option and selecting Delete Credential. This requires you to use a fingerprint for step one and a password for step 2. When this is complete, the policy steps should look like those in Figure 2-31.

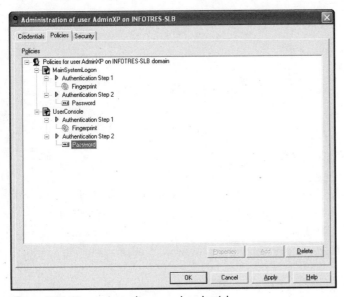

**Figure 2-31:** Fingerprint and password credential

Finally, if you only want to allow the right index finger or the left thumb to provide the fingerprint credentials, you could right-click on the fingerprint credential under step one for both policies, select Properties, and deselect the fingers you don't want to allow. When completed, the screen should look like that shown in Figure 2-32.

Now your authentication steps require you to use either the right index finger or left thumb first; then you need to type the appropriate password for step two. If both of these are not accomplished, identification/authentication will not occur and access will be denied.

# Sample Fingerprint Product Use with Applications and Utilities

One of the benefits of using biometric technology is that the biometric tool can often be used for other purposes. If the biometric device is very easy to use (easier than typing in a password, for example) levels of authentication can be established, and multiple authentications throughout the session can be required without adversely affecting productivity. In the case of the U.are.U Pro product, many uses are possible. Below are some of the ways in which fingerprint technology can be used to create higher levels of security and to make use of the workstation easier.

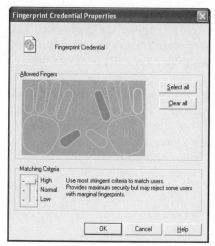

**Figure 2-32:** Right index and left thumb

Because authentication is achieved using only a simple scan of an individual's finger(s), security becomes more convenient. By default, U.are.U places an icon in the Windows tray (see Figure 2-33).

**Figure 2-33:** Lock workstation tray icon

Double-clicking on the DigitalPersona icon places the computer into a locked mode. The screen shown in Figure 2-34 appears.

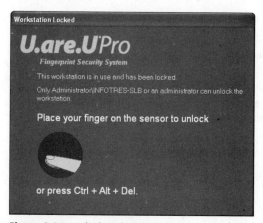

**Figure 2-34:** Locked workstation

The primary difference between this screen and the logon screen is that here, there is indication that the workstation has been locked, and only the current user may unlock the workstation. The Administrator must place his or her finger on the sensor to unlock the workstation. Pressing Ctrl+Alt+Del will allow the user to be changed, but to unlock the workstation, the proper policies must be met.

Using the U.are.U product, the screen saver with a password can be used. When using Windows XP, right-click an open space on the desktop, select Properties, and then click the Screen Saver tab. Select a screen saver from the pull-down menu and click the "On resume, password protect" checkbox. Set an appropriate Wait time, click Apply, and then click OK. When you are finished, your settings should look similar to those in Figure 2-35.

**Figure 2-35:** Screen Saver settings

When the computer has been idle for the Wait time period (in our example, one minute), the screen saver will activate. If you try to type or move the mouse, the Workstation Locked identification screen (Figure 2-34) is displayed. To regain access to the computer, place your finger on the sensor.

One of the benefits of using U.are.U Pro is that users can create templates that allow them to automatically enter information based on placing a finger on the scanner. This can be very useful when a user wants to use his or her fingerprint to authenticate to many secure Web sites requiring different login names and passwords.

## WEB SITE AUTHENTICATION CONTROL

Whether at home or in a corporate environment, many users must interact with several Web sites throughout the course of a workday. Because security is of such high concern today, more and more Web sites are requiring users to identify themselves and to authenticate each and every time they log in to the Web site. To keep up with these multiple logins and passwords, users sometimes resort to using the same password at many different sites, keeping password spreadsheets, or writing down their passwords — any of which is a security risk. Additionally, because users often need to remember many passwords, the ones they choose are easily breached using dictionary-style password crackers, or even brute force password crackers. So, let's take a look at how this can be addressed.

U.are.U allows the user to create a password store on the fly. When a user is prompted for their credentials, they can simply hold down the Ctrl key and place a finger on the sensor. This brings up the One Touch Internet screen. From the One Touch Internet screen, the user can then enter the appropriate credentials. Figure 2-36 illustrates this.

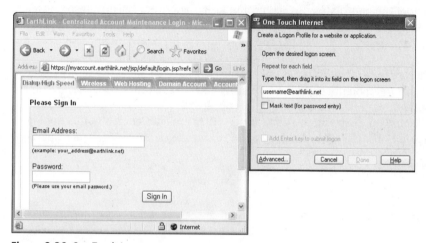

**Figure 2-36:** One Touch Internet

On the left of Figure 2-36 is an Earthlink Web sign-in, and on the right the One Touch Internet dialog box. By typing `username@earthlink.net` in the One Touch Internet dialog box and dragging it to the e-mail address in the Earthlink — Centralized Account Maintenance Login... box, then by typing the password in the One Touch Internet dialog box and dragging it to the Password field on the Earthlink — Centralized Account Maintenance Login... screen, the authentication information can be stored by U.are.U Pro. The next time the user visits the same Web site, they can authenticate simply by placing their fingerprint on the sensor.

## MORE DIFFICULT TO GUESS PASSWORDS

As shown in our example of One Touch Internet, users of U.are.U can use their fingerprints to authenticate to multiple Web sites. This means that not only do they no longer have to remember passwords, they can use completely random, long and difficult to guess passwords when registering. However, there is a drawback.

If the user intends to access the Web site from multiple workstations that do not have fingerprint technology, he will need to be able to manually enter the Web site authentication credentials.

## PGP USAGE FOR ENCRYPTING E-MAILS

E-mail has become one of the most popular and most convenient ways of communicating today, both personally and professionally. However, many of the e-mails sent today are not protected. If they were to get into the wrong hands, the result would be embarrassing to say the least.

Many years ago, the owner of a consulting company told his employees that although e-mail is a great tool, it can also be a great threat, and no e-mail should be sent that you wouldn't want to appear on the front page of a local or national newspaper.

Although the sentiment was sound, the fact is that private and confidential e-mails are sent every day, and this trend will continue. In an effort to ensure privacy, companies have resorted to encrypting and digitally signing their e-mail messages. This is often accomplished using Public Key Infrastructure (PKI) technology. A user obtains a public and private key. The public key is used to encrypt information destined for a specific individual. The individual's private key is the only key that can decrypt the information. In an effort to keep the private key private, many users enter the passphrase needed for the private key each and every time it is needed. As holds true with most passwords or passphrases, the longer and more diverse the password or passphrase, the better.

Because a passphrase can be lengthy, programs that use them often allow the ability to cache the passphrase. This has the potential to pose a security risk. Therefore, it is considered most secure to enter the passphrase each and every time it is needed.

Pretty Good Privacy (PGP) Corporation is one vendor that provides encryption technologies including mail encryption. Using PGP technology and PKI, messages can be encrypted and digitally signed.

The term "digitally signed" refers to the process of ensuring the authenticity of the message's sender.

However, to ensure security, the passphrase should be entered each and every time it is needed. Figure 2-37 illustrates this.

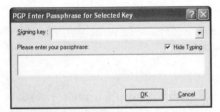

**Figure 2-37**: PGP passphrase

The Signing key information has been intentionally removed.

It is pretty apparent that the passphrase can be a very long combination of letters, numbers, and other associated characters. It would be very difficult to remember if you didn't write it down, and even more cumbersome to have to type it in each and every time a message was to be sent.

One of the benefits of One Touch Internet is that it can also be used to automatically enter long passphrases. Using the same procedure defined above, the passphrase can be entered using One Touch Internet. Subsequent need for the passphrase can be accomplished using the fingerprint-scanning device. Figure 2-38 illustrates this using PGP mail encryption technology.

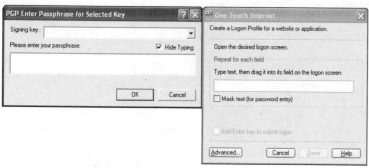

**Figure 2-38:** PGP passphrase

Using One Touch Internet, a very long passphrase can be entered into the "Repeat for each field" entry area. The entered information is then dragged to the passphrase area of PGP. Finally, click the "Add Enter key to submit logon" checkbox, and the next time the passphrase is needed, the user only needs to place a finger on the fingerprint acquisition device.

This procedure can also be used with additional features of PGP. For example, a PGP disk creates a virtual encrypted hard drive.

## PRIVATE SPACE

DigitalPersona's U.are.U Pro product also includes a software program called Private space. Private space creates a virtual secure storage space (similar in nature to the PGP disk). However, as of this writing, Private space does not function on Windows XP.

## UNIQUE USE

Often, the most effective use of a given device is not what the manufacturer originally envisioned for it, but rather some unique implementation that allows the device to provide a niche solution. To illustrate this, two simple examples follow.

**EXAMPLE 1**    Because the One Touch Internet feature is so versatile, the ways in which it can be used can be left up to your imagination. However, one such use could be to provide authentication to a firewall. Because firewalls are the gateway (or road block) into a network, many firewalls use very long, highly diverse passwords. Again, this poses the added probability that the password will be written down. To limit the need to do this, you can set up a specific machine with the appropriate authentication information. Because the U.are.U Pro software can also track usage, greater levels of change control can be achieved. Figure 2-39 illustrates how One Touch Internet can be used in this fashion with a Watchguard Small Office/Home Office (SOHO) firewall. Although this is shown with a SOHO, the logic can traverse other devices.

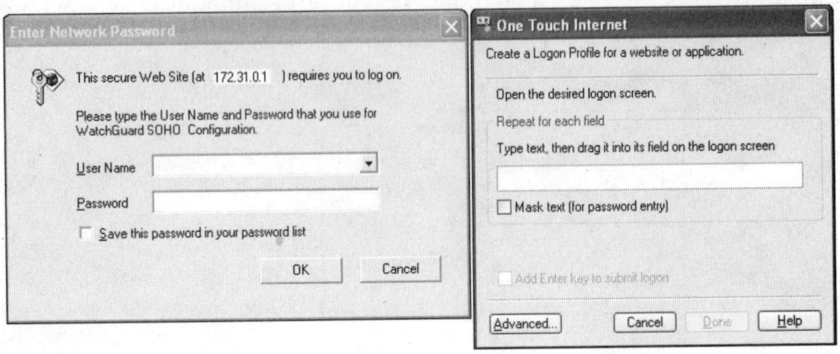

**Figure 2-39:** Watchguard authentication

Because the Watchguard uses a Web-based login, One Touch Internet can provide the necessary information to allow authentication to the Watchguard SOHO. If the only one or two machines were set up with the proper authentication information and logging was turned on, it would be easy to determine who accessed the firewall at any given time. If this is coupled with proper firewall change logging, excellent security and change control is possible.

**EXAMPLE 2**    The U.are.U Pro solution also has the ability to provide additional authentication using the One Touch Internet feature. In our test implementation, a peer-to-peer network exists. Suppose you want to allow full access to a shared resource (FTP for example) for one user, and only read FTP access for other users. The FTP program requires a username and password each time the user wants to connect. One Touch Internet can also be used as previously shown to provide authentication using only the touch of a finger.

For these and many other reasons, when looking for the right fingerprint solution, review the possible uses for the solution to find the best fit.

# Summary

Fingerprint technology has been around for centuries, and a great deal is known about how it can be used (and misused). From as far back as prehistoric times, fingerprints have been used to uniquely identify individuals, and the possibility of two fingerprints producing a match is estimated to be as high as one in 64 billion. Although discovering identical fingerprints is theoretically possible, it is highly unlikely that two individuals with identical fingerprints would cross paths. More likely, an evildoer would try to re-create fingerprints using readily available technology. Requiring multiple finger scans, using smart scanning devices that can distinguish between live and fake fingers, and altering the presentation sequence of multiple fingerprint scans can easily thwart these efforts.

Regardless of the method of fingerprint acquisition, there is no doubt that using biometric fingerprint technology correctly can be quantifiably more secure than password-only security, with the additional benefit of ease of use. These factors, coupled with the bells and whistles implemented by different manufacturers, make biometric fingerprint technology one of the top contenders in the biometric marketplace today.

# Chapter 3

# Face Technology

INDIVIDUALS ARE UNIQUE IN many ways, and the unique characteristics and traits of a given individual are often used to distinguish that person from the others stored in our memories. Although this is based primarily on facial features, other traits are also used to validate our initial assessment. However, in cases where only the face is present, you can still make identification based on that face.

This chapter discusses whether biometric face technology is a viable solution, and answers other questions and issues associated with using a person's face to uniquely identify him or her from others.

## Introduction

Throughout your lifetime, you encounter thousands, maybe even millions, of people. Simply seeing a face briefly once will generally not provide enough of a trigger for you to recall that face on demand. However, that face is typically stored somewhere in your memory nonetheless. How accurate and how much of a trigger is needed for each person varies, but the general concept is the same.

Among the most critical components of identification data stored by humans to recognize a previously encountered person, is the individual's face. Portraits and pictures were painted in times past for the same reasons as pictures are used today — to provide a record of an action at a point in time, to preserve a memory, or to capture the likeness of an individual for personal or historical purposes.

 Most people initially identify a person based on facial features but use additional characteristics and traits to confirm that identification (voice, for example). This is important when implementing biometric technologies as well.

Because faces are used for unique identification, individuals began using their face recognition capabilities to solve common issues and problems. For example, in the old west, likenesses (often crude) of outlaws were sketched out to create wanted posters. These posters were distributed in an effort to track, find, and bring the outlaws to justice. This face sketch and distribute method is still in use today (some still hand-drawn, others computer-generated) where no known pictures of a given face exist.

The methods used to determine criminals' identities based on their face characteristics have been enhanced throughout the years to include mug shot comparisons and surveillance videos identification. When individuals are arrested, they are fingerprinted and photographed for potential future comparisons. Rendered drawings (hand-drawn or computer-generated) are sometimes manually or automatically compared to existing mug shots or surveillance videos in an effort to identify an individual from the recollection of a witness or from a surveillance video or photo. This process is referred to as *matching*.

Although this type of face recognition is quite common in our world today, the additional possibilities of its use can be much broader. Below are some examples; however, many more exist:

- ✓ Lost or missing persons
- ✓ Ensuring single issuance of drivers licenses
- ✓ Firearms authorization
- ✓ Single enrollment in government aid programs
- ✓ ATM authentication
- ✓ Airport screening
- ✓ Bank surveillance
- ✓ Physical access control

Crowd identification could become one of the main uses for face technology. This stems from terrorist attacks on buildings, including the attack of September 11, 2001. The ability to use crowd-based face acquisition, which can be quickly compared to a database of known terrorists, might help avoid future terrorist attacks. Additionally, using such techniques in public transportation areas, major buildings, landmarks, and so on can go a long way toward reducing future terrorist events. However, this chapter's main focus is how face recognition technology can be put to use within a network environment.

Each person's face is unique in its own way (with the exception of identical twins). Even look-alikes differ in some fashion. So, it would stand to reason that using a individual's face for identification would be a simplistic method, and if this identification could be used to identify and authenticate an individual to allow data access, the end result could provide higher levels of security.

Stating that face technology *could* provide higher levels of security is intentional because potential weaknesses and exploits for face identification technology must be addressed. These weaknesses and potential exploits are discussed later in this chapter.

# Technical Description

Although each person's face is different or unique (again, excluding identical twins), there must be some way to electronically capture, store, and process these distinct characteristics. The method in which this is accomplished differs by product manufacturer but in general terms is done by creating a biometric template based on the data obtained from the face scan.

Most face recognition and identification devices do not actually perform a scan. Rather, they capture an image of the face in a picture or video format.

The information is converted to a template or data representation of the captured information. This template can range in size from 100 bytes to 3,000 bytes. After the initial information is stored, subsequent face scans can be compared to the original captured template. If an individual's comparison template matches an existing template, the individual is considered identified. If no match is found, the person is not identified. This process was previously discussed in Chapter 2, including Crossover Error Rates (CERs), False Reject Rates (FRRs), and False Accept Rates (FARs).

Templates are created from information obtained from the structure of a person's face or components of the face.

## Face Structure

Each person's face is made up of peaks and valleys at different altitudes, with features located at varying latitudes and longitudes. If you think of the human face in these terms, understanding how templates can be created using our own unique features becomes easier. A map can be quite descriptive, yet in simple terms it is just a piece of paper. You can think of a face template in much the same manner. You can consider hair, eyes, nose, mouth, ears, eyebrows, mustache, beard, chin, cheeks, forehead, wrinkles, glasses, and so on when creating a face template. However, unlike a map, facial terrain can change each time you create a template. Smiling, frowning, closed eyes, winking, and a number of other facial expressions can alter the template. So, you must make sure that the facial structure remains as constant as possible to ensure quality template creation and comparison.

Users must often re-enroll when their face changes. Such changes can include hairstyle changes, a move from glasses to contacts or vice versa, facial hair growth or shaving, plastic surgery, and so on.

Face information acquisition occurs when the subject's face information is captured and a template is created. The face is often divided into domains. The number and scope of the domains vary depending on technology and implementation.

The technology used to acquire face information and create the template varies, as described in the following section.

# Face Acquisition Technologies

You should understand the different face scan technology types as each may perform better in a given situation. Some face technologies are very susceptible to lighting issues, whereas others are more susceptible to heat, and others are capable of learning. Each may provide a different solution in a given scenario.

### EIGENFACE

Imagine Eigenface in similar fashion to one of those novelty toys that has hundreds of pins. When you place your hand (or, for our purposes, your face) on the pins, it creates an image of your hand in the pins. Eigenface is imprecisely similar.

Eigenface was developed by the Massachusetts Institute of Technology (MIT) and uses a two-dimensional database containing grayscale face images. Combinations of the grayscale images contained in the two-dimensional database are used to represent an individual's face image during the enrollment process. This information is then used to create an enrollment template for future comparison.

A general illustration of an Eigenface is shown in Figure 3-1.

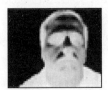

**Figure 3-1:** Eigenface

### THERMAL

More than one type of thermal facial recognition technology is available. One of the methods of thermal scanning technology uses thermal cameras to detect and acquire blood vessel patterns that are located under the skin to create a biometric template. Blood vessel patterns are unique even among identical twins. This form of thermal facial scans is a good method of determining identity compared to conventional face scan technologies because discerning between identical twins becomes possible, which may not be the case with conventional face scan techniques.

Thermal scan blood vessel technology does not have to be confined solely to facial scanning. It can be used to scan multiple areas — for example, thermal blood vessel hand scanning.

A second method of thermal facial recognition uses an infrared camera to detect the thermal heat pattern variations of an individual; however, this method is susceptible to variations in human conditions and environment. For example, if a person exercises just prior to attempting identification, the thermal heat patterns will be different than if that individual were just going about his normal business. In this case, an authorized user might not be granted access; in other words, the system will produce a false negative.

In similar fashion, if the environment temperature varies greatly (as might be the case for open areas, poorly environmentally controlled warehouses, and outside docks) to the extent that the face temperature is dropped or raised sufficiently, the person attempting identification might be falsely accepted or falsely denied.

## LOCAL FEATURE ANALYSIS

Local feature analysis leverages many of a face's features from the different regions of that face. The features are correlated to their relative location on the face and are typically small in size. The features are captured using a pixel format and changes between these pixels are used to plot the differences within a given region. The location of the regions is also used to help form the template's uniqueness. So, a local feature analysis technology might represent the face in pixel format and then break it up into regions using eyes, nose, mouth, cheeks, and so on, and the subsequent regions would be mapped even further based on distinct changes between facial features within each region, represented by the differences in pixel colors.

For example, a face is pixellated. Each eye, the nose, mouth, ears, cheeks, chin, forehead, and so on is separately broken into regions. Within an eye region, the distinct change in feature between an eyebrow and the skin of the eyelid (between the eyelid and the eye and so on) would be mapped accordingly using varying pixel color shades. Each of these regions is then used to create the necessary biometric template — for example, to provide confirmation of a claimed identity for data network login purposes.

Local feature analysis is the most widely used facial biometric technology today and can accommodate for some changes in facial expressions and aging.

## AUTOMATIC FACE PROCESSING

Automatic face processing still uses camera devices (not infrared cameras) to capture face images, as does Eigenface and local feature analysis. However, automatic face processing uses distances and distance ratios derived from predominant facial features. These predominant facial features most often include the eyes, nose, and mouth, and characteristically focus on key features such as the point of the nose and the corners of the mouth.

Automatic face processing is not considered as strong as the other facial recognition technologies; however, documentation suggests that it might perform better in low-light, front-facing image acquisition conditions because it can acquire the key facial points in these types of conditions.

## NEURAL NETWORK

Many who hear the term neural network invariably conjure up an image of some sort of living/growing/learning network. In the case of biometric facial identification, this notion is somewhat true. Neural networks use stored faces for reference purposes. These stored faces are created during the enrollment process. Upon subsequent face acquisitions, the neural network compares the acquired image to the enrolled image. Each image (acquired and enrolled) is used to determine whether a match exists through a voting process. Weights are assigned to each image's unique global features. The acquired image information is used in this voting process to determine whether there is a match with the enrollment image via algorithms that determine the matches of the unique global features. During this matching algorithm/voting process, when an incorrect vote is encountered, the weight assigned to the feature that caused the incorrect vote is modified. This is the method in which the neural network "learns." By systematically adjusting the weights of the features that provide inaccurate votes, the system can weed out those unique global features that do not provide accurate votes.

Because neural networks are capable of learning, they are also potentially capable of reducing the effects associated with issues such as lighting, aging, changing expressions, and other such face recognition issues.

## ACQUISTION TECHNOLOGY NOTES

Some manufacturers use only certain portions of the face, or use a predetermined space within the capture device for the face to fit into. This means that during the initial data template acquisition phase (enrollment), the template captured could contain only certain parts of the face. For example, if a manufacturer uses a predetermined space from which to acquire the template, and the individual whose face information is being acquired is too close, the resulting template might only include part of the person's nose and mouth. If the person were too far away, however, some environmental information could be acquired as part of the template. The environment could represent a change that might cause the user to be rejected. Most manufacturers have addressed or are addressing these issues.

Because manufacturers' face recognition technology is patented, the method in which the template is generated is often not fully known. Nonetheless, some general hypotheses can be made.

- ✓ The more data acquired, the bigger the template (depending on the algorithm).
- ✓ The larger the template, the more data points to compare against.
- ✓ The better the acquiring device's resolution, the better quality the template will be.
- ✓ Distances vary based on face recognition technology and use.

## FAILURE TO ENROLL

Relating to face recognition technology, a Failure to Enroll (FTE) occurs when the acquiring device is unable to obtain a quality image during the enrollment process that contains enough unique facial data. In different implementations, this can be caused by lighting issues (too dim, too bright, direct sunlight), poor focus, distance (too close or too far), positioning (too high, too low, too far left, and so on), or in some cases, perception on the part of the acquiring mechanism that the image for enrollment is not live.

## FALSE MATCH OR FALSE ACCEPT (TYPE 2)

The possibility of a false match or false accept with face recognition technology occurs when two faces from different people create an incorrect identification or match. This is very possible with identical twins, but may also occur in face recognition technologies that do not acquire enough data points. For example, a look-alike could be falsely identified as the person who provided the enrollment template if only a few data points are used and enough of those data points are the same as the enrollment template.

## FALSE NON-MATCH OR FALSE REJECT (TYPE 1)

In face recognition technology, a false non-match can occur when a previously enrolled/valid individual does not create a match during a subsequent acquisition process. This can occur for many of the same reasons as a Failure to Enroll, including changes in lighting, age, hairstyle, disfigurement, plastic surgery, positioning, and so on.

# Accuracy

When combined with passphrases or PINs, face technology biometrics provides strong authentication access controls.

## CROSSOVER ERROR RATE ALSO REFERRED TO AS EQUAL ERROR RATE (EER)

Although Crossover Error Rate (CER) data for facial recognition systems is not widely publicized, you can surmise that the CER for face recognition systems is well known. CER is also referred to as Equal Error Rate (EER).

## ABILITY TO VERIFY RATE

One of the unique benefits of facial recognition technologies is that a very low number of people won't be able to use them (depending on the face recognition technology chosen). This is because most of the problems associated with the Ability to Verify (ATV) rate can be easily overcome. For example, a blind person might have problems with a retina or iris scanner, but if the same person were able to sit in a prearranged chair, the face scanner would most likely be able to acquire an image for both enrollment and subsequent identifications.

Some face recognition systems examine the face image for a few seconds to determine whether the image being presented is live or fake. The determination of live versus fake is often based on eye blinks and other such movements.

# Password Replacement Scheme

Although not truly a biometric technology, another security method bears mentioning here because it leverages an individual's ability to recognize faces.

Generally, human beings have an amazing ability to remember and recognize faces. In fact, tests have shown that a human can remember 10 faces more easily than 10 random characters. This has caused some manufacturers to look at other methods of authentication. For example, Real User Corporation has created a product called PassFace. PassFace is a replacement for traditional passwords. Here's how it works.

During the enrollment process, the user is presented with a number of (up to 10) pictures of people. The user is taken through a review process of each portrait several times. After the initial learning process, the user is asked to pick each portrait out of a group of portraits. After demonstrating the ability to pick the portraits out of a group of portraits several times, the sequence is set. Upon subsequent logins, the user must select the appropriate faces as they are presented to be logged in. What makes this so unique is that many users who can forget a password in minutes, hours, or a few days, are often able to recall their PassFaces even weeks or months later.

One of the security benefits of using a product like PassFaces that leverages our own facial recognition abilities is that it is difficult to pass on to someone else. For example, you would have to be very adept at describing details of at least five or more people in to pass on your PassFace credentials.

PassFaces does have a few drawbacks, however. PassFaces does not work for visually impaired people, and a small number of the population (one in eight million sighted people, according to Real User Corporation) is unable to recall the information sufficiently to use PassFaces.

# Fact/Fiction

Both true and false perceptions exist in relationship to biometric technologies. Some of the beliefs people have relating to face biometric technologies are listed in Table 3-1.

**TABLE 3-1: Face Technology Perceptions**

| Belief | Fact |
| --- | --- |
| Infrared facial scanning can be damaging. | Most infrared technology devices remain within ranges that are not considered harmful. |

| Belief | Fact |
|---|---|
| Some people have a fear of being photographed. | Although an individual might not overcome this fear, there are ways to make system more palatable for the person to use. Depending on the use for facial recognition, the camera can be placed in an inconspicuous (out of sight) place and might be operated in conjunction with user interaction so the user does not know that a facial scan is taking place, or so the user associates the identification process with the user interaction rather than just the face scan. |
| Facial recognition scans violate a person's privacy. Although most people will not have as much of a problem with face scan techniques as they might with other biometric technologies such as retina, fingerprint, iris, and voice, many still have issues concerning privacy. | Many biometric solutions do not actually capture the face, but use the face to create a template. Educating users on how the face recognition technology works might help to reduce this issue. |

# Face Recognition Security Characteristics

When creating a face template, the components (data elements or points) captured can have a dramatic effect on the technology's ability to provide a truly unique template.

The methods used to create biometric templates vary greatly from manufacturer to manufacturer. However, to get a general sense of how a biometric template is built using face recognition technology, refer to the matrix-style template that maps directly to certain face features depicted in Figure 3-2.

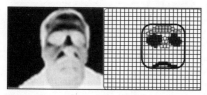

**Figure 3-2:** Simple Face Template example

One of the differences between face biometric technologies and many of the other biometric technologies is that the face can often be reconstructed from biometric face data. As previously noted, this can raise privacy concerns as well as other issues.

Using Figure 3-1 combined with a purely speculative template that leverages only four colors and uses only four regions, a template representation might look something like that shown in Figure 3-2. Because some face scan technologies use a facial scan area as part of their implementation, an outline surrounds the face scan area on the template.

Each colored square represents a different region, and the pattern of the colored squares represents the features within the region. You begin to see how this type of mapping using many pixels of varying shades, and breaking down each region, can differentiate between users. However, using a model as rudimentary as the one depicted makes it apparent that users could incorrectly be matched as other users, not to mention that a picture of a person could very easily fool this type of template creation.

**note**

The sample template model is used solely for the purpose of generically illustrating one potential template creation method. Actual facial recognition systems use much more sophisticated methods.

Table 3-2 indicates some of the additional characteristics of face recognition technology:

**TABLE 3-2: Additional Face Technology Characteristics**

| Characteristic | Ease of use | Error incidence | Accuracy | Acceptance | Security Level | Stability | Cost |
|---|---|---|---|---|---|---|---|
| | Medium | Low | High | Medium | Medium | Medium | Low |

# Strengths

Biometric face recognition technology has several strengths that can make it a good choice depending on the application. In fact, it may be among the fastest growing of the biometric technologies because of its applicability in crowd recognition areas, where obtaining biometric information using other acquisition techniques is impractical.

✓ May not require user interaction

✓ No physical contact with the device required

✓ Can often use standard camera (digital, Web, video, and so on) as long as resolutions are adequate

✓ Easy to use (simply look at it)

✓ Reduced cost over other biometric technologies (excluding infrared cameras); examples include the following:

   ■ Retina (acquisition devices are costly and bulky)

   ■ Iris (special iris camera devices are required)

   ■ Signature (tablets, touch screens, or other devices such as PDAs are needed)

   ■ Fingerprint (requires specific scanner based on manufacturer's implementation)

✓ Face scan technology is highly accepted compared to fingerprint, iris, and retina technologies.

✓ Very low number of users that can't use the technology (low Ability to Verify percentage)

✓ The camera can typically acquire an image from varying distances, whereas other technologies are distance-dependant.

✓ Face scan technology is a good candidate for strong or two-factor authentication schemes.

# Weaknesses

Although facial scanning has many strengths and is considered to be much less intrusive than other biometric technologies, it also has its share of weaknesses:

✓ Twins can be falsely identified as each other.

✓ Degrees of variation (loosely put, degrees of variation is the number of degrees a face presentation can be off and still be correctly acquired for identification).

✓ Lighting, either too bright or too dim, can have a dramatic effect on the acquired face.

✓ Environmental conditions, such as extreme heat or cold, can affect thermal facial scan technologies.

✓ Facial expressions could cause false rejects.

✓ Hair changes can cause false rejects with some facial scan products.

✓ Facial hair growth/shaving might cause a user to be unrecognized, leading to false rejects. During the growth process, the user can intermittently and increasingly experience false rejects.

✓ Glasses can alter a user's ability to be recognized if they are removed or added after enrollment.

✓ Aging of the human face could cause false rejects.

✓ Distance variations might cause false rejects or could prevent enough unique information from being acquired during the enrollment process.

✓ Not considered as secure as some other biometric technologies such as fingerprint, iris, and retina.

✓ Can be easily tricked or faked.

✓ Proof of life refers to the ability of face recognition to ensure that the presented image is living.

You might have noticed that distance is listed as both a strength and weakness. Depending on the face recognition technology and its use, distance can be a plus or a drawback. For example, for surveillance implementations, the ability to obtain information from a long range can be a great strength, whereas problems can occur if a person is too close or too far away from the camera in the case of a technology that fits the face into a predetermined space.

# Countermeasures

As some continuously search for methods to create greater levels of security, another faction constantly seeks ways to foil these security measures. The following list presents some of the methods that you can use to reduce the affects of the weaknesses of facial recognition/identification technologies:

✓ To reduce the potential that twins could be falsely identified, add a second security measure or use thermal facial scanning.

✓ Address degrees of variation issues first by understanding how the system will be used and then selecting a system that can accommodate for its use (within reason).

✓ Address lighting weaknesses by ensuring that proper and consistent lighting is maintained in the acquisition area.

✓ Where possible, control environmental conditions. When controlling environmental conditions is not an option (as might be the case for outdoor use), choose a solution that is not dependant on such conditions.

✓ Overcome facial expression weaknesses by educating the user to present as consistent a facial expression as possible and/or by choosing technologies (such as local feature analysis) that can accommodate some facial expression changes.

✓ Avoid hair change false reject issues by choosing a technology that uses a preset area for acquisition and by positioning users so that only the face and not the hair is presented.

✓ One method of addressing facial hair growth/shaving false reject problems is to re-enroll the user.

✓ To address user false rejects due to the removal of glasses, educate the user and/or re-enroll that user.

✓ Address false reject issues due to aging by selecting a technology that can accommodate for such changes (for example, a neural network), or re-enroll the user.

✓ Address problems with facial recognition caused by distance by educating the user and positioning acquisition devices in such a fashion that the user will generally, automatically, place himself/herself in the proper area, or mark the acquisition area that the user must be in.

✓ To overcome the fact that facial recognition technologies are not considered as secure as some other biometric technologies, choose strong facial recognition technologies and implement additional security measures. For example, mixing face and passwords/PINS or face and voice and so on can allow users to be identified without adding too much burden to the user.

Many implementations currently use passwords. Because adding facial recognition can have minimal effect on a user, many face implementations still use both face and password security.

✓ To reduce the risk of a facial scan/recognition technology being easily tricked or faked, select a robust, detailed technology that tries to determine that the presented face is not a fake, and implement additional security measures.

✓ To verify that the presented face is alive (Proof of Life), select a technology that evaluates items such as expression changes, movement, and eye blinking. Add additional security measures (perhaps requiring real-time interaction).

# Face Technology Uses

Face recognition/identification technology is not for everyone. However, the fact that it does not require physical contact with the device and that it can leverage generally available and inexpensive capture devices (for example, Web cams) makes it appealing for many applications.

## Surveillance

Surveillance has been and will continue to be one of the most effective ways law enforcement (and other) agencies gather information. Phone tapping, following an individual suspected of illegal activities, photographing, and videotaping are all forms of surveillance. However, in many cases, surveillance information uncovers additional, unknown suspects. The methods used to determine an unknown suspect's identity vary depending on the source of the surveillance information.

Where face recognition is concerned, photographic and video surveillance information can be used in conjunction with face recognition technology to assist such surveillance agencies in determining whom they might have gathered intelligence on.

Face recognition, sometimes referred to as face matching technology, is capable of taking this gathered intelligence information and comparing it to known information (a database of known persons) for the purposes of identifying an individual by obtaining a match. To accomplish this, the gathered surveillance information is electronically input (captured via digital means, scanned, and so on) into the recognition system. The face image can be manipulated (enlarged, reduced, lightened, darkened, and so on) to prepare it for the matching phase. The image is then compared to the database of faces. In simplistic terms, a match occurs when the input image, when compared to an existing face image in the database, falls within an acceptable tolerance range.

For example, imagine that a law enforcement agency has had a reputed mob boss under surveillance for several months. In the course of its information gathering it has collected information (taken photographs) on an unknown associate of the mob boss. The local agency sends the information (copies of the photographs) to a national or international agency capable of comparing the information to its database of known persons. The photographs are scanned, and the face recognition system performs match analysis on each known person in the face recognition system database, searching for any responses where 75 percent of the unidentified person's features match. (Most face match technologies provide the ability to adjust the match percentage.)

Several possible matches are found, noted, and the associated information is printed out. The information is sent back to the originating law enforcement agency. In this fashion, the originating law enforcement agency can determine whether the individual on which it has gathered intelligence can be positively identified.

Although the method of comparison varies by manufacturer and technology implementation, the analysis should provide similar results.

Crowd scanningis another form of identification using facial recognition technologies. Simply put, crowds are scanned and the individual faces of each person in the crowd are compared to databases of known faces.

## Identification/Recognition

Identification and recognition are often erroneously used interchangeably. Loosely defined, *identification* is achieved when an unknown person becomes known. *Recognition* occurs when a person claiming a specific identity is "recognized" as being the owner of that identity. Most often, this is accomplished by comparing the acquired credentials of the individual claiming the identity with the information available for that identity.

For example, some Automatic Teller Machine (ATM) applications leverage facial recognition technology. When a person goes to an ATM, that person inserts his bankcard into the ATM. The ATM reads, processes, and forwards the information to a central data repository. Because the bankcard contains the individual's "claimed identity," the camera acquires the person's face information and sends it to the central data repository. The captured face information is compared to the face information obtained during an enrollment process (usually acquired when the person is issued the bankcard) and stored in the central data repository. If the newly acquired face is within acceptable tolerances, the person is considered recognized, and the transaction continues. This process can happen in seconds.

One of the facial matching methods used breaks down the face into different areas or domains, as previously mentioned. Each domain of the acquired facial image is compared to each domain of the original or enrollment image. If enough domains are considered a match, the individual is recognized. However, technology similar to this domain matching technology can be used in a reverse fashion to achieve a different goal (see the next section for details).

## Reverse Identification/Recognition

When an individual witnesses a crime, a police sketch artist is often called in to create a sketch from information obtained from the witness. This poses a few problems:

- ✓ The sketch artist might not be a police officer, so additional expense is incurred.

- ✓ A sketch artist might not be available.

- ✓ After the sketch is complete, it must be turned into an electronic representation (scanned, digitized, and so on).

To address these and other issues, many police agencies use electronic means of creating these police sketches.

Instead of using a face recognition system purely for comparison, some programs also contain a database of known faces broken down by area or domain that can be used to create a digital composite sketch. This sketch is created by selecting the individual area based on the witness's recollection of that feature. In this fashion, a face is built rather than sketched. This means that almost anyone can create the face (including the witness), reducing or eliminating the need to have a special artist draw composite sketches.

A similar approach can be used to determine identity and facial features based on forensic evidence.

Although much of the discussion to this point references face technology and uses for law, the technology can be used simply for access control.

## Access

One facial recognition technology feature is that it does not require interaction with a device for the biometric information (face image) to be obtained. This makes it more acceptable to the general population and a good system to use for physical access control and for systems such as time and attendance.

A user might only need to stop briefly (and look in a general direction) before being identified. Once identified, they can proceed with little or no interaction with the camera.

## Data Protection

Biometric solutions in the area of data protection are growing greatly. As individuals become more dependant on the data contained on their networks, and as the networks become more secure, they store more sensitive information on them. As more sensitive information is stored electronically, more individuals will try to gain unauthorized access to the information. This unauthorized access often comes in the form of internal employees allowing an outside person or group access to the information. Using a biometric authentication solution such as face technology can reduce the ability of external forces to gaining access to sensitive information. Instead of logging on using a simple username and password, face login solutions can provide greater security.

When a user logs on to a network using only a username and password, he or she is using information that user knows. This means that someone might easily be able to obtain this information using common hacking techniques. For example, if the company standard naming convention is first initial and last name (as it is in many companies), all a hacker really needs to do is know the person's name (often obtainable from automated phone directories or operators), and then the hacker only needs to learn a particular user's password. This cuts down on a hacker's work considerably. However, if a company uses the "something you know and something you have (or are)" philosophy, also referred to as two-factor authentication, it can greatly increase security.

An example of two-factor authentication is combining password and biometric authentication. When two-factor authentication is employed, a user must know his or her username and password and must also supply a biometric credential. Again, face recognition technology fits this scenario well because it does not require great user training efforts, does not cost much, and provides an additional level of security.

No matter what the reason for evaluating or implementing face recognition technology, you must consider a few points (discussed in the next section).

# Face Technology Considerations

As withXany technology decision, before you reach your decision you should have a full understanding of the technology options, components, and uses. Relating to face technology, consider the following matters:

- ✓ Cost of the product versus the value of the information to be protected.

- ✓ Any biometric technology should implement strong security measures against tampering. One of the benefits to face technology is that cameras have been around for a long time and can operate in many venues. However, they are also susceptible to tampering. For example, a video playback could be used to gain access to a system even if the system requires movement to prove the image being submitted is actually living.

- ✓ Environmental conditions are a concern, but because camera technology has been around for a long time and cameras can be placed in controlled housings (perhaps environmentally controlled), you can limit extreme temperature, humidity, moisture, and even some device tampering issues.

✓ The solution must support the environment in which it will be used. For example, if the environment is Window 2000 Server with Active Directory and Windows XP workstations, the solution must support that environment.

✓ System requirements must be known and addressed.

✓ You must address the current environment security and how the face recognition technology will fit within the environment.

✓ At a minimum, the selected solution, including software, hardware, enrollment process, and environment should be resistant to false input methods. Relating to face recognition technology, these include the following:

- The solution should require users to move or change their pose during acquisition.

- Hardware must be implemented so that the camera device cannot be spoofed (that is, so no one can splice into the acquisition device's wires and use a video playback, for example).

- The software should be able to implement additional security measures (for example, voice). You could require a user's face information and require the user to repeat a saying or give a verbal password.

- If face and password technology is jointly used, you can implement a keystroke password biometric technology toX increase the security.

- The highest resolution and most detailed analysis will provide the best results.

- How is aging handled?

- How do hairstyle changes, facial hair issues, glasses, and so on affect the solution?

- Are any special requirements needed (lighting, distance, training, and so on)?

✓ The camera device must function in the area of intended use but ideally should also be able to function under a wide range of conditions and in a wide range of areas without adversely affecting the image quality, including the following:

- Portability

- Indoor and/or outdoor use

- Personal and/or public use

- Varying presentations should not cause false accepts and should limit false rejects.

✓ The camera device must also fulfill specific resolution requirements, including the following:

- As the face database grows, how will performance be affected?

- Who else is using the technology?

- What are the scalability requirements/limitations?

- What solution maintenanceX is required?

General and more specific technologyX considerations are discussed in Chapter 11.

## Implementation Criteria

Face technologyX can be used for a broader range of applications than many other biometric technologies. However, this book's mission is to provide you with a good understanding of the biometric technologies and how they can be used for data networks. As such, the focus here is on data network implementation criteria.

You can use face recognition technology to provide greater levels of security for data networks by increasing the security measures associated with the following:

✓ Network logon/authentication

✓ Individual workstation logon/authentication

✓ Application control

✓ Inactivity security

✓ Encryption control

✓ Activity logging

✓ Public access protection (including capturing the faces of rejected users)

However, for any biometric solution to be effective, it must be generally acceptable, minimally intrusive, and, under optimal circumstances, the user should derive some benefit from the biometric technology Ximplementation.

# Network Product Commonalities

Although face recognition technology has many uses, its use for data network authentication can't yet be classified as widespread. Much of this is due to the maturity of the technology. Although faces have been used for recognition since the dawn of mankind, biometric face recognition technology is not considered as mature as fingerprint, iris, or retina technologies. Nonetheless, face recognition technology is projected to grow substantially as the technology becomes more mature.

Don't let its maturity keep you from implementing it if doing so is an appropriate choice. Just make sure the implementation leverages two-factor authentication; you may even want to add a third (second biometric technology) security measure that does not require any additional user interaction. An example might include face, password, and password keystroke technologies. The user's face is scanned, and the user only has to enter a password.

Keystroke biometrics is covered in Chapter 8.

Face biometric network solutions vary greatly. Most provide login authentication using the users' face information. However, some systems only provide login authentication, whereas others implement additional features. And although the acquisition devices may differ (camera versus infrared camera, thermal, and so on), the acquisition method remains the same — the face information is acquired without physical interaction with the device.

Most manufacturers products provide both face and password security protection. This allows a company that simply wants to increase security using biometric face recognition technology to add the solution with minimal impact to the user. The user must still type the password but will not be authorized unless the claimed identity (login name), password, and face image all match.

# Network Product Variations

Face acquisition technologies were discussed earlier in this chapter, but the method in which the biometric templates are generated differs by manufacturer. For example, Eigenface might be the underlying acquisition technology, but one manufacturer might use the Eigenface acquired information to create a biometric template to use for network logins that cannot provide an image of the face if it were reverse engineered. Another manufacturer might store the picture information "as is" and might simply compare the enrollment information and the submission information.

Most of the network product differences for biometric face technology are derived from the method in which the manufacturers view their products. Many companies have face login products, but they come in the form of Software Development Kits (SDKs). This methodology provides great flexibility for companies that can afford the time, effort, and cost of custom development but can leave those companies that do not have such resources wanting more.

On the other hand, some manufactures' face technology provides network login authentication, file encryption, communication security, e-mail encryption, Web authentication, standalone workstation authentication, and inactivity protection (screen saver authentication). However, they are completely modular, must be purchased separately, and in some cases do not all support the same platform(s).

Finally, the methods in which the products are implemented vary from manufacturer to manufacturer. Some manufacturers' products support multiple biometric solutions such as face, voice, electronic signature, keystroke, and fingerprint Other manufacturers' implementations support one biometric technology and passwords, with little control over the authentication steps used. For example, one manufacturer's product might authenticate on face only and only use a password if a user is not recognized, while another manufacturer might allow both face and password and also allow for a password-face image-password combination for higher security.

# Sample Product

This book (where possible) shows you how to install and use a sample biometric product or provides code for future programming of your own biometric solutions. This chapter uses the demo version TrueFace PC from Miros, Inc. The product selected runs on Windows 95/98. It was selected partially to demonstrate a biometric technology application on an older platform, because many Windows 98 installations are still in use today.

TrueFace PC was designed to secure Windows 95 and 98 systems. Newer releases of TrueFace PC (or a similar product) will probably be released to provide security for Windows ME, 2000, and XP.

This sample installation shows the acquisition device installation, TrueFace PC installation, enrollment process, match tuning, live submission tuning, testing, and inactivity (screen saver) security.

Before you begin the installation of TrueFace PC, ensure that your system meets the minimum requirements based on the version you intend to install. For this example, version 1.0 of the TrueFace PC software has the following minimum system requirements:

- ✓ Windows 95/98/98SE/NT
- ✓ 16MB memory
- ✓ 10MB hard drive space available
- ✓ PC camera compatible with Video for Windows
- ✓ Latest patches and fixes

This example's PC camera is the Panasonic Authenticam (camera device only), for which the drivers must first be installed.

## Authenticam Driver Installation

The camera driver software is installed during the Private ID installation.

1. Place the Private ID CD into CD-ROM drive. The menu shown in Figure 3-3 should appear.

2. If the menu does not appear, browse to the CD-ROM drive and select the Setup icon.

3. To enter the Private ID installation, click on the link shown in Figure 3-3.

4. After clicking on the Install Private ID 2.0 selection, you are presented with the InstallShield Wizard status indicator shown in Figure 3-4. This will automatically take you to the Private ID Setup.

5. The Private ID Setup window is shown in Figure 3-5.

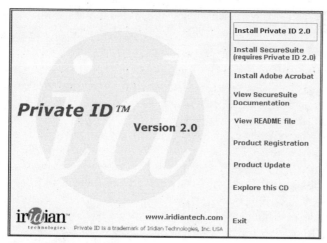

**Figure 3-3:** PrivateID menu

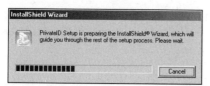

**Figure 3-4:** Status indicator

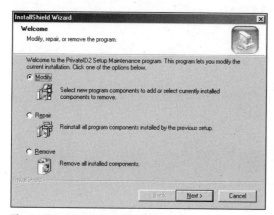

**Figure 3-5:** Private ID Setup screen

Click Next to continue to the license acceptance window illustrated in Figure 3-6.

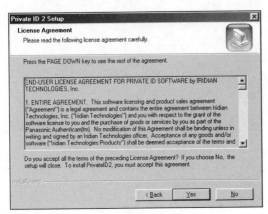

**Figure 3-6:** License acceptance

**6.** Click Yes to accept the license and the program begins the installation process. The Private ID 2 Setup Status window displays the files being copied and the status, as shown in Figure 3-7.

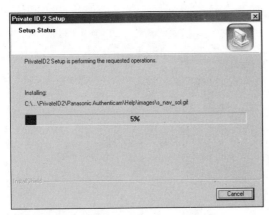

**Figure 3-7:** Setup status

**7.** After all the files have been successfully copied, the Finish screen appears, as shown in Figure 3-8.

Click Finish to complete the Private ID installation. Reboot the PC if you are prompted to do so.

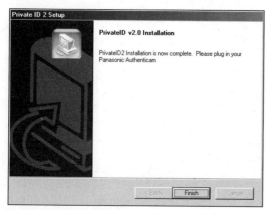

**Figure 3-8:** Private ID Finish screen

Before proceeding to the TrueFace PC installation, verify that the Authenticam camera is functioning by doing the following:

**1.** Selecting it from the start menu, as shown in Figure 3-9.

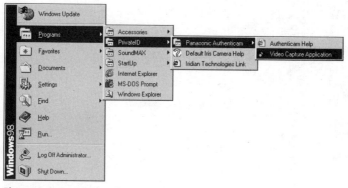

**Figure 3-9:** Start Authenticam

**2.** This brings up the PC-CAM Capture window. Select Devices and Panasonic Authenticam, as shown in Figure 3-10.

**Figure 3-10:** Select Panasonic Authenticam

**3.** The camera should turn on, and a green light located on the lower left of the Authenticam should illuminate. When this light comes on, make sure the shutter is open over the camera lenses and the camera should begin to operate. If you sit directly in front of the camera, you should be able to see yourself in the PC-CAM Capture window. You can also ensure that the device is working properly by clicking on the device test option and selecting Color Bar. The camera should turn on (green light illuminates) if it was off, and a color bar pattern like that shown in Figure 3-11 should appear.

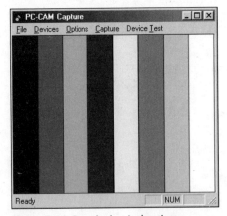

**Figure 3-11:** Functioning Authenticam

With the Authenticam functioning properly, you can proceed to the TrueFace PC Installation and setup procedure.

You will likely use a different camera. Follow the instructions for your camera and ensure that it is functioning properly before you proceed with the TrueFace PC installation. Also, make sure your camera is focused properly.

## TrueFace PC Installation

You can obtain the TrueFace PC demo software by searching the Internet for the key words "TrueFace PC." After you have downloaded the demo, save it to the directory of your choice and extract it within that directory.

**1.** Browse to the directory containing the installation files and double-click on the Setup.exe file. The installation begins with the Welcome screen shown in Figure 3-12.

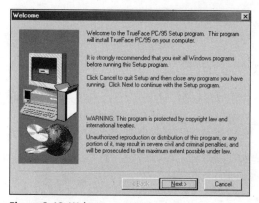

**Figure 3-12:** Welcome screen

**2.** Click Next to bring up the license screen shown in Figure 3-13.

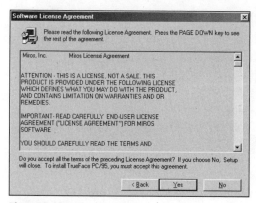

**Figure 3-13:** License window

**3.** Click on Yes to accept the license agreement terms and continue the installation. The Readme Installation window appears, as shown in Figure 3-14.

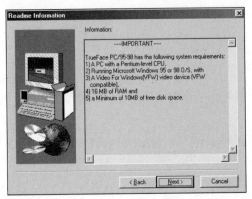

**Figure 3-14:** Readme installation window

**4.** Click Next to continue. The installation proceeds to the installation status screen, as shown in Figure 3-15.

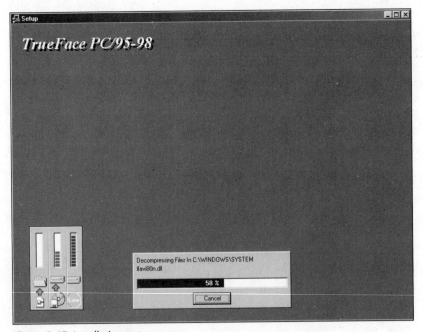

**Figure 3-15:** Installation status screen

**5.** After the files have been installed, the TrueFace PC/95 Reserve Password screen appears, as shown in Figure 3-16.

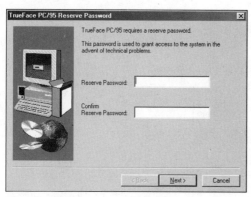

**Figure 3-16:** Reserve password screen

**6.** Enter a strong password twice. Make sure you use a different password than that of the Administrator account. Also, ensure that you can remember the password because it will be needed from time to time. Click Next to proceed to the Enable TrueFace PC/95 Logon Protection screen shown in Figure 3-17.

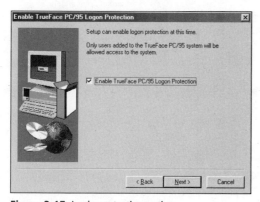

**Figure 3-17:** Login protection option

**7.** Ensure that the checkbox next to Enable TrueFace PC/95 Logon Protection is checked, and click Next to continue. The TrueFace PC/95 Screen window appears, as illustrated in Figure 3-18.

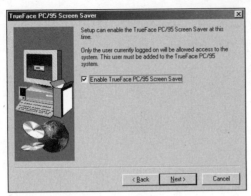

**Figure 3-18:** Screensaver option

**8.** Ensure that the checkbox next to Enable TrueFace PC/95 Screen Saver is checked, and click Next to continue. The TrueFace PC/95 finish installation window appears, as illustrated in Figure 3-19.

**Figure 3-19:** Finish

**9.** Click Finish, and you are presented with the screen shown in Figure 3-20.

**10.** Select the Try First button. This allows you to test the product for 30 days. You are then prompted to reboot the machine.

**Figure 3-20:** Trial Screen

# TrueFace PC Configuration

To configure TrueFace PC, follow these steps:

**1.** After the machine has rebooted, you are presented with the window shown in Figure 3-21. Initially, the Username was blank. As shown in the figure, type Administrator and enter your Reserve Password.

**Figure 3-21:** TrueFace logon window

**2.** After being authenticated, you are presented again with the Trial Screen (shown in Figure 3-20). This screen is presented many times throughout the demonstration. When the screen appears, click on the Try First option each time. After selecting the Try First option the first time, you are presented with the enrollment screen shown in Figure 3-22.

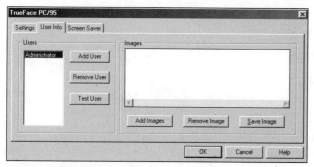

**Figure 3-22:** Enrollment screen

**note**

The TrueFace PC utilities screen shown in Figure 3-22 is located in the Windows control panel.

**3.** To enroll for the Administrator user, click on Add Images to bring up the screen shown in Figure 3-23.

**Figure 3-23:** Image acquisition

**4.** The "TrueFace Micros" acquisition window is displayed on the left-hand side of the display. Clicked on the face within the display window to proceed. The TrueFace Micros acquisition window is displayed on the right of the screen. Again, click on the face to proceed. You are prompted with the following message illustrated by Figure 3-24.

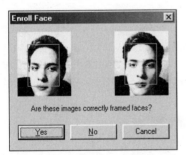

**Figure 3-24:** Enroll Face window

**5.** Ensure that the face is framed properly and click Yes to continue. Notice that there are now two faces entered into the User Info screen shown in Figure 3-25.

Adding several face images from different distances away from the camera is recommended. This is primarily because you will not likely position yourself exactly the same each time you sit down. One of the best methods is to enroll a face image, get up, walk away, come back, reposition, and enroll another image.

**Figure 3-25:** Enrolled User Info

**6.** After enough images have been enrolled, test the user images using the Test User button. The camera will turn on, acquire an image (using the window shown in Figure 3-23), and the image acquisition will occur as was the case for the enrollment process.

When performing the Test User option with detection fraud turned on, make sure you look at the displayed windows (first the left window, then click on the face, then the right window, and click on the face).

After both images have been acquired, a screen similar to Figure 3-26 will display.

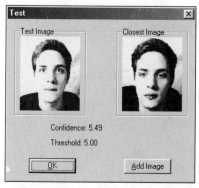

**Figure 3-26:** Confidence rating

7. A confidence rating will display along with the current threshold. The confidence scale is 0 to 10. In this example, the threshold is 5 and the confidence is 5.49. Increasing the threshold increases the security. Do this by selecting the Settings Tab and increasing the threshold values, as shown in Figure 3-27.

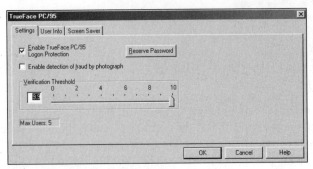

**Figure 3-27:** Changing the threshold

8. You can enable fraud detection by checking the box next to the Enable detection of fraud by photograph (also shown in Figure 3-27). This option makes the process of someone using a photograph to achieve a false accept more difficult. When this option is enabled, the user must look at the acquisition windows, first left then right. If the system does not detect the change, an error message occurs stating that the user did not pass the fraud detection test.

9. Finally, TrueFace has the capability to protect against computer inactivity using a screen saver. Enable this option by selecting the Screen Saver tab and selecting a screen saver option from the pull-down list shown in Figure 3-28.

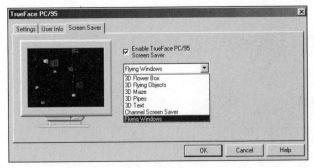

**Figure 3-28:** Enable and select screen saver

**10.** After selecting the screensaver, you can select additional settings to be made by clicking the Settings button shown in Figure 3-29.

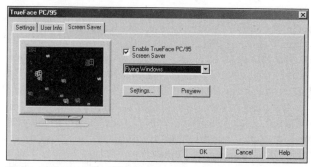

**Figure 3-29:** Settings and preview

**11.** After choosing all the settings, you can view the screen saver option in full screen mode by selecting the Preview button (also shown in Figure 3-29). After the settings have been made for TrueFace PC, make sure the Windows screen saver has the TrueFace PC screen saver selected, as shown in Figure 3-30.

In Figure 3-30, the screen saver is selected to TrueFace PC, the wait (or inactivity timeout) is five minutes, and the password-protected button is not checked. The Password button is not checked because when TrueFace PC screen saver is selected, it will automatically use the settings from TrueFace PC. You can check this button with no passwords set to achieve the same result.

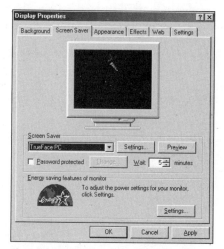

**Figure 3-30:** Windows display properties

TrueFace PC is now installed, enrollment has been performed, the appropriate features are set, the threshold has been raised, and the screen saver option is enabled.

# Summary

This chapter discussed the many topics relating to face recognition/identification technology. The four primary face acquisition technologies are Eigenface, local feature analysis, thermal, and neural network. Each acquisition technology has a place and is used for different face recognition /identification implementations.

Face recognition/identification technology has several uses, including surveillance, crowd scanning, network authentication, and more. Depending on the solution, when a face is scanned it will either be compared to a database of faces or to the face information for the declared individual. In cases where an identity needs to be derived from the characteristics of an unknown face, a database is searched; on the other hand, if a user declares an identity (as is the case for network logins), the acquired face image will likely only be compared to the traits obtained during the enrollment process for the declared user.

The products and solutions that implement face technology are quite varied. Each manufacturer implements different features depending on its use of the technology. Selecting the right technology can be a daunting task, but with the proper information you can make sound selections.

Face recognition technology is relatively new to the biometric network login scene. Testing of different products has shown that face recognition technology can still be tricked relatively easily and, as such, should not be used as the sole means of authentication. Mixing face recognition technology with other forms of security technologies can actually increase the strength of the security model. For more information on two-factor authentication and multibiometrics, see Chapter 10.

Finally, the chapter demonstrated a sample face recognition product by installing the camera drivers and the TrueFace PC software and enrolling and configuring the appropriate options to secure your PC using face recognition technology.

# Chapter 4

# Iris and Retina Vascular Pattern Technology

UNTIL NOW, THIS BOOK has discussed biometric technologies that are secure, but the level of security can pale in comparison (referring to the *crossover error rate*, or *CER*) to what this chapter discusses. Iris and retina vascular pattern biometric technologies raise the bar for the CER. This heightened level of security, however, often comes with more than just a higher price tag.

Despite what some may think, in the grand biometric scheme, iris and retina vascular pattern technologies are not infants. (Retinal vascular pattern uniqueness was noticed as far back as 1930, and iris technologies date back to at least 1936.) Compared to the interest in fingerprints, which dates back to at least the prehistoric era, however, these technologies can be considered infants. And much as occurs with infants, the anticipation of their ultimate potential may fall well short of what they can actually accomplish. Adding to their mystique, retina and iris scanning technologies are often among the most-portrayed technologies seen in movies, primarily because of their "scientific" (and/or futuristic) appeal. Because they do have some history, and because the cost of using them is coming down rapidly, there are definite and encouraging reasons why these technologies may make their way into more mainstream roles. To understand why this may occur, a good understanding of the distinctiveness of each is essential.

## Technical Descriptions

Although each technology can broadly be placed into the eye-biometric technology (purely because they deal with eyes), the underlying technology of each is very different. To help you gain a better understanding of how each technology differs, the following sections look at each in some detail.

### Retina Vascular Pattern Technology

So far, we have looked at face and fingerprint biometric technology, and each deal with an external biometric trait, characteristic, or combination thereof. Retina (and iris) biometric technology changes this pattern by using an internal and unique biometric characteristic. The choice of an internal biometric provides some significant benefits and some unusual negative aspects. However, many of these negative aspects can be overcome with quality education, an understanding and sympathetic mind, and by taking reasonable and well-thought-out precautions.

Retina vascular pattern technology uses the unique pattern formed by the blood vessels behind the eye. Not only is this pattern unique to each individual, but it is also unique to each eye. Even in the case of twins, this pattern could be dramatically different in each twin. Figure 4-1 roughly depicts how the blood vessels are viewed through the eye.

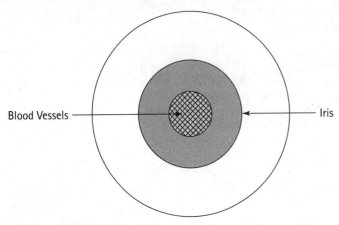

**Figure 4-1:** Looking into the eye

In this figure, the outer white ring represents the eye; the middle, darker ring represents the iris; and the inner ring with the crosshatch pattern represents the blood vessel pattern of the eye. Obviously, a real eye would not have a perfect crosshatch pattern, as shown in Figure 4-1, but rather a pattern more similar to that of Figure 4-2, which illustrates how an actual blood vessel pattern may appear.

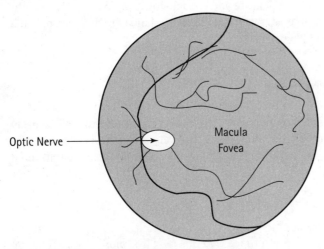

**Figure 4-2:** Retina vascular pattern

Each blood vessel pattern is unique. In the preceding figure, for example, you see different densities and definite distinct patterns. If this were the right eye of a person, the pattern of the left eye would also be different from that shown in Figure 4-2. This also holds true even in the case of identical twins.

## CLASSIFICATION

Unlike fingerprints, for example, retina vascular patterns don't form loops, whorls, and arches and, therefore, are not classified into categories similar to those of fingerprints. the patterns of the blood vessels, however, are very unique and are not determined by genetic factors. This can also help to reduce or eliminate some of the negative responses and potential refusals to use the technology because of the possibility of it being ethnically biased.

## TEMPLATE ACQUISITON

To generate a template with retina scanning technology, a user must typically position himself, specifically his eye, very close to the acquisition device (the retina vascular pattern scanner). This positioning can be approximately one-half inch away from the acquisition device to as close as having the eye socket rest on the acquisition device. The user looks into the acquisition device while the retina vascular patterns are measured. Depending on the acquisition device, the scanning process can take up to five seconds. Additionally, with many devices, any movement may render the scan unusable and an additional scan would be necessary.

During the enrolment process, as many as five (or possibly more) images could be necessary. This means that, compared to some other biometric technologies, the enrollment process is lengthier.

## UNIQUE IDENTIFIICATION

Retina scanners can truly provide unique identification above and beyond that of other biometric devices currently available today. One of the reasons that this is possible relates to the number of data points collected. Because different technologies handle template generation differently, one of the common evaluation points relating to the strength of the technology relates to how many data points are collected. In the case of fingerprint technology, minutiae are collected, and the number of minutiae (unique feature points) collected can generally be equated to the strength of the overall template (to resist false matches and false rejects). In the case of retina technology, as many as 400 data points can be collected, in contrast to fingerprint technology, which can have as few as 30 or 40 minutiae (data points). If this is coupled with the algorithm used, the potential for two individuals to have the same 400 data points in the same order, sequence, and so on greatly increases the individuality of the collected template. The greater the individuality of the template, the less likely is the occurrence of a false match (which should be one of the top items — if not *the* top item — on your security hit list). As is true of other technologies, however, retina technology is not completely infallible.

## RECOGNITION

Retina vascular pattern scanning and comparison technology functions somewhat similar to other biometric technologies in that templates are created for comparison. The type of retina technology can determine how many templates are created (one-to-many). After enrollment has occurred, each time that the retina is scanned, a new template is created and compared to existing enrollment template(s). If the algorithm determines that a match exists, the presenter is considered recognized, or identified. Three common ways of recognizing an individual as the unique provider of the enrollment template (using our terms) are database searching, declaration/match, and submit/validate.

**DATABASE SEARCHING**   With database searching, the presenter's retina is scanned, and a one-time template is created. This template is then compared to the existing database of enrolled individuals, where the templates of known persons exist. If the one-time presentation template produces a match with an existing template, the presenter is informed of whom he is. Using a common movie scenario, for example, if Scott Blaul had previously provided his retina vascular pattern profile (generated template) into the database during an enrollment process, a template uniquely identifying Scott Blaul would exist. Using a database search methodology, the next time that Scott Blaul submitted his eye for retina vascular pattern identification; a new template would be created and then compared to known templates to determine whether a match existed. If a match were found, the system may permit Scott Blaul to enter a facility by providing a verbal message, "Welcome Scott Blaul, you are cleared to enter the facility," and unlocking a door.

**DECLARATION/MATCH**   The second common method of recognition requires users to declare who they are before submitting to the retina scan. This enables the database to check against only one user template, thus increasing response times and speed. However, it also provides a higher level of security because, not only must the user submit to the scan, but the presentation template also is then compared only to that of whom the person states that he or she is instead of to all templates.

One could argue that this does not produce a higher level of security, because someone who could potentially produce a false retina would have to know the source. If you consider, however, that this is very difficult and that, if a database is searched to find a match without declaration, the potential for a false positive increases, the declaration/match method definitely provides greater security.

**SUBMIT/VALIDATE**   The submit/validate method is somewhat the reverse method of the declaration/match method. During this process, the presenter's retina is scanned. The user is then prompted for some other form of identification, such as a passphrase, password, or PIN. In some systems, a combination of these items is used to create the presentation template, and in other systems, it is used to ensure that the matched template is the correct one by comparing the entered passphrase, password, or PIN to the enrolled one matching the appropriate retina vascular pattern template.

The submit/validate method is also a form of two-factor authentication, which is discussed in the chapter on multibiometrics.

After the presented template has been matched with the enrolled template and the appropriate code has been successfully entered, the user is considered recognized.

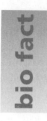

Most manufacturers of biometric products have their own unique (patented) method of performing recognition. This can actually be a positive rather than a negative if you consider what it may take to breach every system.

## FAILURES AND ERRORS

Even though retina vascular pattern biometric technology is (arguably, based on some manufacturers' claims) currently the most secure, the probability still exists that false matches and false nonmatches (rejects) can occur. The likelihood is much less than with other technologies, but it is still possible, even if the number of unique data points collected is substantially higher than that of other technologies.

**FAILURE TO ENROLL (FTE)**    Relating to retina technology, a failure to enroll (FTE) can occur if a given individual cannot create an enrollment template. This can be caused by factors that prohibit the scanning of the retina vascular patterns, including cataracts, eye damage, eye disease, and even refusal. Additionally, although highly unlikely, the possibility exists that a scan would yield a template that lacks sufficient unique data to provide the capability to uniquely identify an individual on comparing it to the current database of known users. This has the potential to produce a false match.

**FALSE MATCH OR FALSE ACCEPT (TYPE 2)**    An example of a false match in retinal technology could occur if two users' templates are not unique enough to sufficiently differentiate one from one another—in essence, a false match could occur if the enrollment template were generated without sufficient uniqueness, thereby potentially providing two identities for one person. Additionally, if the database searching method is used exclusively, the possibility exists that users could be incorrectly identified.

**FALSE NONMATCH OR FALSE REJECT (TYPE 1)**    More realistically, a failure to obtain a valid presentation template or a false nonmatch may occur more often than the other errors. This can be due to any number of factors, including eye placement (too far away, too close), eye movement, colored contacts, and so on.

## ACCURACY

As stated earlier, retina technology accuracy numbers vary widely. This is partially due to the fact that the amount of data available to determine biometric technology accuracy by using retina vascular patterns is very limited compared to the vast array of data available for technologies such as fingerprints. This accounts for varying CER rates.

**CROSSOVER ERROR RATE (CER) OR EQUAL ERROR RATE (EER)**    The accuracy of the retina CER has been stated as anywhere from one in 100,000 to as high as one in one billion, depending on the source. No matter what the actual number is, however, the critics agree that its accuracy is very good.

As you may recall, the CER is the point at which the false match rate and the false nonmatch rate are equal. The accuracy for retina technology if the CER were .0000001, therefore, would equate to around one in one billion (x in 100, where x is .0000001). Compared to a technology such as fingerprint technology, the accuracy of which which is .2 percent, or two in 1,000 (which is considered a relatively secure technology by most), you can see the rather large security advantage to using a technology such as retina vascular patterns.

As is the case with other technologies, the CER is affected (changed) if the sensitivity level increases or decreases. Changing the sensitivity may not be possible with some manufacturers' products.

**ABILITY TO VERIFY RATE (ATV)**    For any number of reasons, the ATV with retina technologies has been listed as low as 85 percent of the population. Some of this is because of items discussed in FTE (such as eye disease), but a good portion of this number may result from the stigma that surrounds eye-related biometric technologies. In any event, if the ATV rating is a higher number, it is considered better than those with lower ATV ratings. One reason why the ATV rating varies, even among retina technologies, relates to how the user must interact with the acquisition device. If users must place their eye on the acquisition device, they are more resistant than if they do not need to physically touch the acquisition device at all. If a user can be a half an inch away from the acquisition device, therefore, and no part of the body must touch it, the person is likely less resistant to the technique.

This is an important factor, because the fewer people who are not verified, the better is the overall security of the system. A high ATV, however, can also lead to higher levels of false matches or false accepts. A system with a high ATV rate and a low false match and false acceptance rate, therefore, would be the most preferred.

Systems with higher ATV rates, low false accept rates, and low false reject rates generally cost more than those that do not have such stringent criteria.

## FACT/FICTION

Like it or not, common beliefs (which may or may not be factual) and misconceptions must be overcome in dealing with biometrics. Some of those related to retina biometric technologies are reflected in Table 4-1:

## TABLE 4-1: Retina Biometrics Fact versus Fiction

| Belief | Fact |
| --- | --- |
| If I must place my eye on the acquisition device, I may pick up some disease. | The fact is that, although it may be unlikely or minimal, something may still possibly be transmitted or picked up from any common or public device. |
| The acquisition device is harmful to the eye. | Correctly constructed retina scanners operate within ranges that are not considered harmful to the eye. |
| Medical information can be gathered by using the technology. | This concern has some validity. Because retina scan technology can be affected by eye disease, if its use were mandatory, the system could (by virtue of FTE) identify users with eye diseases. This, however, is not the only cause of FTE; if, therefore, the reason for FTE was not researched for individuals who could not enroll, medical information would not be obtained. |

## RETINA VASCULAR PATTERN SECURITY CHARACTERISTICS

By now, we hope that you are realizing that retina vascular patterns are very unique and can provide very high levels of identification. As noted previously, whenever a retina is scanned, many data points can be gathered. Because the method of determining uniqueness is typically provided by an algorithm designed to create a template from the unique patterns found, and because this template generation method is very often patented per manufacturer, we are reverting back to our sample template, using logic similar to that in the chapter on fingerprint technology.

Using our simplistic template-generation scheme, as described in Chapter 2, if we plot items in a fashion similar to that of a fingerprint, using only bifurcations and endings, and we then add the capability to plot vessels of a specific diameter along with the optic nerve, our template would look similar to that shown in Figure 4-3.

The fact that the number of data points used can dramatically increase the overall accuracy of identification now becomes very apparent.

In our example, different shades represent different biometric traits. Some relate to branches (or, in fingerprint terminology, bifurcations), some relate to endings (such as those of ridge endings), and the other two are for vessels of a diameter greater than x (where x is a predetermined diameter). Finally, the optic nerve is represented by yet another color/shade.

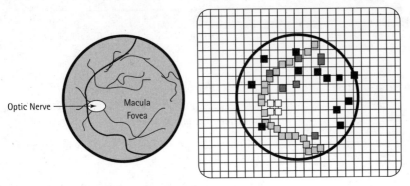

**Figure 4-3:** Simple retina template example

Table 4-2 indicates some of the additional characteristics of retina vascular pattern technology.

**TABLE 4-2: Additional Retina Vascular Technology Characteristics**

| Characteristic | Ease of use | Error incidence | Accuracy | Acceptance | Security Level | Stability | Cost |
|---|---|---|---|---|---|---|---|
| | Low | Low | Very High | Medium-low | High | High | High |

## RETINA STRENGTHS

Retina vascular scanning technology has some definite strengths over some of its biometric counterparts. Some of these strengths include the following:

✓ Retinas are very stable and generally remain unchanged from the time that a person is approximately one year old.

✓ Retina vascular pattern characteristics are very unique.

✓ Many data points can be gathered in small templates.

✓ The retina is difficult to spoof or fake.

✓ The retina is an internal trait that is considered hidden.

✓ Depending on the device, a user may not need to have direct contact.

✓ The retina is not subject to outside influences (except for such things as aging or disease).

## RETINA WEAKNESSES

As strong as the retina is, it does have some inherent weaknesses. These weaknesses include the following:

- ✓ The retina is subject to disease, aging, and severe physical damage.

- ✓ Limited data (compared to other technologies such as fingerprint).

- ✓ Stigma about eye damage and transference of sickness/disease in using the technology still exists with many.

- ✓ Many devices still don't handle glasses and/or contacts well.

- ✓ Higher cost.

- ✓ Still primarily used for physical access devices. This is expected to change, however, as the technology becomes more portable and less costly.

## RETINAL COUNTERMEASURES

Some of the countermeasures for retina technologies must be developed and compiled with time. These relate primarily to the limited amount of data that exists. Most of the weaknesses of the technology can be overcome, however, by using some of the following methods:

- ✓ Use retina acquisition devices that do not require physical contact with the acquisition device. Doing so can reduce the objections related to transference.

- ✓ Uncover objections and research methods to overcome them. If an objection is based on a user being concerned about eye damage, for example, medical references are available that state that, if the scanning technology used falls below specified ranges, it is considered safe.

- ✓ Use the technology only where appropriate. If physical access is required, for example, but only one location needs the highest level of security, use alternative, more-accepted technologies (for example, voice recognition) for lower requirements.

- ✓ Choose technologies that can accommodate glasses and contacts without sacrificing accuracy.

Retina vascular pattern scanning technology is continually being developed. As the devices become smaller and more affordable, the technology is very likely to become more available for computers and networks. If the acquisition devices can become faster, easier to operate, and more convenient for the user, they can provide extremely high security for computers and networks (especially if combined with other options).

# Iris Technology

Although iris biometric technology falls into the eye biometric category, the underlying technology is quite different than that of retina vascular pattern scanning technology. Like retinal technology, however, iris biometric technology is considered an internal biometric trait/characteristic. Because it is an internal trait, it is considered more secure and less tamperproof than external biometric technologies. Nonetheless, it, too, is not immune to being spoofed or faked.

Iris pattern technology uses the unique pattern formed by the iris to uniquely identify an individual from others. Within the past few years, iris identification has been touted to be stronger than even retina technology. In fact, one article claimed that, with more than two million registered users, the false match rate was zero. This is not necessarily surprising if you consider that the numbers can range from one in 131,000 to one in 783,000,000, depending on whose study you read and which data you choose to believe. Even so, the fact remains that iris technology (whether top dog or second fiddle) is considered very secure.

The primary reason that iris technology is considered secure is that, as with retina technology, iris templates are generated by using many data points.

Current iris technology does not capture iris images in color, but rather in black and white. Even without the benefit of color, the iris patterns of different eyes are, in fact, uniquely different.

To demonstrate how iris patterns can differ, we have selected two different iris images of the same person. These images are shown in Figure 4-4, and they illustrate how even the iris patterns of different eyes of the same person are unique.

Same individual

**Figure 4-4:** Iris patterns

In the figure, notice that the irises of the same individual (even with black-and-white images) are still very discernable as quite unique. Simply by using these images, you can determine that the eye on the left has a pattern much different than that of the eye on the right. A dip appears in the lower center of both iris patterns, but the one in the left image is much more pronounced. Additionally, the image on the left contains blank spaces at about two o'clock. These blank spaces do not appear on the right image, but a different pattern on the right image is apparent in the same area.

This type of individuality persists each time that a different iris is scanned.

The images portrayed in Figure 4-4, however, are from standard cameras. Images from an actual iris camera are even more unique and would appear more like the images shown in Figure 4-5.

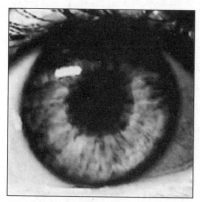

**Figure 4-5:** Iris images

As is the case with retina and fingerprint technology, each iris pattern is unique. But unlike fingerprints, iris patterns contain much more unique data. This is partially because the iris is colored, but mostly simply due to the tremendous amount of unique patterns created by each iris.

The iris appears almost tissuelike, and the folds, rolls, gaps, openings, slits, speckles, and the like (referred to as freckles, furrows, and rings) can be used as data points to uniquely identify an individual. In the preceding figure, for example, the iris appears almost to be rolled, whereas other irises may appear more layered or even multilayered. Because the iris of each eye is different, both irises can be used to create stronger authentication. Scanning irises in succession (for example left, left, right, left, right) is another means of creating even higher security levels. As is the case with retina technology, because each eye differs, the pattern of the left eye and right eye would be different. Additionally, even in the case of identical twins, each iris is unique.

## CLASSIFICATION

To a degree, iris patterns can be likened to multilayered snowflakes; people say that no two snowflakes are the same. The same is thought to be true of irises. Many of the patterns of irises are quite unique, especially compared to other irises, and are not, therefore, classified into categories similar to those of fingerprints. In fact, the patterns of irises have been stated by more than one source as being 100 percent unique. This does not, however, mean that the iris technology of today is capable of making the same claims.

## TEMPLATE ACQUISITON

Iris pattern template acquisition is somewhat similar to that of retina vascular pattern template acquisition. The technologies are similar in that the user must gaze into an acquisition device, and in both cases, the user is looking at a light, but that's really where the similarities end.

Iris scanning devices can typically acquire the image from much greater distances than most retina scanners. The product that we demonstrate later in this chapter, for example can acquire the iris pattern image from 19 inches away from the device. This reduces some of the stigmatism associated with eye-scanning technologies (primarily the transference issues) but does not completely eliminate the stigmatism. Some users still feel that the device can harm their eyes.

Additionally, to acquire the iris image(s), users must be very aware of the device and where they are in relationship to it. That a device can acquire an image from 19 inches away is nice, but if the margin of error is only a half-inch, the user must be within 18½ to 19½ inches away from the device for it to work. Eye movement, angle, and lighting can also affect the capability of the device to obtain a quality image. These factors add to the difficulty in both enrollment (FTE) and post-enrollment identification (FNMR). If a user has difficulty enrolling, therefore, and the enrollment process requires four or more valid enrollment templates, the process can become lengthy and perceived as very intrusive to the user.

Template sizes on average range anywhere from 128 bytes to 512 bytes. Some systems also provide a reduced-size reference pattern to save space and facilitate a speedy analysis.

## UNIQUE IDENTIFIICATION

As do retina scanners, iris scanners can truly provide unique identification. The added benefit that iris scanners provide is that the cost of the acquisition device (iris scanner) is continually dropping. In fact, during the writing of this book, the average cost dropped about eight percent.

Furthermore, even though retina vascular pattern technologies are widely accepted as the most unique and secure biometric technology, some controversy has arisen in stating that iris pattern technology is as secure as — or more secure than — retina scanning. One of the reasons this may be happening is that, because of the pricing of the iris devices, more devices are being put into production, and more data is therefore being gathered. Regardless, most agree that the top two biometric devices providing unique identification are iris and retina technology.

Iris technology, similarly to its cousin, retina technology, gathers many unique data points. The method of evaluating these data components, however, differs between iris and retina. Biometric traits are generally measured in degrees of freedom. To gain a general understanding of how unique an iris is compared to a fingerprint, the delta between degrees of freedom can be measured. In the case of iris technology, you find 250 degrees of freedom, in contrast to 35 degrees of freedom for fingerprints. This means that iris technology has 218 degrees of freedom more than a fingerprint.

*Degrees of freedom* represent the number of independent varieties of a deviation. If 100 shredded strips of paper were randomly dropped from the same distance, for example, the end result would differ each time, and the likelihood of getting the same result is almost impossible.

## RECOGNITION

Iris pattern scanning and comparison technology function somewhat similar to other biometric technologies in that templates are created for comparison. The method by which the template is created, however, is different than that of most other technologies.

A bar code-type bit stream is generated by using the unique characteristics of the iris. The bar code is generated by using mathematical functions derived from iris information. This unique algorithm can be stored in a 521-byte template.

During the enrollment process, the iris can be scanned multiple times to ensure that the generation of the template is within acceptable tolerances. Depending on the software used with the iris-scanning device, a composite template can be used or multiple templates can be stored.

 One of the benefits of storing multiple templates is that the presented template (acquired for purpose of identification-post enrollment) can be compared to all templates, and if it is found to be unique to all four, the user is recognized. If it falls out of range with any one template, however, the user can be denied.

As is the case with retina technology, the type of iris software and its use can determine how many templates are created (one-to-many). After enrollment has occurred, each time that the iris is scanned, a new template is created and compared to existing enrollment template(s). If the algorithm determines a match, the presenter is considered recognized or identified. Three common ways of recognizing an individual as the unique provider of the iris enrollment template are also available.

**DATABASE SEARCHING**    Database searching is provided in much the same way as with retina scanning. Iris scanning was designed to be very fast, however, and, as such, is very well suited to this type of matching. In fact, with some implementations, up to 100,000 templates can be searched per second. Because this method does not require the user to declare an identity prior to comparison, the possibility of a false match is greater for this method than for the other options.

**DECLARATION/MATCH**    The general functionality of the declaration/match method is the same. An important point is that, because the user is declaring his identity in advance, however, the speed at which the comparison occurs is directly related to the speed at which the declaration/ match software/database operates. This may be faster or slower than the preceding method, depending on design characteristics and database size, but it is most likely faster because only one user's enrollment information must be evaluated.

**SUBMIT/VALIDATE**    Submit/validate also functions in a similar fashion to those already defined. But as is the case with most technologies, the manufacturers supporting them are often different, and the features, functionality, design, and size, therefore, must be considered.

We discuss the use of submit/validate technology with multibiometrics in the chapter on multibiometrics.

## FAILURES AND ERRORS

As mentioned previously, the distinction of which biometric technology is the most secure (retina or iris) is being challenged by some. But the fact remains that, until the day that a biometric technology exists that can truly claim 100 percent accuracy (and this ever happening is highly unlikely), the possibility must always exist that errors can occur. You find that this rings true for all biometric technologies. The primary determining factor for which technology becomes most acceptable is likely to be based on such elements as usage, cost, scope, enrollment requirements, and so on.

**FAILURE TO ENROLL (FTE)**   Holding true to form, a failure to enroll (FTE) can occur with iris technology if a given individual cannot create an enrollment template. Some of the causes remain the same as in retina technology, but a few new issues arise as well. The constants are factors that prohibit the scanning of the iris, including eye damage, eye disease, and even refusal. Again, although highly unlikely, the possibility exists that a scan would yield a template that lacks sufficient data to provide the capability to uniquely identify an individual if compared to the current database of known users, creating the potential to produce a false match. In addition to these factors, the following specific requirements are needed to achieve a quality iris scan enrollment:

- ✓ The pupil diameter must be less than 75 percent of the iris.

- ✓ Excessive eye movement, which may prohibit acquisition, must be avoided.

- ✓ Distance from the device may be more difficult to judge.

- ✓ The angle of acquisition may have a greater affect on a user's capability to enroll.

- ✓ Lighting is typically more of an issue.

- ✓ Additionally, specific types of afflictions can affect the capability of an individual to enroll. In approximately 1.8 in 100,000 births, for example, the individual has a condition called *aniridia*, which is the lack of an iris. These individuals cannot use iris recognition technology.

**FALSE MATCH OR FALSE ACCEPT (TYPE 2)**   As is true with the other biometric technologies, a false match in iris technology could occur if two users' templates are not unique enough to allow sufficient differentiation between them. One of the methods that can be used to mitigate a Type 2 error, however, is to compare the enrollment template to those already created during the enrollment process. If the template yields a match to an existing template, the capability to enroll is denied, because the template is not unique enough to differentiate it from that of an already enrolled user. Additionally, the requirement by an enrollment process of a specific number (or greater) of unique data points can help to limit this problem.

**FALSE NONMATCH OR FALSE REJECT (TYPE 1)**   Generally, the primary issue with iris technology is not so much a false nonmatch rate, but rather the capability of the device to acquire the image in the first place. Unlike many other technologies, iris scanning can prove to be problematic. Although this does not truly qualify as a false nonmatch, the fact is that it is a reject of sorts, and our opinion is that it should be considered as such. Therefore, iris scanning technology is among the most difficult to use on a consistent basis.

## ACCURACY

We mentioned earlier that some controversy revolves around which of the eye technologies is the most accurate. But after everything is counted, we would still need to agree that retina technology remains the most accurate, based on CERs, ATVs, FARs, and FRRs. One of the reasons that we believe this is true is because fewer issues are involved in obtaining a good retina image (assuming that the subject is capable of providing a valid image) than in obtaining a good iris image. By no means does this statement indicate that retina vascular pattern scanning is likely to become as popular as iris technology unless the size and prices of the acquisition devices for retina scanning come down. For the price, therefore, iris technology provides the highest level of security. That said, we need to look at the CER and ATV of iris technology.

**CROSSOVER ERROR RATE (CER) OR EQUAL ERROR RATE (EER)** The accuracy of iris CERs has been described as anywhere from one in 131,000 to at least one in 1.2 million. Again, you see a big gap here, but the net result is that the technology is definitely more accurate than fingerprint technology, which is widely accepted as the third most-secure biometric technology available today.

**ABILITY TO VERIFY (ATV) RATE** Although iris technology is definitely less expensive and comes in a smaller form factor than that of retina technology, it, too, has been rated by some as having a low ability to verify (ATV) rate, rivaling that of retina (85 percent). The fact is that iris technology has a high ability to verify after the image is acquired. But the capability to acquire that image is reduced by many factors that can influence the acquisition of a template with iris technology.

As with retina technology, the ATV rate for irises can be low because of the items discussed in the section on FTE (such as lighting, distance, and angle). And although the stigma of transference is all but eliminated, these combined issues place iris-scanning technology in a similar ATV category as retina-scanning technology. With good training and by addressing the distance and angle issues, however, you can increase the ATV rate for iris technology into the 90 percent-plus range.

Remember that a higher ATV rating is better than a lower ATV rating.

## FACT/FICTION

Iris technologies and retina technologies share some of the same facts and fictions, but iris technology carries some of its own unique idiosyncrasies, as shown in Table 4-3.

### TABLE 4-3: Iris Technology Idiosyncrasies

| Belief | Fact |
| --- | --- |
| The acquisition device is harmful to the eye. | Although iris scanners use infrared to help obtain the iris image, the levels are such that they are not harmful to the eye. |

*Continued*

**TABLE 4-3: Iris Technology Idiosyncrasies** *(Continued)*

| Belief | Fact |
|---|---|
| Medical information can be gathered by using the technology. | This concern has some validity. Because iris scan technology can be affected by eye disease, if its use were mandatory, the system could (by virtue of FTE) identify users with eye diseases. This, however, is not the only cause of FTE; if, therefore, the reason for FTE was not researched for individuals who could not enroll, medical information would not be obtained. |
| The eyes are the windows to the soul, and I don't want anyone looking at my soul. | Whether the belief has any foundation, the fact is that the iris information is not even captured, but rather evaluated to create a template. The soul, therefore, remains safe. |
| The iris scanner can monitor my activities. | Although this may be possible, because some devices have a built in camera as well as the iris scanner, closing or covering up the camera lens would prevent this. The iris scanner itself currently is designed to take a "snapshot" of sorts rather than to monitor continually. |

## IRIS PATTERN SECURITY CHARACTERISTICS

The biometric template for each biometric technology is different, and iris pattern technology templates hold true to this diversity. Iris characteristics provide high levels of identification because of the amount of individual data available and the algorithm that is used to create the "biometric bar code." This bar code is created by using wavelet filtering and mapping for iris technology. Although this bar code-style template is somewhat different than that of other technologies, we can still use our simplistic template-generation scheme to generically demonstrate how a template is created.

Before proceeding to the template, however, you should be aware of another important difference between retina and iris technologies. Because iris technology is actually looking at the eye, whereas retina technology is looking through the pupil, enough of the iris must be showing for quality acquisition to occur. Cases have occurred where certain individuals must consciously open their eyes wider to enable the device to acquire an image. This occurs if the eyelid is covering up too much of the iris (even though the device accounts for some of this) so that the device cannot acquire the image.

Using the theme we've built on since Chapter 2, if we plot items in similar fashion to those of a fingerprint, this time using the uniqueness of the iris, our template data collection may look something like what you see in Figure 4-6.

Because one of the differences between iris and other biometric technologies is the bar code-style template, however, we could then use the gathered information to create such a bar code. After the image is acquired, it is used to turn the information into the bar code data stream.

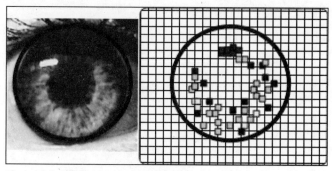

**Figure 4-6:** Simple iris template example

In our example, each different shade represents a different iris trait. After the image is acquired, the information is then turned into a biometric bar code data stream. This bar code data stream becomes the template to be used for verification. After the information is gathered and turned into a template, therefore, the template can be represented by the bar code shown in Figure 4-7.

**Figure 4-7:** Iris bar code

Table 4-4 indicates some of the additional characteristics of iris pattern technology.

**TABLE 4-4: Additional Iris Technology Characteristics**

| Characteristic | Ease of use | Error incidence | Accuracy | Acceptance | Security Level | Stability | Cost |
| --- | --- | --- | --- | --- | --- | --- | --- |
| | Medium | Low | Very High | Medium-Low | Very High | High | Low/medium |

## IRIS STRENGTHS

Iris technology has many of the same strengths as retina technology, as well as some of its own unique strengths. These strengths are as described in the following list:

- ✓ Irises are very stable and generally remain so throughout a person's life.

- ✓ Iris pattern characteristics are very unique, and many say that no two irises could be identical.

✓ Many data points can be gathered in small templates (512K).

✓ The iris is an internal biometric that is relatively difficult to fake or spoof.

✓ Depending on the device, a user may not need to have direct contact.

✓ The iris is not as subject to outside influences as are some other biometrics, such as fingerprints (except for factors such as aging or disease).

✓ Iris technology is considered slightly more user friendly than retina technology

✓ The cost of iris technology is currently less than that of retina technology.

✓ Iris devices may work without the user needing to remove glasses or contacts.

✓ Iris technology can be used on networks for identification/authentication.

✓ Current testing has not revealed a false match.

## IRIS WEAKNESSES

The weaknesses associated with iris technology include the following:

✓ The iris is subject to disease, aging, and severe physical damage.

✓ Persons with aniridia (lack of an iris) cannot participate.

✓ Data is limited compared to that of other technologies, such as fingerprints, but because of the increasing use of the technology, more data is continually compiled.

✓ Depending on the device chosen, glasses and/or contact can affect the device's capability to acquire a valid iris image.

✓ Stigma about eye damage using the technology still exists with many.

✓ Iris technologies involve higher costs than technologies such as fingerprint, voice, and face identification and electronic signatures.

✓ Lighting and other environmental conditions can affect image acquisition.

## IRIS COUNTERMEASURES

Most iris countermeasures can be overcome. Those that can't be overcome (disease, aging, severe physical damage) must be addressed outside the confines of iris scanning technology. To overcome many of the weaknesses, the following countermeasures can be of assistance:

✓ To address disease, aging, and severe image concerns, you can use a biometric engine that can support more than one biometric technology — for example, one that supports both iris and fingerprint technology.

✓ Keep current on newly published iris data. As iris technology becomes more prevalent, more data is sure to become available. As recently as two years ago, iris technology was listed as not capable of scanning through glasses or contacts. This could still be true with some devices but may not be all encompassing.

✓ Use the technology only where appropriate. If physical access is required, for example, but only one location needs the highest level of security, use alternative, more-accepted technologies (for example, voice recognition) for lower requirements.

✓ Choose technologies that can accommodate glasses and contacts without sacrificing accuracy wherever possible.

✓ Continually educate personnel on the device to limit the stigma of potential eye damage. Have an eye doctor (or several) talk to the users.

✓ Ensure that correct environmental conditions exist. This includes adequate lighting.

✓ If necessary, create an environment that gives the user being identified the capability to position himself correctly — for example, through use of an alignment device designed to enable the user to get into position correctly.

Even with all its strengths, iris technology has been faked or spoofed. One such example is listed at www.extremetech.com and is entitled "Body Check: Biometrics Defeated." Although this case was supposedly based on a beta product, the potential that any biometric technology can be fooled exists. Some of the countermeasures that can be taken to reduce those risks associated with iris technology include the following:

✓ To reduce the possibility that a dummy or fake iris can be used to falsify an identification, you can take the following precautionary/countermeasures:

- Enroll and use both eyes for single authentication.

- Use a pattern of eye scanning — for example, left eye first, then right, right, and so on. Change that pattern occasionally.

- Require individuals to declare an identity prior to accepting identification.

- Use combinations of biometric technologies.

- Use a device that can sense an actual eye versus a picture or a fake.

- Switch between eyes occasionally, making sure that you remove the last enrolled iris.

✓ Use multiple means of identification and authentication (for example, fingerprint and password).

✓ Permit identification to occur only from a certain iris-acquisition device rather than from any acquisition device.

✓ Control physical access to iris scanning devices wherever possible.

✓ Do not permit templates to be transmitted without being encrypted.

Following the countermeasure tips in this list can greatly reduce the probability that someone could breach your security mechanism(s).

# Technology Uses and Applications

One of the reasons to implement biometric technologies is identity verification. This task can be accomplished in the background by using database searching or by having a user declare his identity in advance. Another reason to implement biometric technology, however, is to make the environment friendlier for the users. The degree that this is possible often rests on your users and their acceptance of the technology. To address both security and convenience, you must have a good understanding of the available uses and applications.

## Retina

Retina vascular pattern technology is still primarily used to provide very high physical-access control security. This type of security is used where access to a building, site, floor, room, or even safe must ensure not only that the individual is allowed to enter, but that the individual's identity is verified (and most likely logged) prior to allowing access. Therefore, retina technology is used by the military, government, corrections institutions, and private industry to verify and control access to secrets, to develop information, or to ensure the identity of prisoners before they can be transferred or released.

Some correctional institutions even scan visitors on arrival and departure to ensure that a prisoner cannot masquerade as a visitor and escape from the institution.

However, some advances have enabled this technology to be used for other purposes.

Because of its ties to access control, retina-scanning technology has been chosen as a logical choice for applications monitoring an employee's time and attendance. Believe it or not, this has benefits (and potential drawbacks) for both the employer and employee.

Suppose, for example, that you work for a company that develops top-secret gizmos and gadgets. The company is likely to use some form of identity management to ensure that proper access is granted to the facility and/or to certain areas within the facility. If access is granted at the facility level, wouldn't it be nice if the authorizing device automatically "punched you in" to the time and attendance system? This capability is one of the reasons that retina technology may become a logical choice for monitoring time and attendance.

So that's nice — you need to identify yourself only once to enter the building and be clocked in. But what if you are a smoker and the facility is a smoke-free environment (as many are today)? You're allowed to go outside to smoke, but each time that you do, you nust re-identify yourself, giving the employer a log that shows each time that you exit the facility.

As you can probably see, the use of such technology raises some pretty controversial issues.

Retina technology has not yet, however, reached a point where it is widely available for identification and authentication use in data network environments.

We discuss more uses for retinal technology in the chapter on technology solution models.

# Iris

Iris scanning devices can be acquired from several sources. The underlying technology, however, originates from Iridian Technologies. This has both benefits and drawbacks. One of the benefits is that you don't have a lot of different products to choose from (compared to other electronic technologies), so if you need to use iris scanning products, your decision-making process is greatly narrowed. If you're into choices, however, this is not benefit at all.

The drawback to having only one company developing iris technology is that the development pace is not challenged. New developments may therefore be slow in coming. Additionally, the market is dependant on whoever is willing to work with the developer of the technology, and most development companies partner with one or a select number of manufacturers. This is evident if you look for an iris-scanning device for your network — you find only Panasonic's Authenticam (unlike in other technologies, where you often have many choices). The good news is that the pricing of the Authenticam is very reasonable considering the security that it provides.

Other iris scanning devices have been implemented for ATM usage in banks. In some cases, the customer (the user of the ATM) needs only to have his iris scanned (database search), whereas other implementations require a PIN or customer name prior (a declaration) to a search.

We discuss iris ATM implementation and more uses for iris technology in the chapter on technology solution models.

# Implementation Criteria

Although fingerprint technology is one of the most popular biometric technologies used today, iris technology (even with its phobias and weaknesses) is beginning to become more accepted. Much of acceptance derives from the events of September 11, 2001. Since that time, both security and disaster recover/planning issues have taken a front seat in many companies. With the increasing use of iris technology in ATMs and additional development of the technology, it is really only a matter of time before it becomes one of the mainstream solutions for network security. This fire should be further fueled as more software development companies integrate iris technology into their biometric offerings.

Although it is not yet considered mainstream, iris technology offers both a surprisingly sound product and many good features, and we now know that it is very strong as an identification tool. After the iris image is acquired, the authentication process is very quick, even with a large number of templates in the system.

Moreover, as is the case with fingerprint technology, iris technology can be used in many of the following data applications (as well as in others):

- ✓ Network logon/authentication
- ✓ Individual workstation logon/authentication
- ✓ Application control
- ✓ File-level encryption control
- ✓ Folder-level encryption control
- ✓ Mail encryption
- ✓ Password replacement

✓ Activity logging

✓ Public-access protection

# Increased or Decreased Costs?

So can iris technology compete with fingerprint technology (or other technologies) on a cost basis? The answer isn't as simple as yes or no; it truly depends on your evaluation criteria.

## Pure Acquisition Cost

If only the costs of designing the security solution, acquiring the biometric devices, implementation and support are considered, the answer would need to be a resounding no. Most fingerprint, voice, signature, keyboard, and face biometric solutions come in at an acquisition cost of less than $150 per workstation (using only the cost of individual workstation products), whereas the cost for the Authenticam product is currently about $250 per workstation, using the same criteria. What if, however, you evaluate the cost on the level of protection provided?

## Cost Based on Protection Level

Earlier in this chapter, we mentioned the term *degrees of freedom*. As you may recall, degrees of freedom is a measure of the strength (or, more specifically, the potential for duplication) of a biometric technology. Fingerprinting has a rating of 35 degrees of freedom as opposed to 250 degrees of freedom for iris technology. If we use this measurement of strength, actual fingerprint technology costs are approximately equal to $4.29 per degree of freedom.

$150/35 (degrees of freedom) = $ 4.2857 per degree of freedom.

Iris technology, on the other hand, has a cost of $1 per degree of freedom.

$250/250(degrees of freedom) = $1 per degree of freedom.

Based on this measurement, the odds are in favor of iris technology by more than four to one.

 The numbers in the preceding equations are estimates based on current average market prices.

So, if the primary goal is security, the best value is iris technology, although you're not likely to win a cost battle based on that information alone.

## Iris Biometric Savings Example

In the chapter on fingerprint technology, we showed you a cost-savings example based on certain criteria, including a reduction in help-desk costs. Iris biometric technology can be evaluated in much the same fashion. But the cost savings aren't realized as quickly as they are with a cheaper technology. So if you're looking to implement iris technology and looking for a way to justify it, you need to combine both its cost savings and the fact that it provides higher security than other choices (excluding retina vascular pattern technology). Table 4-5 provides a simple example for 150 users.

**TABLE 4-5: Biometric Savings**

| Element | Cost |
| --- | --- |
| Help-desk cost savings | $40,000 (reduction in call volume, number approximated) |
| Iris security advantage | $439.50 |
| Cost to acquire | $37,500 |
| Net gain | $2939.50 (coupled with tighter security) |

This is a very simplistic way of looking at it, and many other costs are involved in implementing biometric technologies. Be sure to use factual numbers and include costs, savings, and new capabilities.

# Sample Product

For our sample product demonstration, installation, authentication, and applications/utilities usage, we use the Panasonic Authenticam with PrivateID software, Version 2.0, from Iridian Technologies. The product is installed on a Windows 2000 workstation connected to a peer-to-peer network for the purpose of sharing hard-drive and printing resources and for encrypting e-mail messages and attachments. We are using TED (developed by TigerTools.net) to encrypt messages for e-mail. Additionally, we show how to use the PrivateID software to encrypt files and folders, as well as to control access to applications.

## PrivateID Installation Example

Before you begin the installation of the Panasonic Authenticam and PrivateID software, make sure that your system meets the minimum requirements of the version that you intend to install. Our installation is using Version 2.0 of the PrivateID software and Version 3.10 of the SecureSuite for Windows 2000 software. Our minimum system requirements, therefore, are as follows:

- ✓ Auto Logon disable (if applicable)
- ✓ Pentium-class processor 333MHZ or higher
- ✓ USB port

✓ Windows 2000

✓ 64 MB RAM (128 recommended)

✓ Internet Explorer 4.0 (Internet Explorer 5.5 or higher recommended)

✓ CD-ROM for installation software

✓ 40MB hard-drive space available (60 recommended)

Although those are the minimum requirements, we recommend that your system is updated with the latest service and security patches and that you are running the current version of IE with the appropriate patch levels.

We also recommend that you close all applications and log on as the administrator before beginning the installation.

Ensure that the Panasonic Authenticam iris scanner/camera is *not* connected.

After you insert the PrivateID installation CD, the first screen that you should see is a Windows-based menu that enables you to select the option you want. The screen is as shown in Figure 4-8.

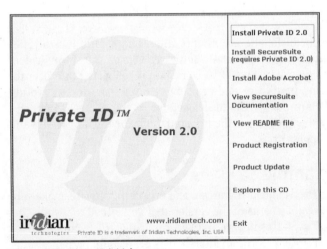

**Figure 4-8:** PrivateID initial screen

If you do not see this screen, you must go to MyComputer, select the appropriate CD-ROM drive, use the Open command, and select the SETUP.EXE file to start the installation. We recommend that you review the documentation before proceeding to the installation. You can do so by selecting the View SecureSuite Documentation option from the PrivateID Windows menu screen.

Adobe Acrobat Reader is required to view the documentation. If you do not have Acrobat Reader installed, you can select the option to Install Adobe Acrobat from the PrivateID screen. You need Internet access, however, because this link directs you to the Adobe Web site.

After reviewing the documentation, you can proceed with the installation. The first step is to install the PrivateID software. Select Install Private ID 2 from the menu. After the installation begins, the next screen you should see is the PrivateID 2 Setup screen, as shown in Figure 4-9.

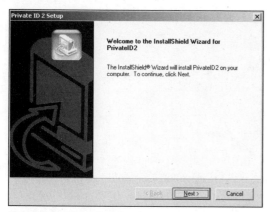

**Figure 4-9:** Private ID 2 Setup screen

After you have verified that you've exited all programs, click Next. You rae presented with the license agreement, as shown in Figure 4-10.

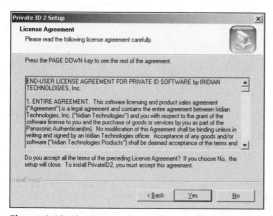

**Figure 4-10:** License agreement

Before you can continue, you must read and accept the license agreement, as is typically the case with most installations. After you have read the agreement, click the Yes button, and the installation continues automatically. The installation should proceed by copying the necessary files, as shown in Figure 4-11.

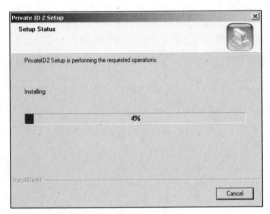

**Figure 4-11:** File installation screen

In our example, the destination folder is F:\Program Files\Iridian Technologies\........ On completion of the file installation, you are presented with the Finish screen, as shown in Figure 4-12.

**Figure 4-12:** Installation finish screen

Clicking Finish completes the installation.

After the installation is completed, connect the Panasonic Authenticam iris scanner/camera to the computer via a USB port (either directly or through a USB hub).

The possibility exists that the Panasonic Authenticam may not be recognized when plugged into a USB hub. If the device is not recognized, try connecting the device directly to the computer.

After you're connected, the Found New Hardware screen should appear, as shown in Figure 4-13.

**Figure 4-13:** The Found New Hardware screen

After the Panasonic Authenticam is recognized, a Digital Signature warning appears. This warning informs the installer that the software does not contain a Microsoft digital signature and that you have no guarantee that the software works correctly with Windows. This message is shown in Figure 4-14.

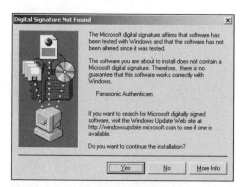

**Figure 4-14:** Digital Signature warning

We select Yes, as we want to continue the installation. At this point, the camera should be recognized. The preceding portion of the installation installed only the Private ID software and enabled the camera to be recognized.

The next step is to install the SecureSuite software. Select Install SecureSuite (requires Private ID 2.0) from the Private ID Initial install screen, as shown previously in Figure 4-8. You are presented with the SecureSuite 3.10 workstation installation wizard, as shown in Figure 4-15.

Click Next to continue to the licensing screen, as shown in Figure 4-16.

**Figure 4-15:** The SecureSuite 3.10 workstation installation wizard

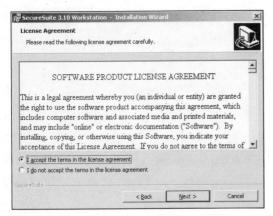

**Figure 4-16:** SecureSuite License screen

Read the license agreement and, if you agree, click the I Accept the Terms in the License Agreement radio button and click the "Next>" button. The next screen that you see is the product serial number screen, as shown in Figure 4-17.

Enter the serial number listed on the back of the CD envelope. The version that we are installing has two serial numbers on the back of the envelope, one for SecureSuite 2.3 (used for Windows 98 or ME) and one for SecureSuite 3.10 (used for Windows 2000). After the serial number is entered, click Next. The customer information entry screen shown in Figure 4-18 appears.

By default, the information is filled in for you. Change the information if necessary or select Next to access the setup type screen, as shown in Figure 4-19.

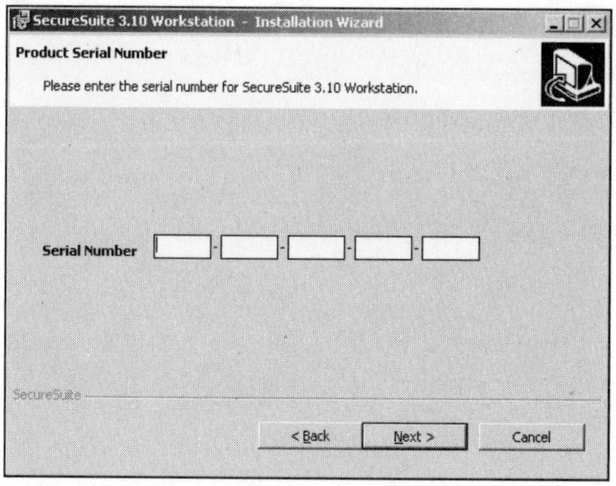

**Figure 4-17:** Serial number entry screen

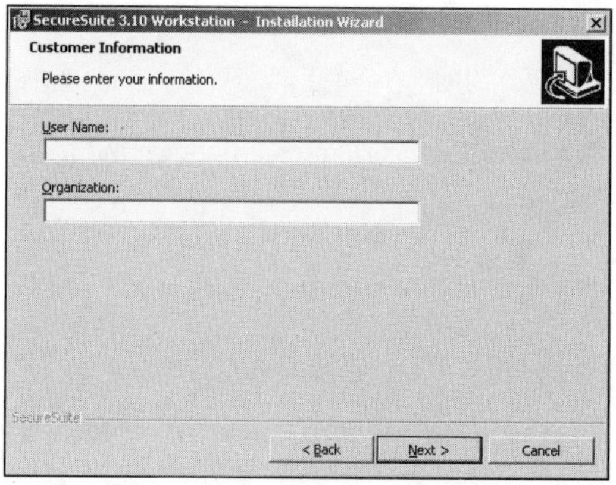

**Figure 4-18:** Customer information entry screen

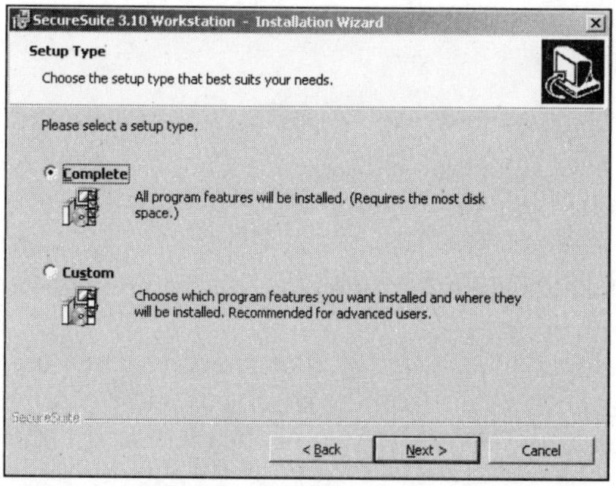

**Figure 4-19:** Setup type screen

Select Complete and click Next. You are presented with the Ready to Install screen, as shown in Figure 4-20.

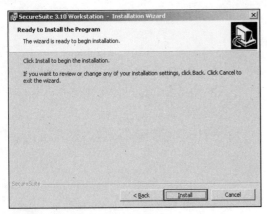

**Figure 4-20:** The Ready to Install screen

Click the Install button to continue. The installation status indication screen, shown in Figure 4-21, indicates the current status of the installation.

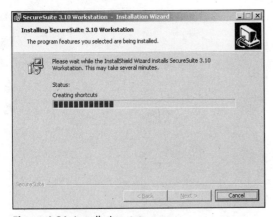

**Figure 4-21:** Installation status screen

Ager the installation process is completed, the Additional Information screen appears, as shown in Figure 4-22.

If you want to review the Readme text file (recommended), simply click Next. If you do not want to review the Readme text file, deselect the option by clicking the check box and ensuring that no check is visible. The computer prompts you to connect the Authenticam. Because the

Authenticam was previously connected, click OK, and the installation continues and completes. The screen shown in Figure 4-23 appears.

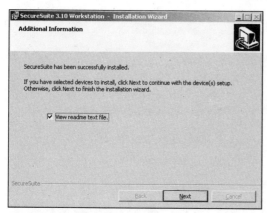

**Figure 4-22:** Additional information

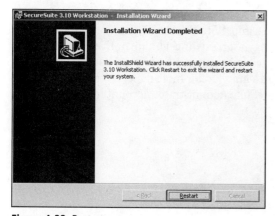

**Figure 4-23:** Restart screen

Click Restart and wait for the computer to reboot.
After the computer has rebooted, you should see the screen shown in Figure 4-24.

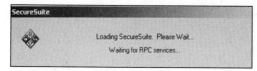

**Figure 4-24:** SecureSuite Initialization

This screen updates several times. After the screen shown in Figure 4-25 appears, click Next.

**Figure 4-25:** Administrator Account setup screen

This marks the beginning of the Administration setup. With Private ID, the very first thing that you must do is set up an administrator. If you try to type an existing administrative account name, however, it informs you that the user name is already in use and that you must select another name. This makes accidentally deleting the standard administrator more difficult. The screen shown in Figure 4-26 is where you enter the Default SecureSuite Administrator Account Information.

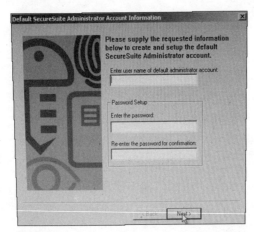

**Figure 4-26:** Default Secure Suite Administrator Account Information

Enter the name of the SecureSuite Administrator. The Administrator name must be different from other usernames that currently exist on the machine. The name Administrator, therefore, cannot be used. We have selected AdminXP, as shown in Figure 4-27.

note

Before hitting the Tab key to move to the first field, ensure that the name that you typed is correct, as you cannot modify it from this screen after you continue.

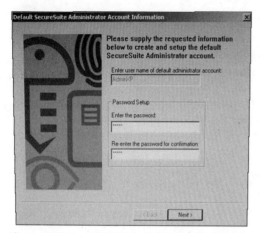

**Figure 4-27:** Completed Default Secure Suite Administrator Account Information

Click Next to continue, and you are prompted with a screen stating that you have successfully set up the administrator account. Click Finish to complete the installation. The following screen should appear (see Figure 4-28).

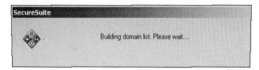

**Figure 4-28:** Building the Domain List

After the Domain List is completed, you are presented with the logon screen, as shown in Figure 4-29.

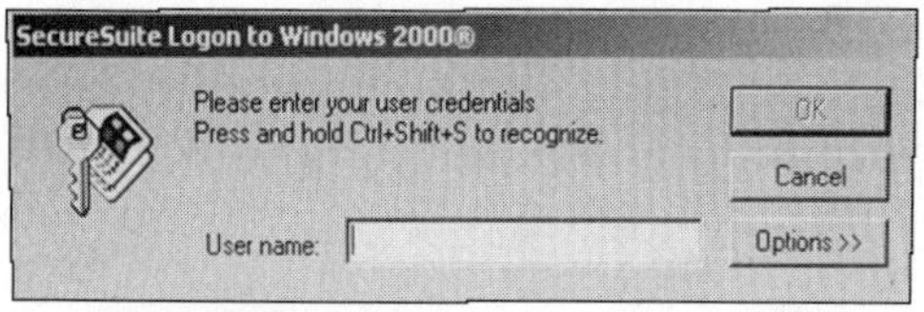

**Figure 4-29:** Logon screen

Notice that you have only a spot for a username on this screen. If you enter an appropriate username here, a second field appears for the password. Clicking the Options tab does not access the password entry, but rather enables you to change domains.

In our example, we entered AdminXP, and after the password field appeared, we entered the appropriate password and were granted access.

The first time that you log in, you enter a password. After a successful login, you can use the SecureSuite User Manager located in the Control Panel to enable enrollment to occur and to remove the capability to use a password if you want.

After access was granted, we were presented with the screen shown in Figure 4-30.

**Figure 4-30:** SecureSuite Welcome screen

From this screen, you see options labeled Register SecureSuite, Using Your Authenticam, Create a New User, and Exit to the Desktop. For now, we choose to exit to the desktop.

## Sample Network Authentication Using Iris Biometrics

Before we can proceed to authentication using our iris camera, we must first enroll. Remember that, right after installation, the first time that we logged in we created our SecureSuite Administrator. After the Administrator was created (as AdminXP), we logged in using only a password. That's because, before we can actually be identified and allowed to log in using the Authenticam, we must enroll.

The enrollment process can be performed either from the SecureSuite User Manager or from My SecureSuite Settings (which enables you to change the current user). We use the SecureSuite

User Manager, because, as we demonstrate later in this chapter, many of the other things that we want to secure can also be accomplished by using the SecureSuite User Manager.

After we installed SecureSuite, with the options that we selected, an icon was placed on the desktop and in the system tray. Either can be used to gain access to the SecureSuite User Manager. We've elected to use the system tray. The system tray icon is as shown in Figure 4-31.

**Figure 4-31:** SecureSuite system tray icon

Click the icon, and you access a menu containing several options. Select the SecureSuite User Manager option. This opens the application shown in Figure 4-32.

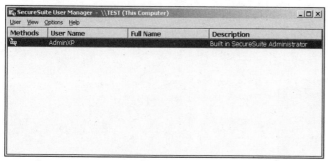

**Figure 4-32:** SecureSuite User Manager

Figure 4-32 also shows why, as we initially logged in, we were required only to use a password. Looking under the methods listed for the username AdminXP in the SecureSuite User Manager, we see a key with an xxx over it. That is the symbol for a password in SecureSuite. The next step is to enroll the appropriate user for the account AdminXP.

The quality of control the you have over the enrollment process has a direct correlation to overall security. The enrollment process must be extremely well coordinated and very precise. Many companies require users to present certain additional identification prior to enrolling as yet another safeguard against potentially enrolling a user who is not who he or she claims to be.

By double-clicking the AdminXP user, we access the User Properties screen, as shown in Figure 4-33.

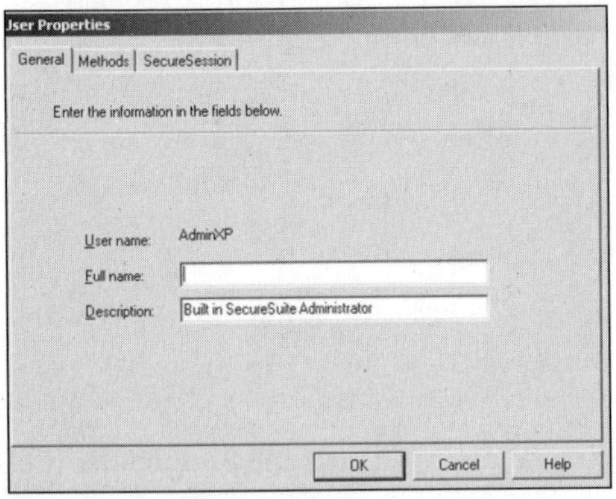

**Figure 4-33:** User Properties screen

Three tabs listed are across the top of the screen: General, Methods, and SecureSession. Currently, the General tab is showing. We can enter a full name (Administrator for SecureSuite) here and click the Methods tab to access the screen shown in Figure 4-34.

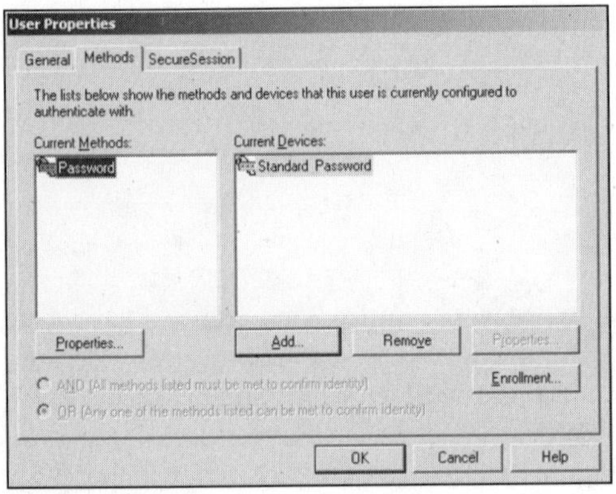

**Figure 4-34:** User Properties-Methods

Both Current Methods and Current Devices list only Password and Standard Password, respectively. To use the Panasonic Authenticam for iris identification, you must add it. Clicking Add reveals that another authentication method is available, as shown in Figure 4-35.

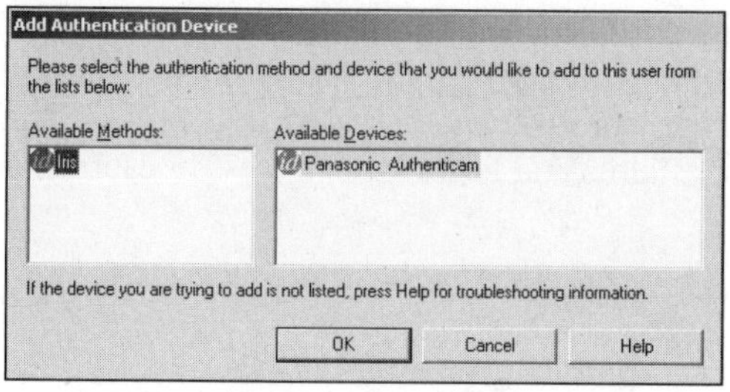

**Figure 4-35:** Available authentication methods

Under Available Methods, Iris is already selected. Clicking OK causes the program to select Iris as one of the authentication methods and starts the enrollment process. The first screen that appears during the enrollment process is an informational screen welcoming you to the enrollment process. The only options here are Next or Cancel. Clicking Next takes you to the Iris Image Enrollment Section, as shown in Figure 4-36.

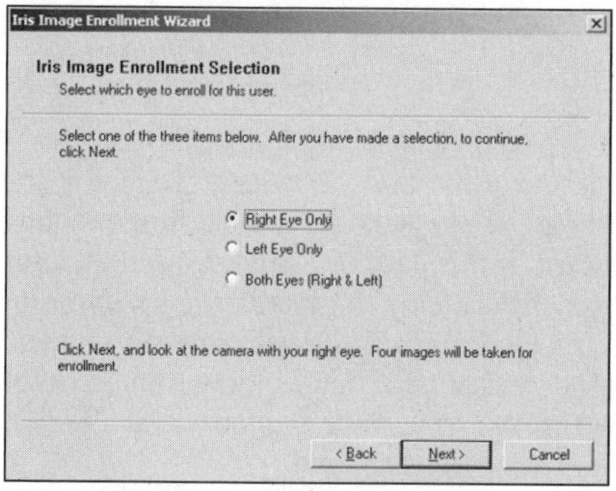

**Figure 4-36:** Iris image Enrollment Section

You can give the user some input here, possibly gaining a greater deal of acceptance by the user. If, for example, during a formal enrollment process (which should supervised), the user reaches this screen, the enrollment supervisor can inform the user that he can make a choice as to which eye(s) to enroll. The user may then choose to enroll the right, left, or both eyes.

After the selection is made, click Next to continue. This particular product responds with a screen that informs the user that, if he wears eyeglasses, to please remove them for the enrollment process. Before a user removes his eyeglasses and clickes Next to continue, this screen would be a good place to emphasize to the enrollee that distance from the camera and the amount of iris available can affect the capability of the device to capture a valid iris image.

The Authenticam emits an orange light directly from the center of the iris-scanning camera (which is the top aperture), and the infrared lights at the bottom of the camera light up. Neither the orange light nor the infrared light turns on until the user proceeds to the next step, however.

The user should be positioned the correct distance (19-21 inches) from the camera and should be able to see the orange light. After the user is properly positioned and has removed any eyeglasses (if appropriate), the user (or the enrollment supervisor) can click Next to continue. The screen shown in Figure 4-37 appears, and the camera lights and begins the process of capturing the iris image.

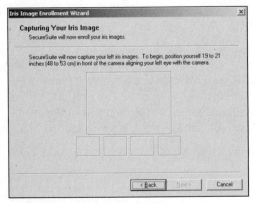

**Figure 4-37:** Iris enrollment acquisition screen

After an iris image is acquired, the light in the center of the camera turns green, and if the computer to which the Authenticam is connected has active speakers, an audible shutter sound (like that of a camera taking a picture) should be heard. If this does not happen, have the user slowly move back and forth, keeping the orange light in the center of the aperture, until the scanner takes a picture. As soon as the Authenticam gets a picture, have the user stop moving and remain in that position until all enrollment templates are captured. If, again, the camera is not capturing the image for the next template, have the enrollee move back and forth again. Repeat this process as necessary until all enrollment templates have been acquired.

After four good enrollment scans are acquired, your screen should look like the one shown in Figure 4-38.

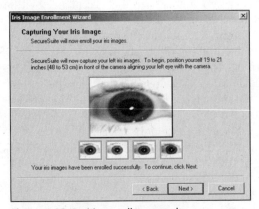

**Figure 4-38:** Positive enrollment result

Click Next on the current screen. A Finish screen appears next, so click Finish. With your enrollment complete, you should now have both authentication options, as shown by Figure 4-39.

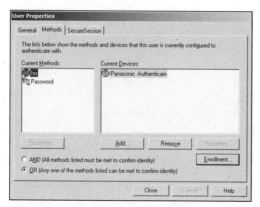

**Figure 4-39:** Dual authentication options

A couple noteworthy items are shown in Figure 4-39. First, notice that both Iris and Password appear under Current Methods and that, near the bottom, are two radio buttons labeled AND and OR. With the current selection of OR, authentication can be performed by using either the iris scan or by typing the password. If the AND button is selected, the user must authenticate by using both iris and the password. This is one method of both creating a higher level of security and ensuring identity.

If your security policy calls for using only the iris for authentication, highlight the password selection and click the Remove option. The administrative user setup using iris scanning is now complete.

## User Administration

The user AdminXP is currently the only user who has enrolled by using SecureSuite for identification/authentication use up to this point. As is the case in using the fingerprint solution, if you intend to use only iris identification/authentication, each user must enroll, and the password option must be removed from each user authentication profile. Other users of this workstation must also enroll, therefore, if they are to use their iris(s) for authentication. This process is completed in much the same way as the initial enrollment. A user with the appropriate rights, however, must run the SecureSuite User Manager. In our example, we open the SecureSuite User Manager by selecting it from the system tray in the same fashion as listed earlier. After we open the User Manager, we select the User option and then select New User, as shown in Figure 4-40.

A New User Welcome screen appears; click Next to continue, and you are taken to a user information entry screen displaying three fields: Username, Full Name, and Description. Enter the appropriate information and click Next. You are taken to the Group Membership screen. Assign the user to the appropriate group(s) and click Next. The final screen is a simple Finish screen; click finish, and the new user is created through SecureSuite.

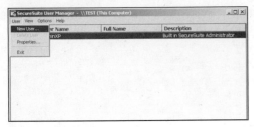

**Figure 4-40:** Adding a new user

Now, what about existing users?

One of the nice features of SecureSuite is the User Conversion Utility, which you can access by choosing Start → Programs → SecureSuite or by double-clicking the SecureSuite shortcut on the desktop that you created during the installation and selecting the SecureSuite User Conversion Utility icon. After you have selected the SecureSuite User Conversion Utility and have entered your authentication credential(s), your screen should look like the one shown in Figure 4-41.

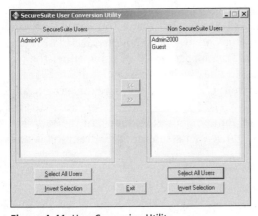

**Figure 4-41:** User Conversion Utility

Converting the users from here is as simple as clicking the names of the users that you want to convert in the Non SecureSuite column and moving them over to the SecureSuite column. After select them and click the arrows (<<) to move the selected users, however, you are given some options. These appear in Figure 4-42.

The top selection (Use), if selected without the Add Characters to Password option, enables a password to be entered into the two appropriate fields. This becomes the password of the converted user. The second option is Use User Name. If this is selected without the Add Characters to Password option, the username is used as the password for the converted user. And, finally, if the Add Characters to Password option is selected, the characters typed into the appropriate entry field are added to the front of the password (Before) or to the end (After), depending on which of these two radio buttons is selected.

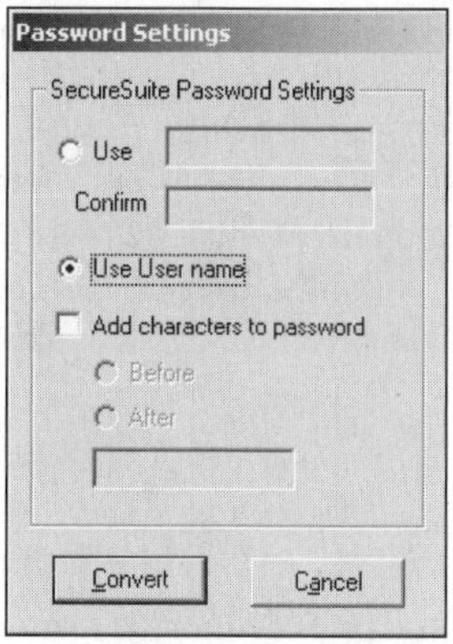

**Figure 4-42:** User conversion options

# Modifying Authentication Steps

After all the users are converted, you need to add the option to enroll each user individually, as previously shown. Selecting the SecureSuite User Manager, selecting the appropriate user, selecting the Methods tab, and adding the Iris option accomplishes this task. After you add the Iris option, the enrollment process begins in the same fashion as previously discussed.

## AUTHENTICATION STEPS

Previously, we mentioned that SecureSuite offers the capability to enable a user to authenticate using his iris, a password, or both. This is accomplished by using the OR or AND options listed at the bottom of the User Properties screen/Method tab. This is important, because if more than one authentication option is possible and the OR radio button is selected, the user can use any of the existing options. Two methods can be used to ensure that the user must authenticate with his iris.

The first method is simply to enroll the user by using only the iris, as previously discussed. After the user is enrolled, remove the password option from the Current Methods by selecting (highlighting) the password option on the User Properties screen's Method tab, in the Current Methods window, as shown in Figure 4-43.

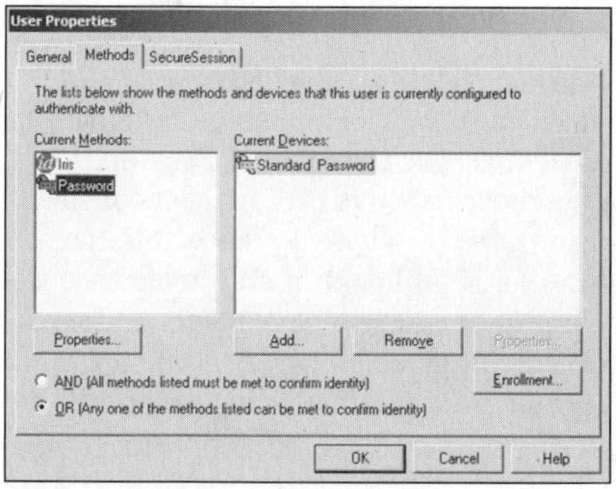

**Figure 4-43:** Removing the password option

After the password method is highlighted, click the Remove button. The password method no longer appears under Current Methods.

The second method of ensuring that the iris must be used as part of the authentication process does not require the removal of the password method. Simply ensure that the user has enrolled with at least one eye (iris), select the AND option (meaning that all methods listed must be met to confirm identity), and then click OK. With this option selected, not only must the user be identified by using the enrolled iris(es), but must also enter the appropriate password. This is considered two-factor authentication.

Repeat this process as necessary for each user, as required.

## Sample Iris Product Usage with Applications and Utilities

The SecureSuite workstation product contains several options that not only provide increased levels of identification, but can also provide some enhanced security features while reducing the burden on the end user. As is the case with the fingerprint technology, the SecureSuite product can help a user manage multiple passwords, create higher levels of security by using a screen saver lock on the workstation, and perform file and folder encryption. The product can also enable you to work with other products such as Tiger Encryption-Decryption (TED) to encrypt text that for insertion into mail messages (or other documents), all the while allowing user authentication only through the use of the iris, the password, or both.

If the network is to be secure, every touch point on the network must also be secure. This includes every node and every device connected to the network, as well as the human factor.

Security is only as good as the weakest link. This does not, however, mean that, if a weak link exists, no other precautions should be taken to increase the security of other areas. External to internal security, internal to external security, and internal to internal security (as well as the many other security measures) must be as strong as possible and as prudent.

The human factor comprises some of the biggest security threats to your network; yet often, only the technological aspects of security are addressed. Biometric solutions offer one means of addressing the human factor.

Users are both creatures of habit and, generally speaking, seek the path of least resistance. If a user, therefore, can select a password that he can remember, such as a loved one, a birth date, an anniversary date, a pet's name, and so on, he usually does select such a password. Even users with the best intentions often use similar logic, replacing specific characters with numbers or special characters in an effort to help thwart the would-be intruder. Hackers, however, know this, too, and are continually devising new methods of guessing passwords. Although it still holds true that guessing an eight-character password by using upper- and lowercase letters, numbers, and special characters may take several years, given the standard computing technology available today, the fact is that too many users (unless required) don't use best practices in selecting passwords. But you already knew this, right?

Although most of the computing industry now knows it, what many fail to realize is that one of the reasons users don't follow best practices is because they must remember so many passwords. Being creatures of habit and generally following the path of least resistance, they resort to using something they know. As you began to see even in using only fingerprint technology, however, you can change this paradigm if you use biometrics for security. The SecureSuite product not only can follow suit, but adds additional features that can create even greater levels of security.

## SCREEN SAVER

SecureSuite can provide greater levels of security by enabling you to use the screen saver in very much the same fashion as you would the fingerprint solution. By right-clicking an open space on the desktop and choosing Properties from the pop-up menu that appears, the user can modify the screen saver settings to help create a more secure environment.

As important as security is, it must be made as convenient for the users as possible to be effective. Users often fail to lock their workstations or set appropriate screen saver levels (with password protection) because they simply don't want to type a long password every time that the system screen saver activates. Therefore, they either choose a less-than-desirable password or they don't activate the screen saver password option. Because SecureSuite and the Panasonic Authenticam can be used to remove the need for a password by replacing it with iris identification, the user no longer needs to remember a lengthy, best-practices password. Therefore, if the user turns on the screen saver with the password-protect option and reduces the number of minutes of inactivity before it activates to as little as one minute, the user is only minimally inconvenienced if the screen saver comes on, because the user can simply re-identify himself by using his iris.

Enabling the screen-saver password in Windows 2000 is accomplished by right-clicking an open space on the desktop, selecting Properties, and then selecting the Screen Saver tab. After the Screen Saver tab opens, simply select a screen saver and check the Password Protected check box. Figure 4-44 shows a completed screen saver configuration.

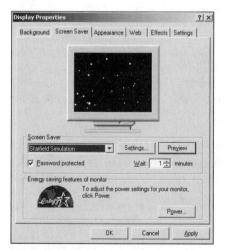

**Figure 4-44:** Screen saver setup

Notice that we have selected the Starfield Simulation option, checked the Password Protected check box, and reduced the Wait time to one minute. If the computer is not used for one minute, the system automatically goes into screen-saver mode, requiring the user to identify himself before system use can continue. The user must hit the Ctrl+Alt+Del keys simultaneously and then perform the appropriate identification procedure, depending on the option(s) selected (iris only, iris and password, iris or password, or password only).

An important point to note is that the capability to require everyone to authenticate by using an iris may not be possible because of factors previously listed in this chapter. A percentage of users, therefore, may need password-only authentication. Working with those users to provide other biometric options, as appropriate, or, at a minimum, ensure that they use very strong passwords is very important.

## LOCKING THE WORKSTATION

Another method of securing a workstation by running the SecureSuite workstation product is to use the Lock Workstation option. This can be done by clicking the diamond-shaped, yellow-and-purple icon that's located in the system tray, as shown earlier in Figure 4-31. Clicking the icon opens the menu shown in Figure 4-45.

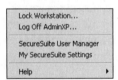

**Figure 4-45:** Locking the workstation

Move the mouse to the Lock Workstation option, and the workstation is now locked. A Computer Locked screen appears, stating `This computer is in use and has been locked`. Additionally, it states that only the user who locked the machine or an administrator can unlock it.

Unlocking the workstation is done in much the same fashion as when the system screen saver becomes active. The user must hit the Ctrl+Alt+Del keys simultaneously and then perform the appropriate identification procedure, depending on the option(s) selected.

## UTILITIES/APPLICATIONS

The SecureSuite product selected for this sample installation offers many features and functions. Among these are the capability to provide authentication to secure Web sites, programs, and other systems by using the current SecureSuite user profile (for example, iris only, password only, or both).

**WEB SITE AUTHENTICATION CONTROL**    Web site authentication is accomplished by enabling the user to create a protected password store for a given Web site the first time that a user visits a secure Web site.

note

A *secure Web site* is defined as a Web site requiring a user ID and password.

After the Web site is registered in the Internet password store, whenever the user returns to that Web site, the user can use SecureSuite (iris, password, or both) to log on to the secure Web site.

Suppose that you needed to log on to your Microsoft Exchange server by using Outlook Web Access (OWA). Depending on your implementation, as you first connect to OWA, you are prompted to log in, as shown in Figure 4-46.

**Figure 4-46:** OWA login screen

You would type your logon information and press Enter. After this is done, you are prompted with the Enter Network Password screen. As this is the first time you are visiting this site since installing SecureSuite, if you press the default hot keys of Ctrl+Shift+F12 simultaneously, an authentication prompt appears. Authenticate by using the appropriate SecureSuite method (iris, password, or both).

After authentication, a window appears asking `Would you like to register this window with secure session support?` Click OK to continue, and the screen shown in Figure 4-47 appears.

**Figure 4-47:** Outlook login

The SecureSession Windows Registration window appears. Notice the Select Field, Enter Information field, and that the first field (User Name) in the Enter Network Password window is highlighted. To register the information for use by SecureSession for subsequent visits to this site, type the username. (For this example, we're using ABCUSER.) Then click the down arrow next to Select Field. A new blank field is provided in Select Field, Enter Information, and the highlighted field moves from the User Name field to the Password field in the Enter Network Password window. Enter the password and click the down arrow next to Select Field again. Again, a blank is presented for the Enter Information field, and the highlight is moved to Domain. After you enter your final information and before you proceed, the screen appears as shown in Figure 4-48.

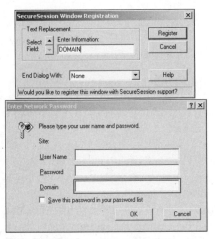

**Figure 4-48:** Information registration

The final window contains the End Dialog With field. This field enables the user to select items such as None, Enter and OK. If successfully authenticated, this field is also executed. For this example, we left the field as None so must click OK before actual logon occurs. If OK is selected in the End Dialog With field, the user is automatically logged on to Exchange after authentication is complete.

Click on the Register button, and SecureSession asks for the name of the registered site. For this example, we enter Exchange Logon, as shown in Figure 4-49.

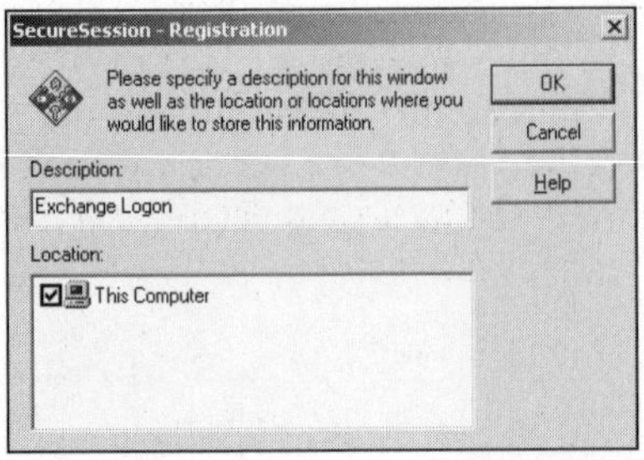

**Figure 4-49:** SecureSession Exchange logon

After you click OK, the final screen instructs you on how to use the SecureSession registered site. This is shown in Figure 4-50.

**Figure 4-50:** SecureSession registration is successful

Clicking OK here returns you to the Enter Network Logon window. At this point, you can press the hot-key sequence (Shift+Ctrl+F12). The authentication screen appears. After you successfully authenticate, the information is automatically entered into the Enter Network Logon window, and because you selected None in the End Dialog With field, clicking OK enables logon to occur.

**MORE DIFFICULT TO GUESS PASSWORDS**    Just as with the fingerprint solution, the iris biometric solution enables you to pick much more difficult-to-guess passwords at your secure Web locations. Although this is an added benefit, it can also pose some unique challenges.

Suppose that a Web site that you frequent requires a password. At work, you have a Panasonic Authenticam and SecureSuite software. You sign on to the secure Web site and change your password to a 16-character password using upper- and lowercase letters, numbers, and special characters. You then register this information in SecureSuite and test it to ensure that authentication occurs using SecureSuite. Everything works great.

Following best practices, you do not write down the password. After you get home, you realize that you need to access the Web site from your home office. But because you didn't write down the password and because it was randomly generated, you can't remember it. Most likely, you cannot accomplish your goal until you have access to the system that you registered the site from.

Or, if it is a Web site that you registered from work and it uses a passphrase for cases when passwords are forgotten, you could change the password so that you can log in. But now your system at work contains the wrong password, so that must be fixed next time that you have access to it. A few other options may make more sense, however.

First, you run SecureSuite at home also. Depending on the level of security, whenever you register a Web site and create a password, you can encrypt the password in a package such as Tiger Encryption-Decryption or PGP and send it, using encryption, to the e-mail address for your home office. This requires documenting the password, however, so after it is sent, all traces must be removed from both systems. At the home system, register the Web site again and delete all traces of the messages by using a strong "wipe" utility such as that contained in PGP.

If your purpose for using a biometric product such as SecureSuite and Authenticam is convenience and won't jeopardize your corporate network or information, you can use the SecureSuite software with a very strong password that you can remember. Ensure that you have valid licensing for all product use.

**TED OR PGP USAGE FOR ENCRYPTING E-MAILS**    SecureSuite also has the capability to help automate the process of encrypting e-mail, files, and folders. Each of these products provides some unique security benefits if combined with SecureSuite.

**PGP**    PGP mail encryption functions much like that outlined in Chapter 2. However, the method of performing the authentication varies. As was the case in our OWA example, after PGP is installed and the public/private keys generated and securely shared as appropriate, creating and sending an e-mail is as simple as opening the e-mail program, typing the e-mail, and hitting the hot key sequence to encrypt the text (if not done automatically). After this occurs, the PGP Enter Passphrase window appears.

The first time that this occurs, pressing and holding the Shift+Ctrl+F12 keys begins the SecureSession registration process, as outlined in the OWA example earlier in this chapter. If a default signing key was selected for PGP, the Signing Key field is populated with the default. After the SecureSession registration screen appears, the Please Enter Your Passphrase field for PGP is highlighted for automatic data entry from SecureSession. Type the passphrase in the SecureSession Windows Registration window's Select Field, Enter Information field.

 One caution here: Because we had only one field for entry, the passphrase was in plain text when it was typed into the field. Although this works, we must note that someone could have viewed this information as it was being typed.

For automatic entry to occur, select the OK option from the End Dialog With field of the SecureSession Windows Registration window. Figure 4-51 shows an example.

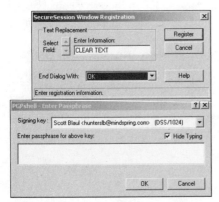

**Figure 4-51:** PGP passphrase example

After the information is entered and the Register button is clicked, SecureSession prompts the user to enter a name for the stored information. Simply enter **PGP mail** here and click OK to continue.

Now, each time that a message needs to be encrypted and the PGPShell - Enter Passphrase dialog box appears, simply hitting Shift+Ctrl+F12 enables the user to use SecureSuite for identification and automatically fills in the PGP information, followed by OK (because the End Dialog With field was set to OK). In this fashion, a very strong passphrase can be used with PGP that encompasses many letters, numbers, and characters in completely random fashion, providing greater security for PGP as well.

**TED**    Because some older e-mail packages do not function automatically with PGP — for example cc:Mail — TED was initially created as a means of encrypting messages outside an e-mail package. TED uses the Clipboard and keys to encrypt messages. After it's encrypted to the Clipboard, the message can be pasted into a document or other text message or directly into the e-mail message itself. This provides the capability to encrypt only certain text in a message that may also contain unencrypted text. Because TED uses a *master password*, SecureSession can be used, in a fashion similar to that demonstrated for PGP, to automatically enter the master password as needed. This enables the master password to be a very strong password — one that a user doesn't need to write down. TED is shown in Figure 4-52.

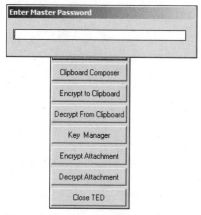

**Figure 4-52:** TED master password

After the master password is displayed, as shown in the figure, pressing the Shift+Ctrl+F12 keys accesses SecureSession Registration. Registration proceeds in a similar fashion to that using a PGP passphrase.

TED is available to you on this book's companion Web site at www.wiley.com/compbooks/ chirillo.

**SECURESUITE FILE ENCRYPTION**    Certain versions of PGP have the capability to perform file encryption and create a PGP disk. File encryption can be accomplished by right-clicking the file to be encrypted, selecting PGP, and selecting one of the following options:

✓ Encrypt

✓ Sign

✓ Encrypt & Sign

This process uses the PGP keys selected to encrypt the file.

If you want to create a secure, encrypted area in which to store files, you can use the PGP disk option. This is accomplished by opening a disk drive/partition/volume with some unused space.

After the drive is open, click File, highlight New, and select PGPdisk Volume to create an encrypted area on the hard drive. You are asked how much space should be allocated. Enter the appropriate information to complete the creation of an encrypted PGP virtual disk. After it's created, whenever the PGP disk is mounted (a passphrase entry is required), the PGP drive has a drive letter assignment like that of other volumes. Simply drag files to the drive to encrypt them.

What if you are a SecureSuite user and do not currently have PGP or another such program? You're in luck. SecureSuite has built-in file and folder encryption. Encrypting files and folders is a simple task using SecureSuite.

To encrypt a file, first locate the file to be encrypted. Right-click the file and select the SecureSuite Secure option from the pop-up menu, as shown in Figure 4-53.

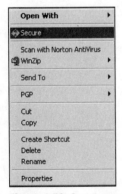

**Figure 4-53:** Secure menu option

After you select the Secure option from the menu, you are prompted to identify yourself through SecureSuite. In the current example, both iris authentication and password appear as Current Methods, with the OR option selected. The authentication screen that appears in Figure 4-54, therefore, provides the capability to use either method.

**Figure 4-54:** Authentication screen

To authenticate by using an iris, the user must hit the Ctrl+Shift+S keys simultaneously to enable the Authenticam. Alternatively, the user can simply type the password for the AdminXP user to accomplish the same goal.

>
> Although both iris and password authentication are shown, we recommend using only iris authentication (and both irises for higher security), where possible. This reduces the possibility that a simple password may be used, which greatly reduces or even eliminates the benefit of the iris authentication. Additionally, using the AND option to require both iris and password can increase security.

After the user has authenticated, the file is encrypted and appears as a sheet with a SecureSuite logo on it, as shown in Figure 4-55.

**Figure 4-55:** Encrypted file

The user who encrypted the file has the capability to decrypt the file. No other user, however, can decrypt the file.

Folder encryption is performed in much the same way as file encryption. Simply locate the folder to be encrypted or create a new folder for encryption. Right-click the folder and select the Secure icon from the menu that appears. SecureSuite displays a Confirm Create SecureFolder warning, as shown in Figure 4-56.

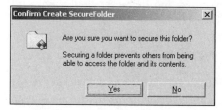

**Figure 4-56:** SecureFolder warning

A very important note here is that others cannot access the folder or its contents. If the documents are to be shared, therefore, another protection method should be used.

After selecting Yes to confirm the creation of a SecureFolder, the user is prompted to authenticate. After a successful authentication, the folder is secured, and a SecureSuite icon appears on it, as shown in Figure 4-57.

**Figure 4-57:** Secured folder

Files and folders can be unsecured/decrypted by the user who secured them. For a file, double-clicking the file and authenticating can accomplish this. This process creates an unsecure copy of the document. To unsecure a folder, right-click the folder. An "unsecure" selection becomes available. Select it and authenticate to begin the unsecure process.

Files and folders must be unsecured before uninstalling SecureSuite; otherwise, the files can never be unsecured and opened again, even if SecureSuite is reinstalled.

**APPLICATION SECURITY**    One of the most powerful features of the SecureSuite product (in our opinion) is the capability of the product to secure applications. What makes SecureSuite unique is that it can secure executable files. This means that authentication can be added to programs that may otherwise run without any authentication. We list two examples why we believe this is a very strong feature of SecureSuite.

**EXAMPLE 1: MICROSOFT MANAGEMENT CONSOLE (MMC.EXE)**    Suppose that you have a need to control access to Microsoft Management Console (MMC). SecureApp can be used to require authentication whenever different options try to access MMC. This can be accomplished by requiring authentication to occur any time that mmc.exe is executed and includes applications and options that call the mmc.exe file. To see how this can be accomplished, review the following method of configuration.

SecureApp can be accessed from the SecureSuite User Manager console by selecting Options and System Properties, as shown in Figure 4-58.

This opens the System Properties screen. This screen has five tabular options. These are (from left to right) General, Devices, Event Logging, Database, and SecureApp. Clicking the SecureApp tab displays the screen shown in Figure 4-59.

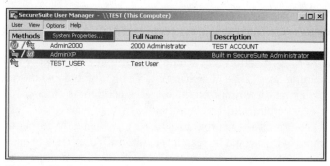

**Figure 4-58:** SecureApp selection

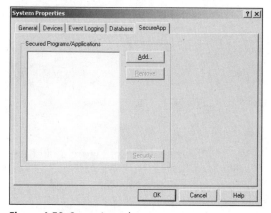

**Figure 4-59:** SecureApp tab

Clicking the Add button opens the Select Program File window. Find and double-click the mmc.exe file. This causes the Access Security for MMC.EXE window to appear, as shown in Figure 4-60.

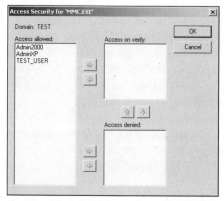

**Figure 4-60:** Access Security for MMC.EXE window

In Figure 4-60, you see three users. Suppose that you want only the AdminXP and Admin2000 users to be able to run mmc.exe after they are verified and no users can run mmc.exe without first being verified.

From the screen shown in Figure 4-60, each admin user would be highlighted and moved to the Access on Verify window. The remaining user (TEST_USER) would be highlighted and moved to the Access Denied window. Finally, clicking the OK button finalizes the configuration.

Now, whenever the administrator users (AdminXP and Admin2000) try to access mmc.exe through any number of methods that call the mmc.exe program, they are prompted to authenticate before they can continue. An example of this would be seen if the AdminXP user tried to open Computer Management from within the Control Panel. The AdminXP user would be prompted to authenticate by using SecureSuite before he or she could continue.

Should the TEST_USER try to run the same program, he or she would be presented with the screen shown in Figure 4-61.

**Figure 4-61:** Insufficient privileges

And, finally, if any of the users were left in the Access Allowed column of Figure 4-60, those user(s) could run the application without authenticating.

Additional applications can be added to SecureApp by performing the same procedure and selecting the appropriate .EXE file.

As a test, we copied the mmc.exe file, and tried to run it. The SecureApp settings also applied to the copied mmc.exe.

**EXAMPLE 2: DATABASE**   Securing a database can be accomplished in much the same manner as outlined for Example 1. Find the database executable file and add it to SecureApp. Ensure that users' access privileges are set appropriately (Allowed, Allowed after Authenticating, or Disallowed).

Ensure that a user cannot access another executable capable of gaining access to the database on the machine. (An example would be that, if a database was stored in a file that was purely a comma-separated value (CSV) file, a standard word processor, spreadsheet program, and so on would be very unlikely to have the capability to open and view the data.) If the intent is to secure both the application and the data, the data should be in a proprietary format (one that only the database application can read).

note

The version of SecureApp shown in here does not support 16-bit applications.

**UNIQUE USE**    Because SecureApp has the capability to control the execution of programs by a user, it can provide some very beneficial functions.

Presume that you have a common-use machine that must have the capability to connect to the Internet for some users and to restrict Internet access for other users. You have chosen SecureSuite and the Authenticam for many reasons, including their capability to provide strong authentication/identification. But because SecureSuite contains SecureApp, you can control Internet access for any user by selecting the Web browser executable file and selecting which users can access the Internet after they are authenticated. Additionally, you place all other users in the Access Denied column. Now, if a user who is allowed to tries to access the Internet, he must authenticate before actually being allowed to browse the Internet. Those who were placed in the Access Denied column, however, are not allowed to access the Internet and are shown a message stating that they do not have the access privileges necessary to perform the function.

**OTHER RECOMMENDED SECUREAPPLICATION USES**    Following are some other uses for SecureApplication:

- ✓ Hyper terminal
- ✓ Telnet
- ✓ Terminal Services
- ✓ Remote connectivity options, such as the following:
  - ▪ America Online (AOL)
  - ▪ Microsoft MSN
  - ▪ Juno
  - ▪ Virtual Private Networks (VPN)
- ✓ Command Prompt (CMD)
- ✓ E-Mail application
- ✓ Remote Assistance
- ✓ Windows Messenger
- ✓ AOL Instant Messenger
- ✓ ICQ

# Questions Raised

In reviewing iris authentication and products such as SecureSuite, many questions can be raised. Some of these questions relate to the human factor of biometric security, while others relate to the technical aspects. The ones that are most important, however, vary from environment to environment. These questions often mark the beginning of the biometric journey for an organization. The destination should ultimately be for a more secure and, hopefully, more user-friendly environment. Nonetheless, through out this process, several questions are sure to be raised. Some of these questions have relatively easy answers, and some take considerable effort to answer; others may require an ongoing search for the answer.

One purpose for displaying a sample product is to help answer some of these questions by using a real-world product. The product itself, however, can spawn new questions. This is especially true for such features as executable-level (.EXE) authorization by using a biometric solution. The following list simply grazes the surface of the possible questions about executable level authorization, using a biometric solution in the hope of providing some kindling for the fire that should become a blaze after some of these questions are asked:

- ✓ What if a duplicate copy is made of the executable?
- ✓ Can the executable be run from another location?
- ✓ How do you protect against other applications that can access the data?
- ✓ How do you protect against a user installing his own application to provide functionality that users would not otherwise be allowed to have?
- ✓ How can the executable be accessed remotely?
- ✓ How can upgrades be handled?

These queries and others should be answered prior to implementing a biometric solution. Furthermore, working with both the manufacturer as well as a knowledgeable consulting firm to assist in answering these questions is important.

# Summary

Eye biometric systems are unique and, as such, can provide some of the highest levels of identification in the field. Although both types mentioned in this chapter provide these very high levels, iris technology is the more accepted of the two. This is primarily because users do not need to be in extremely close proximity to the scanning device compared to retina technology. In addition to its growing acceptance, iris technology manufacturers are beginning to claim that iris technology rivals or even provides higher levels of identification than that of retina technology. Both claim to contain unique characteristics that would make the possibility of false or duplicate identification as unlikely as with the other (one in millions or even one in a billion). Whatever the numbers, we do know that, to date, iris technology has had as many as 2.7 million enrollments in one data store without a single false identification. If these numbers hold true, eye technology could be the manner by which you're identified in the future.

# Chapter 5

# Other Physical Biometrics

THIS CHAPTER IS A DISCUSSION on the less popular biometric technologies. This chapter discusses hand-scan, handprint, and DNA systems for identity and authentication. It also supplies open source (source code available for use and/or modification from its original design free of charge) for your own custom handprint biometric implementations.

## Hand-Scan Geometry

Hand-scan biometricsbeen around for several years, particularly for physical access control and time and attendance. The methodology and usage of hand-scan biometrics is relatively simple and straightforward. First, a user needs to be enrolled in the system's internal template database by placing a hand with the palm facing down on the hand-scan reader, as shown in Figure 5-1. The user's fingertips should be aligned with the guidance pegs that are specifically designed to properly place fingers (typically three of five) for enrollment.

**Figure 5-1:** Recognition Systems, Inc.'s hand scanner collecting data

Upwards of 90 or so measurements are taken from three to four enrollments to create a user template, including length, width, and thickness, plus surface areas of the hand and fingers, by some type of digital camera. Some scanners measure the characteristics of only a few fingers to reduce the template size—which is typically 9 to 50 bytes per user. What's more, newer systems even incorporate temperature-sensing mechanisms.

Probably the most popular hand-scan biometrics systems derive from Recognition Systems, Inc. (RSI). According to the company, a division of Ingersoll-Rand, RSI is the worldwide leader in biometric access control, time and attendance, and personal identification products. The company, founded in 1986, pioneered the commercialization of biometrics using its patented hand geometry. This technology verifies identity by the size and shape of the hand. The widespread use of Recognition Systems' HandReaders in access control and time and attendance applications has established RSI as the market leader in biometric verification.

Recognition Systems' HandReaders provide improved security, accuracy, and convenience for these three important applications: For access control, the HandReaders ensure that the person who enters isn't merely carrying someone else's access card or personal identification number (PIN). For time and attendance, the HandReaders improve payroll accuracy and simplicity by eliminating "buddy-punching." For personal identification, the HandReaders guarantee that the people on a site actually belong there.

"Buddy-punching" is a term used to describe a time and attendance technique whereby one employee punches in or out for a coworker who is not present.

HandReaders are fast, easy to use, and reliable. As of mid-2002, more than 70,000 units had been installed throughout the world in a wide variety of applications. More than 18,000 employees at San Francisco International Airport have depended on HandReaders for tarmac access since 1993, with more than 100 million transactions having occurred. The 1996 Olympic Games used the HandReaders to protect access to the Olympic Village. More than 65,000 people were enrolled and more than one million transactions were handled in 28 days. More than 900 HandReaders control client and employee access to special areas of Italian banks, and more than 100 units perform similar functions in Russia. The HandReaders now play a vital role in a border-crossing system for frequent travelers. The program, called INSPASS, is currently being expanded at United States airports. In the United Kingdom, the prisons rely on HandReaders for prisoner tracking. Universities use HandReaders for their on-campus meal programs, to safeguard access to dormitories, and to protect their computer centers. Veteran's hospitals throughout the United States use HandReaders to protect drug dispensaries. HandReaders enable members to access clubs around the globe without having to remember to carry a card. Schools and daycare centers use hand readers to verify the identity of parents and safeguard the children left in their care. The list goes on.

RSI can attribute the majority of its success, profitability, and growth to three specific markets:

✓ **Access control** — RSI brings the true security and convenience of biometric technology within reach of most access-control applications. The HandKey II uses field-proven hand geometry technology that verifies an authorized person in less than one second. The benefits of biometric security were once reserved for high-security applications, but the HandKey II changes that. Tens of thousands of HandKeys are already installed in applications that range from health clubs and daycare centers to laboratories and prisons. Its ease of use and reliability has made HandKey the biometric standard for the access control industry. The lower cost of the HandKey II now makes the choice even easier.

✓ **Time and attendance** — RSI now brings the accuracy and convenience of biometric technology easily within reach of most time and attendance applications. HandReaders have proven to be a practical and precise security solution.

- Beyond a simple time clock, the HandPunch 1000 brings an enterprise solution to small companies, as well as to companies that have small, multiple locations and minimal supervision.

- The HandPunch 2000 and 3000 provide definable data management keys that allow data collection when employees punch.

- The HandPunch 4000 lets you tailor the system to meet your precise needs.

The systems transmit data to the time and attendance host PC through a variety of options, depending on the model.

✓ **Personal identification** — This is a project-oriented market. The HandKey is used as a means to positively identify a person holding a transaction card, driver's license, national identification card, passport, visa, or other documents. Current installations are in place at the Immigration and Naturalization INSPASS stations at JFK, Newark, and Toronto airports, as well as in the Food Services systems at the University of Georgia. Banks, both domestic and international, are looking into this approach as a way to put a person's bank account on a memory card. Programs are also being planned for biometric identification and verification of government benefits recipients.

## Market

Although hand-scan biometrics is a slow-growing technology, estimates project revenues to grow to approximately $50 million in 2005, which is approximately 2 to 5 percent of the entire biometric market. The primary reason for the minimal forecast is limited usages and aptness mainly for access control and time and attendance applications.

## Hand-Scan Strengths and Weaknesses

Among the strengths for hand-scan geometry biometrics are ease of use, resistance to fraud, size of the template, and user acceptance.

✓ **Ease of use** — The submission of the biometric is straightforward and, with proper training, can be done with little misplacement. The only exception may be elderly clientele or those with arthritic hands, who may be unable to easily spread their fingers and place their hand on the unit's surface. The unit also works fairly well with dirty hands.

✓ **Resistant to fraud** — Short of casting a model of an enrolled person's hand and fingers, it would be difficult and time-consuming to submit a fake sample. Because much of the value of hand scan is as a deterrent in time and attendance scenarios, attempting a fake submission would rarely be worth the effort.

✓ **Template size** — Using RSI as the standard bearer of hand-scan technology, a template size of 9 bytes is extremely small (much smaller than most other biometric technologies).

By contrast, finger-scan biometrics require 250 to 1,000 bytes, and voice-scan biometrics commonly require 1,500 to 3,000 bytes. This much smaller space requirement facilitates storage of a large number of templates in a standalone device, which is how many hand-scan devices are designed to work. It also facilitates card-based storage, as even magstripe cards have ample room for 9-byte samples.

✓ **User perceptions** — As opposed to facial scan or eye-based technologies, which can encounter some resistance, the use of hand geometry is not problematic for the vast majority of users. It bears very little of the stigma of other authentication methods.

Hand-scan weaknesses include the older design, cost, and accuracy.

✓ **Static design** — As opposed to other biometrics, which can take advantage of technological breakthroughs such as silicon development or camera quality, hand-scan has remained largely unchanged for years. Its size precludes it from being used in most logical access scenarios, where compact design may be a prerequisite.

✓ **Cost** — Hand-scan readers cost approximately $1,400 to $2,000, placing them toward the high end of the physical security spectrum. Finger-scan readers, whatever strengths and weaknesses they may have, can be much less expensive, in the $800 to $1,200 range.

✓ **Accuracy** — Although generally more reliable than behavioral biometrics such as voice or signature, hand geometry, in its current incarnation, cannot perform one-to-many searches; instead, it is limited to one-to-one verification. This limits its use in many different applications.

# Handprint Biometrics

Capturing and analyzing an image of your hand — very similar to fingerprinting — is the basis of handprint biometric technology. The design was created to take the developments of current technology (larger storage space and faster processing) into consideration.

There are 14 finger bones, 5 bones in the palm, and 8 bones in the wrist. These bones are controlled not only by the muscles in the hand, but also by muscles in the forearm. This arrangement provides for a wide range of movement, strength, and precision. The hand palms (and feet soles) do not get suntanned. Nor do the palms sweat when you get too hot. They only sweat when you are stressed. No matter what the temperature, if you are relaxed, you will normally have dry palms. Get stressed out on the arctic tundra and you will have sweaty palms. This unusual pattern evolved for better survival in stressful situations when increased grasping action of weapons was needed. When the hand and fingers sweat, the little ridges swell and provide better gripping action.

Handprinting (shown in Figure 5-2) compares the ridges and lines of your hand, including each and every fingerprint, which is considered to be unique. Hand and fingerprints are made up of ridges and furrows. The ridges are the raised portions and the furrows are the lower portions. The difference between the ridges and furrows creates enough space to enable the creation of patterns.

For more information on these patterns, refer to Chapter 1.

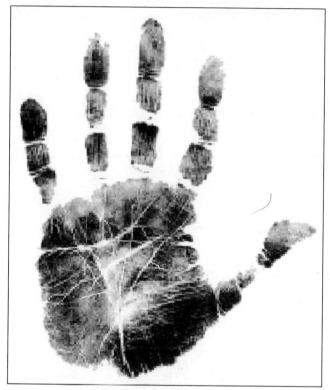

**Figure 5-2:** Handprint scanner template

## Security Characteristics

The components used to determine uniqueness of a user's handprint depend on the ridges that are used to create a differential template. A template contains the values calculated from the fingerprints and actual palm print.

Vertical and horizontal lines may appear on the palms and fingers. The deeper, longer, and clearer the vertical and horizontal lines, the better use in creating a good template; however, templates do expire, as injury and age conditions affect individual, unique prints.

Hands and fingers, especially fingertips, have thousands of nerve endings per square inch and are our major sensors for the physical world. They receive temperature, texture, and pressure sensations, and send them to the brain so that we can form a more accurate mental model of the world around us. Our fingers are like antennae for the brain.

Table 5-1 indicates some of the additional characteristics of handprint technology.

**TABLE 5-1: Additional Characteristics of Handprint Technology**

| Characteristic | Ease of use | Error incidence | Accuracy | Acceptance | Security Level | Stability | Cost |
|---|---|---|---|---|---|---|---|
| | High | Injury, print condition, age | Medium | Medium | Medium | High | Low |

## STRENGTHS

Biometric handprint technology strengths are equivalent to those of fingerprinting, including the following:

✓ Handprints are easy to use — simply place a hand on a scanner.

✓ Many handprint technologies are designed not only for security, but to make multiple authentications to disparate systems easier.

✓ Identification on some systems may be set up to only occur from your personal flatbed scanner.

✓ Considered stronger than password protection alone.

## WEAKNESSES

Because fingerprint technology is one of the oldest and most well known technologies, a good amount of information is publicly available on how to defeat fingerprint technology.

✓ Handprints are easily copied/reproduced to fake a legitimate scan.

✓ An actual hand that may no longer be attached to the owner can be used to gain access.

✓ Fingerprint technology is not considered as secure as retinal or iris biometric technologies.

# Sample Handprint Biometric Applications

Depending on your requirements, a biometric handprint system implementation can be custom developed. The sections that follow discuss various methods of kernel development for proprietary usages and general authentication, such as for network or workstation logon, and program applications.

## TIGERHANDPRINT ANALYSIS CUSTOM SOURCE KERNEL

This section contains topics on configuring TigerHandprint Analysis for custom handprint authentication. For convenience, the authentication, learning, and template modules have been combined into two forms, and each is examined separately.

Visual Basic 6 or higher is recommended for customizing TigerSign source for proprietary implementations. The complete source can be downloaded from www.wiley.com/compbooks/chirillo.

**SCANNER INTEROPERABILITY AND LAYERED APPROACH**    The handprint scanner kernel (see Figure 5-3) adheres to a layered approach for interoperability of different vendor devices that support the *TWAIN (Technology Without an Interesting Name) standard*. This scanning control is easy to use and can acquire images from most TWAIN-compliant devices.

The TWAIN scanner interface is an industry standard interface that is used by Windows for the transfer of data, usually graphical in nature, from scanning devices (flatbed scanners, digital cameras, hand scanners, and so on) directly into applications that can make use of this data.

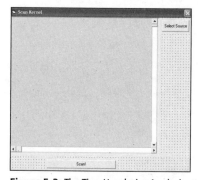

**Figure 5-3:** The TigerHandprint Analysis scanning kernel

Not all PC development software is universally shipped with scanners; therefore, TWAIN drivers and interface software may not be present on all PCs. TWAIN access features built into your software should always be supplied as optional menu items or as on-demand features that are either unavailable or trapped by your application if `TWAIN.DLL` or `TWAIN32.DLL` is not found on the target machine.

The following open source code is provided as a foundation to your proprietary handprint authentication implementations. The scanning kernel contains one form and one class module with appropriate commenting. The form control source is shown in the following extract, frmMain:

```
Private Declare Function TWAIN_AcquireToFilename Lib "TWAIN32d.DLL" (ByVal
hwndApp As Long, ByVal bmpFileName As String) As Integer
Private Declare Function TWAIN_IsAvailable Lib "TWAIN32d.DLL" () As Long
Private Declare Function TWAIN_SelectImageSource Lib "TWAIN32d.DLL" (ByVal
hwndApp As Long) As Long
Dim ScrollAreaScan As CScrollArea

Private Sub cmdScan_Click()
Dim Ret As Long, PictureFile As String
PictureFile = App.Path & "\temp.bmp"
'Picture file is the temporary file "temp.bmp"
Ret = TWAIN_AcquireToFilename(Me.hwnd, PictureFile)
If Ret = 0 Then
'If the scan is successful
picScan.Picture = LoadPicture(PictureFile)
'Load the temporary picture file
ScrollAreaScan.ReSizeArea
'Resize the picture control
Kill PictureFile
'Delete the temporary picture file
Else
MsgBox "Scan was not successful!", vbCritical, "Scanning..."
End If
End Sub

Private Sub cmdSelect_Click()
TWAIN_SelectImageSource (Me.hwnd)
End Sub

Private Sub Form_Load()
Set ScrollAreaScan = New CScrollArea
Set ScrollAreaScan.VBar = VScroll
Set ScrollAreaScan.HBar = HScroll
Set ScrollAreaScan.InnerPicture = picScan
Set ScrollAreaScan.FramePicture = Picture1
End Sub
```

Here is the class modules source:

```
Option Explicit

Public WithEvents VBar As VScrollBar
Public WithEvents HBar As HScrollBar
Public WithEvents InnerPicture As PictureBox
```

```
Public WithEvents FramePicture As PictureBox

Const DFC_SCROLL = 3                    ' Scroll bar

Private Type RECT
    Left As Long
    top As Long
    Right As Long
    Bottom As Long
End Type


Private Type POINTAPI
    x As Long
    y As Long
End Type


Private Declare Function DrawFrameControl Lib "user32" (ByVal hdc As Long,
lpRect As RECT, ByVal un1 As Long, ByVal un2 As Long) As Long
Private Declare Function GetCursorPos Lib "user32" (lpPoint As POINTAPI) As
Long
Private Declare Function SetCursorPos Lib "user32" (ByVal x As Long, ByVal y
As Long) As Long
Private Declare Function GetWindowRect Lib "user32" (ByVal hwnd As Long,
lpRect As RECT) As Long


Private Sub SetScrollBar()
    ' See if we need the vertical scroll bar.
    If InnerPicture.Height <= FramePicture.ScaleHeight Then
        VBar.Enabled = False
    Else
        ' Set scroll bar properties.
        InnerPicture.top = 0
        VBar.Min = 0
        VBar.Max = FramePicture.ScaleHeight - InnerPicture.Height
        VBar.LargeChange = FramePicture.ScaleHeight
        VBar.SmallChange = FramePicture.ScaleHeight / 5
        VBar.Enabled = True
    End If

    ' See if we need the vertical scroll bar.
    If InnerPicture.Width <= FramePicture.ScaleWidth Then
        HBar.Enabled = False
    Else
        ' Set scroll bar properties.
```

```
            InnerPicture.Left = 0
            HBar.Min = 0
            HBar.Max = FramePicture.ScaleWidth - InnerPicture.Width
            HBar.LargeChange = FramePicture.ScaleWidth
            HBar.SmallChange = FramePicture.ScaleWidth / 5
            HBar.Enabled = True
        End If
    End Sub
End Sub
Private Sub VBar_Change()
    InnerPicture.top = VBar.Value
End Sub
Private Sub VBar_Scroll()
    InnerPicture.top = VBar.Value
End Sub
Private Sub HBar_Change()
    InnerPicture.Left = HBar.Value
End Sub
Private Sub HBar_Scroll()
    InnerPicture.Left = HBar.Value
End Sub
Sub ReSizeArea()
    VBar.TabStop = False: HBar.TabStop = False
    InnerPicture.Left = ((FramePicture.Width) - InnerPicture.Width) / 2
    InnerPicture.top = (FramePicture.Height - InnerPicture.Height) / 2
    SetScrollBar
End Sub
```

**TEMPLATE COMPARISON**    After creating a user template, further scans will be analyzed for comparison authentication using the template comparison kernel shown in Figure 5-4. As with the scanning kernel, the comparison kernel also contains one form and one module.

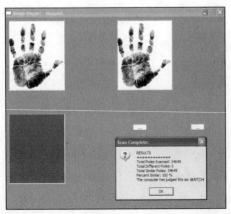

**Figure 5-4:** The TigerHandprint Analysis template comparison kernel

The following is a source extract from the form that can be modified for your own proprietary uses:

```
Private Sub Command1_Click()
Dim x As Long, y As Long
Dim c As Long, d As Long
Dim p1 As Long, p2 As Long
Dim R1 As Long, B1 As Long, G1 As Long
Dim R2 As Long, B2 As Long, G2 As Long
Dim t As Long, r As Integer
Dim per As Long, msg As String
Picture3.Cls

t = Text1.Text

Form1.Caption = "Image Mapper - Mapping"

Do Until y > Picture1.Height Or y > Picture2.Height

p1 = Picture1.Point(x, y)
p2 = Picture2.Point(x, y)

RGB_get p1, R1, B1, G1
RGB_get p2, R2, B2, G2

Diff r, R1, R2, B1, B2, G1, G2, t
If r = 0 Then
d = d + 1
Picture3.PSet (x, y), vbBlue
Else
Picture3.PSet (x, y), vbRed
End If
c = c + 1
x = x + 15
If x > Picture1.Width Or x > Picture2.Width Then x = 0: y = y + 15
Loop

per = 100 - ((d / c) * 100)

msg = msg & "RESULTS" & vbCrLf
msg = msg & "==============" & vbCrLf
msg = msg & "Total Pixles Scanned: " & c & vbCrLf
msg = msg & "Total Different Pixles: " & d & vbCrLf
msg = msg & "Total Similar Pixles: " & (c - d) & vbCrLf
msg = msg & "Percent Similar: " & per & " %" & vbCrLf
If per > 75 Then
```

```
msg = msg & "The computer has judged this as: SIMILAR"
Else
msg = msg & "The computer has judged this as: DIFFERENT"
End If

Form1.Caption = "Image Mapper - Mapped"

MsgBox msg, 0 & 32, "Scan Complete:"
End Sub

Private Sub Command2_Click()
Dim x As Long, y As Long
Dim p1 As Long, p2 As Long
Dim R1 As Long, B1 As Long, G1 As Long
Dim R2 As Long, B2 As Long, G2 As Long
Dim t As Long, r As Integer
Picture3.Cls

t = Text1.Text

Form1.Caption = "Image Mapper - Mapping"

Do Until y > Picture1.Height Or y > Picture2.Height

p1 = Picture1.Point(x, y)
p2 = Picture2.Point(x, y)

RGB_get p1, R1, B1, G1
RGB_get p2, R2, B2, G2

If G1 = -1 Then GoSub 20

Diff r, R1, R2, B1, B2, G1, G2, t
If r = 0 Then
Picture3.PSet (x, y), RGB(R1, B1, G1)
Else
Picture3.PSet (x, y), vbRed
End If

20

x = x + 15
If x > Picture1.Width Or x > Picture2.Width Then x = 0: y = y + 15
Loop
```

```
Form1.Caption = "Image Mapper - Mapped"

End Sub

Private Sub Command3_Click()
Dim x As Long, y As Long
Dim p1 As Long, p2 As Long
Dim R1 As Long, B1 As Long, G1 As Long
Dim R2 As Long, B2 As Long, G2 As Long
Dim Ra As Long, Ba As Long, Ga As Long
Picture3.Cls

t = Text1.Text

Form1.Caption = "Image Mapper - Mapping"

Do Until y > Picture1.Height Or y > Picture2.Height

p1 = Picture1.Point(x, y)
p2 = Picture2.Point(x, y)

RGB_get p1, R1, B1, G1
RGB_get p2, R2, B2, G2

Ra = (R1 + R2) / 2
Ba = (B1 + B2) / 2
Ga = (G1 + G2) / 2

If Ga = -1 Then GoSub 10

Picture3.PSet (x, y), RGB(Ra, Ba, Ga)

10

x = x + 15
If x > Picture1.Width Or x > Picture2.Width Then x = 0: y = y + 15
Loop

Form1.Caption = "Image Mapper - Mapped"

End Sub

Private Sub Command4_Click()
On Error GoTo Killer
CommonDialog1.ShowOpen
```

```
Picture1 = LoadPicture(CommonDialog1.FileName)
Exit Sub
Killer:
MsgBox "Error!", 0 & 16, "Error:"
End Sub

Private Sub Command5_Click()
On Error GoTo Killer
CommonDialog1.ShowOpen
Picture2 = LoadPicture(CommonDialog1.FileName)
Exit Sub
Killer:
MsgBox "Error!", 0 & 16, "Error:"
End Sub

Private Sub Picture1_Resize()
If Picture1.Width > 3255 Or Picture1.Height > 3255 Then
MsgBox "That picture is too big to be analysed!", 0 & 16, "Error:"
Picture1.Width = 3255
Picture1.Height = 3255
Exit Sub
End If
Picture3.Width = Picture1.Width
Picture3.Height = Picture1.Height
End Sub

Private Sub Picture2_Resize()
If Picture2.Width > 3255 Or Picture12Height > 3255 Then
MsgBox "That picture is too big to be analysed!", 0 & 16, "Error:"
Picture2.Width = 3255
Picture2.Height = 3255
Exit Sub
End If
End Sub
```

The following module source is associated with the main template comparison form:

```
Type COLORRGB
  red As Long
  green As Long
  blue As Long
End Type
```

```
Function RGB_get(ByVal CVal As Long, r As Long, B As Long, G As Long) As
COLORRGB
G = Int(CVal / 65536)
B = Int((CVal - (65536 * G)) / 256)
r = CVal - (65536 * G + 256 * B)
End Function

Function Diff(Result As Integer, R1 As Long, R2 As Long, B1 As Long, B2 As
Long, G1 As Long, G2 As Long, Tol As Long)
If R1 > R2 + Tol Or B1 > B2 + Tol Or G1 > G2 + Tol Or _
R1 < R2 - Tol Or B1 < B2 - Tol Or G1 < G2 - Tol Then
Result = 0 'False
Else
Result = 1 'True
End If
End Function
```

The simple methodology used behind the sourced handprint kernels can be outlined in a few simple steps:

1. Start the scanner kernel.

2. Select TWAIN-compliant scanner source (for example, flatbed scanner).

3. Scan; the template will be stored as temp.bmp.

4. (Optional) Add routines for user registration template development from the results of three initial scans.

5. When the user attempts to authenticate to a program or system, initialize the template comparison kernel to compare the scanned results (see Figure 5-5).

6. (Optional) Add password authentication after a successful match for strong or two-factor authentication.

7. The user is granted access.

**Figure 5-5:** Comparing the user handprint with the master template

# DNA Biometrics

Most of us have heard the term DNA, generally in the context of forensic evidence to determine the identity (or maybe, more accurately, to exclude an individual as a possible suspect) in a crime. One reason why DNA evidence is used so frequently is that it exists in all living cells. Therefore, any cells left at a crime scene will contain DNA (although in some instances not enough DNA is present in the left-behind cells to be used). Another reason why DNA is frequently used is that the characteristics of DNA for each person are unique, and are considered to be very accurate in determining the identity of the DNA provider.

## DNA Biometric Technology

DNA is an acronym for deoxyribonucleic acid, and is present in each and every human cell (as well as in the cells of other living things). The DNA of each person is unique, and provides a very accurate method of identifying an individual. As a biometric identification authentication technology, DNA has some ground to cover before it can be widely and securely used; however, DNA technology is promising. DNA is discussed here as it relates to humans and biometric identification and authentication technologies. To understand why DNA can be used as an identification tool, it is important to have a good understanding of DNA and its potential uses.

## Understanding DNA

Deoxyribonucleic acid is a hereditary substance found in all living cells. DNA is composed of four bases called *nucleotides*. These nucleotides are subelements contained within DNA. The nucleotides are denoted by the letters A, T, C, and G. The order of these nucleotides provides the necessary information for cell function, including which cells grow, die, what they produce (for example, hair), and when.

Chemical bonds connecting the nucleotides together form a chain of sorts, also referred to as a *strand*. Determining the order of the nucleotides along the DNA strand is called *DNA sequencing*. A DNA sequence can be performed on a single nucleotide, multiple nucleotides, or all four, using various methods. Forensic scientists use sequencing to match samples from known persons to samples found at crime scenes.

It is also possible to use the DNA of both parents of a person to determine that person's DNA. However, in the case of identical twins, the DNA may match (the importance of this is discussed later). Figure 5-6 is a simple illustration of a sample DNA sequence pattern using only one of the bases.

While the example shows only one base (for example, C), in actuality, the DNA chains are typically much longer. So, if you were to include all four bases (nucleotides) when coupled with a much longer chain, you'd have a chain that closely resembles that of a human, and begin to see how DNA can be used to uniquely identify a person. However, like other biometric technologies, DNA biometric technology has its strengths and weaknesses.

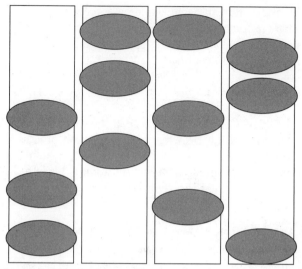

**Figure 5-6:** Sample DNA sequence

## DNA Strengths

The strength of DNA as a biometric identification tool lies primarily in the uniqueness of the DNA sequence. With all four bases included (A, T, C, and G), and with much longer DNA chains than that depicted in Figure 5-6, the possibility of duplicating DNA sequences is extremely remote (except in cases such as identical twins). DNA, as a tool for identity verification and management, is considered to be very strong.

Using logic similar to that of fingerprint, retina, or iris technology, where up to 400 data points are collected, it is feasible that substantially more data points might be collected with DNA technology. This has the potential to be even more secure than the biometric technologies previously discussed. However, some inherent weaknesses must be overcome before DNA technology can be used as a biometric identification and authentication tool for networks.

## DNA Weaknesses

A primary reason for using a biometric trait for authentication is that, typically, a biometric trait is directly connected to the person to be identified. However, with DNA technology, the biometric trait is removable. Because DNA is contained in hair, skin, blood, and so on, it is susceptible to being faked by substitution. Because DNA is contained in items such as hair that shed on their own, it would be very easy for someone to obtain such a sample from the owner without the owner's knowledge. Many examples of this have been used to convict criminals in cases where a single strand of hair, a drop of blood, or a fingernail fragment (and many more examples) have been left at a crime scene.

A person wishing to acquire the DNA of another human being would potentially only have to acquire one such DNA-containing object (a hair, for example). Once obtained, the DNA-containing object could potentially be used to falsely identify an individual — this is a very real threat.

Another weakness relating to DNA biometric identification and authentication lies in the acquisition device. Although microchips are being designed and evaluated that may provide the technology in the future, commercially available network authentication using DNA is currently not available.

DNA identification and authentication for data networks is also not a good choice for sole identification. The primary reason for this is that unless the DNA material submission process is closely guarded, substitute DNA samples would provide easy authentication (false match) for someone masquerading as an authorized user. Consequently, DNA identification is likely to be used in conjunction with another biometric method such as iris, retina, fingerprint, and so on.

Recently, television commercials have depicted users having to authenticate using fingerprint, iris, password, and hair samples. Although overstated, many companies investing in biometric technologies are using multifactor biometrics as a method to mitigate the weaknesses of a single technology.

## TEMPLATE ACQUISITON

Although no widely accepted DNA acquisition devices are available for data networks today (based on our research), it is possible and likely that in the relatively near future some will begin to surface. It is also anticipated that such devices will attempt to mask or conceal the actual DNA information through encryption, or other means, in an effort to protect an individual's actual DNA information.

Bio Fact: DNA acquisition devices are currently under development, but as of this writing, not readily available to the general public. These include microchip devices capable of comparing DNA samples.

## FACT VERSUS FICTION

In discussing DNA identification as a possibility for network authentication with many potential users, some of the common beliefs and misconceptions are the same as with other biometric technologies (such as fingerprint, iris, and retina), and some new concerns also surface, as shown in Table 5-2:

### TABLE 5-2: Belief versus Reality

| Belief | Fact |
|--------|------|
| If the DNA authentication device has to be shared, and many people are placing "samples" on the device, the potential exists to transfer germs and the like. | The fact is that although it might be unlikely or minimal, it is still possible for something to be transmitted or picked up from any common or public device. |
| The users' DNA information is stored, and could potentially be used against them at a later date. | Because the acquisition devices are not in widespread use, it is difficult to state with certainty that this cannot or will not happen. However, if DNA biometric network authentication technology holds true to form (as with other biometric technologies), the captured information will not be stored, but rather some form of encrypted or otherwise manipulated form of the information will be stored. For example, algorithm could be used to convert the information before transmitting the captured information from the DNA acquisition device to any other device. |
| Genetic information will be collected and stored. | If acquisition occurs so that the actual DNA information is not stored, this is unlikely. |

Table 5-3 shows additional characteristics of DNA technology.

### TABLE 5-3: Characteristics of DNA Technology

| Characteristic | Ease of use | Error incidence | Accuracy | Acceptance | Security Level | Stability | Cost |
|----------------|-------------|-----------------|----------|------------|----------------|-----------|------|
| | Medium | False submission, insufficient DNA in submitted material | Very high | Low | High | High | High |

## DNA COUNTERMEASURES

Many of the common countermeasures used with other biometric technologies will also apply to DNA technology when available, including the following:

- ✓ Use DNA acquisition devices that do not require the subject to have physical contact with the device. Doing so can reduce the objections related to transference.

- ✓ Uncover objections and research methods to overcome them. For example, if one objection is based on false information that actual DNA information will be stored, train the users on what actually occurs.

- ✓ Use at least one physical biometric technology, such as iris or retina scanning, in conjunction with DNA.

# Summary

This chapter looked at physical biometric technologies that are typically out of favor or uncommon when compared to other types in this category. It looked at the differences between hand-scan and handprint, and discussed DNA systems for identity and authentication.

In addition, the chapter briefly reviewed open source coding for your own custom handprint biometric implementations for various methods of kernel development, such as for network or workstation logon, and program applications. The complete source can be found at this book's companion Web site, www.wiley.com/compbooks/chirillo.

# Chapter 6

# Signature and Handwriting Technology

SIGNATURE RECOGNITION IS BECOMING better liked in the industry, and the dynamic identification of handwriting speeds and pressures has significantly improved the accuracy of this biometric type. For smaller budgets, this technology can be a cost-effective solution for analyzing and authenticating signature dynamics.

This chapter presents a discussion of signature recognition used in biometric systems for user authentication. It also outlines common uses, examines pilot applications, and develops a custom signature system kernel to use for proprietary purposes.

## Technical Description

Signature verification uses behavioral characteristics and monitors a signature's contour (C), speed (S), and pressure (P). The natural formulation of an autograph with the combination of C+S+P makes it individually unique. Computers can automatically compare a signature with a stored master template to measure accuracy (A) and verify a person's identity. Some systems can also be configured to quantify a percentage of error (%E) to accommodate fluctuations between signatures and create a level of precision acceptance. The result can be formulated as follows:

```
C+S+P(%E) = A
```

Measuring the shape of a signature, the speed of signing, pen pressure, and pauses is known as dynamic signature verification (DSV).

bio fact

Signature recognition systems are aware that signatures will not be perfect matches. As a result, some systems will likely reject perfect-matching templates or ask for further verification, because these could suggest foul play.

Signature verification and authentication can also be used to certify documents. When an individual signs a document using a signature recognition program, such as from PenOp, a token is attached. This token tracks the time of the signature as well as the contents of the document. The use of a biometric token can provide an alert mechanism upon alteration of the document. Cyber-SIGN (www.cybersign.com) and Communication Intelligence Corp. (www.penop.com) provide the most popular token systems.

✓ Cyber-SIGN—According to Cyber-SIGN Inc., Cyber-SIGN is a software technology for authentic electronic signatures and secure user verification. With Cyber-SIGN, online identity is securely authenticated and a trusted electronic signature is created. The software is an uncomplicated biometric authentication system that increases data security and enables trusted document authorization. Cyber-SIGN authenticates a person, not a machine or software key. Cyber-SIGN analyzes the shape, speed, stroke order, off-tablet motion, pen pressure, and timing information captured during the act of signing. Unlike a password, personal identification number (PIN), or keycards—identification data that can be forgotten, lost, stolen, or shared—the handwritten signature's captured values are unique to an individual and virtually impossible to duplicate. Advantages of Cyber-SIGN include the following:

- Cyber-SIGN provides reliable personal identification with your signature alone.

- Cyber-SIGN uses biometrics to confirm the computer user's identity. A computer user simply signs on a tablet and can be positively identified around the clock and from anywhere in the world.

- Cyber-SIGN is the only signature verification technology that uses the timing of changes in pressure, shape, direction, speed, and velocity in the signature verification process, and the only integration system that presumes biometric identification is done only from a secure server.

- A Cyber-SIGN application transforms the hand-written signature into a secure, private, computerized personal identifier.

✓ Sign-On—According to Communication Intelligence Corp., Sign-On is the first logon security utility for handheld organizers that uses biometric signature verification to keep the data on your device safe. Sign-On will allow you and only you to gain access to the data on your organizer. Just sign your name or create a personalized drawing or design, and Sign-On will verify your signature or personalized design to unlock the device. Advantages of Sign-On include the following:

- Sign-On is the first signature solution to capture, verify, and encrypt your signature directly on the handheld device.

- Your own personal signature is used to secure the device and your data.

- Setting up Sign-On is a snap; just sign your name a few times to create your recognition template.

- All signature data and templates are encrypted for secure storage using the Triple DES algorithm.

- To unlock the device, just sign your name once. Sign-On compares the signature to the templates and lets you and only you gain access to the device.

- Unlike traditional password protection systems, your signature cannot easily be guessed or forgotten.

# Valyd eSign Signature Authentication

Among the most common signature technologies used today that are covered in the sample applications section of this chapter is Valyd, Inc.'s eSign. eSign was launched in the first quarter of 2000 and has been thoroughly field-tested and refined during the past 18 months. Significant customer installations have been completed in the U.S. and other markets for financial services, healthcare, manufacturing, and government organizations.

According to the manufacturer, the eSign software was designed to be an authentication framework that uses a combination of security technologies. It combines the best features of each, staying consistent with electronic signature legislation. The eSign framework was built using an open architecture and standard component technologies to create a truly scaleable authentication framework compatible with most widely used software platforms.

This framework also includes the capability of maintaining the integrity of a document or other content to which an electronic signature is bound. Any change in content after signing invalidates the signature, indicating to the parties involved that something has changed.

## NETWORK SECURITY: SECURE LOGON

Relying on password-based security for corporate networks and intranets is an extremely dangerous practice. Passwords form an inherently weak security layer that can be breached or inadvertently/deliberately compromised.

Valyd network security solutions use advanced authentication techniques to ensure secure and reliable logon access to your network. This robust form of authentication can prevent both hostile external attacks and internal security compromises.

## DESKTOP AUTHENTICATION

The eSign Desktop allows you to sign and securely transmit documents using a choice of signing methods, including digital signature and electronic handwritten signature. Multiple authentication mechanisms such as strong password, signature, and others are supported. In addition, document contents are protected from unauthorized alteration or tampering.

Some business benefits include the following:

✓ Legally valid electronic signatures

✓ Execute transactions and contracts online

✓ Paperless business processes

## SOLUTIONS

You can utilize eSign technologies in numerous ways, including network security, workflow, banking, insurance, government, and healthcare.

**NETWORK SECURITY**   All organizations have data and resources on their network that require restricted access. Unauthorized access and misuse of data is, unfortunately, common. Almost all networks use passwords and login IDs for securing access. Passwords form at best a weak protection layer; they are shared or compromised too easily.

eSign can be used in place of, or in addition to, passwords for access to corporate networks. Such a system can be used for logon as well as for access control of selected data or resources. Logon authentication based on eSign can be used for LAN, WAN, intranet, or virtual private network (VPN)-based corporate networks. Key network security benefits include login authentication using handwritten signatures and restricted access to private resources.

**WORKFLOW**   In spite of widespread office automation and ubiquitous use of e-mail, businesses still use fax and courier/parcel services. One of the key reasons why documents are printed and sent using these services is the need to authenticate the document using signatures.

With eSign, electronic documents can be authenticated and sent in electronic form, saving time and money for the organization while ensuring document integrity and authenticity. From a create, print, sign, fax/courier cycle, you move to a create, eSign, and e-mail cycle.

Electronic documents offer easier storage, retrieval, and archival facilities, making the entire process efficient and easy. The same can be applied to other office procedures such as purchase orders, invoices, reports, and so on. eSign also provides an audit trail as to whom, when, and why for easy retrieval and accountability.

**BANKING**   With higher customer expectations and increased competition, banks are gearing up to the challenge by leveraging information technology (IT) to increase operational efficiencies as well as to offer new value-added services to customers. eSign could be a critical tool in helping banks to improve process efficiencies, save time, reduce costs, and to offer value-added services to clients.

High-value, repeat individual customers and corporate customers require a higher level of servicing. The transaction value and the potential benefits easily justify the cost of integrating eSign into the system.

**INSURANCE**   Each business process in insurance has its own paper trail that includes forms, policies, claims, and adjuster reports. In the past few years, efforts have been made to reduce paperwork as well as document processing time and cost. The use of computers and electronic forms and processes by insurance agents has led to significant savings in time and money. However, as these processes are digitized, a secure, dependable, and fast authentication solution is required. eSign fits the bill perfectly. Key insurance usage benefits include the following:

✓ Huge savings in processing time leading to improved efficiency and employee productivity

✓ Savings on document processing and storage costs

✓ Better response times resulting in higher customer satisfaction

✓ Audit trail for increased accountability for all employees

✓ Easy archival and faster search and retrieval functions

**GOVERNMENT**    Governments are embracing IT in a bid to increase productivity and efficiency. Whether for document management across departments or in specific applications such as information and benefit disbursal, electronic initiatives in improving efficiency, responsiveness, and accountability have yielded encouraging results.

Typical applications for eSign include the following:

✓ Online submission of forms, filing of returns, and so on

✓ Workflow automation and document management across offices

✓ Archival and retrieval of documents and records (for example, land registration records)

Benefits to these applications in government include speeding up approval processes, increasing accountability by tracking documents and workflow, and reducing fraud.

**HEALTHCARE**    The Health Care Desktop Information Nondisclosure Act of 1999 and the Medical Information Privacy and Security Act (MIPS) introduced in 2000 are calculated efforts to encourage the use of digital signatures in the distribution of medical records over the World Wide Web. They define strict penalties for individuals who compromise other people's confidential medical records. These acts further establish one's right to keep medical records private.

The need for confidentiality and highly secure access to medical records placed online requires an authentication technology that is highly secure, dependable, and easy to use (for medical personnel, patients, and so on). eSign fits the bill perfectly. eSign user profiles are collected and stored on the server, which houses the records. To log in, the user must sign and be authenticated by the server. eSign can also be used to authenticate a trusted source for generating and storing the documents and approving them at different levels. Key healthcare benefits include the following:

✓ Consistent with the Health Insurance Portability and Accountability Act (HIPAA) and MIPS Act

✓ Secure access to online medical records

✓ Authenticates medical reports and processes them electronically

✓ Ability to encrypt files and records and create encrypted folders

# TigerSign Custom Signature Recognition

TigerSign is our feature custom signature recognition software and will be examined and piloted later in this chapter. The source is available as a kernel module for you to customize for your own proprietary implementations. TigerSign is the first on-screen, mouse-signing, behavioral biometric system that also supports tablets and touch-screens.

With TigerSign, you can implement signature recognition in any application, adjust the error-acceptance level, and combine it with two-factor or strong authentication by adding a logon password, passphrase, or PIN.

For details on combining TigerSign with another method into a two-factor authentication scheme, see Chapter 9.

# Classification

Many signature types exist in the computing world. You may already be accustomed to digital signatures, digitized signatures, and e-mail signatures. When this text refers to signatures, it's talking about biometric signature recognition.

- ✓ **Digital signature** — A digital signature is an electronic signature used to guarantee the identity of an individual sending a message or the signer of a document, provide non-repudiation services (to ensure that the message sender cannot deny it later), and at times to ensure message integrity. A digital certificate contains the digital signature from a certificate-issuing authority, enabling a user to verify that the certificate is real.

- ✓ **Digitized signature** — A digitized signature is really just an image of a person's hand-written signature or "wet signature." Sometimes a vendor or application requires an individual to sign a hand-written signature using a special computer input device, such as a digital pen and pad (for example, when making a credit card purchase at a store). The digitized representation of the entered signature may also be compared to a previously stored copy of the handwritten signature for verification.

- ✓ **E-mail signature** — An e-mail signature is basically text and/or pictures that are automatically added to the end of an e-mail message you create and send. Some e-mail signature uses include creating custom signatures for different audiences, such as for friends or business associates, or adding boilerplate text to the message, such as an explanation of how you want others to respond or legal information.

- ✓ **Biometric signature** — Biometric signature recognition authenticates an individual by comparing a signature with a master template. The signature image is calculated by measuring the shape of a signature, the speed of signing, and even pen pressure. This biometric method is classified as a behavioral system.

## Signature Recognition Strengths and Weaknesses

Scanning signatures is becoming a popular biometric system, especially for document authentication and financial applications. Some of this system's strengths include the following:

- ✓ **User acceptance** — Signature recognition resides in the middle-to-upper region (refer to Chapter 1) of user acceptance primarily for being a noninvasive technology. Individuals need not worry because signing is not threatening nor does it invade one's privacy.

- ✓ **Ease of use** — Creating a signature is a natural and simple process for a user.

✓ **Flexibility** — Signatures don't have to be exactly the same as what's stored in the master template, and templates can be easily updated in this biometric system.

✓ **Advancements** — Some systems also calculate pen pressure for improved identification.

Some of signature scanning biometric technology's weaknesses include the following:

✓ **False negatives and false positives** — Given that signatures can vary widely from time-to-time, the programmable error rate (%E) in this biometric system must be flexible. This suppleness makes the system prone to increased false-positive (authenticating an imposter) error rates. On the other hand, firm programmable %E rates don't allow for greater fluctuations in someone's signature; therefore, the system may be prone to increased false-negative (not authenticating a valid user) error rates.

✓ **Unfamiliar uses** — Users are typically not used to signing on a screen or with a tablet/pen combination. At times, users sign their names with or without a middle initial, and sometimes individuals sign only with their first initial and last name. These fluctuations make captured signatures appear unlike their wet signature counterparts and increase the system's error rates.

# Technology Uses and Applications

One of the first issues to resolve when trying to decide which signature authentication technology to use is the type of system best suited for your environment. The following list describes some general criteria that can be used when making a system selection:

✓ Cost

✓ Marketplace acceptance of your signature options

✓ Tamper-resistant and forgery security measures

✓ Does the system(s) support strong authentication? Can it be implemented in a two-factor scheme authentication?

✓ The system should be minimally affected by humidity and temperature within reasonable expectations.

✓ System performance is a concern for any biometric system and should be tested, preferably, in a live environment.

✓ Is the system scalable for your growth concerns?

✓ Are certain systems easier to maintain and keep up than others? What maintenance is required, and how frequently should it occur?

✓ What is the contingency plan if the technology fails?

# Sample Product Pilots

The sample product installation, authentication, and applications/utilities usage presented in the following sections will use eSign by Valyd and TigerSign's custom source kernel. These products will be installed on a Windows XP Professional workstation.

Visit `www.valyd.com`, `www.TigerTools.net`, and `www.InfoTRESS.com` for more information on these products.

## Valyd eSign Desktop 3.0

This section discusses installing and configuring eSign Desktop 3.0 for signature authentication.

To successfully install eSign on Windows NT (4.0 and later), the system should be upgraded with Win NT service pack 3.5 or later. For MS Office: If Microsoft Office is not loaded properly, some eSign files may not install properly. To rectify this, reinstall MS Office properly and repair eSign by choosing the Repair option in the eSign installation.

### INSTALLATION

eSign Desktop requires a 32-bit windows operating system; for example, Windows 95 (Build 708 or higher), Win NT 4.0 (build 1381 with Service Pack 4 or higher), or Windows 98/2000/XP/Me, IE 5.0 and above for Digital Signature compatibility, HotSync for using Palm-based signing and Microsoft ActiveSync for Pocket PC, and/or Schlumberger CSP for Schlumberger smart cards. Your system should also have a minimum of 20MB free space on the hard disk. Take the following steps:

1. Power up the system and execute the eSign setup file. After setup locates the associated .cab files, the Welcome screen (see Figure 6-1) will display. Click Next to begin the installation.

2. After reading the license agreement, click Yes to accept the terms and continue the installation.

3. Enter your name, company name, and product serial number from Valyd to register the software and enable it on your system, as shown in Figure 6-2.

**Figure 6-1:** eSign Desktop installation wizard

**4.** Next, as illustrated in Figure 6-3, select from the following component options you would prefer eSign to support:

- eSign for Microsoft Word — Biometric signature capture and verify for MS Word 97/2000/XP

- eSign for Microsoft Excel — Biometric signature capture and verify for MS Excel 97/2000/XP

- eSign for Microsoft Outlook — Biometric signature capture and verify for MS Outlook 2000/XP

- eSign for Outlook Express — Biometric signature capture and verify for Outlook Express 4.0/5.0

- eSign for Adobe PDF — Biometric signature capture and verify for Adobe Acrobat 4.0/5.0

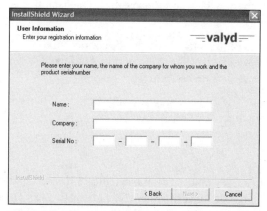

**Figure 6-2:** eSign installation wizard user input and software registration

Also, select from the following input device options you would prefer eSign to support:

- WinTab32 Compliant Digital Pad — Use Wintab32 compliant device as the signature-capturing device.

- Palm Device — Use a Palm handheld connected to your desktop computer as a signature capture device.

- Pocket PC — Use a Pocket PC handheld connected to your desktop computer as a signature capture device.

After making your component selections, click Next to continue.

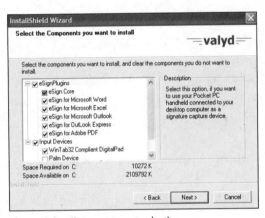

**Figure 6-3:** eSign component selection

5. The next screen has you verify your component selections. After doing so, click Next.

6. Verify the installation path. If you wish to change the path where Setup will install eSign, click Browse and choose the path you wish to use. Click Next to continue.

7. Choose the program folder to which to install the software files. The default is eSign Desktop 3.0. Click Next to continue.

8. Depending on whether you've opted to use a handheld device connected to your desktop computer as a signature capture device, you will see the optional mobile device setup screen. Click to acknowledge the handheld to continue.

9. Restart your system before moving forward with eSign configurations. When you're ready, select to Reboot your system and click Finish.

## CONFIGURATION

With eSign Desktop, you can sign using an X.509 standard digital certificate ID and biometric signature. If you do not already have a third-party digital certificate, you can create one. Your options when using eSign with a pre-selected component such as MS Word, Excel, or Outlook include signing, encrypting, or decrypting and incorporate the following steps:

1. To begin, you need to create a self-signed digital ID. Open the eSign Preferences Manager shown in Figure 6-4, and click browse. The Preferences Manager will list all predefined digital IDs — if any exist — on your system (see Figure 6-5).

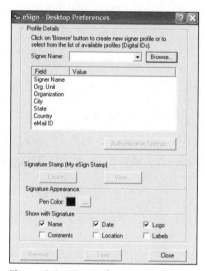

**Figure 6-4:** eSign Preferences Manager for creating a self-signed digital ID

**Figure 6-5:** Browsing for any potential digital IDs

2. Click Create New to create a self-signed digital ID, as shown in Figure 6-6.

**Figure 6-6:** Creating a self-signed ID

When you've finished completing the fields, click OK and then Yes to add the certificate to the eSign Root Store (shown in Figure 6-7).

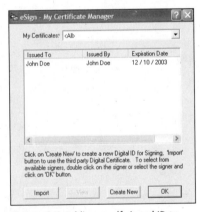

**Figure 6-7:** Adding a self-signed ID to the Root Store

**3.** With the selected ID, click Authentication Settings from the main Preferences Manager window (see Figure 6-8).

You can set the type of Authentication for Signing to Password only or Biometrics only or Password or Biometrics to gain access to the Digital ID of the profile for signing. You can change your profile's password by clicking on Change Password.

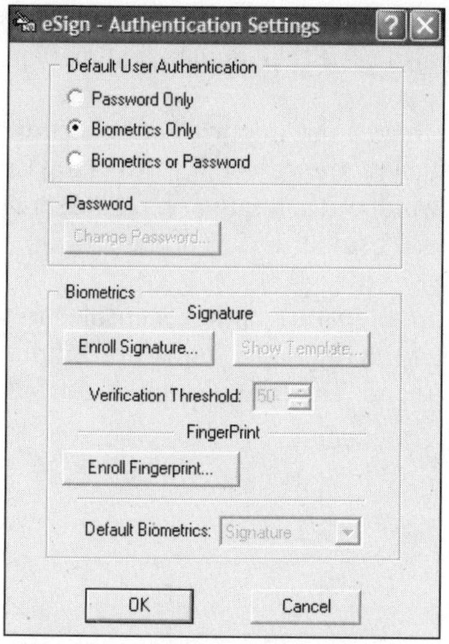

**Figure 6-8:** Configuring authentication settings for a new self-signed ID in the Root Store

Signature enrollment (Figure 6-9) of the user is done to enable the signature verification process to gain access to the profile's Digital ID for signing. Verification of the captured signatures is done against the enrolled signature template (eSign card). To enroll, click the Enroll option and provide five consistent signature samples. To re-enroll for an already created profile, click the Re-enroll option. You can also set a percentage level (50 to 100 percent) for *Signature Verification Threshold*, a set level for signature acceptance. Setting a higher percentage level indicates a higher level of security.

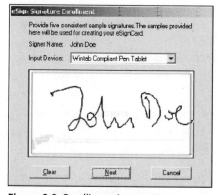

**Figure 6-9:** Enrolling a signature

You can optionally enroll your unique fingerprint by clicking Enroll Fingerprint and providing four fingerprint samples of the same finger. You can also set either Fingerprint or Signature as Default Biometrics.

The eSign stamp is a password-protected signature that can be imported onto documents. You can create an eSign stamp using the Create option in the Preferences window. Clicking Create displays a signing window. For Signing on the signing window, there are several acceptable input methods. Already created signature stamps can be viewed using the View option.

**HANDWRITTEN SIGNATURES**     By default, the Biometric Signature option is enabled in the signing window. If you do not want to sign, you can deselect the Biometric Signature option. You can select the signature-input device from the drop-down menu. The options include the following:

- ✓ Wintab Pen Tablet
- ✓ My eSign Stamp
- ✓ Palm
- ✓ Pocket PC

Each of these options is explained in detail in the following sections. You can also create an eSign Card (handwritten signature template) that will be used for verification of your signature. To create an eSign Card, click Enroll and sign five times as consistently as possible. At the end of the fifth signature, you will be informed that the sign card has been successfully created.

**USING PALM**     My eSign for Palm O/S, which is installed on the Palm device, captures the signature and transfers it to the eSign application running on the desktop. The application is installed on the desktop along with the eSign software and then, using the HotSync, is downloaded onto the device. This completes the installation process.

**USING MY ESIGN**     To use these steps:

1. Tap the application icon on the Palm device to launch My eSign.

2. Sign in the Signature capture area using the stylus.

3. Tap the OK button after the signature is done. A message is displayed indicating that the signature has been saved and will be displayed on the Desktop on the next HotSync operation.

4. Place the device on the cradle and press the HotSync button on the cradle. Your signature will display on the Desktop eSign application.

**USING THE WINTAB-COMPLIANT DIGITIZER TABLET**     Make sure that the Wintab Digitizer Tablet is installed along with the necessary drivers. To sign using the Wintab Pen Tablet, select the Pen Tablet option from the drop-down menu and sign using the pen. Look at the tablet rather than at the screen, and practice a few times for best results.

**USING POCKET PC**   My eSign for Pocket PC (Windows CE), which is installed on the Pocket PC device, captures a signature on the Pocket PC device and transfers it to the eSign application, which is running on the desktop computer. My eSign Application is installed on the PC desktop along with the eSign Desktop. Select the Add/Remove programs from the Tools menu of Microsoft ActiveSync, and click OK. My eSign will immediately be installed on the device.

## My eSign Application

1. Select the My eSign Application (shown in Figure 6-10) from your Pocket PC's Start Menu or tap the My eSign application icon by pressing the MENU Button on your Pocket PC.

2. Sign in the Rectangular area using the stylus.

3. Use the Clear button if you want to sign again.

4. Tap the OK button after completing the signature. The signature is saved and can be transferred onto eSign Desktop.

**Figure 6-10:** My eSign Application for capturing Signatures on the Pocket PC

**USING ESIGN STAMP**   The eSign stamp is a password-protected signature that can be imported onto documents. You can create an eSign stamp using the Create option in the Preferences window. This signature is used as a stamp to import onto the documents when required.

**SIGNING USING DIGITAL IDS**   To sign a document using your digital ID, select My eSign from the taskbar or click on the corresponding icon. If you have multiple profiles stored, select the profile you want to sign with and click OK. If you want to sign only with a digital ID, uncheck the check box Biometric Signature. Enter your profile password when prompted, and your signature will be placed onto the document. Ensure that you have a valid digital ID associated with that profile before signing. Signing may not take place if the Digital Certificate is expired or revoked.

**ENCRYPTING A FILE**    eSign Desktop 3.0 allows you to encrypt a file using the intended recipient's public key, ensuring confidential transmission. To encrypt a file, follow these steps:

1. Click on the Encrypt icon, or select Encrypt File from the My eSign menu.

2. The currently opened file is taken as the input for encryption. You can also browse and select other files by clicking on the Browse button.

3. Select the receiver ID from the certificate store containing all the Digital Certificates. Multiple recipients can also be selected.

4. Click OK to start the encryption process. You will be prompted as to whether you wish to retain the original unencrypted file. The encrypted file will be stored under the same name with an .esd extension and can be securely sent to the recipient.

**DECRYPTING A FILE**    To decrypt an encrypted file sent to you, click on the decrypt icon or select Decrypt File from the My eSign menu. eSign uses the private key corresponding to the public key that has been used to encrypt the file. Browse to select the file to be decrypted, and click OK. The decrypted file will be stored under the same name without an .esd extension.

## Sample Signature Biometric Applications

Depending on your requirements, implementing a biometric signature system can be an onerous task; however, using the products discussed, the process can be quite simplistic. This part of the chapter discusses various methods of configuring, customizing, and using the eSign and TigerSign products for general signature authentication, such as for network or workstation logon, and program application uses, such as with MS Word, Excel, and Outlook e-mail.

### TIGERSIGN CUSTOM SOURCE KERNEL

This section discusses configuring TigerSign for custom signature authentication. For convenience, the authentication, learning, and template modules have been combined to one form (as illustrated in Figure 6-11), but each will be examined separately.

Visual Basic 6 or higher is recommended for customizing TigerSign source for proprietary implementations. You can download the complete source from www.wiley.com/compbooks/chirillo.

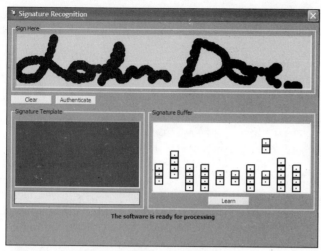

**Figure 6-11** The TigerSign modules for signature authentication, learning, and template creation

**SIGNATURE BUFFER**    When you first use TigerSign, you should create a template by signing a signature in the Sign Here field and then clicking Learn (as shown in Figure 6-12) to save the image within the system buffer. At that point, enter a unique user initial or character code in the pop-up box to represent that user within the system, and then click Enter.

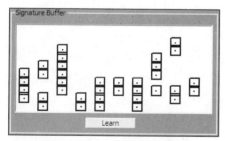

**Figure 6-12** TigerSign signature buffer for capturing a handwritten image

The system will store the buffer image to a template in file DATA.rec on your hard drive. If you peruse this file, you'll notice a series of bits used to represent and recreate the latest images. This data is exposed and could potentially be translated for unauthorized reuse. Refer to Chapter 9 for encryption techniques and strong authentication tools that will mitigate such an instance.

The signature buffer source module can be customized from Form frmMain:

```
Begin VB.Frame frameArea3
        BackColor       =    &H00808080&
        Caption         =    "Signature Buffer"
        Height          =    2895
        Left            =    4200
        TabIndex        =    10
        Top             =    2520
        Width           =    4935
    End

Private Sub buttonLearn_Click()
    Me.TeachLabelText.FontBold = False
    Me.TeachLabelText.Caption = "Enter the user initial or character code"
    Me.buttonLearn.Visible = False
    Me.buttonRecognise.Visible = False
    Me.buttonClearScreen.Visible = False
    Me.buttonLearnConfirm.Visible = True
    Me.buttonLearnCancel.Visible = True
    Me.inputLearnCharacter.Visible = True
    Me.inputLearnCharacter.Text = ""
    Me.inputLearnCharacter.SetFocus
    Me.buttonLearnConfirm.Enabled = False
End Sub

Begin VB.Label TeachLabelText
        BackColor          =    &H8000000C&
        Caption            =    "Enter User Initial or Character Code"
        BeginProperty Font
            Name           =    "Tahoma"
            Size           =    8.25
            Charset        =    0
            Weight         =    700
            Underline      =    0       'False
            Italic         =    0       'False
            Strikethrough  =    0       'False
        EndProperty
        Height         =    255
        Left           =    3120
        TabIndex       =    12
        Top            =    5520
        Width          =    3855
    End
```

```vb
Private Sub inputLearnCharacter_GotFocus()
    Me.inputLearnCharacter.SelStart = 0
    Me.inputLearnCharacter.SelLength = Len(Me.inputLearnCharacter.Text)
End Sub

Private Sub inputLearnCharacter_KeyUp(KeyCode As Integer, Shift As Integer)
    If Len(Me.inputLearnCharacter.Text) = 1 Then
        Me.buttonLearnConfirm.Enabled = True
        Me.buttonLearnConfirm.SetFocus
    ElseIf Len(Me.inputLearnCharacter.Text) > 1 Then
        Me.inputLearnCharacter.Text = ""
        Me.buttonLearnConfirm.Enabled = False
    Else
        Me.buttonLearnConfirm.Enabled = False
    End If
End Sub


Private Sub buttonLearnConfirm_Click()
Dim Filename_Database As String
Dim Filename_buttonLearn As String
Dim Buffer_DrawArea As Variant
Dim strbuttonLearnText As String
Dim intCounter As Integer
Dim strBuffer As String
    FileSystem.ChDir (App.Path)
    userTemplateArea.Cls
    strbuttonLearnText = Me.inputLearnCharacter.Text
    intCounter = 0
    Filename_Database = "DATA" & recordFileExtension
    Filename_buttonLearn = Filename_Database
    intCounter = intCounter + 1
    Call GraspRawData
    If strData = "" Then
        Call buttonClearScreen_Click
        Me.buttonLearn.Enabled = Not Me.buttonLearn.Enabled
        MsgBox "A signature was not detected in the Sign Here Area.", _
vbExclamation, "Warning"
        GoTo buttonLearnConfirm_SkipbuttonLearn
    End If
    Open Filename_buttonLearn For Binary As #1
        strBuffer = Space(5)
        Get #1, , strBuffer
    Close #1
    If strBuffer = "recPK" Then
        strRECpk = ""
        strBuffer = ""
```

```
    Open Filename_buttonLearn For Binary As #1
        strBuffer = Space(5)
        Get #1, , strBuffer
        strRECpk = strRECpk & strBuffer
        strBuffer = Space(22)
        While Not EOF(1)
            Get #1, , strBuffer
            strRECpk = strRECpk & strBuffer
        Wend
    Close #1
    strRECpk = Mid(strRECpk, 1, Len(strRECpk) - 22)
    i = 3
    strRECpk = strRECpk & strbuttonLearnText
    strRECpk = strRECpk & ","
    For j = 1 To 10
        strRECpk = strRECpk & Chr(BinToDec(Mid(strData, i - 2 + ((j - 1) *
10), 2)))
        strRECpk = strRECpk & Chr(BinToDec(Mid(strData, i + 0 + ((j - 1) *
10), 8)))
    Next j
    Open Filename_buttonLearn For Binary As #1
        Put #1, , strRECpk
    Close #1
Else
    Open Filename_buttonLearn For Append As #1
        Write #1, strbuttonLearnText & "," & strData
    Close #1
End If
buttonLearnConfirm_SkipbuttonLearn:
    Me.TeachLabelText.FontBold = True
    Me.TeachLabelText.Caption = strCaption
    Me.buttonLearnConfirm.Visible = False
    Me.buttonLearnCancel.Visible = False
    Me.inputLearnCharacter.Visible = False
    Me.buttonLearn.Enabled = False
    Me.buttonLearn.Visible = True
    Me.buttonRecognise.Visible = True
    Me.buttonClearScreen.Visible = True
End Sub
```

As an antitheft mechanism, TigerSign will hide all data and on-screen images if another program
is loaded or executed on the same screen.

**AUTHENTICATION MODULE**    The Sign Here authentication module (shown in Figure 6-13) is your signature pad. You can sign with your mouse, touchpad, tablet, touch screen, or via third-party remote controller software using your Pocket PC or Palm handheld.

**Figure 6-13:** The TigerSign authentication module is used to create and sign your signature for processing

The authentication pad captures your signature in a digitized format on your screen in pixels—similar to the methods used in graphics and image software except that the speed at which you sign is factored in. The system analyzes the peaks, slopes, and velocity of your signature and formulates an image to be stored in the template and used for authentication. As a result of these calculations, the on-screen image may look somewhat dissimilar to your written signature. After signing the screen, click Authenticate to proceed to the template database-matching module discussed next.

The Sign Here authentication source module can be customized from Form frmMain:

```
Begin VB.Frame frameArea1
      BackColor       =    &H00808080&
      Caption         =    "Sign Here"
      Height          =    1935
      Left            =    120
      TabIndex        =    8
      Top             =    120
      Width           =    9015
      Begin VB.PictureBox userDrawArea
         BackColor        =    &H00C0C0C0&
         DrawStyle        =    2  'Dot
         BeginProperty Font
            Name          =    "MS Sans Serif"
            Size          =    8.25
            Charset       =    0
            Weight        =    400
            Underline     =    0    'False
            Italic        =    0    'False
            Strikethrough =    0    'False
         EndProperty
         Height           =    1575
         Left             =    120
         ScaleHeight      =    1515
```

```
              ScaleWidth    =    8715
              TabIndex      =    11
              Top           =    240
              Width         =    8775
         End
      End


Private Sub userDrawArea_MouseDown(Button As Integer, Shift As Integer, x As
Single, y As Single)
    currentlyDrawing = True
    userDrawArea.DrawWidth = 17
    userDrawArea.PSet (x, y)
    If Not Me.buttonLearn.Enabled Then
        Me.buttonLearn.Enabled = True
        Me.buttonRecognise.Enabled = True
        Me.buttonClearScreen.Enabled = True
    End If
    If Not Me.buttonRecognise.Enabled Then
        Me.buttonRecognise.Enabled = True
    End If
End Sub

Private Sub userDrawArea_MouseMove(Button As Integer, Shift As Integer, x As
Single, y As Single)
    userDrawArea.DrawStyle = vbSolid
    userDrawArea.DrawWidth = 17
    If currentlyDrawing Then
        userDrawArea.PSet (x, y)
        If Not fMainForm.buttonLearn.Enabled Then
            Me.buttonLearn.Enabled = True
            Me.buttonRecognise.Enabled = True
            Me.buttonClearScreen.Enabled = True
        End If
    End If
End Sub

Private Sub userDrawArea_MouseUp(Button As Integer, Shift As Integer, x As
Single, y As Single)
    currentlyDrawing = False
    Call GraspRawData
End Sub

Private Sub buttonRecognize_Click()
Dim Filename_Database As String
Dim strbuttonRecognised As String
Dim intMatch As Integer
```

```
Dim intMaxMatch As Integer
Dim intCounter As Integer
Dim boolFindLastFile As Boolean
Dim boolNoMoreFileLeft As Boolean
Dim buffer As String
Dim Buffer_DatabaseArea As Variant
Dim strBuffer As String
   FileSystem.ChDir (App.Path)
    strbuttonRecognised = ""
    intMaxMatch = 0
    intCounter = 0
    c = 0
    On Error GoTo buttonRecognise_FileClose
    Filename_Database = "DATA" & recordFileExtension
    If Filename_Database <> "" Then
        Me.AppTemplateArea.Cls
        Open Filename_Database For Binary As #1
            i = 0
            strBuffer = Space(5)
                Get #1, , strBuffer
                arrRawData(i) = strBuffer
                i = i + 1
            strBuffer = Space(22)
            While Not EOF(1)
                Get #1, , strBuffer
                arrRawData(i) = strBuffer
                i = i + 1
            Wend
            arrRawData(i - 1) = ""
            Close #1
            i = 0
            strBuffer = ""
            If arrRawData(0) = "recPK" Then
                i = i + 1
                strbuttonRecognised = ""
                intMaxMatch = 0
                intCounter = 0
                c = 0
                While arrRawData(i) <> ""
                    a = 190
                    b = 190
                    d = 0
                    intMatch = 0
                    Me.AppTemplateArea.Cls
                    arrTagData(i - 1) = Mid(arrRawData(i), 1, 1)
                    arrRawData(i - 1) = ""
```

```
                        For j = 1 To 10
                            arrRawData(i - 1) = arrRawData(i - 1) & _
DecToBin(Asc(Mid(arrRawData(i), 3 + ((j - 1) * 2), 1)), 2) & _
DecToBin(Asc(Mid(arrRawData(i), 4 + ((j - 1) * 2), 1)), 8)
                        Next j
                        i = i + 1
                        For ii = 1 To 10
                        For jj = 1 To 10
                            If Mid(arrRawData(c), d + 1, 1) = vbBlack Then
                                If Mid(strData, d + 1, 1) = vbBlack Then
                                    intMatch = intMatch + 1
                                Else
                                    intMatch = intMatch - 1
                                End If
                            Else
                                If Mid(strData, d + 1, 1) <> vbBlack Then
                                    intMatch = intMatch + 1
                                Else
                                    intMatch = intMatch - 1
                                End If
                            End If
                            d = d + 1
                            b = b + (Me.AppTemplateArea.Height - 200) / 10
                        Next jj
                        b = 190
                        a = a + (Me.AppTemplateArea.Width - 200) / 10
                        Next ii
                        If intMaxMatch < intMatch Then
                            intMaxMatch = intMatch
                            strbuttonRecognised = arrTagData(c)
                            intCounter = c
                            Me.progressRecognition.Value = intMaxMatch
                            If intMaxMatch > 90 Then
                                GoTo buttonRecognise_FileClose
                            End If
                        End If
                        c = c + 1
                    Wend
                    arrTagData(i - 1) = ""
                    arrRawData(i - 1) = ""
                Else
                    strbuttonRecognised = ""
                    intMaxMatch = 0
                    intCounter = 0
                    c = 0
                    Open Filename_Database For Input As #1
```

```
            While Not EOF(1)
buttonRecognize_SkipLine:
        a = 190
        b = 190
        d = 0
        intMatch = 0
        Me.AppTemplateArea.Cls
            If EOF(1) Then
                GoTo buttonRecognise_FileClose
            End If
            Input #1, arrRawData(c)
            If Len(arrRawData(c)) < 102 Then
                GoTo buttonRecognise_SkipLine
            End If
            arrTagData(c) = Mid(arrRawData(c), 1, 1)
            arrRawData(c) = Mid(arrRawData(c), 3)
            For i = 1 To 10
            For j = 1 To 10
                If Mid(arrRawData(c), d + 1, 1) = vbBlack Then
                    AppTemplateArea.PSet (a, b)
                    If Mid(strData, d + 1, 1) = vbBlack Then
                        intMatch = intMatch + 1
                    Else
                        intMatch = intMatch - 1
                    End If
                Else
                    If Mid(strData, d + 1, 1) <> vbBlack Then
                        intMatch = intMatch + 1
                    Else
                        intMatch = intMatch - 1
                    End If
                End If
                d = d + 1
                b = b + (Me.AppTemplateArea.Height - 200) / 10
            Next j
            b = 190
            a = a + (Me.AppTemplateArea.Width - 200) / 10
            Next i
            If intMaxMatch < intMatch Then
                intMaxMatch = intMatch
                strbuttonRecognised = arrTagData(c)
                intCounter = c
                Me.progressRecognition.Value = intMaxMatch
                If intMaxMatch > 90 Then
                    GoTo buttonRecognise_FileClose
                End If
            End If
```

```
                            End If
                            c = c + 1
                    Wend
buttonRecognise_FileClose:
                    Close #1
                End If
        End If
    Me.buttonRecognise.Enabled = False
    Me.progressRecognition.Value = 0
    If strbuttonRecognised <> "" Then
        AppTemplateArea.Cls
        With AppTemplateArea
        .ForeColor = vbWhite
        End With
        a = 190
        b = 190
        d = 0
        For i = 1 To 10
        For j = 1 To 10
            If Mid(arrRawData(intCounter), d + 1, 1) = vbBlack Then
                AppTemplateArea.PSet (a, b)
                AppTemplateArea.Line (a - 110, b - 110)-(a + 110, b - 110)
                AppTemplateArea.Line (a + 110, b - 110)-(a + 110, b + 110)
                AppTemplateArea.Line (a + 110, b + 110)-(a - 110, b + 110)
                AppTemplateArea.Line (a - 110, b + 110)-(a - 110, b - 110)
            End If
            d = d + 1
            b = b + (Me.AppTemplateArea.Height - 200) / 10
        Next j
        b = 190
        a = a + (Me.AppTemplateArea.Width - 200) / 10
        Next i
    End If
    If strbuttonRecognised <> "" Then
        Me.textResult.Caption = intMaxMatch & "% match with user '" &
strbuttonRecognised & "'"
        Me.textResult.ToolTipText = intMaxMatch & "%"
        Me.DrawWidth = 2
    End If
End Sub
```

**TEMPLATE DATABASE**    The template database calls up the closest-matching image stored from the saved buffer templates to the image in the authentication Sign Here module. The system will report the match in a percentage after calculating C+S(%E) = A, as shown in Figure 6-14.

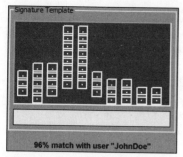

**Figure 6-14:** The TigerSign template database finds the closest stored match

At this point, depending on your preprogrammed policy, the user could be presented with a login password for two-factor authentication (see Chapter 10) to log into the system or to access a program or file, or maybe sign again if your %E is programmed to accept a closer match.

The template database and match percentage source module can be customized from Form frmMain:

```
Begin VB.Form frmMain
    BackColor       =   &H00808080&
    BorderStyle     =   3  'Fixed Dialog
    Caption         =   "Signature Recognition"
    ClientHeight    =   6495
    ClientLeft      =   45
    ClientTop       =   600
    ClientWidth     =   9240
    DrawStyle       =   5  'Transparent
    FillColor       =   &H00C0FFFF&
    FillStyle       =   2  'Horizontal Line
    BeginProperty Font
        Name            =   "Tahoma"
        Size            =   8.25
        Charset         =   0
        Weight          =   400
        Underline       =   0    'False
        Italic          =   0    'False
        Strikethrough   =   0    'False
    EndProperty
    ForeColor       =   &H80000018&
    Icon            =   "frmMain.frx":0000
    LinkTopic       =   "Form1"
    MaxButton       =   0   'False
    MinButton       =   0   'False
    MouseIcon       =   "frmMain.frx":0442
    ScaleHeight     =   6495
```

```
ScaleWidth       =    9240
ShowInTaskbar    =    0    'False
StartUpPosition =    2    'CenterScreen
Begin MSComctlLib.ProgressBar progressRecognition
    Height          =    375
    Left            =    240
    TabIndex        =    14
    Top             =    4920
    Width           =    3735
    _ExtentX        =    6588
    _ExtentY        =    661
    _Version        =    393216
    BorderStyle     =    1
    Appearance      =    0
    Scrolling       =    1
End


Begin VB.Frame frameArea2
    BackColor       =    &H00808080&
    Caption         =    "Signature Template"
    Height          =    2895
    Left            =    120
    TabIndex        =    9
    Top             =    2520
    Width           =    3975
End
Begin VB.Label textResult
    BackColor       =    &H00808080&
    Caption         =    "Signature Recognition Ready..."
    BeginProperty Font
        Name            =    "Tahoma"
        Size            =    8.25
        Charset         =    0
        Weight          =    700
        Underline       =    0    'False
        Italic          =    0    'False
        Strikethrough   =    0    'False
    EndProperty
    Height          =    225
    Left            =    3120
    TabIndex        =    13
    Top             =    6240
    Width           =    3975
End
```

```
    Begin VB.Menu mnuPopUp
        Caption          =    "mnuPopUp"
        Visible          =    0    'False
        Begin VB.Menu mnuPopUp_About
            Caption          =    "&About"
        End
        Begin VB.Menu mnuPopUp_Close
            Caption          =    "&Close"
        End
    End
End

Private Sub GraspRawData()
Dim bool1stScan As Boolean
Dim ax As Integer
Dim ay As Integer
Dim bx As Integer
Dim by As Integer
bool1stScan = True
strData = ""
c = 0
Me.userTemplateArea.Cls
For i = 1 To userDrawArea.Width Step 100
    For j = 1 To userDrawArea.Height Step 100
        If userDrawArea.Point(i, j) = vbBlack Then
            userTemplateArea.PSet (i, j)
            If Not bool1stScan Then
                If i < ax Then
                    ax = i
                    End If
                If i > bx Then
                    bx = i
                    End If
                If j < ay Then
                    ay = j
                    End If
                If j > by Then
                    by = j
                    End If
            Else
                bool1stScan = False
                ax = i
                bx = i
                ay = j
                by = j
            End If
        End If
```

```
Next j, i
If bx - ax <> 0 And by - ay <> 0 Then
    a = 190
    b = 190
    Me.userTemplateArea.Cls
    For i = ax To bx - (bx - ax) / 10 Step (bx - ax) / 10
        For j = ay To by - (by - ay) / 10 Step (by - ay) / 10
            If userDrawArea.Point(i, j) = vbBlack Then
                userTemplateArea.PSet (a, b)
                userTemplateArea.Line (a - 110, b - 110)-(a + 110, b - 110)
                userTemplateArea.Line (a + 110, b - 110)-(a + 110, b + 110)
                userTemplateArea.Line (a + 110, b + 110)-(a - 110, b + 110)
                userTemplateArea.Line (a - 110, b + 110)-(a - 110, b - 110)
                strData = strData & userDrawArea.Point(i, j)
                c = c + 1
            Else
                strData = strData & 1
                c = c + 1
            End If
            b = b + (Me.userTemplateArea.Height - 200) / 10
        Next j
        b = 190
        a = a + (Me.userTemplateArea.Width - 200) / 10
    Next i
End If
End Sub
Private Function StatusWindow(Optional ByVal strBuffer As String) As String
Dim Status_OpenButton As String
Dim Status_buttonLearnButton As String
Dim Status_buttonLearnConfirmButton As String
Dim Status_buttonLearnCancelButton As String
Dim Status_buttonRecogniseButton As String
Dim Status_buttonClearScreenButton As String
Dim Status_ExitButton As String
Dim Status_DrawArea As String
Dim Status_DatabaseArea As String
Dim Status_DataArea As String
Dim Status_Form As String
    Select Case strBuffer
    Case "OpenButton": strBuffer = Status_OpenButton
    Case "buttonLearnButton": strBuffer = Status_buttonLearnButton
    Case "buttonLearnConfirmButton": strBuffer =
```

```
Status_buttonLearnConfirmButton
    Case "buttonLearnCancelButton": strBuffer = Status_buttonLearnCancelButton
    Case "buttonRecogniseButton": strBuffer = Status_buttonRecogniseButton
    Case "buttonClearScreenButton": strBuffer = Status_buttonClearScreenButton
    Case "ExitButton": strBuffer = Status_ExitButton
    Case "DrawArea": strBuffer = Status_DrawArea
    Case "DatabaseArea": strBuffer = Status_DatabaseArea
    Case "DataArea": strBuffer = Status_DataArea
    Case "Form": strBuffer = Status_Form
    End Select
    StatusWindow = strBuffer
End Function


Private Function BinToDec(strBin As String) As Integer
i = Len(strBin)
While i > 0
    If Mid(strBin, i, 1) = "1" Then
        BinToDec = BinToDec + 2 ^ (Len(strBin) - i)
    End If
    i = i - 1
Wend
End Function


Private Function DecToBin(intDec As Integer, intDigit As Integer) As String
Dim intTemp As Integer
While intDec > 0 And intDigit > 0
    intDigit = intDigit - 1
    intTemp = intDec Mod 2
    If intTemp Then
        DecToBin = "1" & DecToBin
        intDec = (intDec - 1) / 2
    Else
        DecToBin = "0" & DecToBin
        intDec = intDec / 2
    End If
Wend
While intDigit
    intDigit = intDigit - 1
    DecToBin = "0" & DecToBin
Wend
End Function
```

Chapter 10 further discusses customizing TigerSign and adding components. Additionally, see the appendix in the back of this book for the full source listing.

## USING ESIGN DESKTOP IN MS WORD 97/2000/XP AND EXCEL 97/2000/XP

When eSign Desktop is installed onto a system, a plug-in for MS Word/Excel is automatically installed. On opening the application, you will be able to view the following icons (see Figure 6-15):

✓ Sign Document

✓ Preferences

✓ Encrypt File

✓ Decrypt File

The same options can also be accessed from the My eSign drop-down menu from the main menu of the MS Word/Excel application.

**Figure 6-15:** eSign Desktop control menu in MS Excel

Macro Security is applicable to Office 2000 and Office XP only. When you open MS Word after eSign Desktop installation, a security-warning window appears. If the macro security (from menu Tools/Macro/Security) setting is set to either High or Medium in your system, the security-warning window appears. Macros from eSign document template are digitally signed and are safe. Checking Always trust macros from this source will mark these macros as safe and avoid displaying the security warning window in the future. Click Enable Macros to proceed.

**CREATING A SIGNATURE**    To Sign an MS Word/Excel document, click on the My eSign icon (or select it from the drop-down menu, with the cursor on the location where you wish to place the signature). A signature placeholder is created on the document. Double click on the signature placeholder to get the signing window.

**DIGITAL SIGNATURES**    Select the Signer Profile in case of multiple user profiles. The Digital Certificate details of the selected profile are displayed in the signing screen. If you choose to sign without enabling biometric signatures, you will be prompted to give your profile password. After you do so, your digital signature will be embedded in the document along with the profile name, date, and time. The Digital Certificate will be attached to the signature.

**HANDWRITTEN SIGNATURES**    To add your handwritten signature, enable the Biometric Signature check box and select the Signature input device. To use a Wintab 32 pen tablet, simply pick up the pen and sign. Use the clear option if you are not satisfied with the signature, and sign again. Capturing signatures using PDAs is illustrated in earlier sections.

   If you have a pre-enrolled sign card, the signature made will be matched against the same. If verified, a message indicating successful signature verification is displayed. If the signature does not match the sign card, you can choose to place the signature onto the document by giving your profile password or sign again to authenticate the signature successfully. Please note that the signature on verification will indicate that biometric verification was not successful.

**VERIFICATION**    Verification of signatures requires eSign Desktop 3.0 or eSign 3.0 Viewer to be installed on the system. To verify an eSigned signature, double click on the signature. The authentication information includes the following:

- ✓ Whether the document has been modified after signing
- ✓ Whether the Digital ID is valid
- ✓ Whether biometric signature verification has been successful

   The signer details are displayed along with the handwritten signature, if available. Additionally, the signer's Digital Certificate can be viewed by clicking on Show Certificate. In addition to the basic functions previously mentioned, the eSign MS Word plug-in also has the following features:

- ✓ **Sectional signing** — The eSign MS Word plug-in allows a user to sign in multiple sections created in a document such that each section is treated as an independent document. This is especially true in cases where the same document is being signed by multiple signatories and should permit a second or third signer to add comments without affecting the first signer's signature. For example, the first signer (for example, John) can create a section and authenticate it with his signature and forward it to the second signer (for example, Nancy), who can then add her comments to the second section and authenticate it with her signature, and so on.

✓ **Freezing of a section/document**—The plug-in allows the signer to choose whether he/she wants to freeze a particular section or document. Freezing is accomplished through the act of signing and immobilizes the chosen section or the entire document and does not allow any changes or modifications to be made. In a multiple signatory scenario, any of the signatories can freeze the section they want to protect.

✓ **Encryption and decryption of files**—MS Word files can be encrypted using the intended receiver's public key, ensuring confidential transactions. To encrypt a document, click on the encrypt icon or select encrypt from the My eSign menu. The default file is the currently open file. You can also browse and select the file that has to be encrypted. You have the option of saving the original file or deleting it. To decrypt an encrypted document, simply click on the Decrypt icon or select Decrypt file from the My eSign menu. Browse and select the file to be decrypted, and click OK.

**SHEET-WISE SIGNING IN EXCEL**   The eSign MS Excel plug-in allows a signer to create multiple sheets in an Excel Workbook such that each sheet is treated as an independent workbook. This is especially true in cases where the same Excel workbook is being signed by multiple signatories and should permit a second or third signer to add comments without affecting the first signer's signature. For example, the first signer (for example, John) can create a sheet, authenticate it with his signature, and forward it to the second signer (for example, Nancy), who can then add her comments to the second sheet and authenticate it with her signature, and so on.

**ENCRYPTION AND DECRYPTION OF EXCEL FILES**   MS Excel files can be encrypted using the intended receiver's public key, ensuring confidential transactions. To encrypt a workbook, click on the Encrypt icon or select Encrypt File (shown in Figure 6-16) from the My eSign menu. The default file is the currently open file. You can also browse and select the file that has to be encrypted. You have the option of saving the original file or deleting it. To decrypt an encrypted document, simply click on the Decrypt icon or select Decrypt File from the My eSign menu. Browse and select the file to be decrypted, and click OK.

---

## TROUBLESHOOTING WORD

After installing eSign, if the eSign Desktop icons are not visible in the Word tool bar, do the following:

1. Right click on the toolbar and ensure that eSign option is selected.

2. If eSign is not listed in the menu, check for eSign3.dot file in the MS Word startup path (usually `c:\Program Files\Microsoft Office\Office\startup`).

3. If this is not present, close the MS Word application and copy the `eSign3.dot` file from the eSign folder (generally `c:\Program Files\eSign Desktop 3.0`) to the MS Word startup path.

## TROUBLESHOOTING EXCEL

Before you begin signing in Excel, you must ensure that you exit design mode by clicking on the Exit Design Mode icon in the control toolbox bar. (Please note that without exiting design mode, you will be unable to use eSign.) After installing eSign, if eSign Desktop icons are not visible in the Excel tool bar, do the following:

1. Right click on the toolbar, and ensure that the eSign option is selected.

2. If eSign is not listed in the menu, check for the `eSign3.xla` file in the MS Excel startup path
(usually `c:\Program Files\Microsoft office\office\xlstart`).

3. If this is not present, close the MS Excel application; copy the `eSign3.xla` file from the eSign folder (generally `c:\Program Files\eSign Desktop 3.0`) to the MS Excel startup path.

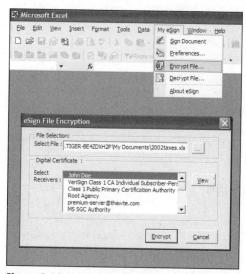

**Figure 6-16:** Using eSign Desktop to encrypt an MS Excel file

## USING ESIGN DESKTOP 3.0 IN MS OUTLOOK

The eSign plug-in for MS Outlook automatically loads the My eSign toolbar in Outlook's new mail window.

**CREATING A SIGNATURE**   Place your cursor in the body of a new mail where the signature needs to be placed, and click on the My eSign button. A signature placeholder appears in the body of the mail. When you are ready to sign, double click on this placeholder to sign the document.

**DIGITAL SIGNATURES** On double clicking the placeholder, the eSign signature screen appears. Select the Signer Profile in case of multiple user profiles. The Digital Certificate details of the selected profile are displayed in the signing screen. If you choose to sign without enabling biometric signatures, you will be prompted to give your profile password. After you do so, your digital signature will be embedded in the document along with the profile name, date, and time. The Digital Certificate will be attached to the signature.

**HANDWRITTEN SIGNATURES** To add your handwritten signature, enable the Biometric Signature check box and select the Signature input device. To use a Wintab32 pen tablet, simply pick up the pen and sign. Use the clear option if you are not satisfied with the signature, and sign again. Capturing signatures using PDAs is illustrated in earlier sections.

If you have a pre-enrolled sign card, the signature made will be matched against the same. If verified, a message indicating successful signature verification is displayed. If the signature does not match the sign card, you can choose to place the signature onto the document by giving your profile password or sign again to authenticate the signature successfully. Please note that the signature on verification will indicate that biometric verification was not successful.

**VERIFICATION** Verification of signatures requires eSign Desktop 3.0 or eSign 3.0 Viewer to be installed on the system. To verify an eSign signature, double-click on the signature. The authentication information includes the following:

✓ Whether the document has been modified after signing

✓ Whether Digital ID is valid

✓ Whether biometric signature verification has been successful

The signer details are displayed along with the handwritten signature, if available. Additionally, the signer's Digital Certificate can be viewed by clicking Show Certificate.

**TROUBLESHOOTING ESIGN WITH OUTLOOK** If the My eSign signature button is not available on the tool bar, go to the Tools menu in the Outlook main window and click Options. The Add option here is to add needed missing add-ins (in this case, the eSign add-in). Go to the location where eSign Desktop has been installed, and select esOLAddIn.dll. This adds eSign functionality to Outlook.

Ensure that the Outgoing mails format in the MS Outlook Options is set to HTML before using eSign in the mails. If you are using MS Word as the editor for composing messages, such e-mails need to be opened in Outlook that also has MS Word as its editor. Otherwise, the eSigned mail will be shown as invalid.

If you see a dialog box with the message Current Security settings do not permit ActiveX controls to initialize and run properly, you will need to alter the security settings for ActiveX controls. To alter the security settings, follow these steps:

**1.** Start Outlook, go to the Tools Menu, and then select Options/Security/Zone Settings.

**2.** A message box will appear. Click OK to continue.

**3.** Click the Custom Level button, and scroll down to the following options:

- Initialize and script ActiveX controls not marked as safe — Enable this option.
- Run ActiveX controls and Plug-ins — Enable this option.

Ensure that the Outgoing mail format in the MS Outlook Options is set to HTML format before using eSign in e-mails.

# Summary

More signature recognition biometrics are being implemented in authentication policies. The dynamic identification of handwriting speeds and pressures is improving, and smaller-budget projects are justifying a cost-effective on-screen or tabletized signature recognition solution for authenticating signature dynamics.

This chapter discussed signature recognition used in biometric systems for user authentication primarily for file and program access control. It also examined pilot applications and reviewed TigerSign, a custom signature system kernel to use for your own proprietary purposes.

Be sure to visit Chapter 9 for adding login capabilities with signature recognition and creating two-factor or strong authentication schemes.

# Chapter 7

# Voice Recognition

Voice recognition is actually comprised of two separate types of technologies — namely, voice-scan and speech recognition. Voice-scan is used to authenticate a user based on his or her voice characteristics, while speech recognition is used for the technological comprehension of spoken words. Both play a role in voice recognition biometrics, and the science of vocology is the underlying motivation, which is what this chapter discusses. In addition, this chapter looks at a sample voice system and components of a development kit for custom design.

## The Speaking Voice and Factors to Consider

Analyzing sound waves can produce a series of voice patterns that are based on frequency, intensity, and time, among other factors. Your voice involves the anatomy of your larynx, and the elements of your voice are affected by its components, in addition to any potential disorders or obstructions. According to the Center for Laryngeal and Voice Disorders at Johns Hopkins, the larynx is positioned in the anterior neck, slightly below the point where the pharynx divides and gives rise to the separate respiratory and digestive tracts. Because of its location, the larynx plays a critical role in normal breathing, swallowing, and speaking. Damage to the larynx or its tissues can result in interference with any or all of these functions.

The framework of the larynx is comprised mainly of two cartilages: the upper thyroid cartilage (whose anterior prominence is often noticed — the Adam's apple) and the lower and smaller cricoid cartilage. The vocal folds lie in the center of this framework in an anterior-posterior orientation. When viewed from above, the right and left folds appear as a v-shaped structure with the aperture between the v forming the entrance to the trachea. At the rear of the larynx, on each side, each vocal fold is attached to a small arytenoid cartilage. Many small muscles also attach to the arytenoids. These muscles contract or relax during the various stages of breathing, swallowing, and speaking, and their action is vital to the normal function of the larynx.

Phonation is a complicated process in which sound is produced for speech. During phonation, the vocal folds are brought together near the center of the larynx by muscles attached to the arytenoids. As air is forced through the vocal folds, they vibrate and produce sound. Contracting or relaxing the muscles of the arytenoids can alter the qualities of this sound. As the sound produced by the larynx travels through the throat and mouth, it is further modified to produce speech.

## How Vowels Are Formed

According to the National Center for Voice and Speech, as you phonate, your vocal folds produce a complex sound spectrum made up of a wide range of frequencies and overtones. As this spectrum travels through the various-sized areas in the vocal tract, some of these frequencies resonate more than others. Larger spaces in the vocal tract resonate at lower frequencies, whereas smaller spaces resonate at higher frequencies.

The two largest spaces in the vocal tract, the throat and mouth, produce the two lowest resonant frequencies, or *formants*. These formants are designated as F1 (the throat/pharynx) and F2 (the mouth). In singing or speaking, it is these two formants that are controlled by shaping the resonant areas with lip and tongue movements to produce vowels.

## Which Formant Frequencies Result in Which Vowels?

The vowel chart illustrated in Figure 7-1, adapted from the work of G.E. Peterson and H.L. Barney in 1952, shows the frequency regions for F1 and F2, which result in the 10 English vowel sounds.

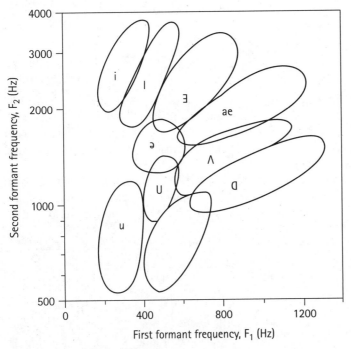

**Figure 7-1:** Vowel chart with frequency regions

The vowels [backwards D], [i], and [u] represent the three extremes of F1-F2 locations in the vowel chart and tongue placement. The other seven vowels are placed within these extremes. The three "corner vowels" are easy to remember by tongue placement, as follows:

✓ For the [backwards D], or "ah" sound, as in *father*, the tongue is low and back.

✓ For the [i], or "ee" sound, as in *keep*, the tongue is high and front.

✓ For the [u], or "oo" sound, as in *loot*, the tongue is high and back.

Note, too, that the vocal tract shape [backwards c] (as in the word *us*) is located at the center of the vowel chart. It is often referred to as the neutral vowel because the tongue is neither high nor low, forward nor back. Make this sound. Do you see why scientists can use a tube shape to mimic the vocal tract for speech simulation research? The vocal tract is roughly uniform in cross-sectional shape from bottom (just above the larynx) to top (lips).

# Individual Differences in Vowel Production

A rich area of research involves the study of differences among individuals in regard to formant frequencies. These differences are attributable to differences in size, age, gender, and speech habits. Differences can also be observed between speaking and singing and between singers due to the variability of training techniques. Often, the singer must balance vowel intelligibility with a beautiful quality of sound.

# Rules for Modifying Vowels

The acoustic differences that enable us to distinguish between the various vowel productions are usually explained by a source-filter theory. The *source* is the sound spectrum created by airflow through the glottis, which varies as the vocal folds vibrate. The *filter* is the vocal tract itself, the shape of which can be controlled by the vocalist. We perceive vowels on the basis of the vocal tract's two lowest formant frequencies.

### FOUR RULES FOR MODIFYING VOWELS

The following rules assist you in modifying vowels:

1. **All formant frequencies decrease uniformly as the length of the vocal tract increases.** This rule is good common sense; larger objects resonate sound at lower frequencies. For this reason, one uses long organ pipes, long strings, large drums, and big loudspeakers to produce low notes. We cannot change our vocal tracts' lengths greatly, however. A 10 percent increase or decrease (roughly speaking) is possible by lowering or raising the larynx and by protruding or retracting the lips. This produces a comparable percentage shift in the formant frequencies. The result is a darker (or brighter) coloring of the vowels. To convince yourself of this, try phonating an [a] vowel and gradually lower your larynx by attempting to yawn; then try extending your lips forward as far as possible during an [a]. You should hear similar changes. That is, the vowel sounds darker as it is modified toward [backwards c].

2. **All formant frequencies decrease uniformly with lip rounding and increase with lip spreading.** In the preceding exercise, you probably had to round your lips to protrude them because there is only so much tissue to work with. Lip rounding is similar to partially covering the mouth. In both cases, the effective tube length increases (acoustically). This lowers all the resonant frequencies. This time, try phonating an [a] and gradually

cover half of your mouth with your hand. The vowel again changes toward [backwards c]. The term *covered sound* likely originated as a result of musicians covering the mouth ends of their instruments, particularly brass players. In singing, we usually don't cover our mouths with the hand, but we can cover it by rounding the lips. Combined with larynx height adjustments, lip rounding or spreading can be very effective in darkening or brightening vowels. In addition to these front-end and back-end modifications, jaw lowering can be used to modify vowels. In particular, F1, the first formant, can be raised substantially by lowering the jaw. Two other rules are applicable to vowel formation in which either the front half (the mouth) or the back half (the pharynx) is narrowed.

3. A mouth constriction lowers the first formant and raises the second formant. This creates a more diffuse vowel spectrum. The acoustic energy is spread out over both low and high frequencies, as in the vowels [i] and [e].

4. A pharyngeal constriction raises the first formant and lowers the second formant. This makes the vowel spectrum more compact, as in the case of [a] or [o].

# Spectral Analysis

A sound *spectrograph* is a laboratory instrument that displays a graphical representation of the strengths of the various component frequencies of a sound as time passes. Voice researchers use the spectrograph as a tool for analyzing vocal output. In current research, it is used for identifying the strength and frequencies of formants and for real-time biofeedback in voice training and therapy.

The spectrograph performs two main kinds of voice analysis: *wideband* (also called *broadband*, with a bandwidth of 300 to 500 Hz) and *narrowband* (with a bandwidth of 45 to 50 Hz).

## WIDEBAND SPECTROGRAMS

Wideband spectrograms, when used for normal speech with a fundamental frequency of around 100 to 200 Hz, pick up energy from several harmonics at once and add them together, as illustrated in Figure 7-2. The fundamental frequency (Fo) can be determined from the graphic by counting the number of individual vertical lines per unit time. Also, the frequencies and relative strengths of the first two formants (F1 and F2) are visible as dark, blurry concentrations of energy.

The wide bandwidth in this type of analysis allows for excellent time resolution; you can see the energy peaks from each individual vocal fold vibration in the graph. However, the wide bandwidth also means that this kind of spectrogram cannot single out individual harmonics. For the wideband spectrograph, frequency components within a 300 to 500 Hz bandwidth are not easily distinguished.

## NARROWBAND SPECTROGRAMS

The narrowband spectrogram has different strengths. Unlike the wideband spectrogram, it can pick out individual harmonics, but its time resolution is not good enough to isolate each individual vibration cycle, and the formant structure of the sound is not rendered as clearly as with a wideband analysis. Notice the dark horizontal stripes representing each harmonic in Figure 7-3. Also notice that the large clusters of formant energy that you saw in the wideband spectrogram are not present.

Time waveform and broadband spectrogram of [i e a o u].

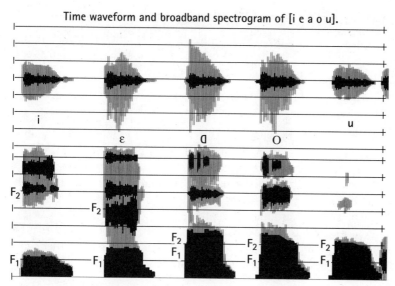

**Figure 7-2:** Broadband spectrogram

Time waveform and narrowband spectrogram of [i e a o u].

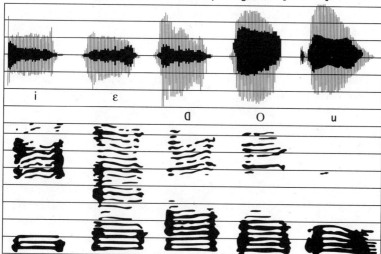

**Figure 7-3:** Narrowband spectrogram

Although the spectrograph is often used in voice recognition research, it can also serve as a helpful tool in the voice clinic to provide feedback as part of a voice therapy or training program.

# Factors Influencing Fundamental Frequency

The human voice is classified into various types, based on pitch, timbre, and other factors that influence perception of someone's voice or how that voice can be used. This section explains some of the physiological factors that influence the pitch and timbre of voices.

## IS IT BODY SIZE?

The most obvious influence on pitch is the size of the sound-producing apparatus. You can observe from an orchestra's instruments that smaller objects tend to make higher-pitched sounds, and larger ones produce lower-pitched sounds. Assuming that small people would make high sounds and large people would make low sounds is logical. And, to some extent, this assumption is borne out by the facts. Baby cries have an Fo of around 500 Hz (roughly corresponding to the note B4). Child speech ranges from 250 to 400 Hz (notes B3 to G4), adult females tend to speak at around 200 Hz (about G3), and adult males around 125 Hz (B2).

So, relating body size to Fo does seem to make sense. However, think about the fact that big opera singers don't always make low sounds; there are very large sopranos and some rather short, slender basses. Body weight and height can't be the only determining factors.

## IS IT LARYNGEAL SIZE?

Perhaps a measurement of something more relevant to the voice source itself, such as the size of the larynx, would be more helpful. Although men, on average, have a larynx that is about 40 percent taller (measured along the axis of the vocal folds) than that of women, this does not explain all of the difference between male and female Fo. However, a size difference inside the larynx does explain the full difference (see Figure 7-4).

## VOCAL FOLD LENGTH

If you assume that the vocal folds are "ideal strings" with uniform properties, their Fo is governed by the equation shown in Figure 7-5.

The key variable here is the length of the part of the vocal folds that is actually in vibration, which is called the *effective vocal fold length*. If you examine this quantity for men and women, you find that men have a 60 percent longer effective fold length than women, on average, which fully accounts for the Fo difference between the sexes.

## VOCAL TRACT LENGTH

Along with pitch, another variable used to classify voices is their quality, or timbre. A fuller treatment of voice qualities is available in the next section. To review, the preceding sections explain that formant frequencies and timbre are related to the length of the vocal tract. Different vocalists have different vocal tract lengths, of course, and speakers and singers can control tract length to a limited extent by raising or lowering the larynx. A longer tract results in a darker-sounding voice, whereas shorter tracts make the voice sound brighter. Keep in mind, however, that the length of the vocal tract is largely determined by nature. Some are born with necks that are swan-like, while others are quite short.

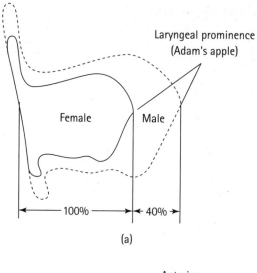

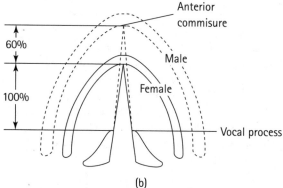

**Figure 7-4:** Narrowband spectrogram

# Voice Qualities and Recognizing Distinctiveness

Voices are as distinctive as faces—no two are exactly alike. Some of the traits that make voices unique can be formed into well-defined categories; fundamental frequency (high and low) and intensity (loud or soft) are examples. Other attributes fall into a general set of characteristics called *vocal qualities*. Register generally falls into this category, although it tends to be quantal rather than continuous perceptually. Characteristics such as tightness, resonance, or nasality aren't easily defined—perhaps because they tend to be present along a continuum.

An equation for an individual's unique voice might look something like this: *Voice Quality = vocal tract configuration + laryngeal anatomy + learned component*.

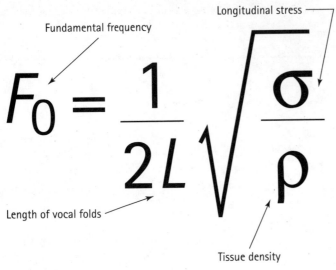

Fundamental frequency

Longitudinal stress

$$F_0 = \frac{1}{2L} \sqrt{\frac{\sigma}{\rho}}$$

Length of vocal folds

Tissue density

**Figure 7-5:** Fundamental frequency equation

The shape of an individual's vocal tract is partly genetic and partly learned. Necks are long or short; pharynxes may be narrow or wide. Although these attributes are genetically determined (except for configurations due to trauma or disease), individuals can also manipulate vocal tract shape. Highly trained singers have many tricks to change the contours of their vocal tracts to improve the sound coming out of their mouths. Lip rounding lengthens the vocal tract, for example.

Similarly, laryngeal anatomy is partially determined at birth: genes determine the length of one's vocal folds. However, the general hydration of vocal fold tissues or muscular agility of laryngeal muscles can be partly controlled by vocal health and training.

The learned component of the equation could also be called *vocal habits*. These would be items such as rhythm, rate of speech, and vowel pronunciation. Rhythm includes mannerisms such as periodic pauses to search for the right word, whereas rate refers to the speed of an individual's syllables and speech. (The average rate of speech for English speakers in the United States is about 150 words per minute.) A speaker's habits also influence how much air pressure is used to produce sound and how laryngeal muscles open and close the vocal folds.

So don't be surprised that family members often sound alike. After all, for most, the home and the gene pool of siblings, parents, and children are shared.

## DESCRIBING PERCEIVED VOCAL QUALITIES

The average person easily recognizes familiar or famous voices, yet would have difficulty describing them in words. Language has not been as well developed for vocal characteristics as it has for appearance. People can be tall, bald, or wrinkled, but how do you describe how they sound?

Despite their training, vocologists and voice researchers also disagree about exact descriptions of vocal qualities, and voice recognition software must accommodate for this. Table 7-1 lists terms suggested by Dr. Ingo Titze at the Eighth Vocal Fold Physiology Conference in April 1994. The list is likely incomplete and does not necessarily reflect a consensus of the conference or the field of vocology as a whole.

### TABLE 7-1: Vocal Terms

| Voice Quality | Perception | Physiologic Component |
|---|---|---|
| aphonic | No sound or a whisper | The inability to set vocal folds into vibration; caused by lack of appropriate power (air pressure) or a muscular/tissue problem of the folds. |
| biphonic | Two independent pitches | Two sources of sound (for example, true folds and false folds or two folds and whistle due to vortex in air). |
| bleat (see flutter) | | |
| breathy | Sound of air is apparent | Noise is caused by turbulence in or near glottis, caused by loose valving of laryngeal muscles (lateral cricoarytenoid, interarytenoid, and posterior cricoarytenoid). |
| covered | Muffled or darkened sound | Lips are rounded and protruded or the larynx is lowered to lower all formants to obtain a stronger fundamental. |
| creaky | Sounds like two hard surfaces rubbing against one another | A complex pattern of vibrations in the vocal folds creates an intricate formation of subharmonics and modulations. |
| diplophonic | Pitch supplemented with another pitch one octave lower; roughness usually apparent | A period doubling, or Fo/2 subharmonic |
| flutter | Often called bleat because it sounds like a lamb's cry | Amplitude changes or frequency modulations occur in the 8 to 12 Hz range. |
| glottalized | Clicking noise heard during voicing | Forceful adduction or abduction of the vocal folds during speech. |
| hoarse (raspy) | Harsh, grating sound | Combination of irregularity in vocal fold vibration and glottal noise generation. |
| honky | Excessive nasality | Excessive acoustic energy couples to the nasal tract. |
| jitter | Pitch sounds rough | Fundamental frequency varies from cycle to cycle. |
| nasal (see honky) | | |

*Continued*

**TABLE 7-1: Vocal Terms** *(Continued)*

| Voice Quality | Perception | Physiologic Component |
|---|---|---|
| pressed | Harsh, often loud (strident) quality | Vocal processes of the arytenoid cartilages are squeezed together, constricting the glottis and causing low airflow and medial compression of the vocal folds. |
| pulsed (fry) | Sounds similar to food cooking in a hot frying pan | Sound gaps caused by intermittent energy packets below 70 Hz; formant energy dies out prior to re-excitation. |
| resonant (ringing) | Brightened or ringing sound that carries well | Epilaryngeal resonance is enhanced, producing a strong spectral peak at 2500 to 3500 Hz; in effect, formants F3, F4, and F5 are clustered. |
| rough | Uneven, bumpy sound appearing to be unsteady and short-term but persisting over the long-term | Modes of vibration of the vocal folds are not synchronized. |
| shimmer | Crackly, buzzy | Short-term (cycle-to-cycle) variation in a signal's amplitude. |
| strained | Effort apparent in voice; hyperfunction of neck muscles; entire larynx may compress | Excessive energy focused in laryngeal region. |
| strohbass | Popping sound; vocal fry during singing | Sound gaps caused by intermittent energy packets below 70 Hz; formant energy dies out prior to re-excitation. |
| tremerous | Affected by trembling or tremors | Modulation of 1 to 15 Hz in either amplitude or pitch due to a neurological or biomechanical cause. |
| twangy | Sharp, bright sound | Often attributed to excessive nasality, but probably also has an epilaryngeal basis. |
| ventricular | Very rough (Louis Armstrong-type voice) | Phonation using the false folds anterior rather than the vocal folds; unless intentional due to damage to the true folds; considered an abnormal muscle pattern dysphonia. |
| wobble | Wavering or irregular variation in sound | Amplitude and/or frequency modulations in the 1 to 3 Hz range. |
| yawny | Quality akin to sounds made during a yawn | Larynx is lowered and pharynx is widened, as people do when yawning. |

# Fluctuation and Perturbation: Other Factors for Voice Systems

The terms *fluctuation* and *perturbation* are used in voice science to describe disturbances, or changes in the voice output. A perturbation is generally understood to be a small, temporary change in the vocal system; a fluctuation is a more significant change and tends to indicate that the voice is somehow unstable. Here are some descriptions of common terms used to describe various kinds of vocal fluctuations and perturbations. Notice that the following truly are descriptive terms rather than precise, scientific measurements:

- ✓ **Jitter** — Short-term changes in Fo (pitch). In this context, short-term means within a single vibration cycle.

- ✓ **Shimmer** — Short-term changes in amplitude (loudness).

- ✓ **Vibrato** — A "cultured" or artistic fluctuation, usually introduced purposefully by a performer. Vibrato involves changes in pitch of plus or minus 0 to 3 percent, occurring 4.5 to 6.5 times per second (that is, at a rate of 4.5 to 6.5 Hz). The vibrato rate can vary with many factors, including vocal intensity, the vocal conditioning of the singer, pitch, and the amount of pitch changes in the music being sung.

- ✓ **Trill** — A deliberate attempt by a singer to alternate back and forth between a given base note and the note either a half step or whole step above it.

- ✓ **Trillo** — A rapid repetition of the same note accomplished with the cricoarytenoid muscles; the voice stops and starts very quickly. The vocal folds are rapidly approximated (held close together) and then separated so that no vibration can occur and then approximated again, and so on.

These definitions point to a gray area in the field of vocology. Some variation in voicing is desirable and considered to be important artistically (as vibrato in singing). Too much variability can lead to unintelligibility, however, and no variability (such as computer simulated speech) produces highly unnatural phonation.

# That Was Then, This Is Now

Although voice technology is extremely scientific and still in its infancy, voice-scan and voice-recognition systems have proven to be highly accurate, and voice authentication has become an emergent technology for authentication. Deon Scheepers, from ATIO Corporation, is commonly quoted for identifying the following reasons for implementing voice-authentication systems:

- ✓ Accuracy (claimed as high as 99.9 percent)

- ✓ Low cost

- ✓ No hardware or software required

- ✓ No need to hire specialists to install the system for you

✓ Device independent

✓ You pay only for the services used

✓ Speed (verification in less than half a second, regardless of where in the world the person is located)

✓ Ease of use (no PINs or passwords to remember; voice verification service is available around the clock; the only requirement is access to a phone, or a microphone if you are on the Web, and the voice is something that you carry with you at all times)

✓ Unobtrusive (no need to disclose personal information)

Some of the most popular voice systems today are offered from the following companies, among others:

✓ **Anovea** (www.anovea.com) — Anovea designs and builds speaker-verification systems for real-world applications. It develops its own core technology, including speaker-verification and speech-compression algorithms, and provides this powerful technology to customers in the form of speaker-authentication products, developer resources, and consulting services.

✓ **Graphco Tech (a.k.a. G-TEC at** www.graphcotech.com) — G-TEC is an advanced technology and systems-development company focused on being a leading provider of secure access, biometric identification, surveillance, and secure data-hosting solutions. G-TEC's advanced technology applications offer products and systems that increase security, safety, and peace of mind for individuals, businesses, and enterprises through authorized access, biometric identification, and secure information-exchange solutions.

✓ **SentryCom** (www.voiceprove.com) — SentryCom designs, develops, and markets biometric voice authentication solutions that accurately verify a person's claimed identity. The company's core technology is based on its proprietary and patented Voice Authentication Engine (VAE), designed to increase and enhance security while improving end users' privacy and confidence. SentryComs' solutions generate a positive return on investment by reducing exposure to security breaches through unauthorized access and exploiting the opportunities generated by being able to use the Internet and telephone networks safely.

✓ **T-NETIX** (www.t-netix.com) — T-NETIX is a leading provider of specialized call-processing and fraud-control software technologies and is the nation's largest provider of corrections industry-related telecommunications services. The services offered include specialized call-processing and billing services for use by correctional institutions; direct local and long-distance call processing for correctional facilities; and value-added telecommunications services, such as preconnection restrictions, digital recording, jail and inmate management systems, video booking, and call-processing systems hardware.

✓ **VeriVoice** — See the following section, "Sample Product Demo."

✓ **Voicevault** (`www.voicevault.com`) — Voicevault is a world leader in the application of voice verification. Voicevault provides an entrusted third-party service, which enables you to verify customers by their voices over the phone (Voicevaultphone), Web (Voicevaultweb), or Internet (Voicevaultnet) in less than a second, regardless of where in the world the speaker is located. Voicevault's voice-verification engine, which offers you a replacement and enhancement for PINs, passwords, and so on, represents the best in terms of value, accuracy, and speed of verification. The key benefits of Voicevault are that it reduces costs and fraud, increases security, and improves overall efficiency.

✓ **Voice Security** (`www.voice-security.com`) — Voice Security Systems, Inc., was formed in 1999 to market products resulting from research and development of voice-authentication technology. The concept originated with the idea of a voice-controlled garage door opener. This led to other iterations of the security device. The challenge to this technology in developing a self-contained, microprocessor-based, access-control firmware has always been cost. Ten years of research and development culminated in a technology that is innovative and cutting-edge. Voice Security Systems' founders applied for their first U.S. patent in 1997 and were awarded U.S. Patent 5,835,894 in November 1998. Voice Security Systems, Inc., was also awarded U.S. Patent 6,161,094 in December 2000. Voice Security Systems holds exclusive rights to this intellectual property. Voice Security Systems' Voice Protect speaker-verification technology uses a person's voice print to uniquely identify individuals by using biometric speaker-verification technology.

# Sample Product Demo

As implied by its name, VeriVoice specializes in developing voice biometric security solutions. The biometrics voice verification technology at the heart of the VeriVoice Security Lock (SL) was developed after more than a decade of research, including security-enhancing studies at government facilities. VeriVoice is the owner of U.S. Patent 5,142,565, which is "a system and method for controlling data communication between a host computer and a remote device when it is desirable to effect verification with a biometric such as voice." VeriVoice also holds the exclusive license on U.S. Patent 5,526,465, which provides algorithms for developing accurate, high-performance, and scalable speaker-verification systems.

## VeriVoice

The VeriVoice SL is a patented voice-verification technology that provides a fast, highly accurate, and customizable solution for identification of enrolled users. The SL has two implementations, one for recording and verification over a microphone and one for recording and verification over a telephone. In addition, with the VeriVoice Developer's Toolkit, you can easily include robust voice verification in your next application.

The product can be used to do the following:

✓ Protect your corporate intranet

✓ Control access to your Web site

✓  Protect a database

✓  Control phone access to your company's 401(k) program

✓  Control entrance to a building or facility

✓  Secure your PC

What's more, VeriVoice SL accurately verifies in noisy environments and over cordless and cellular telephones. With the Developer's Toolkit, accuracy levels can be fine-tuned to meet the security requirements of the project.

## HOW THE SYSTEM WORKS

Using VeriVoice SL begins with the one-time enrollment of a user's voice. A model of the user's voice is developed from a series of phrases. Depending on the application, this enrollment can be taken over a telephone or from a microphone connected to a PC.

After enrollment, signing onto the system is a fast and secure process. VeriVoice SL prompts the user for a set of random digits spoken over the telephone or into a microphone. Prompting for a randomly generated sequence of numbers enhances security by eliminating hacking with digital recorders. Also, there is no password to be discovered or to forget. Verification takes less than one second.

The product is used to enhance security of any password-protected, keycard, or token-locked system.

## VERIVOICE INSTALLATION

Apps.exe is a self-extracting zip archive. Double-click Apps.exe to start a WinZip Self-Extractor dialog box. By default, extraction take places on the C drive. The C drive option should be changed only if the system folder (Windows or WINNT, for example) is on a different drive. If you change the default Unzip to a folder from C, you must edit the VeriVoice.ini file (see the "Changing the Default Drive" section). Click Unzip to install the demonstration software. After installation is complete, click Close in the dialog box to exit the WinZip Self-Extractor application.

## PREPARING TO RUN THE DEMONSTRATION

A quality microphone is essential to the construction of a quality voiceprint (voice template). Noise cancellation microphones are very good in environments with ambient noise, but they tend to produce more breath noise and wind noise. Make sure that the pickup is placed slightly to the side of your mouth to minimize these noises.

## MICROPHONE CALIBRATION

The first step in achieving a quality voiceprint is to have a correctly adjusted microphone. The VeriVoice vMicSetup wizard leads you through a series of steps to adjust your microphone.

With respect to this demo, you can start vMicSetup in one of the following three ways:

1. Click the desktop shortcut, launch it from EnrolDemo by selecting Microphone Setup from the Tools entry on the menu bar, or launch it from VerifyDemo by selecting Microphone Setup from the Tools entry on the menu bar.

2. Click the Shortcut to vMicSetup to start the microphone setup wizard. You are presented with the screen shown in Figure 7-6.

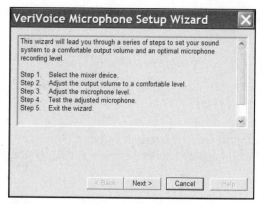

**Figure 7-6:** VeriVoice Microphone Setup Wizard

3. Click the Next button to proceed to the audio mixer selection illustrated in Figure 7-7.

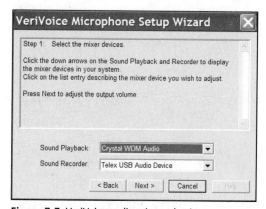

**Figure 7-7:** VeriVoice audio mixer selection

4. After you have chosen the Playback and Recorder device, click the Next button to proceed to the adjust output volume section (see Figure 7-8).

**Figure 7-8:** Adjusting the output volume

5. Click the Open Volume Control button to display an output volume control (as shown in Figure 7-9). Click the Play Sound button to play a short audio file and adjust the slider bar as needed.

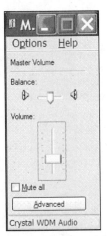

**Figure 7-9:** Output volume control

6. After you set the output volume, click the Next button to proceed to the adjust microphone level section, as shown in Figure 7-10.

7. Click the Adjust Microphone button, and you are prompted to say a five-digit numerical sequence. The wizard records your response and evaluates the quality of the recording. If the recording is unsuitable, you are prompted again. This process continues until a suitable setting is achieved or the microphone is found to be unsuitable. You can pause the adjustment process by clicking the Pause button. An interruption window appears. You can elect to stop adjustment or to continue. Click No to stop the adjustment process or click Yes to resume adjustment.

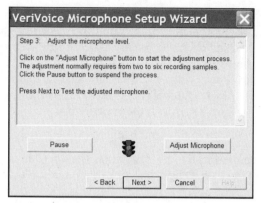

**Figure 7-10:** Adjusting the microphone level

**8.** After the microphone is adjusted, an adjustment complete window appears. Click OK and then click Next to proceed to the test microphone level section, as shown in Figure 7-11.

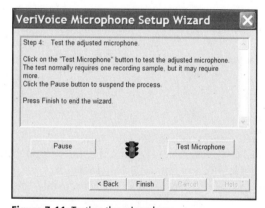

**Figure 7-11:** Testing the microphone

**9.** You can test the microphone settings by clicking the Test Microphone button. As in calibration, you are prompted to say a five-digit numerical sequence. You are informed whether the settings are adequate; if an inadequacy occurs, you are prompted for a numerical sequence again. If testing does not measure an acceptable setting, it continues until stopped. You can stop the testing anytime by clicking the Pause button.

This step can be suspended in the same fashion as previously explained. If the microphone was just adjusted, you can skip this step. This step is useful if you want to test the adjustment of a microphone without actually doing the adjustment step. Click Finish to end the wizard.

## ENROLLMENT

Click the shortcut to EnrollDemo to start the enrollment process. Enter the name that you want for an enrollment template in the User ID field and click OK. You are asked to repeat 12 five-digit phrases. A level bar indicates relative recording strength as you repeat the phrases. Message feedback is given if a phrase is not suitable for enrollment. Normally, messages indicate that you spoke too softly, too loudly, or too soon after the beep queue. After all 12 phrases are recorded, an enrollment record is created. You may then test the enrollment with the VerifyDemo.

## VERIFICATION

Click the shortcut to VerifyDemo to start the verification process. Enter the template name that you chose during the enrollment process in the User ID field and click OK. You are asked to speak a random five-digit phrase. A level bar indicates relative recording strength as you speak the phrase. You are provided with feedback on the success or failure of your voice verification. To test again, just click OK.

## CHANGING THE DEFAULT DRIVE

If you install to a drive other than C, you must edit four lines in the `VeriVoice.ini` file. Locate the [NGM] section in `VeriVoice.ini` in the Windows folder and change C to the chosen drive letter in the following four lines:

```
TemplateDir=C:\Apps\VeriVoice\Templates
MessageDir=C:\Apps\VeriVoice\Sounds
ProgramsDir=C:\Apps\VeriVoice\Programs
TraceDir=C:\Apps\VeriVoice\LogData
```

## VOICE VERIFICATION DEMONSTRATION

This system is designed to recognize (authenticate) you based on the unique properties of your voice and, as such, requires correct and cooperative use, as outlined in the following steps. As you use the system, remember that it is working for you. You are not trying to fool it.

Use the following instructions whenever you enroll (create a voiceprint) and during verifications (normal use):

1. **Match the prompt's speed.** Speaking at the same speed (cadence) as the voice prompt is best. Speak clearly and consistently. Speak the digits at a constant volume. Speaking too quickly or too slowly can decrease the effectiveness of the system.

2. **Speak into or toward the microphone.** Position yourself in front of or near the attached or embedded microphone, as you would under normal use. Keep a comfortable and constant distance between your mouth and the microphone. Do not speak too closely into the microphone and do not turn your head away.

3. **Repeat the numbers as they were given.** After you are prompted to repeat the five-digit sequence of numbers, repeat the exact numbers in the order given. If you say a wrong digit or say a digit in the wrong order during verification, you may decrease the system's effectiveness.

4. **Minimize noise.** Minimize lip-smacking, deep breaths, and background noise as much as possible.

The following procedures are recommended for testing the accuracy of the demonstration. After you have enrolled, do the following:

1. Test against your template in a cooperative manner at least 10 times. This tests the system's accuracy in its normal intended use (identifying a bona fide user under normal conditions).

2. Have an imposter challenge your template at least 10 times.

3. Do not disguise your voice in an attempt to test the system. Even disguised, it is still your voice, and the system may or may not recognize you. Furthermore, a disguised voice gives you an inaccurate perception of the false acceptance and rejection rates.

---

## Verivoice faqs

**What is a false accept and a false reject?**

*A false accept is when the system permits an unauthorized user to log into an account (for example, you log in claiming to be someone else and the system accepts it). A false reject is when you try to log into your account and the system thinks that you are not you.*

**What are the false accept and false reject rates for the VeriVoice SL?**

*The false accept and false reject rates are plus or minus 1.5 percent. This is a very loaded question, because many companies do not use comparable tests to develop this number.*

**What control is there over adjusting this rate to control the accuracy of the verification?**

*The software enables the system administrator to adjust this.*

**How do I integrate the VeriVoice SL into my application?**

*You integrate the VeriVoice SL into your application through a very simple application program interface (API) that has approximately five function calls.*

**What tools can I use to call the VeriVoice SL API?**

*Use function calls in C.*

**Are Unix, Linux, and Mac OS versions available?**

*Linux should be available soon.*

**Is the VeriVoice SL multithreaded?**

*Yes. Verivoice SL was built from the beginning to be multithreaded.*

# Custom Speech Recognition Development

As previously mentioned, voice-scan authenticates a user based on his or her voice characteristics, whereas speech recognition is used for the technological comprehension of spoken words. The latter of the two can be used with an authentication system to add additional security for command execution, such as opening files and performing system functions. This section is a brief examination of a voice recognition developing kit (see Figure 7-12) that can be customized for proprietary development. This kit contains three main framework modules: recognizing, enrolling, and administering speech patterns and templates.

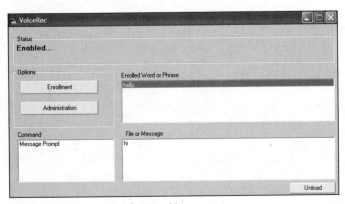

**Figure 7-12:** Custom speech recognition

## Recognizing Speech From Your System's Microphone

The first module contains the main form and routines for using the Microsoft Direct Speech Recognition and Microsoft Direct Text-to-Speech controls to recognize speech from your microphone.

The following is the source for the voice module functions and declarations (see Voice.zip):

```
Option Explicit
Private Declare Function SetWindowPos Lib "user32" (ByVal hwnd As Long, ByVal
hWndInsertAfter As Long, ByVal x As Long, ByVal y As Long, ByVal cx As Long,
ByVal cy As Long, ByVal wFlags As Long) As Long
Private Const SWP_NOMOVE = &H2
Private Const SWP_NOSIZE = &H1
Private Const HWND_TOPMOST = -1
Private Const HWND_NOTOPMOST = -2
Private Sub Command5_Click()
End
End Sub
Private Sub DirectSR1_PhraseFinish(ByVal flags As Long, ByVal beginhi As Long,
ByVal beginlo As Long, ByVal endhi As Long, ByVal endlo As Long, ByVal Phrase
```

```
As String, ByVal parsed As String, ByVal results As Long)
    Dim noth
    List1.ListIndex = -1
    For i = 0 To List1.ListCount
        If Phrase = "" Then
            List1.ListIndex = -1
            List2.ListIndex = -1
            List3.ListIndex = -1
            Exit Sub
        End If
If Phrase = List1.List(i) Then
            List1.ListIndex = i
            List2.ListIndex = i
            List3.ListIndex = i
            Label4.Caption = "Currently executing command: " + List3.List(i)
            Timer1.Enabled = True
            If List3.Text = "Open" Then
            noth = Shell(List2.List(i), vbNormalNoFocus)
            ElseIf List3.Text = "Delete" Then
            Kill List2.Text
            ElseIf List3.Text = "Message Prompt" Then
            MsgBox (List2.Text)
            End If
        End If
    Next i
End Sub
Private Sub Form_Load()
    Dim junk, windir$
    Label4.Caption = ""
    windir = Space(144)
    junk = getwindir(windir, 144)
    windir = Trim(windir)
    i = InStr(windir$, vbNullChar)
    windir$ = Mid$(windir$, 1, i - 1)
    words = windir$ & "\words.txt"
    dirs = windir$ & "\dirs.txt"
    descrip = windir$ & "\desc.txt"
    test = Dir(words)
    If test = "" Then
        Open words For Output As #1
        Close #1
    End If
    test = Dir(dirs)
    If test = "" Then
        Open dirs For Output As #1
```

```
        Close #1
    End If
    test = Dir(descrip)
    If test = "" Then
        Open descrip For Output As #1
        Close #1
    End If
    Call loadfiles
    Label4.Caption = "Currently Enabled"
    SetWindowPos hwnd, HWND_TOPMOST, 0, 0, 0, 0, SWP_NOMOVE + SWP_NOSIZE
End Sub
Private Sub Form_Unload(Cancel As Integer)
    Call savefiles
    Set Form1 = Nothing
    Set Form2 = Nothing
    Set Form3 = Nothing
    End
End Sub
Private Sub command1_click()
    Form2.Show
End Sub
Private Sub Command2_Click()
    Form3.Show
End Sub
Private Sub Timer1_Timer()
Label4.Caption = "Currently Enabled"
Timer1.Enabled = False
End Sub
```

Here's the Main Module source:

```
Option Explicit
Public line, test, words, descrip, dirs As Variant
Public count, pos, length, i As Integer
Public Declare Function getwindir Lib "kernel32" Alias "GetWindowsDirectoryA"
(ByVal lpBuffer As String, ByVal nSize As Long) As Long
Public Sub loadfiles()
    Form1.DirectSR1.Deactivate
    Form1.DirectSR1.GrammarFromFile (words)
    Form1.DirectSR1.Activate
    Open words For Input As #1
        Do Until EOF(1)
            Line Input #1, line
            If line <> "" Then
                test = Left(line, 8)
```

```
                If test = "<start>=" Then
                        line = Mid(line, 9, (Len(line) - 8))
                        Form1.List1.AddItem (line)
                        Form2.List1.AddItem (line)
                End If
            End If
        Loop
    Close #1
    Open dirs For Input As #1
        Do Until EOF(1)
            Line Input #1, line
            If line <> "" Then
                Form1.List2.AddItem (line)

                count = 0: pos = 0
                Do
                    pos = InStr(pos + 1, line, "\")     'find how many "\"s
there are
                    If pos = 0 Then Exit Do             'in the full dir
                    count = count + 1
                Loop Until pos = 0

                For i = 0 To count - 1                      'using the last
result, gets
                    pos = InStr(pos + 1, line, "\") + 1 'position of the last
"\"
                Next i                                     'and add 1 so it is
pos after "\"

                length = Len(line) - pos + 1                'length of filetitle
                Form2.List3.AddItem (line)
            End If
        Loop
    Close #1
    Open descrip For Input As #1
        Do Until EOF(1)
            Line Input #1, line
            If line <> "" Then
                Form1.List3.AddItem (line)
                Form2.List2.AddItem (line)
            End If
        Loop
    Close #1
line = ""
End Sub
```

```
Public Sub savefiles()
    Dim data As Variant
    Open words For Output As #1
        data = "[Grammer]" & vbCrLf & "type=cfg" & vbCrLf & "[<start>]" &
vbCrLf
        Form1.List1.ListIndex = -1
        For i = 0 To Form1.List1.ListCount
            If Form1.List1.List(i) <> "" Then
                data = data & "<start>=" & Form1.List1.List(i) & vbCrLf
            End If
        Next i
        Print #1, data
    Close #1
    Open dirs For Output As #1
        data = ""
        Form1.List1.ListIndex = -1
        For i = 0 To Form1.List1.ListCount
            If Form1.List2.List(i) <> "" Then
                data = Form1.List2.List(i) & vbCrLf
                Print #1, data
            End If
        Next i
    Close #1
    Open descrip For Output As #1
        data = ""
        Form1.List1.ListIndex = -1
        For i = 0 To Form1.List1.ListCount
            If Form1.List3.List(i) <> "" Then
                data = Form1.List3.List(i) & vbCrLf
                Print #1, data
            End If
        Next i
    Close #1
End Sub
```

# Enrolling a Word or Phrase and Applying it to a Command

This module is used to enroll a word or phrase and apply a command (for example, open or delete a file) or message prompt when called.

Here's the enrollment template source code for the voice module:

```
Option Explicit
Dim CommandType As String
Private Declare Function SetWindowPos Lib "user32" (ByVal hwnd As Long, ByVal
hWndInsertAfter As Long, ByVal x As Long, ByVal y As Long, ByVal cx As Long,
```

```
ByVal cy As Long, ByVal wFlags As Long) As Long
Private Const SWP_NOMOVE = &H2
Private Const SWP_NOSIZE = &H1
Private Const HWND_TOPMOST = -1
Private Const HWND_NOTOPMOST = -2
Private Sub Form_Load()
    Label1.Caption = "Word/Phrase:"
    Label3.Caption = "Command:"
    Command1.Caption = "Save"
    Command2.Caption = "Close"
    Command3.Caption = "Browse"
    Text1 = ""
    Text3 = ""
    SetWindowPos hwnd, HWND_TOPMOST, 0, 0, 0, 0, SWP_NOMOVE + SWP_NOSIZE
End Sub
Private Sub command1_click()
    Dim count, pos, i, length As Integer
    Dim line, test As Variant
    Form1.List1.AddItem (Text1.Text)
    Form1.List2.AddItem (Text3.Text)
    Form1.List3.AddItem (CommandType)
    Form2.List1.AddItem (Text1.Text)
    Form2.List2.AddItem (CommandType)
    Call savefiles
    Form1.List1.Clear
    Form1.List2.Clear
    Form1.List3.Clear
    Form2.List1.Clear
    Form2.List2.Clear
    Form2.List3.Clear
    Call loadfiles
  Text1.Text = ""
  Text3.Text = ""
  Option1 = True
End Sub
Private Sub Command2_Click()
    Unload Me
End Sub
Private Sub Command3_Click()
    On Error Resume Next
    CommonDialog1.Filter = "All Files"
    CommonDialog1.ShowOpen
    If Err.Number = cdlCancel Then Exit Sub
    Text3 = CommonDialog1.FileName
End Sub
```

```
Private Sub Form_Unload(Cancel As Integer)
    Set Form3 = Nothing
End Sub
Private Sub Option1_Click()
If Option1 = True Then
CommandType = "Open"
End If
End Sub
Private Sub Option3_Click()
If Option3 = True Then
CommandType = "Delete"
End If
End Sub
Private Sub Option4_Click()
If Option4 = True Then
CommandType = "Message Prompt"
End If
End Sub
```

## Administering Enrollments

Use this module to sort and administer enrollments. You can view and delete enrolled words and/or phrases with their associated commands.

Here's the source for the administration form:

```
Option Explicit
Dim SendText As String
Private Declare Function SetWindowPos Lib "user32" (ByVal hwnd As Long, ByVal
hWndInsertAfter As Long, ByVal x As Long, ByVal y As Long, ByVal cx As Long,
ByVal cy As Long, ByVal wFlags As Long) As Long
Private Const SWP_NOMOVE = &H2
Private Const SWP_NOSIZE = &H1
Private Const HWND_TOPMOST = -1
Private Const HWND_NOTOPMOST = -2
Private Sub Command6_Click()
End Sub
Private Sub Form_Load()
    Label1.Caption = "Word/Phrase"
    Label3.Caption = "File/Message"
    Command1.Caption = "Close"
    Command2.Caption = "Delete"
    SetWindowPos hwnd, HWND_TOPMOST, 0, 0, 0, 0, SWP_NOMOVE + SWP_NOSIZE
End Sub
Private Sub List1_Click()
    List2.ListIndex = List1.ListIndex
```

```
        List3.ListIndex = List1.ListIndex
End Sub
Private Sub List2_Click()
    On Error GoTo exitsub
    List1.ListIndex = List2.ListIndex
    List3.ListIndex = List2.ListIndex
exitsub:
End Sub
Private Sub command1_click()
    Form2.Hide
End Sub
Private Sub Command2_Click()
    Dim index As Integer
    index = List3.ListIndex
    On Error Resume Next
    List1.RemoveItem List1.ListIndex
    List2.RemoveItem List2.ListIndex
    List3.RemoveItem List3.ListIndex
    Form1.List1.RemoveItem (index)
    Form1.List2.RemoveItem (index)
    Form1.List3.RemoveItem (index)
    Call savefiles
    Form1.List1.Clear
    Form1.List2.Clear
    Form1.List3.Clear
    Form2.List1.Clear
    Form2.List2.Clear
    Form2.List3.Clear
    Call loadfiles
End Sub
Private Sub List1_DblClick()
    MsgBox Form1.List2.List(List3.ListIndex)
End Sub
Private Sub List2_DblClick()
    MsgBox Form1.List2.List(List3.ListIndex)
End Sub
Private Sub List3_Click()
On Error GoTo exitsub
List1.ListIndex = List3.ListIndex
List2.ListIndex = List3.ListIndex
exitsub:
End Sub
Private Sub List3_DblClick()
    MsgBox Form1.List2.List(List3.ListIndex)
End Sub
```

# Development Kit requirements and Quick-code tutorial

This kit is based on the Microsoft Direct Speech Recognition and Microsoft Direct Text-to-Speech controls that you can download from `http://activex.microsoft.com/activex/controls/agent2/actcnc.exe`. From within your programming environment, simply add the Direct Speech Recognition and Direct Text-To-Speech control to your form by right-clicking the toolbox and selecting Components. Select the Microsoft Direct Speech Recognition and Microsoft Direct Text-To-Speech items and click OK. Following is an excellent tutorial submitted by John T. Yung, entitled *Writing Your First Speech Recognition Program*.

*I recently came upon a project where a program can take in voice commands and perform tasks, such as opening a program or a file in Windows, without any mouse or keyboard input. At first, I thought that some fancy coding stuff was going on that was out of my league. On closer investigation, it was not. In fact, programming voice recognition into a software is very simple, and I am going to demonstrate how in this article.*

*Microsoft has been developing voice recognition for a few years and now has a Web site specializing in that (`www.microsoft.com/speech`). To start programming voice command recognition, you must have the Microsoft Speech Recognition Engine installed. To download a copy, visit this site: `www.microsoft.com`.*

1. *Start a project in Visual Basic. Select Standard EXE and, after all the given codes and forms are loaded, go to Project → Components.*

2. *In the Components dialog box, find and select Microsoft Direct Speech Recognition (DirectSR). Remember that this option is available only if you have the Microsoft Speech Engine installed. An icon button that looks like an ear should appear in the Toolbox bar; that is the Speech Recognition component. Click the ear icon and drag it onto the form. Now your form will have the DirectSR component icon, also shown in the code window.*

3. *Now, in the code window of the form with the DirectSR, select DirectSR from the top-right drop-down menu. (Pull down the menu to the right of that, and you can see the various methods, events, and properties the DirectSR component provides.)*

4. *In this article, the one DirectSR that we concern ourselves with is the PhraseFinish procedure. This is the procedure that is called by DirectSR after it has finished processing a voice command.*

*After you select PhraseFinish, the following code is put in place for you:*

```
Private Sub DirectSR1_PhraseFinish(ByVal flags As Long, _
```

```
        ByVal beginhi As Long, ByVal beginlo As Long, ByVal endhi
As Long, _
        ByVal endlo As Long, ByVal Phrase As String, ByVal parsed
As String, _

    ByVal results As Long)
```

There are a lot of parameters, you say? The only one that we need to be concerned with is the Phrase parameter. This parameter string contains the recognized word that was processed by the DirectSR engine.

5. Now we need to input a set of words for the Speech Engine to recognize. DirectSR has two ways for you to feed the words in during the form's Onload procedure:

- *DirectSR1.GrammarFromString* takes in a string variable that contains the words.

- *DirectSR1.GrammarFromFile* takes in a file path of a file that contains the words in text format.

*DirectSR1.GrammarFromString* provides the greatest flexibility because you can dynamically add words to the engine and still add words from a file such as *DirectSR1.GrammarFromFile* by putting the text in the file into a variable.

In the form's Load function, input the following code:

```
Dim totaldata As String

totaldata = totaldata _
    & "<start>=Notepad" & vbCrLf _
    & "<start>=Volume" & vbCrLf _
    & "<start>=Media Player" & vbCrLf

    DirectSR1.GrammarFromString (totaldata)

    DirectSR1.Activate
```

6. So this is how the string looks. For each line that contains a word, a "*<start>=*" tag is used to signify a word that follows for the DirectSR to recognize. The sample code uses three terms: Notepad, Volume, and Media Player. We use these terms for the voice command to load these programs. In addition, *DirectSR1.Activate* is used to start the engine to begin recognizing voice commands. *DirectSR1.Deactivate* stops the engine from recognizing voice commands.

*Continued*

## Development Kit requirements and
## Quick-code tutorial *(Continued)*

7. *All we need to do now is return to the PhraseFinish procedure to parse the command. Remember that the Phrase parameter is all we need to be concerned about, and study the following code:*

```
Dim sFile As String
Dim noth As Long

Select Case Phrase
        Case "Notepad"
        sFile = "\system32\notepad.exe"

        noth = ShellExecute(0, "OPEN", _
                Environ ("SystemRoot") & sFile, "", "", 1)
        Case "Volume"
        sFile = "\system32\sndvol32.exe"

        noth = ShellExecute(0, "OPEN", _
                Environ("SystemRoot") & sFile, "", "", 1)

        Case "Media Player:
        sFile = "C:\Program Files\Windows Media
Player\mplayer2.exe"

        noth = ShellExecute(0, "OPEN", _
                sFile, "", "", 1)


End Select
```

8. *Here is the lowdown: If the DirectSR recognizes a sound, it processes the sound into a word that may closely match the one that you provided. If it matches, the Phrase variable contains the matched word. The code we used is a Select Case just for the Phrase variable for the words that we fed into the engine in the Load function. After a match occurs, we use an API function* ShellExecute() *to load the program.*

   *To declare the API, put the following code on top of the form module:*

```
Declare Function ShellExecute Lib "shell32.dll"
    Alias "ShellExecuteA" (ByVal hwnd As Long, ByVal
    lpOperation As String, ByVal lpFile As String, ByVal
    lpParameters As String, ByVal lpDirectory As String,
```

```
ByVal nShowCmd As Long) As Long
```

9. *The core of the sample is basically done; however, as you know, nothing is really done without some style with the graphical user interface (GUI). Let's put a button on the form to toggle a start and stop function for the recognition. Also, let's create a label to show the status of the engine and the recognized word.*

   *Place a label on the form.*

10. *Next, place a button on the form and double-click the button to open the code. Use this code:*

```
Private Sub Command1_Click()
    Select Case Command3.Caption
    Case Is = "Disable"
        DirectSR1.Deactivate
        Command3.Caption = "Enable"
        Label1 = "Disabled"
    Case Is = "Enable"
        DirectSR1.Activate
        Command3.Caption = "Disable"
        Label1 = "Ready"
    End Select
End Sub
```

*The code is straightforward, a select case to test the button's caption. If you disable or deactivate the engine, set the button caption to Enable and set the label caption to read Disabled. If you enable or activate the engine, set the button caption to Disable and set the label caption to read Ready.*

11. Finally, we show the Phrase in the label so that the user knows what was spit out by the speech engine. We can accomplish by putting the following code in the PhraseFinish procedure:

```
If Phrase <> "" Then
    Label1.caption = "Matched word is " & Phrase

Else : Label1.caption = "No word matched"

End If
```

*Save your project. Press F5 and let the baby run. Say the command **Notepad** and watch the program open. As you can see, this is only the beginning, and the potential of voice command is as far as your imagination can take you.*

# Summary

This chapter explained the science of vocology as the underlying motivation of voice-scan and voice-recognition technologies. It also described and compared these technologies in regard to their roles in voice-recognition biometrics. Finally, it looked at an example deployment of VeriVoice — a voice verification system — and components of a development kit for custom design with a quick-code tutorial designed to get you underway for prompt proprietary development.

# Chapter 8

# Keyboard/Keystroke Dynamics

BEHAVIORAL BIOMETRICS DIFFER FROM physical biometrics in that behavioral biometric technologies use a method whereby individuals do something to uniquely identify or recognize themselves, as shown in the chapters on signature and voice biometrics. Keystroke dynamics use much the same logic.

This chapter explains keystroke dynamics technology, how it functions, and how using nothing more than a standard keyboard and keystroke dynamics can help achieve greater levels of security.

## Keystroke/Keyboard Dynamics Biometric Technology

Many of us have witnessed the philosophy on which keystroke biometrics is built. Remember when you were first introduced to typing, perhaps in a high school typing class? From the beginning of the very first class (when you actually began to type), it became apparent that individuals learn at different paces. This was often evidenced by the unsynchronized striking of the typefaces on the paper even if, say, the lesson asked you to type the letters "aaa," "bbb," "ccc," "ddd," "eee," and so on, in succession. Even with a teacher leading the charge by calling out the letters, the typing "band" was seldom, if ever, truly synchronized.

The primary reason synchronization is not truly attainable is that people type differently. Whether it's the length of time a person strikes a key, the length of time between key strikes, the pressure used to strike the key, or even the pattern used to type different phrases, peoples' typing patterns differ. This is the premise on which keystroke dynamics is built.

### Understanding Keystroke Dynamics

In uncomplicated terms, keystroke biometric technology is based on the different ways people type. If two people sit down and type the same phrase, it is extremely difficult for them to exactly match the keystroke pattern of the other, even if they type at the same speed. Even if they sound synchronized, differences will occur.

When individuals type a phrase, they use their combined/learned typing skills. The method in which they type will differ based on the following criteria:

- ✓ Typing speed
- ✓ Accuracy

✓ Length of time a key is pressed

✓ Time between key presses

✓ Pressure with which the key was pressed (requires a pressure-sensitive keyboard)

Two users can have the same typing speed and no errors when typing a simple phrase. However, the length of time each key is pressed and the time between key presses won't match exactly because individuals have a propensity for a given set of words, letters, and numbers, as well as weaknesses (relative to their strengths) relating to other words, letters, and numbers. One example would be an individual who types better with the left hand than the right. Even the fastest and most accurate typist will admit to having more difficulty with certain characters than others.

## EXPERIMENT

To test this philosophy without any biometric technology, get two (or more) family members together. On the same computer, have both of them type the following phrase.

`I live at 1957 Applecrest Blvd. Crestwave, 55055.`

As each person is typing the phrase, note the differences in speed, the number of errors each produces, the key pressure (do they type hard, soft, or somewhere in between?), the length of time each presses a key, and pauses in between key depression. You will very quickly witness how keystroke dynamics works.

This test can also be run while any one of a number of keystroke monitoring programs that exist is running on the PC.

## KEYSTROKE DYNAMICS CHALLENGE

Currently, keystroke biometric technology is used primarily as a mechanism to add security and a level of unique identification to standard password/pass code/PIN-style authentication methods. This is accomplished by implementing software at individual workstations, on servers, at the enterprise directory level, or by using a combination of these methods.

The challenge with keystroke dynamics is to as accurately as possible capture the keystrokes so that the potential of two individuals' keystrokes being close enough to cause a match is reduced. Without special keyboards, this is accomplished with software that monitors each keystroke, pressed duration, elapsed time between keystrokes, and accuracy or number of errors.

During the enrollment process, a user must type his password several times for the keystroke biometric software to obtain sufficient information on the user's typing habits, style, and traits. These traits are captured for future reference and, as with other biometric technologies, the method used for biometric template generation differs by manufacturer. However, the biometric template is typically protected using a strong encryption method or other such algorithms.

Users must type as they normally would to obtain the best keystroke dynamics template. Altering their normal typing rhythms can lead to reduced security.

## Keystroke Strengths

Keystroke technology is appealing to many organizations because it can require very little additional end-user training, and, outside of the enrollment process, the user is minimally inconvenienced. Keystroke biometric technology strengths include the following:

- ✓ Except where pressure-sensitive keyboards are required, keystroke biometric technology does not require any special hardware equipment.

- ✓ Keystroke technology can be layered on top of, integrated with, or can replace existing password technology with its own password/passphrase/PIN keystroke technology.

- ✓ Typically, the user can easily change the password depending on the implementation settings.

- ✓ Minimal user training or retraining is required.

- ✓ The cost is usually very low compared to that of other biometric technologies.

- ✓ Currently available biometric keystroke technologies do not require a large amount of overhead.

- ✓ A biometric keystroke solution typically contains the ability to alter the security level associated with the keystroke technology. Adjusting this might simply require the user to type more passwords/passphrases/PINs during the enrollment process to provide more data, while in other keystroke implementations, this might set the comparison rates and tolerances to lower percentages.

- ✓ Keystroke technology is high speed (compared to some of the other biometrics technologies).

- ✓ This technology can be leveraged with other biometric technologies in a multibiometric solution to differentiate between identical twins and look-alikes.

## Keystroke Weaknesses

Keystroke biometric technology currently has many weaknesses, mostly because keyboard/keystroke dynamics technology is relatively new compared to other biometric technologies. Many of these weaknesses are also normally associated with standard password protection. This is because keystroke dynamics technology (relating to network security) is most often integrated with, layered on top of, or used as a replacement for standard password authentication. Keystroke technology weaknesses include the following:

✓ Users' typing skills can change over time, causing the user to become unrecognized (false reject).

✓ Because programs exist that can monitor keystrokes, the possibility exists that a replay attack or playback can provide sufficient data to trick the keystroke biometric solution, leading to a false accept.

✓ Although difficult, one user matching both the password and the keystroke dynamics of another user is not impossible. This could lead to a false accept.

✓ Remote access and portability might be difficult to achieve on some systems.

✓ Different keyboards can pose challenges to both the user and the biometric keystroke technology. On a different keyboard, a user might not be identified because that user could enter the information differently enough to cause a false reject. Additionally, the timing of some keyboards (clock speeds) may differ enough between systems to cause false rejects.

✓ Because keystroke technology leverages password-type authentication technology, the enrollment process is often not monitored. This can lead to false enrollment of users.

✓ Keystroke technology is not considered as mature as other biometric technologies because it has not been around as long.

✓ Because keystroke technology does not get rid of the need for passwords and should still be used in conjunction with strong password policies, it does not reduce the costs associated with password resets and help desk password issues.

✓ Keystroke dynamics technology generally does not provide the end user with additional convenience. However, it is feasible that multiple passwords could be used on non-keystroke-enabled systems, and password replacement could occur using only the keystroke login password/security.

## FACT/FICTION

As with the other biometric technologies, some common beliefs (some false, some true) exist about keystroke dynamics technology. Thoroughly understanding these and anticipating additional beliefs is important to properly educate users.

### TABLE 8-1: Beliefs and Facts about Keystroke Dynamics Technology

| Belief | Fact |
|---|---|
| No one can gain access when using keystroke biometrics technology, even if the password is known. Therefore, I don't have to protect my password. | Although an intruder gaining access to a system running keystroke biometric technology is difficult, the fact remains that someone can either replay or match the entry pattern; therefore, passwords must be kept secret. |

| Belief | Fact |
| --- | --- |
| Because it is more difficult for an intruder to obtain access when using keystroke dynamics, passwords do not have to be changed. | Although it may be more difficult for a user to gain access when using keystroke dynamics, the fact remains that changing passwords regularly, and requiring unique, new passwords (not simply adding or changing a character) makes it more difficult for hackers. |
| When using keystroke technology, strong passwords are not important. | Although using keystroke technology does add an additional level of protection, strong passwords or strong passphrases are still highly recommended. |

Refer to Table 8-2 for general characteristics of keystroke biometrics.

### TABLE 8-2: Keyboard Technology Characteristics and Dynamics

| Characteristics | Ease of Use | Error Incidence | Accuracy | Acceptance | Security Level | Stability | Cost |
| --- | --- | --- | --- | --- | --- | --- | --- |
| Keyboard Dynamics | High | Mistype, change in rhythm, change in pressure | Medium | High | Medium Low | Medium | low |

Keystroke technology is not yet considered mature. Additionally, the amount of data available for determining crossover error rate (CER) is limited. Therefore, you can still find CERs for keystroke technology that range from 2 percent and up. We have seen CERs at greater than 16 percent. For more information on CER refer to Chapter 1.

## KEYSTROKE COUNTERMEASURES

Although keystroke dynamics might seem heavy on weaknesses, remember that keystroke technology is additive to standard password technology; many of the weaknesses can be greatly reduced using some common countermeasures. Because keystroke dynamics uses password/passphrase/PIN-type authentication technology as its root, many of the weaknesses are the same as those for standard password/passphrase/PIN authentication technology. The list below provides some countermeasures available for keystroke dynamics technology:

✓ **Users typing skills change** — Have the users re-enroll periodically. This can often be accomplished automatically by requiring periodic password changes/periodic re-enrollments.

✓ **Playback attacks** — Implementing pressure-sensitive keyboards can reduce the possibility of using keystroke-monitoring tools for playback attacks, because many do not have the ability to track the information associated with pressure-sensitive keyboards.

✓ **Pattern matching** — You can minimize this weakness by implementing pressure-sensitive keyboards and increasing the sensitivity, where possible.

✓ **Remote access** — To ensure remote access, select and implement a system that incorporates and/or supports the remote access technologies to be used in the environment (for example, VPN, wireless, and so on), and can accurately validate users typing biometrics from multiple sources (however, this can also create an additional weakness because such a system might not be as sensitive as a nonremote solution).

✓ **Different keyboards** — Where possible, use similar keyboards. Additionally, selecting a product that determines a user's pattern on many keyboards can limit this issue. However, such a product is probably not as strong as one that is more sensitive.

✓ **Unmonitored authentication process** — To address this issue, formalize, monitor, and manage the enrollment process. Require formalized re-enrollment. Remember that this can be administratively unfeasible in large or very distributed organizations.

✓ **User convenience** — If user convenience is a concern, selecting a product that includes a Software Development Kit (SDK) might provide the solution. Using the SDK might allow development of user conveniences such as WEB and encryption authentication username and password replacement using the keystroke biometrics credentials.

For an additional measure of security, implement a solution that checks for and monitors other software programs that monitor keystrokes.

Another method that can be used with some keystroke technologies is to intentionally type and then substitute characters. For example, typing test0, then backspacing over the 0 and replacing it with a 1 can provide an additional level of security. However, many products (such as the one shown in the example that follows) view this as an error and require the user to re-start the authentication process.

# Sample Product Implementation

BioPassword, from Net Nanny Software International, Inc., increases Windows security by adding keystroke dynamics to the Windows logon process.

BioPassword is software-based and does not require any special keyboards or other equipment. BioPassword operates on Microsoft Windows XP, Home or Professional, Windows 2000 Professional, and Windows NT 4.0.

This example shows the installation of BioPassword, as well as the enrollment process. After enrollment has been accomplished, you will see how to increase the security level from the default installation value.

Before you begin the installation of BioPassword, make sure your system meets the minimum requirements. For all versions of Windows, the following minimum system requirements are recommended:

✓ Windows XP Home or Professional, Windows 2000 Professional, Windows NT 4.0

✓ 64MB memory

✓ 7MB hard drive space available

✓ 133MHz or higher Pentium or Pentium-compatible Processor (Intel, AMD, and so on)

✓ Standard keyboard, mouse, and monitor

✓ Latest patches and fixes

## BioPassword Software Installation

The BioPassword software can be electronically downloaded after purchase. Before beginning the installation, ensure that you are logged on to the PC with Administrator rights. After the download is complete, begin the software installation by double-clicking the downloaded file icon. In this case, BioPassword will be installed on a PC with Windows XP Professional.

**1.** After you double-click the file icon (BP127LP4508.exe), the installation begins with the InstallShield Wizard screen shown in Figure 8-1.

**Figure 8-1:** InstallShield Wizard

**2.** The installation proceeds automatically. The next screen shows what operating system was detected, as illustrated in Figure 8-2.

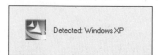

**Figure 8-2:** OS Detection

**3.** In this example, Windows XP is the detected operating system. The installation again proceeds automatically to the BP-127 BioPassword Logon Protection Setup window shown in Figure 8-3.

**Figure 8-3:** BioPassword Logon Protection Setup

**4.** In this example, Fast User Switching is enabled. To install BioPassword, Fast User Switching must be disabled. Consult the Windows documentation for instructions on how to disable Fast User Switching.

Here, disable Fast User Switching by selecting Start → Control Panel → User Accounts → Change the way users log on and off, and by deselecting the checkbox next to the Use Fast User Switching option and clicking the Apply Options button. The end result is shown in Figure 8-4.

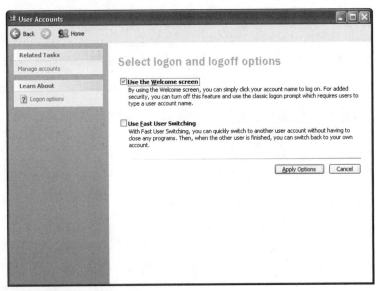

**Figure 8-4:** Disable Fast User Switching

**5.** After Fast User Switching has been disabled, you can again begin the installation process. The BioPassword installation process again displays the screens shown in Figures 8-1 and 8-2, and proceeds automatically. Again, the BP-127 BioPassword Logon Protection screen is shown; however, it now displays a username and password strength recommendation screen, as illustrated in Figure 8-5.

**Figure 8-5:** Password Strength

**6.** To continue the installation, click the OK button. The next screen that appears is the Setup Welcome screen shown in Figure 8-6.

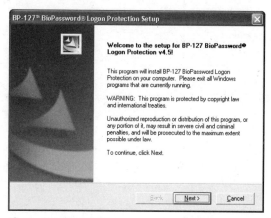

**Figure 8-6:** Setup Welcome

**7.** Click Next and the installation continues to the license agreement screen shown in Figure 8-7.

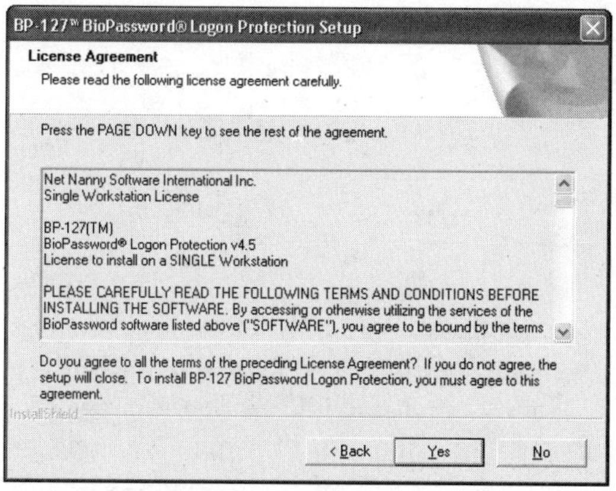

**Figure 8-7:** License Agreement

8. Select Yes to continue the installation. The installation proceeds to the License Key entry screen shown in Figure 8-8.

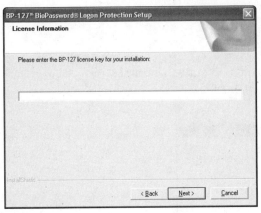

**Figure 8-8:** License Key Entry

9. Enter the license key obtained from the purchase information for BioPassword. After successfully entering the license key information, click the Next button to continue the installation. The Read Me window is displayed, as illustrated in Figure 8-9.

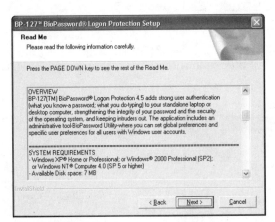

**Figure 8-9:** Read Me

10. View the information in the Read Me file by scrolling down. An overview of the product and the system requirements, as well as other types of information, is provided. Here you can make sure one final time that the system has met the minimum requirements. Click Next to continue with the installation. The Choose Destination Location screen appears, as shown in Figure 8-10.

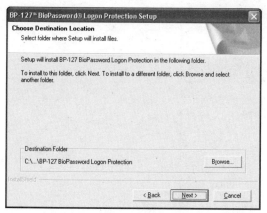

**Figure 8-10:** Choose Destination Location

**11.** Change the location to which BioPassword files will be copied, or simply click Next to continue the installation using the default location. The installation process continues, and the Select Program Folder window appears, as shown in Figure 8-11.

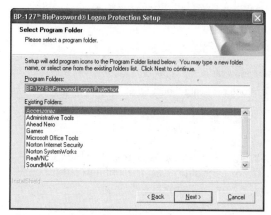

**Figure 8-11:** Select Program Folder

**12.** Select an existing folder to contain the BioPassword program icons, or click Next without any changes to create the BP-127 BioPassword Logon Protection program folder, and place the BioPassword program icons into it. The installation continues and the Administrator Account Verification window is displayed, as shown in Figure 8-12.

**Figure 8-12:** Account Verification Window

**13.** Type in the administrator account username and password for the PC. This example uses an administrator account named XPAdmin with a password of hardpass (all lowercase, no quotes). After successfully entering the account information and clicking OK, the Challenge/Response Questions and Answers window is displayed, as shown in Figure 8-13.

This example uses a simple password to easily depict the process. However, using a strong password is highly recommended. A strong password would be at least eight characters long and would contain upper and lowercase letters, numbers, and special symbols.

**14.** Because BioPassword is based on typing rhythms, a user must be able to type in his normal typing rhythm. If an administrator cannot do this, the Challenge/Response Questions and Answers will allow the administrator access.

A user may not be able to type using his or her normal rhythms in the event of hand or finger injuries, as well as other afflictions.

Type challenge and response information that is easy for you to remember, but difficult for anyone else to guess. For example, use a question that only you know the answer to, such as your secret hiding place.

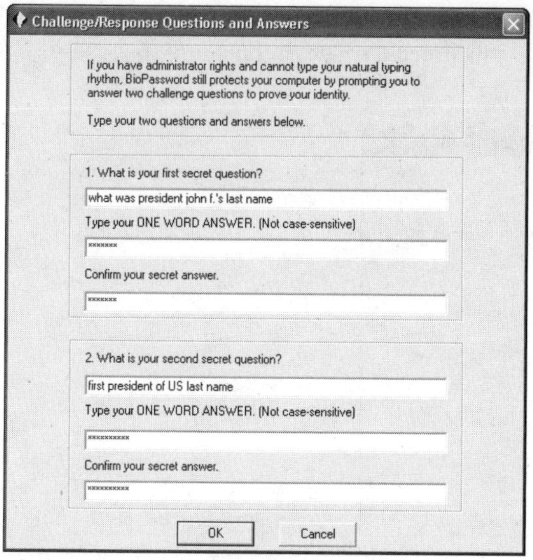

**Figure 8-13:** Challenge/Response

Select two of these types of secret questions, and enter both the questions and answers in the appropriate fields (only 56 characters can be used for the questions). (This example uses common information to enable user understanding; however, we strongly advise against using any information that might be easily guessed.) After the information has been entered, click Next to display the Start Copying Files window shown in Figure 8-14.

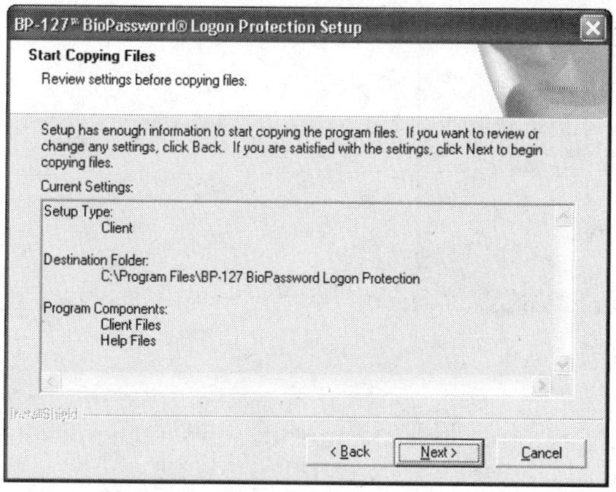

**Figure 8-14:** Start Copying Files

**15.** Confirm the settings in the window before continuing. If no changes are required, click Next to start the file copy Setup Status process shown in Figure 8-15.

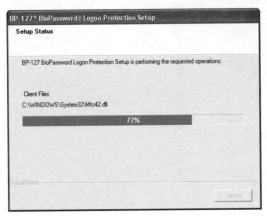

**Figure 8-15:** Setup Status

**16.** Upon successful completion of the file copy process, the Finish screen is displayed, as illustrated in Figure 8-16.

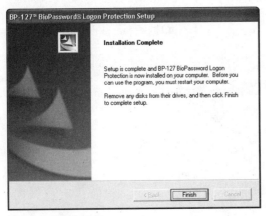

**Figure 8-16:** Finish Screen

**17.** Click Finish to bring up the Password Strength recommendation screen previously shown in Figure 8-5. Again, click OK to continue. A Warning message appears, indicating that the system will be rebooted. This message is shown in Figure 8-17.

**Figure 8-17:** Reboot Warning

**18.** Click OK to continue and the PC reboots. After the system has rebooted, you will be prompted with the Log On to Windows screen shown in Figure 8-18.

**Figure 8-18:** Windows Logon

**19.** Re-enter your username and password (XPAdmin and hardpass in this example). After successfully entering the information, hit Enter or select OK to continue. The User Registration/first time user entry screen appears, as shown in Figure 8-19.

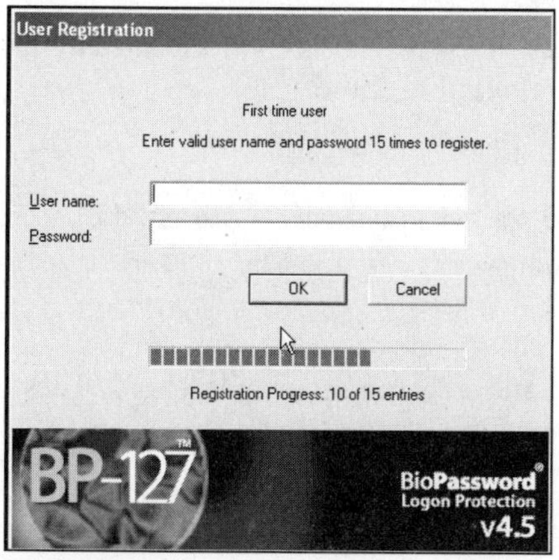

**Figure 8-19** First Time User Enrollment

**20.** This is the beginning of the enrollment process. The username and password must be successfully entered 15 times (the default for BioPassword) for enrollment to occur. Based on the information in Figure 8-19, ten entries have been successfully made, and five entries remain.

Entering `XPAdmin` and `hardpass` 15 times completes the enrollment process. An indication that the process was successful is displayed as shown in Figure 8-20.

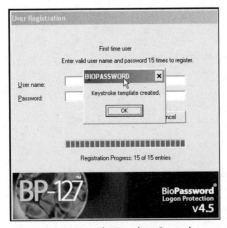

**Figure 8-20:** Keystroke Template Created

**21.** Click the OK button to log on to the PC.

Upon subsequent logins, the user will simply have to accurately enter the login credentials in the appropriate manner to be authenticated.

# Modifying BioPassword Defaults

Additional users are created as they would normally be using User Accounts located in the Control Panel. A user logging in for the first time will be required to enroll.

> The enrollment process should be formal, tracked, monitored, and supervised by appropriate security team and management members, at the very least during the initial enrollment process.

BioPassword defaults to 15 enrollment entries and a default security level of 3. These settings can be modified using the BioPassword utility shown in Figure 8-21.

**Figure 8-21:** Starting BioPassword Utility

Executing the utility brings up the screen shown in Figure 8-22.

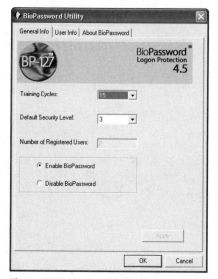

**Figure 8-22:** BioPassword Utility General Info

From the General User tab of the BioPassword utility, you can change the Training Cycles (number of accurate templates required during enrollment, 10 to 20), the Default Security Level (keystroke dynamic strength, 1 = lowest through 10 = highest), and the ability to enable or disable BioPassword use.

Selecting the BioPassword Utility's User Info tab displays the information shown in Figure 8-23.

**Figure 8-23:** BioPassword Utility User Info

Within the BioPassword Utility User Info screen, you can enable Authentication and modify the security setting for each user individually or collectively by selecting the appropriate user and changing the settings, or by clicking the Select All Users button and changing the Authentication and/or Security settings. In this fashion, users' security levels can be adjusted individually or disabled. For example, if only Administrator accounts need to use BioPassword, BioPassword could be enabled for the Administrator accounts using a high security level (8 or higher), and disabled for standard user accounts.

## BioPassword Notes

Although BioPassword increases the level of security associated with passwords, it does not increase user convenience. In fact, it can actually decrease user convenience because the enrollment process requires users to enter their credentials ten to twenty times. Additionally, costs due to password resets (both help desk and lost productivity) are not reduced because users will still lose or forget their passwords.

However, it is our opinion that the additional security benefits outweigh the intrusiveness and inconvenience associated with the template generation, because this only occurs during the enrollment process or when the password is changed.

Finally, the Challenge/Response Questions and Answers provide a means for a user with Administrator rights who can't type using his or her normal typing rhythms to gain access. The username and password of that administrative user are still required, but after entering the correct information three times with a different typing rhythm, the Administrative user can select the Assistance button and then be prompted with a Challenge/Response screen. When the Administrative user enters the responses correctly, access is granted.

# Summary

This chapter briefly explained how the method in which users type is used by keystroke dynamics technology to assist in uniquely identifying an individual. Even the typing of identical twins will probably vary enough to allow them to be uniquely and individually identified.

This chapter illustrated how keyboard/keystroke dynamics can be used to strengthen password/passcode/passphrase security, noting that it is vitally important that users type normally during both the enrollment process and for subsequent authentications. The chapter discussed strengths and weaknesses of keyboard/keystroke dynamics technology and listed some common counter-measures that can be employed to reduce some of these weaknesses.

The "Sample Product Implementation" section illustrated how keyboard/keystroke dynamics technology can be implemented on a standalone workstation. This section described the installation process, enrollment process, and tuning. Although the illustration was depicted for a standalone workstation, the knowledge, understanding, and methodologies can be applied to larger, more integrated, network-based implementations using the appropriate solution.

Keyboard/keystroke dynamics can be used to strengthen password-type security; however, it does not provide the benefits of additional user convenience and reduced support costs due to password resets, as is the case with many of the other biometric technologies. Keystroke technology is unlikely to become as accepted as many of the other biometric technologies. However, if the goal is purely to add additional security with limited end-user training and no additional hardware at a reasonable cost, keyboard/keystroke dynamics is a good choice.

# Chapter 9

# Hiding Data with Passphrases

As we briefly discussed in Chapter 1, strong or two-factor authentication is identifying oneself via two of the three methods of something you *know* (for example, a password), something you *have* (for example, a swipe card or token), and something you *are* (for example, your fingerprint). Given that many passwords can be easily cracked and most first-level authentication and identification programs or systems can likely be circumvented, strong authentication is becoming more of a de facto standard in secure computing environments. Some sensitive computing locations even mandate multi-factor authentication, which combines all three methods (something you know, have, and are) before encountering access control mechanisms that are protecting confidential information.

Hiding data, or, more appropriately, the art of hiding information within other messages or images, which is known as *steganography*, is basically replacing unused bits of a file with bits of a hidden message. This chapter presents a discussion of ways to utilize this technology by using biometric images (as shown in Figure 9-1) and to secure the decoding process by using a passphrase for inclusion in a strong authentication scheme.

 The term *steganography* means "covered writing." The practice dates back to ancient Greece, where messages were etched into wooden tablets and then covered with wax or created by shaving a messenger's head and then tattooing a secret message on it, letting his hair grow back, and then shaving it again after he arrived at the receiving party to reveal the message.

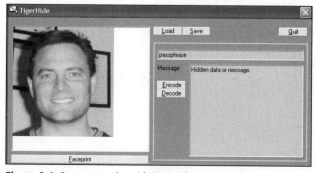

**Figure 9-1:** Steganography with TigerHide

# Technically Speaking: Pixels, Bits, Binary, and Hex

Before discussing the kernel elements of steganography for a biometric authentication scheme, we want to review the technical descriptions of pixels, bits, binary, and hex. A *pixel* (picture element) is a point in an image. Graphic video cards display images on monitors made up of thousands or even millions of pixels. The pixels are so small and jam-packed that, at a distance, they appear as one image on-screen. The number of bits used to represent each pixel decides how many colors can be displayed. Using an 8-bit mode means that eight bits are used for each pixel, and the more bits that you use per pixe,l the better is the quality of the imaging. For example, 32-bit true-color video cards use 32 bits per pixel, enabling them to display more than 16 million different colors.

A *bit* is actually an abbreviation for *binary digit*, which represents the smallest unit of information on a computer. A bit is comprised of the value 0 or 1. On a similar note, a *byte* is eight consecutive bits. Data entered into applications running on a computer commonly use decimal format. Decimals are numbers that we use in everyday life that do not have a decimal point in them (for example, 1, 16, 18, 26, and 30) — any random number. After decimal numbers are entered into the computer, the system converts them into binary format, 0s and 1s, which basically correlates to electrical charges — charged versus uncharged. IP addresses, for example, are subnetted and calculated by using *binary* notation.

The eight bits that make a potential number are equated in the following manner:

| Bit: | 1 | 2 | 3 | 4 | 5 | 6 | 7 | 8 |
|---|---|---|---|---|---|---|---|---|
| Value: | 128 | 64 | 32 | 16 | 8 | 4 | 2 | 1 |

Look at the number 224. If a bit is used, it is charged with a 1; otherwise, use 0, as follows:

| Bits: | 1 | 1 | 1 | 0 | 0 | 0 | 0 | 0 |
|---|---|---|---|---|---|---|---|---|
| Value: | 128 | 64 | 32 | 16 | 8 | 4 | 2 | 1 |

Add the decimal value of the bits: 128 + 64 + 32 = 224. The binary value 11100000 equates to the decimal value 224, as follows:

| Decimal | Binary |
|---|---|
| 224 | 11100000 |

The *hexadecimal* system is a form of binary shorthand. Internet-working equipment, such as routers, use this format while formulating headers to easily indicate Token Ring numbers, bridge numbers, networks, and so on to reduce header sizes and transmission congestion. Typically, *hex* is derived from the binary format, which is derived from decimal. Hex was designed so that the eight bits in the binary 11100000 (Decimal = 224) equates to only two hex characters, each representing four bits.

To clarify, take a look at the binary value for 224 again: 11100000.

In hex, you break this eight-bit number into four-bit pairs, as follows:

1110          0000

Each bit in the four-bit pairs has a decimal value, starting from left to right: 8, 4, 2, and then 1 for the last bit, as follows:

8 4 2 1          8 4 2 1
1 1 1 0          0 0 0 0

Now we add the bits that are "on," or that have a 1 in each of the four-bit pairs, as follows:

8 4 2 1 = 8 + 4 + 2 + 0 = 14          8 4 2 1 = 0 + 0 + 0 + 0 = 0
1 1 1 0               0 0 0 0

In this example, the decimal values that represent the hex characters in each of the four-bit pairs are 14 and 0. To convert these to actual hex, use Table 9-1. Using this chart, the hex conversion for the decimals 14 and 0 (14 for the first four-bit pair and 0 for the second four-bit pair) equals e0.

**TABLE 9-1: Sample Hex Comparison Chart**

| Decimal | Binary | Hex |
| --- | --- | --- |
| 0 | 0000 | 0 |
| 1 | 0001 | 1 |
| 2 | 0010 | 2 |
| 3 | 0011 | 3 |
| 4 | 0100 | 4 |
| 5 | 0101 | 5 |
| 6 | 0110 | 6 |
| 7 | 0111 | 7 |
| 8 | 1000 | 8 |
| 9 | 1001 | 9 |
| 10 | 1010 | a |
| 11 | 1011 | b |

*Continued*

**TABLE 9-1: Sample Hex Comparison Chart** *(Continued)*

| Decimal | Binary | Hex |
|---------|-----------|-----|
| 12 | 1100 | c |
| 13 | 1101 | d |
| 14 | 1110 | e |
| 15 | 1111 | f |
| 16 | 0001 0000 | 10 |
| 17 | 0001 0001 | 11 |
| 18 | 0001 0010 | 12 |
| 19 | 0001 0011 | 13 |
| 20 | 0001 0100 | 14 |

 For the full hex conversion chart, visit the companion Web site at www.wiley.com/ compbooks/chirillo.

This last example converts the decimal number 185 to binary, as follows:

| Bits: | 1 | 0 | 1 | 1 | 1 | 0 | 0 | 1 | |
|-------|-----|----|----|----|---|---|---|---|-------|
| Value: | 128 | 64 | 32 | 16 | 8 | 4 | 2 | 1 | = 185 |

The binary for 185 is 10111001 (bits, as indicated above).
Now convert the binary number 10111001 to hex, which you break into 4-bit pairs, as follows:
1011          1001

Each bit in the four-bit pairs has a decimal value, starting from left to right: 8, 4, 2, and then 1 for the last bit, as follows:

8 4 2 1        8 4 2 1
1 0 1 1        1 0 0 1

Now, add the bits that have a 1 in each of the four-bit pairs, as follows:

8 4 2 1 = 8 + 0 + 2 + 1 = 11        8 4 2 1 = 8 + 0 + 0 + 1 = 9
1 0 1 1        1 0 0 1

Using the hex chart, the hex conversion for the decimals 11 and 9 (11 for the first four-bit pair and 9 for the second four-bit pair) = b9, as shown here:

| Decimal | Binary | Hex |
| --- | --- | --- |
| 185 | 10111001 | b9 |
| 224 | 11100000 | e0 |

## Examining the Hex of a Hidden Message

As discussed earlier, an encoded image or file can replace unused bits of a file with bits of a hidden message. With that said, a standard unconcealed message file's hex dump might look like the one shown in Figure 9-2. By using any hex editor, you can clearly read the message within the file. Similarly, the hex dump of an image file without an encoded message is as shown in Figure 9-3. Compare it with that of the same image that includes an encoded "hidden" message using steganography, as shown in Figure 9-4. Obviously, the file size of the last image increases to accommodate the hidden message. What's more, the message is encrypted—which adds to the size of the file as well—to further protect it from prying eyes through means such as *steganalysis,* which is the art of discovering steganographic data.

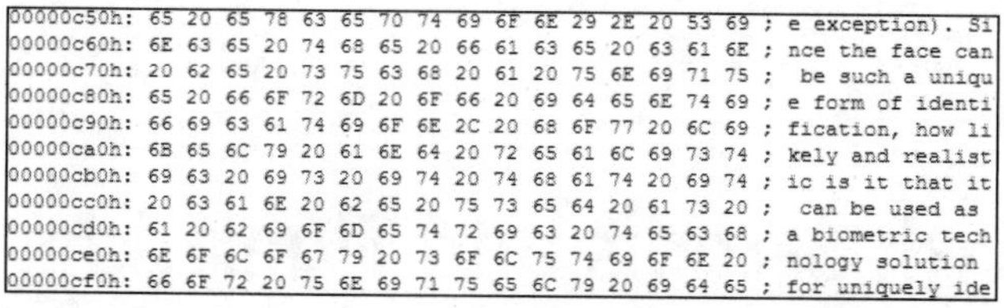

```
00000c50h: 65 20 65 78 63 65 70 74 69 6F 6E 29 2E 20 53 69 ; e exception). Si
00000c60h: 6E 63 65 20 74 68 65 20 66 61 63 65 20 63 61 6E ; nce the face can
00000c70h: 20 62 65 20 73 75 63 68 20 61 20 75 6E 69 71 75 ;  be such a uniqu
00000c80h: 65 20 66 6F 72 6D 20 6F 66 20 69 64 65 6E 74 69 ; e form of identi
00000c90h: 66 69 63 61 74 69 6F 6E 2C 20 68 6F 77 20 6C 69 ; fication, how li
00000ca0h: 6B 65 6C 79 20 61 6E 64 20 72 65 61 6C 69 73 74 ; kely and realist
00000cb0h: 69 63 20 69 73 20 69 74 20 74 68 61 74 20 69 74 ; ic is it that it
00000cc0h: 20 63 61 6E 20 62 65 20 75 73 65 64 20 61 73 20 ;  can be used as
00000cd0h: 61 20 62 69 6F 6D 65 74 72 69 63 20 74 65 63 68 ; a biometric tech
00000ce0h: 6E 6F 6C 6F 67 79 20 73 6F 6C 75 74 69 6F 6E 20 ; nology solution
00000cf0h: 66 6F 72 20 75 6E 69 71 75 65 6C 79 20 69 64 65 ; for uniquely ide
```

**Figure 9-2:** Hex strings of file with unconcealed text message

```
00000000h: 42 4D 68 EC 01 00 00 00 00 00 36 00 00 00 28 00 ; BMhì......6...(.
00000010h: 00 00 C8 00 00 00 D2 00 00 00 01 00 18 00 00 00 ; ..È...Ò.........
00000020h: 00 00 00 00 00 00 12 0B 00 00 12 0B 00 00 00 00 ; ................
00000030h: 00 00 00 00 00 00 34 38 36 37 3A 36 39 3C 37 3E ; ......4867:69<7>
00000040h: 3E 3A 41 3C 3B 40 38 38 3E 36 35 3D 32 33 3C 30 ; >:A<;@88>65=23<0
00000050h: 33 39 2D 32 36 2B 30 36 2A 2F 38 2C 30 39 2D 32 ; 39-26+06*/8,09-2
00000060h: 38 2D 31 35 2D 31 33 2D 30 34 2D 30 34 2B 2E 35 ; 8-15-13-04-04+.5
00000070h: 2B 2D 38 2D 2F 38 2E 30 34 2B 2C 32 2A 2E 32 2B ; +-8-/8.04+,2*.2+
00000080h: 2F 33 2B 2F 34 2D 30 35 2C 2F 35 2C 30 36 2C 31 ; /3+/4-05,/5,06,1
00000090h: 36 2A 2F 35 29 2F 37 2A 32 39 2D 35 51 4C 58 74 ; 6*/5)/7*29-5QLXt
000000a0h: 7F 8B 72 84 8D 7E 83 8C 87 91 A1 5F 73 8C 52 50 ; □‹r„□~ƒŒ‡'¡_sŒRP
000000b0h: 65 80 7E 90 73 8A 98 76 80 8B 90 90 99 86 8E 91 ; e€~□sŠ˜v€‹□□™†Ž'
000000c0h: 5F 61 66 48 4C 5A 53 60 76 70 7F 98 71 88 A2 6C ; _afHLZS`vp□˜qˆ¢l
000000d0h: 88 A2 6C 87 A0 68 85 9D 66 83 9A 67 84 9B 6C 88 ; ˆ¢l‡ h…□fƒšg„›lˆ
000000e0h: 9E 6D 88 A0 6E 89 A6 72 8B A9 73 8A AB 77 8E B3 ; žmˆ n‰¦r‹©sŠ«wŽ³
000000f0h: 7D 96 B9 83 9F BC 8A A7 C0 8D AC C4 94 B0 C7 9C ; }–¹ƒŸ¼Š§À□¬Ä”°Çœ
00000100h: B4 CA 9F B5 C9 9F B6 CA 9F B6 CC 9F B9 CE 9F B9 ; ´ÊŸµÉŸ¶ÊŸ¶ÌŸ¹ÎŸ¹
00000110h: CE A0 BA CF A3 BE D1 A2 BD D0 A2 BC D1 A4 BF D4 ; Î ºÏ£¾Ñ¢½Ð¢¼Ñ¤¿Ô
00000120h: A6 C1 D6 AA C3 D7 AC C5 D8 AB C3 D8 AA C2 D8 AA ; ¦ÁÖªÃ×¬ÅØ«ÃØªÂØª
00000130h: C1 D7 A9 BF D8 AD C1 D8 AC C1 D7 AA BF D6 AC C0 ; Á×©¿Ø-ÁØ¬Á×ª¿Ö¬À
00000140h: D6 AB C0 D5 AA BE D3 AC BE D4 AD C0 D4 AC C0 D5 ; Ö«ÀÕª¾Ó¬¾Ô-ÀÔ¬ÀÕ
00000150h: AB BF D4 AA BF D2 AB C0 D4 AA C0 D5 AB C0 D6 AD ; «¿Ôª¿Ò«ÀÔªÀÕ«ÀÖ-
00000160h: C2 D7 AE C3 D7 AE C1 D7 AE C0 D6 AE C2 D6 AF C2 ; Â×®Ã×®Á×®ÀÖ®ÂÖ¯Â
00000170h: D6 AE C1 D5 AE C1 D5 AE C1 D5 B0 C2 D6 B2 C3 D7 ; Ö®ÁÕ®ÁÕ®ÁÕ°ÂÖ²Ã×
00000180h: B0 C2 D7 AF C2 D8 AF C1 D8 AB BE D7 AB BE D7 AB ; °Â×¯ÂØ¯ÁØ«¾×«¾×«
00000190h: BF D8 AB BF D8 AB BF D9 AB BF DA AD C0 DA AE C1 ; ¿Ø«¿Ø«¿Ù«¿Ú-ÀÚ®Á
```

**Figure 9-3:** Hex strings of image without encoded hidden message

```
00000000h: 42 4D 16 53 04 00 00 00 00 00 36 00 00 00 28 00 ; BM.S......6...(.
00000010h: 00 00 75 01 00 00 FD 00 00 00 01 00 18 00 00 00 ; ..u...ý.........
00000020h: 00 00 E0 52 04 00 00 00 00 00 00 00 00 00 00 00 ; ..àR............
00000030h: 00 00 00 00 00 00 FF FF FF FF FF FF FF FF FF FF ; ......ÿÿÿÿÿÿÿÿÿÿ
00000040h: FF FF FF FF FF FF FF FF FF FF FF FF FF FF FF FF ; ÿÿÿÿÿÿÿÿÿÿÿÿÿÿÿÿ
00000050h: FF FF FF FF FF FF FF FF FF FF FF FF FF FF FF FF ; ÿÿÿÿÿÿÿÿÿÿÿÿÿÿÿÿ
00000060h: FF FF FF FF FF FF FF FF FF FF FF FF FF FF FF FF ; ÿÿÿÿÿÿÿÿÿÿÿÿÿÿÿÿ
00000070h: FF FF FF FF FF FF FF FF FF FF FF FF FF FF FF FF ; ÿÿÿÿÿÿÿÿÿÿÿÿÿÿÿÿ
00000080h: FF FF FF FF FF FF FF FF FF FF FF FF FF FF FF FF ; ÿÿÿÿÿÿÿÿÿÿÿÿÿÿÿÿ
00000090h: FF FF FF FF FF FF FF FF FF FF FF FF FF FF FF FF ; ÿÿÿÿÿÿÿÿÿÿÿÿÿÿÿÿ
000000a0h: FF FF FF FF FF FF FF FF FF FF FF FF FF FF FF FF ; ÿÿÿÿÿÿÿÿÿÿÿÿÿÿÿÿ
000000b0h: FF FF FF FF FF FF FF FF FF FF FF FF FF FF FF FF ; ÿÿÿÿÿÿÿÿÿÿÿÿÿÿÿÿ
000000c0h: FF FF FF FF FF FF FF FF FF FF FF FF FF FF FF FF ; ÿÿÿÿÿÿÿÿÿÿÿÿÿÿÿÿ
000000d0h: FF FF FF FF FF FF FF FF FF FF FF FF FF FF FF FF ; ÿÿÿÿÿÿÿÿÿÿÿÿÿÿÿÿ
000000e0h: FF FF FF FF FF FF FF FF FF FF FF FF FF FF FF FF ; ÿÿÿÿÿÿÿÿÿÿÿÿÿÿÿÿ
000000f0h: FF FF FF FF FF FF FF FF FF FF FF FF FF FF FF FF ; ÿÿÿÿÿÿÿÿÿÿÿÿÿÿÿÿ
00000100h: FF FF FF FF FF FF FF FF FF FF FF FF FF FF FF FF ; ÿÿÿÿÿÿÿÿÿÿÿÿÿÿÿÿ
00000110h: FF FF FF FF FF FF FF FF FF FF FF FF FF FF FF FF ; ÿÿÿÿÿÿÿÿÿÿÿÿÿÿÿÿ
00000120h: FF FF FF FF FF FF FF FF FF FF FF FF FF FF FF FF ; ÿÿÿÿÿÿÿÿÿÿÿÿÿÿÿÿ
00000130h: FF FF FF FF FF FF FF FF FF FF FF FF FF FF FF FF ; ÿÿÿÿÿÿÿÿÿÿÿÿÿÿÿÿ
00000140h: FF FF FF FF FF FF FF FF FF FF FF FF FF FF FF FF ; ÿÿÿÿÿÿÿÿÿÿÿÿÿÿÿÿ
00000150h: FF FF FF FF FF FF FF FF FF FF FF FF FF FF FF FF ; ÿÿÿÿÿÿÿÿÿÿÿÿÿÿÿÿ
00000160h: FF FF FF FF FF FF FF FF FF FF FF FF FF FF FF FF ; ÿÿÿÿÿÿÿÿÿÿÿÿÿÿÿÿ
00000170h: FF FF FF FF FF FF FF FF FF FF FF FF FF FF FF FF ; ÿÿÿÿÿÿÿÿÿÿÿÿÿÿÿÿ
00000180h: FF FF FF FF FF FF FF FF FF FF FF FF FF FF FF FF ; ÿÿÿÿÿÿÿÿÿÿÿÿÿÿÿÿ
00000190h: FF FF FF FF FF FF FF FF FF FF FF FF FF FF FF FF ; ÿÿÿÿÿÿÿÿÿÿÿÿÿÿÿÿ
```

**Figure 9-4:** Hex strings of image with encoded hidden message

# Steganography with S-Tools and TigerHide

*TigerHide* is simply a source software development tool of kernel modules that you can freely modify to use in your own development. Other precompiled steganography programs and trial software can be downloaded from the Internet, such as the well-liked S-Tools from `www.pcworld.com/downloads/file_download/0,fid,4699,fileidx,1,00.asp`.

## S-Tools

Since the advent of computers, there has been a vast dissemination of information, some of which needs to be kept private and some of which does not. Steganography Tools (S-Tools) brings you the capability of concealing files within various forms of data. The key to most steganography applications is digital data, such as a scanned image or a sampled sound. Most computer data must be 100 percent accurate to function correctly, but digitally sampled data need not be. By making subtle alterations to sampled data, you can conceal information while retaining nearly all the content of the original sample.

S-Tools users can opt to encrypt their information by using the strongest state-of-the-art encryption algorithms currently known within the academic world so that even an enemy equipped with a copy of S-Tools cannot be completely sure that data is hidden unless he has your secret passphrase. You could use S-Tools to conceal private or confidential information that you don't want falling into the wrong hands. You could use it to send information to another individual via a broadcast network, such as Usenet. By agreeing on a passphrase, you can keep the information out of unauthorized hands. Alternatively, you could use S-Tools to verify your copyright of an image by storing an encrypted copyright statement in the graphic and extracting it in the event of a dispute. In short, S-Tools enables you to place private information in an inconspicuous "envelope" that does not arouse suspicion.

## HOW DATA IS HIDDEN IN PICTURES

All computer-based pictures are composed of an array of dots (pixels) that make up a very fine grid. Each one of these pixels has its own color, represented internally as separate quantities of red, green, and blue. Within Windows, each of these color levels may range from 0 (none of the color) to 255 (a full amount of the color). A pixel with a red, green, blue (RGB) value of 0 0 0 is black, and one with a value of 255 255 255 is white.

S-Tools works by "spreading" the bit pattern of the file that you want to hide across the least-significant bits (LSBs) of the color levels in the image. For a 24-bit image, this is simple because 24-bit images are stored internally as RGB triples, and all you need to do is spread your bits and save out the new file. The drawback to this is that 24-bit images are uncommon at the moment and would, therefore, attract the attention of those whose attention you are trying to avoid. They are also very large, as they contain three bytes for every pixel (for a 640 x 480 image, this is 640 x 480 x 3 = 921,600 bytes).

Hiding anything within a 256-color image is considerably more difficult. This is because the image may already have more than 200 colors, and meddling with it may carry it to way more than the maximum of 256.

An image with 32 or fewer colors can never exceed 256 colors, no matter how much you meddle with it. To see this, visualize the three LSBs of an RGB triple as a three-bit number. As you pass through it in your hiding process, you can change it to any one of eight possible values, the binary digits from 000 to 111, one of which is the original pattern. If one color can expand to up to eight colors, how many distinct colors can you have before you are in danger of exceeding the limit of 256? 256/8 equals 32 colors. You have no guarantee that 32 colors is your upper limit for every file that you want to hide, however. If you're lucky, the file does not change a color to all its eight possible combinations, so then you can keep one more of the original colors. In practice, however, you often find pictures being reduced to the minimum of 32 colors.

S-Tools tries to reduce the number of image colors in a manner that preserves as much of the image detail as possible. It usually does a good job of preserving the image detail, too; you often cannot tell the difference between a 256-color scanned image and one reduced to 32.

The actual color reduction algorithm is the one used in the *ppmquant* program, a part of the pbmplus graphics toolkit (based on a median-cut color-map generator from Paul Heckbert's paper, *Colour Image Quantization for Frame Buffer Display*, SIGGRAPH '82 Proceedings, page 297). The advanced picture-hiding options enable you to tune the behavior of this algorithm to your taste. You do, however, require knowledge of how it works to use these options effectively.

## HOW S-TOOLS HIDES YOUR DATA

You may have noticed while using S-Tools that you can hide multiple files in one object. How does S-Tools process these files before hiding them? If you have selected compression, the files are individually compressed and stored together with their names. If you are not using compression, just the raw file data is stored along with the names. Then S-Tools appends some random information onto the front of the data to prevent two identical sets of encryption. The entire lot is then encrypted by using the passphrase that you chose to generate the key. (Actually, MD5 is used to hash the passphrase down to 128 evenly distributed key bits.) The encryption algorithms all operate in Cipher Feedback Mode (CFB).

Hiding the data by just spreading it across the available bits in a linear fashion would be too easy, so S-Tools seeds a cryptographically strong pseudo-random number generator from your passphrase and uses its output to choose the position of the next bit from the cover data to use.

For example, if your sound file had 100 bits available for hiding and you wanted to hide 10 bits in it, S-Tools would not choose bits 0 through 9 because that would be trivially detectable by a potential enemy. Instead, it may choose bits 63, 32, 89, 2, 53, 21, 35, 44, 99, and 80. Or it may choose others; the choices depend on the passphrase that you enter. As you can see, the potential enemies' job has just become very difficult indeed.

## OPENING A PICTURE FILE

Use Windows Explorer to locate the picture file that you want to open and drag it over an empty space in the S-Tools window. Make sure that you let go of the file over an empty space; otherwise, S-Tools thinks that you want to hide the file in the object below the mouse pointer. S-Tools knows only about .BMP and .GIF files.

GIF files can have advanced features such as multiple images (used for animation) and transparent colors (used in Web pages). S-Tools quite happily reads these files, but those advanced features are lost as the file is saved back to disk.

## HIDING DATA IN A PICTURE

Use Windows Explorer to select all the files that you want to hide, drag them over the open picture file that you want to hide them in, and let go.

If you have opted to compress the files, you may experience a short pause while compression takes place. After S-Tools checks to make sure that the picture has enough space to hold the hidden data, you are presented with the security dialog box that you can use to choose the level and type of protection that you require for your hidden data.

After you have chosen your desired security options, another dialog box appears in which you can choose how S-Tools processes your picture during the hiding process (see Figure 9-5).

Finally, the hiding process starts and you can check on its progress by watching the Actions window. You are completely free to do other things while the hiding is taking place, including hiding other files in the same picture. After the hiding process is complete, another picture window appears that you can use to prove to yourself that the altered picture still looks the same as the original.

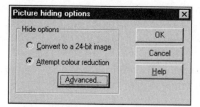

**Figure 9-5:** S-Tools security options

## CUSTOMIZING FILE COMPRESSION

S-Tools enables you to enable/disable the compression of the files that you are hiding and also to set the level of compression that is used. Use the File → Properties menu option to display the dialog box shown in Figure 9-6.

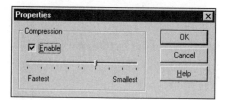

**Figure 9-6:** File compression properties in S-Tools

## SAVING A PICTURE

Click your right mouse button over the picture file that you want to save. Choose either the Save or Save As pop-up menu option to save to disk. The Save option saves the picture with its original file name; the Save As option enables you to choose a new name for the picture.

If you choose a new name for the picture, make sure that the file name ends in either .BMP or .GIF (capital letters or lowercase — it does not matter). S-Tools looks at this part of the file name to decide whether to save the picture as a .BMP or .GIF file.

## REVEALING A HIDDEN FILE

Position the mouse pointer over the object from which you want to reveal data and click the right button. Choose the Reveal option from the context-menu that appears. (The Reveal option always appears on the menu, regardless of whether data hidden is in the object. This is because S-Tools can't tell whether you have data hidden until you try to reveal something.) The security dialog box appears, and you must enter the same passphrase and encryption algorithm that was used to hide the data in the first place.

Whether you get these details correct or not, the Reveal task appears in the Actions window so that you can check on its progress. If you get the passphrase wrong, S-Tools displays the task only briefly before automatically killing it. If you get it right, you can monitor the task's progress before it completes, and a Revealed Archive window appears.

# TigerHide

Adhering to one of the themes of this book, TigerHide provides you with kernel module sources for proprietary steganography development and implementations. By taking a biometric face print and applying a passphrase, you can conceal hidden messages within an image.

The source is broken down into several modules to accommodate the following actions:

✓ Snapping a face print with a digital camera or Web camera

✓ Loading an image

✓ Calculating a numeric seed based on a passphrase

✓ Encoding a message

✓ Saving an image

✓ Decoding a message

The complete source code for the modules in this section can be downloaded from this book's companion Web site at www.wiley.com/compbooks/chirillo.

## SNAPPING A FACEPRINT WITH A DIGITAL OR WEB CAMERA

The first piece of the steganography puzzle — in regard to our discussion here — is to acquire a biometric face print. The following module source can be used as a generic foundation for snapping an image with a digital camera or Webcam that's already configured to work with your system. The code utilizes the Wang Laboratories and Kodak Imaging Controls, from IMGSCAN.OCX — which comes as part of MS Imaging and can be used to capture input from any TWAIN-compatible device.

Following is the source for picture taking (see FacePrint.zip on the companion Web site):

```
Private Sub mnuFileTakePicture_Click()
    'Take a picture
    On Error GoTo Err_Init
    Dim s As String
    Screen.MousePointer = vbHourglass
    s = App.Path & "\picture.bmp"
    DeleteFile s
    TakePicture s
    Status "Picture stored under " & s
    Screen.MousePointer = vbNormal
    Exit Sub

Err_Init:
```

```vb
    HandleError CurrentModule, "mnuFileTakePicture_Click", Err.Number,
Err.Description
    Screen.MousePointer = vbNormal
End Sub
Private Sub InitWebServer()
    'Initialize the web server - set the port, start it listening.
    On Error GoTo Err_Init

    sckWebCam.Item(0).Close
    sckWebCam.Item(0).LocalPort = LocalPort
    sckWebCam.Item(0).Listen
    Status "Listening for picture requests on port " & LocalPort
    Exit Sub

Err_Init:
    HandleError CurrentModule, "InitWebServer", Err.Number, Err.Description
End Sub


Private Sub sckWebCam_ConnectionRequest(Index As Integer, ByVal requestID As
Long)
    'New incoming picture request. Hook them up to an unused connection.
    On Error GoTo Err_Init

    Dim i As Long, FoundOne As Boolean

    'Look for an unused slot
    For i = 1 To sckWebCam.Count - 1
        If sckWebCam(i).Tag = "" Then
            FoundOne = True
            Exit For
        End If
    Next i

    'If we didn't find one, load up a new one
    If FoundOne = False Then
        i = sckWebCam.Count
        Load sckWebCam(i)
    End If

    'Accept the connection
    sckWebCam(i).Tag = "INUSE"
    sckWebCam(i).Accept requestID

    Exit Sub

Err_Init:
```

```
    HandleError CurrentModule, "sckWebCam_ConnectionRequest", Err.Number,
Err.Description
End Sub

Private Sub sckWebCam_DataArrival(Index As Integer, ByVal bytesTotal As Long)
    On Error GoTo Err_Init
    'Get the data. Totally ignore it, because it doesn't matter what they
    ' requested, they're gonna get a WebCam shot back anyway.
    'We're using the existence of incoming data, as our indicator that it's time
    'to take a picture and send back the result.
    Dim s As String, FileName As String

    'Get their incoming data, but throw it away.
    sckWebCam(Index).GetData s

    'Take the picture
    FileName = App.Path & "\" & Format$(Ctr, "0000") & " " & Format$(Now,
"YYYYMMDDHHMMSS") & ".bmp"
    TakePicture FileName
    If FileExists(FileName) = False Then
        'Send the old file, because we're currently scanning
    Else
        'Load the picture into the byte array
        Ctr = Ctr + 1
        If LoadFile(FileName, LastImage) = False Then
            Status "Unable to load picture " & FileName & "!"
            Exit Sub
        End If
        DeleteFile FileName
    End If

    'Send the picture via Winsock
    If sckWebCam(Index).State = sckConnected Then
        s = "HTTP/1.0 200 OK" & vbCrLf & _
            "Content-Length: " & UBound(LastImage, 1) & vbCrLf & _
            "Content-Type: image/bmp" & vbCrLf & vbCrLf
        sckWebCam(Index).Tag = Ctr
        sckWebCam(Index).SendData s
        sckWebCam(Index).SendData LastImage
    End If

    Exit Sub

Err_Init:
```

```
        HandleError CurrentModule, "sckWebCam_DataArrival", Err.Number,
Err.Description
        Resume Next
End Sub


Private Sub sckWebCam_Close(Index As Integer)
        'Close the connection, and mark the slot as unused.
        On Error GoTo Err_Init
        sckWebCam(Index).Close
        sckWebCam(Index).Tag = ""
        Exit Sub


Err_Init:
        HandleError CurrentModule, "sckWebCam_Close", Err.Number, Err.Description
End Sub


Private Sub sckWebCam_SendComplete(Index As Integer)
        'Done sending the picture.
        On Error GoTo Err_Init
        Status "Sent picture " & sckWebCam(Index).Tag & " to slot " & Index & " -
" & sckWebCam(Index).RemoteHostIP & " " & sckWebCam(Index).RemoteHost
        sckWebCam_Close Index
        Exit Sub


Err_Init:
        HandleError CurrentModule, "sckWebCam_SendComplete", Err.Number,
Err.Description
End Sub
```

## LOADING AN IMAGE

This module source calls up Windows Explorer to load a faceprint image into the steganography image editor (see Figure 9-7).

Here's the source to use to load an image into memory (see TigerHide.zip on the companion Web site):

```
Dim sFilename As String


' Show dialog
    With CDialog
        .DialogTitle = "Open image"
        .Filter = "Windows Bitmap (*.bmp)|*.bmp|CompuServe Graphics
Interchange (*.gif)|*.gif"
        .ShowOpen
        sFilename = .FileName
```

```
End With

' Load image
If sFilename <> "" Then
    picImage.Picture = LoadPicture(sFilename)
    imgWidth = picImage.Picture.Width
    imgHeight = picImage.Picture.Height
    If imgWidth > picImage.ScaleWidth Then imgWidth = picImage.ScaleWidth
    If imgHeight > picImage.ScaleHeight Then imgHeight =
picImage.ScaleHeight
    imgLoaded = True
End If
```

**Figure 9-7:** Loading a biometric face print into TigerHide

## CALCULATING A NUMERIC SEED BASED ON A PASSPHRASE

This module source is used for a passphrase control that calculates a numeric seed. The passphrase must be used to encode and reinstated to decode a hidden message. If you support passwords, you should adhere to common password guidelines. Passwords and accounts should not be shared and should be actively managed separately. Password policies should be enforced and should include provisions for changing passwords (among other things), such as the following:

✓ At least every three to six months

✓ Immediately after a password is relinquished

✓ As soon as a password has been compromised or even suspected of a compromise

In changing passwords, choose one of at least eight characters; at least two must be letters, and at least one should be a nonletter character. Any new passwords must differ from the old ones by at least three characters. Use the following general password guidelines instituted by the U.S. government:

✓ Passwords must contain at least eight nonblank characters.

✓ Passwords must contain a combination of letters (preferably a mixture of upper- and lowercase letters), numbers, and at least one special character within the first seven positions.

✓ Passwords must contain a nonnumeric letter or symbol in the first and last positions.

✓ Passwords must not contain the user login name.

✓ Passwords must not include the user's own or a close friend's or relative's name, employee number, Social Security number, birth date, telephone number, or any information about the user that the user believes could be readily learned or guessed.

✓ Passwords must not include common words from an English dictionary or a dictionary of another language with which the user has familiarity.

✓ Passwords must not contain commonly used proper names, including the name of any fictional character or place.

✓ Passwords must not contain any simple pattern of letters or numbers, such as *qwertyxx*.

Here's the source for numeric seed calculation (see TigerHide.zip on the companion Web site):

```
Dim Value As Long
Dim ch As Long
Dim shift1 As Long
Dim shift2 As Long
Dim i As Integer
Dim str_len As Integer

shift1 = 3
shift2 = 17
str_len = Len(password)

For i = 1 To str_len
    ch = Asc(Mid$(password, i, 1))
    Value = Value Xor (ch * 2 ^ shift1)
    Value = Value Xor (ch * 2 ^ shift2)
    shift1 = (shift1 + 7) Mod 19
    shift2 = (shift2 + 13) Mod 23
Next i

CalculateSeed = Value
```

## ENCODING A MESSAGE

This module source encodes a hidden message within a faceprint in the steganography image editor (see Figure 9-8). A passphrase or password must be incorporated to successfully complete the encoding process.

Following is the source for encoding a message (see TigerHide.zip on the companion Web site):

```
On Error Resume Next

    Dim i As Integer
    Dim offset As Integer
    Dim bit As Byte

    Dim X As Long
    Dim Y As Long
    Dim C As Integer
    Dim strPosition As String

    Dim pixel As Long
    Dim R As Byte
    Dim G As Byte
    Dim B As Byte

    offset = 1
    For i = 1 To 8

        ' Get random position and color channel
        Do
            X = Int(Rnd * imgWidth)
            Y = Int(Rnd * imgHeight)
            C = Int(Rnd * 100) Mod 3
            strPosition = "[" & C & "," & X & "," & Y & "]"
            colPositions.Add strPosition, strPosition
            If Err = 0 Then Exit Do
        Loop

        ' Get the Red-Green-Blue value of the pixel
        pixel = picImage.Point(X, Y)
        R = pixel And &HFF&
        G = (pixel And &HFF00&) \ &H100&
        B = (pixel And &HFF0000) \ &H10000

        ' Determine wether bit is 0 or 1
        If Value And offset Then bit = 1 Else bit = 0

        ' Add bit to the selected channel
```

```vb
    Select Case C
        Case 0
            R = (R And &HFE) Or bit
        Case 1
            G = (G And &HFE) Or bit
        Case 2
            B = (B And &HFE) Or bit
    End Select

    ' Update the pixel in the image
    picImage.PSet (X, Y), RGB(R, G, B)

    offset = offset * 2

Next i

Dim strMessage As String
    Dim i As Integer
    Dim message_length As Byte
    Dim seed As Long

    If imgLoaded = False Then
        MsgBox "Load an image first!"
        Exit Sub
    End If

    ' Initialize randomizer
    seed = CalculateSeed(CStr(txtPassword.Text))
    Rnd -1
    Randomize seed

    Set colPositions = New Collection

    ' Prepend the TAG to the message
    strMessage = Steganography_Tag & txtMessage.Text

    message_length = Len(strMessage)

    ' Store message length
    EncodeByte message_length

    ' Store message
    For i = 1 To message_length
        EncodeByte Asc(Mid(strMessage, i, 1))
```

```
Next i

While colPositions.Count
    colPositions.Remove 1
Wend
Set colPositions = Nothing

' Update the image
picImage.Picture = picImage.Image
```

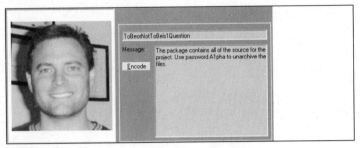

**Figure 9-8:** Encoding a biometric face scan with a secret message

## SAVING AN IMAGE

This module source calls up a Windows dialog box control to save a biometric faceprint image with an encoded message from the steganography image editor.

Here's the source to use for saving the encoded image (see TigerHide.zip on the companion Web site):

```
Dim sFilename As String
    ' Show dialog
    With CDialog
        .DialogTitle = "Save image"
        .Filter = "Windows Bitmap (*.bmp)|*.bmp"
        .DefaultExt = ".bmp"
        .ShowSave
        sFilename = .FileName
    End With
    ' Save image
    If sFilename <> "" Then
        SavePicture picImage.Picture, sFilename
    End If
```

## DECODING A MESSAGE

After an image has been encoded and saved, this module source decodes the hidden message within a faceprint in the steganography image editor (loaded on the recipient station). Again, the unique passphrase or password used in the encoding process must be entered to successfully complete the decoding process.

Following is the source for decoding an encoded message (see TigerHide.zip on the companion Web site):

```
On Error Resume Next

    Dim Value As Integer
    Dim i As Integer
    Dim offset As Integer
    Dim bit As Byte

    Dim X As Long
    Dim Y As Long
    Dim C As Integer
    Dim strPosition As String

    Dim pixel As Long
    Dim R As Byte
    Dim G As Byte
    Dim B As Byte

    offset = 1
    For i = 1 To 8

        ' Get random position and color channel
        Do
            X = Int(Rnd * imgWidth)
            Y = Int(Rnd * imgHeight)
            C = Int(Rnd * 100) Mod 3
            strPosition = "[" & C & "," & X & "," & Y & "]"
            colPositions.Add strPosition, strPosition
            If Err = 0 Then Exit Do
        Loop

        ' Get the Red-Green-Blue value of the pixel
        pixel = picImage.Point(X, Y)
        R = pixel And &HFF&
        G = (pixel And &HFF00&) \ &H100&
        B = (pixel And &HFF0000) \ &H10000

        ' Determine wether bit is 0 or 1
```

```
        Select Case C
            Case 0
                bit = (R And &H1)
            Case 1
                bit = (G And &H1)
            Case 2
                bit = (B And &H1)
        End Select

        ' Increase byte value
        If bit Then
            Value = Value Or offset
        End If

        offset = offset * 2

    Next i

    DecodeByte = Value

Dim strMessage As String
    Dim i As Integer
    Dim message_length As Integer
    Dim seed As Long

    If imgLoaded = False Then
        MsgBox "Load an image first!"
        Exit Sub
    End If

    ' Initialize randomizer
    seed = CalculateSeed(CStr(txtPassword.Text))
    Rnd -1
    Randomize seed

    Set colPositions = New Collection

    ' Read the message length
    message_length = DecodeByte

    For i = 1 To message_length
        strMessage = strMessage & Chr(DecodeByte)
    Next

    If Left(strMessage, 3) = Steganography_Tag Then
```

```
        txtMessage.Text = Mid(strMessage, 4)
    Else
        txtMessage.Text = ""
    End If

    While colPositions.Count
        colPositions.Remove 1
    Wend
    Set colPositions = Nothing
```

# Summary

This chapter talked about the use of strong or two-factor authentication for identifying oneself by using two of the following three methods: something you know, something you have, and something you are. With that said, it touched only the tip of the iceberg by describing the use of steganography with passphrases for biometric faceprint authentication and by providing source code modules for custom proprietary TigerHide implementations in your own authentication schemes.

Hiding data with steganography and replacing unused bits of a file with bits of a hidden message is a useful way to secure the decoding process of a secret message for inclusion in a multi-factor authentication scheme. The next chapter explores other common two- and multi-factor authentication schemes that you can implement with some of the other biometric technologies discussed throughout this book.

# Chapter 10

# Multibiometrics and Two-Factor Authentication

THIS CHAPTER LOOKS AT general two-factor and multifactor biometrics authentication schemes that you can implement with other biometric technologies discussed throughout this book. To recap, *strong*, or *two-factor, authentication* is identifying oneself via two of the three methods of something you *know*, something you *have*, and something you *are*. Similarly, *multibiometrics* refers to identifying oneself via two or more biometric technologies, and frequently adding something you *know* (for example, a password) for much stronger authentication. Finally, *multifactor authentication* is a system that combines all three methods (something you know, have, and are). These methods are employed with strict access-control policies in secure environments.

## Access Control

The National Institute of Security Technology (NIST) lists the eight major elements of computer security:

✓ Computer security should support the mission of the organization.

✓ Computer security is an integral element of sound management.

✓ Computer security should be cost-effective.

✓ Computer security responsibilities and accountability should be made explicit.

✓ System owners have computer security responsibilities outside their own organizations.

✓ Computer security requires a comprehensive and integrated approach.

✓ Computer security should be periodically reassessed.

✓ Computer security is constrained by societal factors.

*Continued*

## Access Control *(Continued)*

Whether or not all of the security controls or elements are in place, administrative and secure systems accessibility require strict management in a protected environment. Encryption, passwords, and access control systems should be implemented and monitored. A variety of access control techniques and combinations thereof can be implemented for different environments, including the following:

- ✓ Discretionary Access Control (DAC) — Restricting access to data based on the user and/or access levels to which they belong. A user or process given discretionary access to information is capable of passing that information along to another user.

- ✓ Mandatory Access Control (MAC) — Multilevel security technique that prevents a user from making information available subjectively. All users and data resources are classified with a security label; access is denied if the user's label does not match that of the resource.

- ✓ Lattice-Based Access Control — Every user and data resource is associated with an ordered set of classes. Resources of a particular class can only be accessed by those whose associated class is as high as, or higher than, that of the resource.

- ✓ Rule-Based Access Control — Every access request is compared to conditions with the user's rights to grant or deny access.

- ✓ Role-Based Access Control — Every user is assigned a role, and each role is assigned specific levels of access privileges that are inherited by the user.

- ✓ Access Control Lists (ACLs) — Databases or tables that contain individual access rights for each resource and to each user (for example, a collection of users who have been given permission to use an object and the types of access they have been permitted).

These access control techniques have been theorized into representative models, including the following:

- ✓ Bell-LaPadula Model — Mandatory access control by determining access rights from different security levels and discretionary access control by cross-referencing access rights from a matrix.

- ✓ Clark-Wilson Model — Achieving data integrity with the well-formed transaction that prevents users from manipulating data, and separation of duties that prevents users from making unauthorized changes.

✓ Biba Model — Protecting data integrity by specifying that a subject cannot execute objects with a lower level of integrity, modify objects that have a higher level of integrity, or request service from other subjects that have a higher level of integrity.

✓ U.S. Defense Department's National Security Agency Orange Book — Specifications that account for the system's security policy, accountability mechanisms in the system, and the operational and life cycle assurance of the system's security.

Upon approval, accounts should be created and access rights and permissions should be implemented by way of the file and data owner's method (each data resource is assigned an owner [administrator] who is responsible for its rights and permissions), the principle of least privilege (every user should be granted the minimum level of permissions — just enough to do his or her job), and/or separation of duties and responsibilities (power control, where the same person who creates accounts shouldn't also approve the creation of accounts, grant access rights, and so on). Upon activation, account usage or accesses should be logged, journaled, and monitored.

# Multibiometrics and Multifactor Biometrics

Several products on today's market already provide multibiometrics capabilities — centrally managing different authentication and biometric systems — and many more companies are developing systems as well. This chapter reviews a few of the most popular multibiometrics products, including BioNetrix Authentication Suite, BioID, and SAF2000. Biometrics is a growing technology for secure identification and authentication (see Figure 10-1), and combining two or more biometric systems with passwords and tickets or tokens — generally termed multifactor biometrics — provides for a strong, secure login foundation. A discussion of developing and custom-designing your own proprietary multifactor biometrics solution is also presented.

## BioNetrix Authentication Suite

According to BioNetrix Systems Corporation (www.bionetrix.com), its BioNetrix Authentication Suite integrates seamlessly with its BioNetrix Single Sign On (SSO) solution and extends SSO functionality to include SSO with the industry's broadest set of strong authentication methods, including smart and proximity cards, tokens, and biometrics (fingerprint, face, voice, iris, and signature).

Administrators set and enforce varying methods and levels of security for both initial user sign-on events and events throughout the workflow process. For example, an individual may gain entry to numerous applications during an initial sign-on event, but may be required to pass additional authentication tests (intrasession authentication) before completing a sensitive transaction within an application.

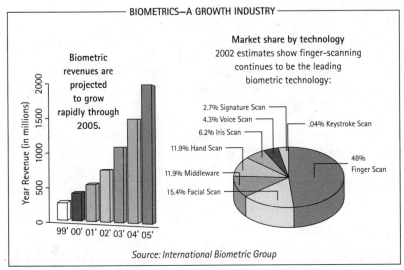

**Figure 10-1** Biometric growth projections through 2005

This combined solution gives today's organizations security assurance while protecting their IT investments with increased productivity and convenience and decreasing support (help desk) costs by mitigating the password legacy.

# BioID

According to HumanScan GmbH (www.bioapi.org), their BioID product is a revolutionary biometric technology that uses face, voice, and lip movement to identify a person.

BioID solutions represent an advanced, people-oriented solution: With BioID, instead of typing in a password or using a PIN, the user simply looks into a standard video camera and says his or her name to get authenticated. Features include the following:

✓ True multimodality

✓ The ability to analyze three biometric traits simultaneously — face, voice, and lip movement

✓ Low-cost implementation, requiring only a standard USB camera and microphone

✓ Ease of use and unobtrusive recognition (users simply look into the camera and say, for example, their name)

BioID technology provides the basis for many biometric security products and solutions, either existing or under development.

# SAF2000

According to SAFLINK Corporation (www.saflink.com), based in Bellevue, Washington, its product, SAF2000 for the Enterprise, integrates secure, multibiometric access to enterprise-wide network environments.

The suite provides Microsoft Windows with a more efficient solution to password-related problems, allowing administrators to focus on more important IT issues. SAF2000 is a scalable add-on module that supports and enhances Windows networks using biometric authentication, the most advanced and effective form of user identification on the market.

SAF2000 enhancements include the following:

✓ An event log that records all user enrollments, changes to user data, account deletions, and workstation updates. All events are time stamped with the user's name.

✓ SAFserver supports multiple databases and directory service protocols for secure storage of user profiles.

✓ Encrypted biometric algorithms — which use the maximum number of available bits from the operating system — enhance authentication security and user privacy.

✓ A developer's toolkit incorporates positive biometric identification into custom applications.

Administrators will appreciate the flexibility and efficiency that SAF2000 provides. Features such as SAFtransactions, a developer's toolkit, and extended Windows functionality, provide a diverse and reliable authentication solution.

Basically, the SAF2000 Enterprise security suite incorporates fingerprint recognition, voice verification, and facial image recognition technologies in a single system to provide a multibiometric foundation that can adapt to meet strong authentication needs.

For more information on the SAF2000 suite, see Chapter 12, case study #1.

# Custom Development

Software Development Kits (SDKs) are programming kernels that enable programmers to develop applications for proprietary platforms. Customarily, SDK packages include APIs, programming tools, and documentation.

## FOR FINGERPRINT SCANNING

Many biometric companies, such as Authentec, Inc. (www.authentec.com), offer SDKs for finger-print development. According to the company, AuthenTec has created a number of solution-enabling kits that make design-in quick and easy. It backs all of its kits with application engineering support, and its specialists can help you get your application off the ground fast. To get started, contact AuthenTec or your authorized AuthenTec representative or distributor with regard to:

✓ **Technology Evaluation Kits (TEKs)** — Used by potential users or developers of products incorporating AuthenTec fingerprint sensor solutions, and by others who want to understand and familiarize themselves with this exciting technology. TEKs include a sensor module, matching algorithms, demonstration software, and user guides.

✓ **Software Developer's Kits (SDKs)** — Intended for engineers who want to create software applications that incorporate AuthenTec's fingerprint authentication technology. SDKs include a sensor module, source libraries (DLLs), object code, algorithms, drivers, underlying API, tools/utilities/debuggers, and software developer guides.

✓ **Reference Design Kits (RDKs)** — Contain the material needed to produce mechanical designs necessary to support manufacturing of printed wiring boards and housing for integration of AuthenTec's fingerprint sensors. RDKs include a sensor module, schematics, bill of materials, board layout and netlists, mechanicals and drawings, software binaries (driver, algorithms, applications), and customizable user documentation.

✓ **Embedded Developer's Kits (EDKs)** — Provide the hardware, software, and documentation for developing standalone, embedded security systems. EDKs include user interface display and keyboard, power module, processor/sensor board, schematics, bill of materials, gerber files, embedded software suite, programmer guides, user guides, and more.

## FOR SIGNATURE RECOGNITION

For signature recognition software development solutions, you can look to Cyber-SIGN's selection of kits at www.cybersign.com. According to the company, these include the following:

✓ **Enterprise SEAL SDK** — The Enterprise Signature Enabled Application Library SDK is a programmer's application development toolkit designed to aid in developing enterprise (TCP/IP client/server) applications utilizing the Cyber-SIGN Dynamic Signature Verification algorithm. You can create applications that are capable of securely verifying identity using the handwritten signature, when captured in real time, using digitizing pads, and against stored signature templates. The SEAL SDK consists of API libraries, sample programs, development files, and other related documents. Software for client/server (TCP/IP) communication is provided, and at each client site, a digitizing tablet is required. Cyber-SIGN is the technology leader for enterprise (TCP/IP client/server) biometric signature verification. No other signature verification technology includes pressure in the identification algorithm, and no other signature verification stores the sensitive biometric data only on a secure server. The user provides sample enrollment signatures at start-up, creating a biometric template that is stored in a commercially available database and on a secured Cyber-SIGN server. During use, to confirm the user's identity, the encrypted data from a subsequently written signature is compared at the server with the secured template.

✓ **Personal (Standalone) SDK** — The Personal SDK is a programmer's application development toolkit designed to aid in developing standalone (non-networked) applications utilizing the Cyber-SIGN Dynamic Signature Verification algorithm. This SDK is valuable for using on a PDA, in conjunction with SmartCARDS, or in any non-networked application. Formerly known as ID-007, the SDK consists of DLL libraries, API sample programs, development files, and other related documents. You can create applications that are capable of securely verifying identity using the handwritten signature, when captured in real time, against stored signature templates. Cyber-SIGN is the technology leader for biometric signature verification. No other signature verification technology includes pressure in the identification algorithm. The user provides sample enrollment signatures at start-up, creating a biometric template that is stored for use to confirm the user's identity from a secured template.

✓ **Enterprise NRD SDK** — The Enterprise Non-Refutable Document SDK is a programmer's application development toolkit that provides the programming tools needed to compliment the Enterprise SEAL SDK when the goal is to create an application that includes the ability to sign and secure — with the handwritten signature — any electronic document. The Enterprise NRD SDK consists of source functions, sample programs, development files, and other related documents that allow the development of an application to sign documents, authenticate identity, and then protect each document with encryption and checksum. This SDK is designed to aid in developing enterprise (TCP/IP client/server) NRD applications utilizing the Cyber-SIGN Dynamic Signature Verification algorithm. This SDK is for use in a client/server environment. You can create applications that are capable of securely verifying identity using the handwritten signature, when captured in real time, using digitizing pads, and against stored signature templates. Software for client/server (TCP/IP) communication is provided, and a digitizing tablet is required at each client site. Cyber-SIGN is the technology leader for enterprise (TCP/IP client/server) biometric signature verification. No other signature verification technology includes pressure in the identification algorithm, and no other signature verification stores the sensitive biometric data only on a secure server. The user provides sample enrollment signatures at start-up, creating a biometric template that is stored in a commercially available database and on a secured Cyber-SIGN server. During use, to confirm the user's identity, the encrypted data from a subsequently written signature is compared at the server with the secured template.

## FOR FACIAL RECOGNITION

Identix's (www.identix.com) embedded software developer toolkits provide you the flexibility to integrate biometric security into your own application or existing network and hardware security solutions. Fully customizable and easy to implement, these solutions are built on powerful algorithms to secure every point of action.

Now you can build your own state-of-the-art applications based on FaceIt, an award winning facial recognition engine. The brand most associated with facial recognition around the globe, FaceIt is based on patented local feature analysis. The SDKs contain face finding and face recognition technologies designed for either one-to-one matching or one-to-many matching.

## SAMPLE DEVELOPMENT KIT

As an example of a complete working development kit with source, the Anveshak system by Vikrant Thakker is presented here. You can use this kit to develop a single or multifactor biometric system, and you can even add a two-factor login dialog. The Anveshak project is an open system that you can use to analyze and classify handwritten characters and input patterns. It analyzes the input pattern in terms of mouse movement information as well as the speed with which the information was entered.

**ANVESHAK EXAMPLE GOAL**   One of the ways to input text on the small devices is to write characters on a small touch pad or directly on the screen. This project's goal is to examine how this is accomplished, and to implement an algorithm that performs single-character recognition.

Single characters are considered rather than entire words or sentences because the touch pad is so small that writing entire words is difficult. The task of recognizing single characters is also much simpler. It is true that when you get entire words instead of single characters, you can use this extra information in combination with a dictionary to analyze the characters, but the problems that arise when you need to find baselines and segment the characters automatically are much more difficult, so you lose what you gained earlier. The algorithm must be able to recognize numerals as well as upper- and lowercase letters. The most common characters in the ASCII table must be supported. Recognition speed is almost equally as important as the recognition rate (the ratio of correctly specified characters) if the user should accept the method of writing on a tablet as a way to input characters. However, recognition speed and recognition rate are two goals that cannot be totally fulfilled at the same time because a recognition system with a high recognition rate with most algorithms also tends to be slow in execution.

**GENERAL DESCRIPTION**    Anveshak is used for user authentication and data input via mouse. The system is self-contained. However, data can be exchanged with other systems through external interface, if required. The system can be functionally divided into the following subsystems:

✓ Character recognition subsystem

- Train the computer on the standard samples provided.

- Accept input as handwritten characters from the user.

- Map the pattern inputted to one of the standard patterns.

- Output the result in plain text as well as through an audio device.

✓ Signature recognition subsystem

- For every new user, collect a sample of his or her signature.

- Store the input pattern in a way that preserves the information about mouse movement.

- For an existing user, accept the signature in the same format as during training.

- Map the pattern input with the standard signature patterns.

- Authenticate the user if successful, or else deny access.

- Output the result in plain text as well as through an audio device.

**CHARACTER RECOGNITION BASICS**    In the 1950s, electronic tablets that could capture coordinate data of pen-tip movements were invented. This created much activity in the field of online character recognition. This activity lasted through the 1960s, ebbed in the 1970s, but was renewed in the 1980s. The growing market of hand-held computers has further increased interest in this research area.

Online recognition means that the recognition is performed while the user writes. Data is captured using electronic tablets and the user is given direct feedback on the recognized characters. In contrast, offline recognition is performed afterwards — that is, on a grey-level bitmap obtained by scanning a paper document. There is, however, no clear line between these two recognition types regarding the algorithms used. An online system could easily use algorithms meant for an offline system by simply converting all the information to a bitmap (and, of course, losing a lot of information in the process about acceleration, slope, and where the stroke started and ended). There are also ways to extract information from a bitmap image to produce guesses regarding to how the character strokes were drawn. Both approaches have their advantages and disadvantages:

✓ In online recognition, you are given much more information to work with. You can get ordered sequences of points grouped into strokes by scanning from pen-down to pen-up, as compared to the unordered bitmap you obtain from a scanned document. You can get time stamp on all the sampled points , so that entities like pen-tip speed and acceleration can be calculated.

✓ Due to the fact that you have immediate contact with the user, the online recognition system may also have the ability to learn and adjust in real time to enhance recognition rate. The user could also show the recognition system how he likes to draw certain letters, to facilitate learning. An offline system could, of course, also learn, but it must do it without feedback from the user regarding what is correct or incorrect.

✓ If your task is to produce a user-independent recognition system, then it could be overkill to use all information (acceleration, pressure, and stroke order, for example) obtained from an online system, since these entities tend to vary greatly between different persons and even between different samples of one person's handwriting. This problem is easily fixed by ignoring the unnecessary information. In a signature verification system, however, these pieces of information might be crucial in order to verify the signature.

✓ A big problem with online systems is that the user is required to use special equipment when inputting data. Writing with a plastic pen-tip on a hard slippery touch pad is not the same as writing on a regular piece of paper. Problems may also arise if the user has to wait for an online recognition system because the system is slow; the thought process would be interrupted.

**HANDWRITING PROPERTIES**   The most important feature of an alphabet is that the differences between different characters are larger than the differences between different samples of a specific character produced by perhaps different writers. One might argue that, in this respect, the English alphabet was badly constructed from the beginning. For example, the letters "I" and "l" (or the letter "O" and the number "0") are sometimes difficult to tell apart. You must see them in the right context.

In single-character recognition, however, where you input one character at a time, you have no context, so you must find other ways to separate characters of numerous meanings. Some information may be available if you look at the characters already written, but because the user doesn't see these characters anymore, one cannot expect the user to remember and stick to, for example, a certain character size. The Graffiti system used on 3Com's Palm Pilot uses two fields for input, one for letters and one for numerals. All letters written in the letter field will be lowercase unless you precede the letter with a special shift symbol. All characters written in the numeral field will be interpreted as numerals (with some exceptions for math symbols like +, - and so on). The Jot system, developed by Communication Intelligence Corporation, has the input field divided in the middle by an imaginary line. Characters written on one side of the line will be recognized as lowercase letters and on the other side you write numerals. Characters overlapping the two regions will be interpreted as uppercase letters.

**CHARACTER PROPERTIES**   How you input your characters greatly affects several factors, including the input speed (the time it takes to write a character), the recognition speed (the time it takes for the system to analyze what you wrote) and the recognition rate (the rate of correctly classified characters) and the speed of enrolling a new user. First, there is the choice between multiple-stroke characters or single-stroke characters. Single-stroke characters are easy from an implementer's point of view. There is no question when one character is finished and the next begins.

You simply examine the pen-down and pen-up actions. This leads, however, to a somewhat strange-looking alphabet, since every character must be completed without lifting the pen. For example, Graffiti uses a kind of single-stroke character set.

Characters with multiple strokes are easy from the user's point of view since he doesn't have to adjust to a new way of writing. There are, however, problems with this. It often takes the user more time to input multiple stroke characters compared to someone who has learnt the new one-stroke characters. There is also no obvious way of knowing when the character is finished, since you use the same area for every character. One can require the writer to make a short pause between every character, but that also reduces speed.

**SYSTEM REQUIREMENTS**    Requirements of the system can be enlisted as:

- ✓ User interface for inputting a pattern.

- ✓ Pattern recognition algorithm.

- ✓ User interface for displaying the result in a pertinent manner.

- ✓ Character Recognition. If the system is trained for a particular user, it gives more than 90 percent accuracy for that user. For generic cases, the accuracy is about 70 percent. The training practically takes 2 to 3 minutes on an Intel Pentium III.

- ✓ Signature Recognition. The accuracy of the system varies between 50 to 70 percent and is highly susceptible to the training pattern it receives. The training practically takes 2 to 3 minutes. These values have been found empirically and are contingent because they depend on the nature of the process and the design of the system.

## General Specifications

- ✓ The system is implemented using Visual Basic 6.0.

- ✓ The system has been tailored to work on the Windows platform using Microsoft SQL as a database.

- ✓ For the audio enable output, the machine should also have Microsoft Voice Text installed.

**OPERATIONAL FEASIBILITY**    Anveshak is designed to be used by end-users with little computer background. So, its basic operation is kept as simple as possible. Online help with each screen makes it possible for a new user to use Anveshak more easily. The study for the two major subparts of the system follows.

Character Recognition. The character recognition part of the system enables any user to input characters with almost 70 to 90 percent accuracy. Hence, when used as a method of input with PDA devices, the system improves efficiency to a great extent. It provides a totally new way of inputting, which is just not present in any current PDA model. Right now, the system accepts input through mouse movement. The rate of error, which is currently about 30 percent for generic user, can be reduced to 10 percent if the system is trained for a particular user.

**Signature Recognition.**This subsystem can be used as a generic authentication system in place of common password-based authentication systems. Every user's signature is unique and can be described by its graphical pattern and time pattern (speed). The time-based pattern recognition reduces the chance of intrusion. Users may have problems signing in with a mouse, but with a stylus, the system shows greater usability.

**TECHNICAL STUDY**     Anveshak is a tool that enhances handwritten character recognition in security systems. Hence, the following utilities must be implemented by the system:

- ✓  A GUI and method for graphical input — For the system, we need a tool that has a method for graphical input, with which we can grab the input given by the mouse. Visual Basic is a technology having such facility, and with its components, it is very easy to create and maintain GUI.

- ✓  Algorithm for recognition of character/signature — To determine the correct character out of all the possible answers, a pattern recognition algorithm is needed. Here, we have implemented an algorithm that looks at the mouse movement and calculates the slope difference instead of looking at the pixels for recognizing the characters. The mouse movement algorithm is many times faster compared to the pixel algorithm; it is also simple and very elegant.

- ✓  A method for audio output — As Anveshak gives output in visual as well as audio form, it uses Text To Speech (TTS) technology. The Microsoft Voice Text is used for this module.

**TOOLS, PLATFORMS, AND LANGUAGES USED**     Currently, the system is tailored to work only on a Windows platform with MS SQL as a database. Since Visual Basic, with its ready-to-use GUI components, is one of the most popular programming languages for Rapid Application Development, all the coding will be done using Microsoft's Visual Basic 6.0 as a front-end and MS SQL for storing the data as a back-end. One point to remember is that this is not a database application, and the main purpose of this program is only to implement the logic of character recognition. Hence, the database selected is MS SQL, which is easy to use with Visual Basic. This might change in the future, by writing the code using the platform-independent language, Java; however, the use of Java poses certain restrictions on the algorithm. This is due to the fact that Java programs are interpreted and therefore not as fast as a program that is, for example, written in C or VB. Since recognition speed is important, this is clearly a problem. For the audio enable output, the machine should also have Microsoft Voice Text installed.

**PROGRAM LOGIC**     This program uses the database file Data.mdf. Each letter would have 100 movements made of 2 digits. When the form loads, these numbers would be put in an Alphabet array. When you draw a letter, the program compares your movement to each letter's movements. The letter with the highest match is the letter recognized. The movement is compared using the Direction function — you input the mouse position and the previous mouse position and a number indicating the direction is calculated. By adding more possible directions, the program becomes more accurate.

**SOURCE (SEE *DEVKIT.ZIP*)**    Following is the source for the sample development kit. Use this hard copy when you need to reference specific routines within the software suite. We'll start by listing the connection and public modules source that tie in the data files and declarations of public functions:

```
Public conn As ADODB.Connection
Public rsChar As ADODB.Recordset
Public Sub Main()
On Error GoTo merr
Dim str1 As String
Set conn = New ADODB.Connection
On Error GoTo errOff97
str1 = "provider=microsoft.jet.oledb.4.0;data source="
str1 = str1 & App.Path & "\data.mdb"
errOff97:
str1 = "provider=microsoft.jet.oledb.3.51;data source="
str1 = str1 & App.Path & "\data.mdb"
conn.Open str1
Set rsChar = New ADODB.Recordset
rsChar.Open "select * from MastChar", conn, adOpenStatic, adLockOptimistic
Load frmMain
frmMain.Show
Exit Sub
merr:
MsgBox Err.Description, vbOKOnly, "Anveshak"
End Sub


Public BuffArray(100) As String      ' Creates an array of 100 elements
Public strFile As String             ' Stores the complete line in the array
Public Distort As Single
Public Difference As Integer         ' Gets the difference of the previous and
the current position of mouse
Public Score() As Single             ' After comparison with the array, each
unit is increased when a matched direction is found
Public Highest As Integer            ' The alphabet that has the highest score
Public HighScore As Single           ' The amount of highest score
' WriteLet is a boolean...
' If "writeLet = True" then this means that the user has not
' completed drawing a character.
' And if "WriteLet=False" then this means that user has completed
' drawing a character.
Public Ans As String     ' This variable is used to store the User Response for
a 'Quit' message
Public tm As Integer     ' This stores the time taken by user to draw one
character
Public Type LetterType
```

```
        Direc(100) As Integer
End Type
'Dim Alphabet(25) As LetterType
Public Alphabet(250) As LetterType
Public WriteLet As Boolean  ' This is used to know whether the user has
completed drawing a character or not
Public HoldX As Integer, HoldY As Integer ' Store the current position value
of X and Y
Public LetterMovement(200) As Integer
'Dim Letter(-1 To 25) As String
Public Letter() As String
Public NumLet As Integer
Public WriteFile As Boolean ' if true then allow  Read and write from the
database file, if false then close the database file
Public Function Direction(X1 As Integer, Y1 As Integer, X2 As Integer, Y2 As
Integer) As Integer

    ' This Function returns the value of Direction by calculating
    ' old and current X and Y  values
    'x1 and y1 are the center points

ReDim Letter(-1 To rsChar.RecordCount) As String
Dim Slope As Single
' Here we get old and current X (x1,x2) and Y (y1,y2) values,
' And on using the formula we calculate the slope
' Based on the return value of slope, we assign a particular
' value to the direction
' x1 is the old X value
'x2 is the current X value
If X2 - X1 = 0 Then
    Slope = 50
Else
    Slope = -(Y2 - Y1) / (X2 - X1)
End If
If Slope <= 0 And Slope > -0.5 Then
    Direction = 0
ElseIf Slope <= -0.5 And Slope > -1 Then
    Direction = 1
ElseIf Slope <= -1 And Slope > -2 Then
    Direction = 2
ElseIf Slope < -2 Then
    Direction = 3
ElseIf Slope > 2 Then
    Direction = 4
ElseIf Slope <= 2 And Slope > 1 Then
```

```
            Direction = 5
    ElseIf Slope <= 1 And Slope > 0.5 Then
            Direction = 6
    ElseIf Slope <= 0.5 And Slope > 0 Then
            Direction = 7
    End If
    ' y1 is the Old Y value,
    ' y2 is the current Y value
    If Y2 > Y1 Then
            Direction = Direction + 8
    End If
    End Function
    Public Sub LoadAll()
    Dim strFileLine As String
    Dim Count As Integer
    Dim i As Integer
    Dim Start As Integer
    ReDim Letter(-1 To rsChar.RecordCount) As String
    'Each alphabet is stored in an array named Letter(-1 to rsChar.RecordCount)
    Letter(-1) = ""
    If rsChar.RecordCount > 0 Then
    rsChar.MoveFirst
    For i = 0 To rsChar.RecordCount - 1 Step 1
        Letter(i) = rsChar!Char
        If rsChar.EOF = False Then rsChar.MoveNext
    Next
    End If
    Dim a As Integer
    ' Each Letter has 100 movements, each of 2 digits,
    ' So this part is to read the movements
    ' Due to this we get the different percentage of different characters, if we delete this part each
    character will show the same probability
    Start = 2
    If rsChar.RecordCount > 0 Then
    rsChar.MoveFirst
    Count = 0
    For i = 0 To rsChar.RecordCount - 1 Step 1
        strFileLine = rsChar!String
        For a = Start To 200 Step 2
            Alphabet(Count).Direc(Int(a / 2)) = Val(Mid(strFileLine, a, 2))
        Next a
        Start = 1
        Count = Count + 1
    If rsChar.EOF = False Then rsChar.MoveNext
    Next
```

```
End If
End Sub
Public Sub MouseDown()
' Store the current X and Y values when the mouse button is clicked down
'Tmr.Enabled = True
tm = 0
WriteLet = True
HoldX = X
HoldY = Y
End Sub
```

## Following is the main module form:

```
Private Sub cmdAbout_Click()
Unload Me
frmAbout.Show
End Sub


Private Sub cmdQuit_Click()
Ans = MsgBox("Do you want to Quit ?", vbYesNo, "Anveshak")
If Ans = vbYes Then
        End
ElseIf Ans = vbNo Then
    Exit Sub
End If
End Sub


Private Sub cmdRecog_Click()
Unload Me
Load frmOCR
frmOCR.Show
End Sub


Private Sub cmdSign_Click()
Unload Me
Load frmSign
frmSign.Show
End Sub


Private Sub cmdTeach_Click()
Unload Me
Load frmTeach
frmTeach.Show
End Sub
```

**This is the character recognition module form:**

```
Private Sub chkSound_Click()
MsgBox "UNDER CONSTRUCTION !!!", vbOKOnly, "Anveshak"
End Sub

Private Sub cmdAbout_Click()
Unload Me
frmAbout.Show
End Sub

Private Sub cmdBack_Click()
Unload Me
frmMain.Show
End Sub

Private Sub cmdCLS_Click()
picDraw.Cls
lblRes.Visible = False
End Sub

Private Sub cmdHelp_Click()
MsgBox "UNDER CONSTRUCTION !!!", vbOKOnly, "Anveshak"
End Sub

Private Sub cmdSubmit_Click()
lblRes.Visible = True      ' Display the result
End Sub

Private Sub Form_Activate()
' If no characters are taught to computer, then display an appropriate message
If rsChar.RecordCount = 0 Then
MsgBox "Note if this is your first time using the program you should probably
" & vbNewLine & "edit every letter because right now they are custom to my
handwriting." & vbNewLine & "So you should edit it to yours to make it more
accurate.  Also a letter " & vbNewLine & "is finished once you release the
mouse so be careful on letter like 'i'.", vbOKOnly, "Anveshak"
End If
End Sub

Private Sub Form_Load()
Dim i As Integer
Call LoadAll
```

```
'Add the list of taught characters in the combo box
For i = 0 To rsChar.RecordCount - 1 Step 1
    cmbLetList.AddItem Letter(i), i
Next i
End Sub


Private Sub picDraw_MouseDown(Button As Integer, Shift As Integer, X As
Single, Y As Single)
' Store the current X and Y values when the mouse button is clicked down
' Enable and start the timer, so that we can know the time taken by user to draw a character
Call MouseDown
Tmr.Enabled = True
picDraw.CurrentX = X
picDraw.CurrentY = Y
End Sub


Private Sub picDraw_MouseMove(Button As Integer, Shift As Integer, X As
Single, Y As Single)
Dim Direc As Integer
Dim BuffX As Integer, BuffY As Integer
Static Count As Integer

If WriteLet = True Then
    Count = Count + 1
    If Count Mod 2 = 0 Then
        If NumLet < 200 Then
            BuffX = X    ' Stores the new current value of X
            BuffY = Y    ' Stores the new current value of Y
' The direction value is calculated and stored in the variable Direc
            Direc = Direction(HoldX, HoldY, BuffX, BuffY)
            HoldX = X
            HoldY = Y

            picDraw.Line -(BuffX, BuffY)


            LetterMovement(NumLet) = Direc

            NumLet = NumLet + 1
        Else
            lblStatus.Caption = "Letter Limit"
        End If
    End If
End If
```

```
End Sub

Private Sub picDraw_MouseUp(Button As Integer, Shift As Integer, X As Single,
Y As Single)
Dim i As Integer
Dim F As Integer
ReDim Letter(-1 To rsChar.RecordCount) As String
ReDim Score(rsChar.RecordCount) As Single

frmOCR.Cls
```

'stretch or compress array to fit 100 into the BuffArray

```
Distort = NumLet / 100
For i = 0 To 100
    BuffArray(i) = LetterMovement(Int(i * Distort))
Next i

If WriteFile = False Then
    'calculate the score for each letter
    For F = 0 To rsChar.RecordCount - 1
        Dim Total As Integer
        For i = 0 To 100

            If BuffArray(i) > Alphabet(F).Direc(i) Then
                Difference = BuffArray(i) - Alphabet(F).Direc(i)
            Else
                Difference = Alphabet(F).Direc(i) - BuffArray(i)
            End If

            'exceptions because the where the circle ends
            If BuffArray(i) = 0 And Alphabet(F).Direc(i) = 15 Then
                Difference = 1
            ElseIf BuffArray(i) = 0 And Alphabet(F).Direc(i) = 14 Then
                Difference = 2
            ElseIf BuffArray(i) = 1 And Alphabet(F).Direc(i) = 15 Then
                Difference = 2
            ElseIf BuffArray(i) = 1 And Alphabet(F).Direc(i) = 14 Then
                Difference = 3
            End If

            Score(F) = Score(F) + (8 - Difference)
            Total = Total + 8
        Next i
        'put score into percent
```

```
        Score(F) = Score(F) / Total * 100
        Total = 0

If rsChar.RecordCount > 0 Then
rsChar.MoveFirst
    rsChar.Move (F)
        ' frmOCR.Print rsChar!Char & ": " & CInt(Score(F)) & "%"
        'lblRes.Caption = rsChar!Char & ": " & CInt(Score(F)) & "%"
        lblRes.Visible = False
        lblRes.Caption = rsChar!Char
End If

    '  frmOCR.Print Letter(F) & ":  " & CInt(Score(F)) & "%"
    Next F


    Highest = 0
    HighScore = Score(0)

    For i = 1 To rsChar.RecordCount - 1
        If Score(i) > HighScore Then
            Highest = i
            HighScore = Mid(Score(i), 1, 2)
        End If
    Next i
    frmOCR.Print ""
    If HighScore < 50 Then
        If rsChar.RecordCount > 0 Then
            rsChar.MoveFirst
            rsChar.Move (Highest)
            ' frmOCR.Print "?" & rsChar!Char & "?  Percent: "; CInt(HighScore)
& "%"
            ' lblRes.Caption = "?" & rsChar!Char & "?  Percent: " & CInt(HighScore) & "%"
            lblRes.Visible = False
            lblRes.Caption = rsChar!Char
        End If
            'frmOCR.Print "?" & Letter(Highest) & "?  Percent: "; CInt(HighScore) & "%"
        '        TS.Speak (Letter(Highest))
    Else
    If rsChar.RecordCount > 0 Then
            rsChar.MoveFirst
            rsChar.Move (Highest)
            'frmOCR.Print rsChar!Char & "  Percent: "; CInt(HighScore) & "%"
    lblRes.Visible = False
```

```
            lblRes.Caption = rsChar!Char
        End If
            ' frmOCR.Print Letter(Highest) & "  Percent: "; CInt(HighScore) & "%"
            '    TS.Speak (Letter(Highest))
    End If
    lblStatus.Caption = "Drawing"


End If
WriteFile = False
WriteLet = False   ' This tells the computer that we have completed drawing a
character
NumLet = 0
End Sub


Private Sub Tmr_Timer()
tm = tm + 1      ' This increments the variable tm by 1, so as to get the value
of total time taken to draw the character
End Sub


Private Sub tmrStatusPause_Timer()
lblStatus.Caption = "Drawing"
tmrStatusPause.Interval = 0
End Sub
```

This is the signature recognition module form:

```
Option Explicit
Private Sub cmdBack_Click()
Unload Me
frmMain.Show
End Sub


Private Sub cmdRecog_Click()
If Trim(txtSign.Text) = "" Then
    MsgBox "Enter the UserName", vbOKOnly, "Anveshak"
End If
End Sub


Private Sub cmdCLS_Click()
picDraw.Cls
lblRes.Visible = False
End Sub


Private Sub cmdExit_Click()
```

```
Ans = MsgBox("Do you want to Exit ?", vbYesNo, "Anveshak")
If Ans = vbYes Then
    End
Else
    Exit Sub
End If
End
End Sub


Private Sub cmdHelp_Click()
MsgBox "UNDER CONSTRUCTION !!!", vbOKOnly, "Anveshak"
End Sub


Private Sub cmdSubmit_Click()
' Displays the result
If Trim(lblRes.Caption) = Trim(txtSign.Text) Then
    MsgBox "Login Successfull !", vbOKOnly, "Anveshak"
ElseIf Trim(lblRes.Caption) <> Trim(txtSign.Text) Then
    MsgBox "Invalid User !", vbOKOnly, "Anveshak"
End If
End Sub


Private Sub Form_Activate()
' If no characters are taught to the computer, then display an appropriate message
If rsChar.RecordCount = 0 Then
MsgBox "Note if this is your first time using the program you should probably
" & vbNewLine & "edit every letter because right now they are custom to my
handwriting." & vbNewLine & "So you should edit it to yours to make it more
accurate.  Also a letter " & vbNewLine & "is finished once you release the
mouse so be careful on letter like 'i'.", vbOKOnly, "Anveshak"
End If
End Sub


Private Sub Form_Load()
Dim i As Integer
Call LoadAll
For i = 0 To rsChar.RecordCount - 1 Step 1
    cmbLetList.AddItem Letter(i), i
Next i
End Sub


Private Sub picDraw_MouseDown(Button As Integer, Shift As Integer, X As
Single, Y As Single)
' Store the current X and Y values when the mouse button is clicked down
```

' Enable and start the timer, so that we can know the time taken by user to draw a character

```
Call MouseDown
Tmr.Enabled = True
picDraw.CurrentX = X
picDraw.CurrentY = Y
End Sub


Private Sub picDraw_MouseMove(Button As Integer, Shift As Integer, X As
Single, Y As Single)
Dim Direc As Integer
Dim BuffX As Integer, BuffY As Integer
Static Count As Integer


If WriteLet = True Then
    Count = Count + 1
    If Count Mod 2 = 0 Then
        If NumLet < 200 Then
            BuffX = X    ' Stores the new current value of X
```

BuffY = Y  ' Stores the new current value of Y
' The direction value is calculated and stored in the variable Direc

```
            Direc = Direction(HoldX, HoldY, BuffX, BuffY)
            HoldX = X
            HoldY = Y


            picDraw.Line -(BuffX, BuffY)


            LetterMovement(NumLet) = Direc

            NumLet = NumLet + 1
        Else
            lblStatus.Caption = "Letter Limit"
        End If
    End If
End If
End Sub


Private Sub picDraw_MouseUp(Button As Integer, Shift As Integer, X As Single,
Y As Single)
Dim i As Integer
Dim F As Integer
```

```
ReDim Letter(-1 To rsChar.RecordCount) As String
ReDim Score(rsChar.RecordCount) As Single
frmOCR.Cls
```

'stretch or compress array to fit 100 into the BuffArray
```
Distort = NumLet / 100
For i = 0 To 100
    BuffArray(i) = LetterMovement(Int(i * Distort))
Next i


If WriteFile = False Then
```
'calculate the score for each letter
```
    For F = 0 To rsChar.RecordCount - 1
        Dim Total As Integer
        For i = 0 To 100


            If BuffArray(i) > Alphabet(F).Direc(i) Then
                Difference = BuffArray(i) - Alphabet(F).Direc(i)
            Else
                Difference = Alphabet(F).Direc(i) - BuffArray(i)
            End If
```

'exceptions because the where the circle ends
```
            If BuffArray(i) = 0 And Alphabet(F).Direc(i) = 15 Then
                Difference = 1
            ElseIf BuffArray(i) = 0 And Alphabet(F).Direc(i) = 14 Then
                Difference = 2
            ElseIf BuffArray(i) = 1 And Alphabet(F).Direc(i) = 15 Then
                Difference = 2
            ElseIf BuffArray(i) = 1 And Alphabet(F).Direc(i) = 14 Then
                Difference = 3
            End If

            Score(F) = Score(F) + (8 - Difference)
            Total = Total + 8
        Next i
```
'put score into percent
```
        Score(F) = Score(F) / Total * 100
        Total = 0


If rsChar.RecordCount > 0 Then
rsChar.MoveFirst
    rsChar.Move (F)
        ' frmOCR.Print rsChar!Char & ": " & CInt(Score(F)) & "%"
        'lblRes.Caption = rsChar!Char & ": " & CInt(Score(F)) & "%"
```

```
              lblRes.Visible = False
              lblRes.Caption = rsChar!Char
        End If

            ' frmOCR.Print Letter(F) & ": " & CInt(Score(F)) & "%"
        Next F

        Highest = 0
        HighScore = Score(0)

        For i = 1 To rsChar.RecordCount - 1
            If Score(i) > HighScore Then
                Highest = i
                HighScore = Mid(Score(i), 1, 2)
            End If
        Next i
        frmOCR.Print ""
        If HighScore < 50 Then
            If rsChar.RecordCount > 0 Then
                rsChar.MoveFirst
                rsChar.Move (Highest)
            ' frmOCR.Print "?" & rsChar!Char & "? Percent: "; CInt(HighScore)
& "%"

            ' lblRes.Caption = "?" & rsChar!Char & "? Percent: " & CInt(HighScore) & "%"
                lblRes.Visible = False
                lblRes.Caption = rsChar!Char
            End If
            'frmOCR.Print "?" & Letter(Highest) & "? Percent: "; CInt(HighScore) & "%"
          '        TS.Speak (Letter(Highest))
        Else
        If rsChar.RecordCount > 0 Then
                rsChar.MoveFirst
                rsChar.Move (Highest)
                'frmOCR.Print rsChar!Char & " Percent: "; CInt(HighScore) & "%"
                lblRes.Visible = False
                lblRes.Caption = rsChar!Char
            End If
            ' frmOCR.Print Letter(Highest) & " Percent: "; CInt(HighScore) & "%"
          '        TS.Speak (Letter(Highest))
        End If
        lblStatus.Caption = "Drawing"

End If
```

```
WriteFile = False
WriteLet = False  ' This tells the computer that we have completed drawing a
character
NumLet = 0

End Sub

Private Sub Tmr_Timer()
tm = tm + 1
End Sub

Private Sub tmrStatusPause_Timer()
lblStatus.Caption = "Drawing"
tmrStatusPause.Interval = 0      ' This increments the variable tm by 1, so as
to get the value of total time taken to draw the character
End Sub
```

This is the teaching enrollment module form:

```
' This form is concerned with the teaching part of the Anveshak
'Option Explicit
Dim BuffArray(100) As String    ' Creates an array of 100 elements
Dim strFile As String           ' Stores the complete line in the array
Dim Distort As Single
Dim Difference As Integer       ' Gets the difference of the previous and the
current position of mouse
Dim Score() As Single           ' After comparison with the array, each unit
is increased when a matched direction is found
Dim i As Integer
Dim F As Integer
Dim Highest As Integer          ' The alphabet that has the highest score
Dim HighScore As Single         ' The amount of highest score

Private Sub cmdBack_Click()
Unload Me
frmMain.Show
End Sub

Private Sub cmdClear_Click()
picDraw.Cls
End Sub

Private Sub cmdCLS_Click()
picDraw.Cls
lblRes.Visible = False
```

```
End Sub

Private Sub cmdEdit_Click()
ReDim Letter(-1 To rsChar.RecordCount) As String
'If cmbLetList.ListIndex <> -1 Then
If Trim(txtChar.Text) <> "" Then
    WriteFile = True
    picDraw.Cls
'   lblStatus.Caption = "Editing: " & Letter(cmbLetList.ListIndex)
    lblStatus.Caption = "Teaching: " & txtChar.Text
Else
    MsgBox "Please write a lettet to teach.", vbCritical, "Anveshak"
End If
End Sub

Private Sub cmdExit_Click()
Ans = MsgBox("Do you want to Exit ?", vbYesNo, "Anveshak")
If Ans = vbYes Then
    End
Else
    Exit Sub
End If
End
End Sub

Private Sub cmdHelp_Click()
MsgBox "Sorry for inconvinience ! UNDER CONSTRUCTION !!!", vbOKOnly,
"Anveshak"
End Sub

Private Sub cmdWorks_Click()
frmWorks.Show 1     ' Opens and Displays the form frmWorks
End Sub

Private Sub Form_Activate()
If rsChar.RecordCount = 0 Then
MsgBox "Note if this is your first time using the program you should probably
" & vbNewLine & "edit every letter because right now they are custom to my
handwriting." & vbNewLine & "So you should edit it to yours to make it more
accurate.  Also a letter " & vbNewLine & "is finished once you release the
mouse so be careful on letter like 'i'.", vbOKOnly, "Anveshak"
End If
End Sub

Private Sub picDraw_MouseDown(Button As Integer, Shift As Integer, X As
```

```vb
Single, Y As Single)
Call MouseDown
Tmr.Enabled = True
picDraw.CurrentX = X
picDraw.CurrentY = Y
End Sub

Private Sub picDraw_MouseMove(Button As Integer, Shift As Integer, X As
Single, Y As Single)
Dim Direc As Integer
Dim BuffX As Integer, BuffY As Integer
Static Count As Integer

If WriteLet = True Then
    Count = Count + 1
    If Count Mod 2 = 0 Then
        If NumLet < 200 Then
            BuffX = X    ' Stores the new current value of X
            BuffY = Y    ' Stores the new current value of Y
            Direc = Direction(HoldX, HoldY, BuffX, BuffY)
            HoldX = X
            HoldY = Y

            picDraw.Line -(BuffX, BuffY)


            LetterMovement(NumLet) = Direc

            NumLet = NumLet + 1
        Else
            lblStatus.Caption = "Letter Limit"
        End If
    End If
End If
End Sub

Private Sub picDraw_MouseUp(Button As Integer, Shift As Integer, X As Single,
Y As Single)
Dim BuffArray(100) As String
Dim strFile As String
Dim Distort As Single
Dim Difference As Integer
Dim Score() As Single
Dim i As Integer
Dim F As Integer
```

```
Dim Highest As Integer
Dim HighScore As Single
ReDim Letter(-1 To rsChar.RecordCount) As String
ReDim Score(rsChar.RecordCount) As Single
frmOCR.Cls

If cmbLetList.ListIndex <> -1 Then
'stretch or compress array to fit 100 into the BuffArray
Distort = NumLet / 100
For i = 0 To 100
    BuffArray(i) = LetterMovement(Int(i * Distort))
    If WriteFile = True Then
        Alphabet(cmbLetList.ListIndex).Direc(i) = LetterMovement(Int(i *
Distort))
    End If
Next i
ElseIf cmbLetList.ListIndex = -1 Then
Distort = NumLet / 100
For i = 0 To 100
    BuffArray(i) = LetterMovement(Int(i * Distort))
    If WriteFile = True Then
        Alphabet(0).Direc(i) = LetterMovement(Int(i * Distort))
    End If
Next i
End If '

If WriteFile = False Then
    'calculate the score for each letter
    For F = 0 To rsChar.RecordCount - 1
        Dim Total As Integer
        For i = 0 To 100

            If BuffArray(i) > Alphabet(F).Direc(i) Then
                Difference = BuffArray(i) - Alphabet(F).Direc(i)
            Else
                Difference = Alphabet(F).Direc(i) - BuffArray(i)
            End If

            'exceptions because the where the circle ends
            If BuffArray(i) = 0 And Alphabet(F).Direc(i) = 15 Then
                Difference = 1
            ElseIf BuffArray(i) = 0 And Alphabet(F).Direc(i) = 14 Then
                Difference = 2
            ElseIf BuffArray(i) = 1 And Alphabet(F).Direc(i) = 15 Then
                Difference = 2
```

```
            ElseIf BuffArray(i) = 1 And Alphabet(F).Direc(i) = 14 Then
                Difference = 3
            End If

            Score(F) = Score(F) + (8 - Difference)
        Total = Total + 8
    Next i
    'put score into percent
    Score(F) = Score(F) / Total * 100
    Total = 0

If rsChar.RecordCount > 0 Then
rsChar.MoveFirst
    rsChar.Move (F)

        ' frmOCR.Print rsChar!Char & ": " & CInt(Score(F)) & "%"
        'lblRes.Caption = rsChar!Char & ": " & CInt(Score(F)) & "%"

        lblRes.Visible = False
        lblRes.Caption = rsChar!Char
End If


        ' frmOCR.Print Letter(F) & ": " & CInt(Score(F)) & "%"


    Next F

    Highest = 0
    HighScore = Score(0)

    For i = 1 To rsChar.RecordCount - 1
        If Score(i) > HighScore Then
            Highest = i
            HighScore = Mid(Score(i), 1, 2)
        End If
    Next i
    frmOCR.Print ""
    If HighScore < 50 Then
        If rsChar.RecordCount > 0 Then
            rsChar.MoveFirst
            rsChar.Move (Highest)

        ' frmOCR.Print "?" & rsChar!Char & "? Percent: "; CInt(HighScore) & "%"
        ' lblRes.Caption = "?" & rsChar!Char & "? Percent: " & CInt(HighScore) & "%"
```

```
            lblRes.Visible = False
            lblRes.Caption = rsChar!Char
       End If


            'frmOCR.Print "?" & Letter(Highest) & "?  Percent: "; CInt(HighScore) & "%"
      '          TS.Speak (Letter(Highest))


    Else
    If rsChar.RecordCount > 0 Then
            rsChar.MoveFirst
            rsChar.Move (Highest)


            'frmOCR.Print rsChar!Char & "  Percent: "; CInt(HighScore) & "%"


            lblRes.Visible = False
            lblRes.Caption = rsChar!Char
       End If


          ' frmOCR.Print Letter(Highest) & "  Percent: "; CInt(HighScore) & "%"
      '          TS.Speak (Letter(Highest))


    End If


    lblStatus.Caption = "Drawing" '
Else
rsChar.AddNew

    For F = 0 To rsChar.RecordCount
       For i = 0 To 100
            If Val(Alphabet(F).Direc(i)) < 10 Then
                strFile = strFile & "0"
            End If
            strFile = strFile & Alphabet(F).Direc(i)
                If i = 100 Then
                     strFile = strFile & Alphabet(F).Direc(i)
                     Tmr.Enabled = False


            rsChar!String = strFile
            rsChar!Char = txtChar.Text
            rsChar!Time = tm
            rsChar.Update
                End If
       Next i
       If F <> rsChar.RecordCount Then
            strFile = strFile & vbNewLine
       End If
```

```
    Next F

    lblStatus.Caption = "Letter Saved"
    tmrStatusPause.Interval = 1000

    Call LoadAll    ' This will reallocate the elements in array

'End If

'Call Teach
End If
WriteFile = False
WriteLet = False    ' This tells the computer that we have completed drawing a
character
NumLet = 0

End Sub

Private Sub Tmr_Timer()
tm = tm + 1
End Sub

Private Sub tmrStatusPause_Timer()
lblStatus.Caption = "Drawing"
tmrStatusPause.Interval = 0
End Sub
```

# Two-Factor Authentication with Passwords, Tickets, and Tokens

User identification and authentication is our focus for a strong login framework. The most common methods include strong passwords, tickets, and tokens. These elements can be added to your biometric systems for two-factor authentication. There are several products on the market today that already combine different authentication techniques for a two-factor system. As an example, we'll look at BioLogon from Identix, Inc.

## BioLogon

According to Identix, Inc. (www.identix.com), their product offers the complete solution for your entire desktop and network fingerprint authentication needs. A complete multifactor authentication solution, BioLogon will provide fingerprint and password support (see Figure 10-2). The result is increased security, lower administrative costs, and added convenience.

**Figure 10-2:** Using BioLogon for strong authentication at the desktop

BioLogon offers complete multifactor authentication of biometrics, plus a complete multifactor authentication providing fingerprint and password support. In addition, you'll find that the software provides seamless integration into a network's OS for central administration, configuration, and maintenance of user account and security policies (see Figure 10-3).

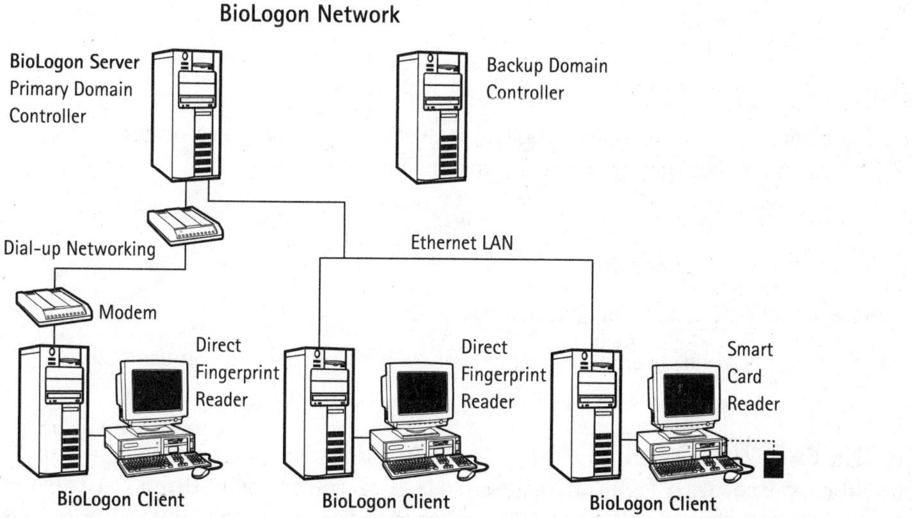

**BioLogon Network**

BioLogon Server
Primary Domain
Controller

Backup Domain
Controller

Dial-up Networking

Ethernet LAN

Modem

Direct
Fingerprint
Reader

Direct
Fingerprint
Reader

Smart
Card
Reader

BioLogon Client

BioLogon Client

BioLogon Client

**Figure 10-3:** BioLogon can be configured to provide strong authentication for network and local logon

BioLogon features include:

✓ Flexibility. BioLogon provides flexible and granular account and resource management, allowing you to control how network resources are accessed and by whom.

✓ Simplicity. BioLogon's centralized credential store allows enrolled users to log on quickly to shared resources from any workstation within the domain. User biometric account credentials are easily established, with enrollment generally taking less than 15 seconds.

✓ Return on investment. Your organization saves time and money by eliminating the 50 percent or more of help desk calls related to lost, stolen, and forgotten passwords.

✓ Server redundancy and load balancing and credential replication across domain controllers.

✓ Secure network communication channel, with support for up to 128-bit encryption.

✓ Local and remote user/workstation policy administration for enterprise-wide management from any location.

✓ Multiple user account login methods, including biometrics and smartcard/PIN combinations.

✓ The self-enrollment tool adds a fingerprint enrollment control to the standard Windows Security dialog to allow non-BioLogon users to enroll biometrically without contacting the domain administrator.

✓ Portable fingerprint authentication management to biometrically enroll on each computer that has a fingerprint reader attached and then, using fingerprint authentication, to log on to all domains in the network.

## Strong Passwords

Passwords and accounts should not be shared and should be actively managed separately. Password policies should be enforced, and they should contain specifications that require users to change passwords as follows:

✓ At least every three to six months.

✓ Immediately after a password is relinquished.

✓ As soon as a password has been compromised or even suspected of a compromise.

### REMEMBER THE PASSWORD RULES

Passwords should contain at least eight characters (sixteen are recommended). At least two of these characters must be letters and at least one should be a number or symbol. Any new passwords must differ from the old ones by at least three characters. Use the following general password guidelines instituted by the U.S. government:

✓ Passwords must contain at least eight nonblank characters.

✓ Passwords must contain a combination of letters (preferably a mixture of upper- and lowercase letters), numbers, and at least one special character within the first seven positions.

✓ Passwords must contain a nonnumeric letter or symbol in the first and last positions.

✓ Passwords must not contain the user's login name.

✓ Passwords must not include the user's own or a close friend's or relative's name, employee number, Social Security number, birth date, telephone number, or any information about him or her that the user believes could be readily learned or guessed.

✓ Passwords must not include common words from an English dictionary or a dictionary of another language with which the user has familiarity.

✓ Passwords must not contain commonly used proper names, including the name of any fictional character or place.

✓ Passwords must not contain any simple pattern of letters or numbers such as "qwertyxx".

For all practical purposes, we'll explain techniques for managing logins and passwords with Windows servers and internetworking equipment such as Cisco routers. We'll also look at adding login dialogs to our own custom projects.

## USER LOGIN AND PASSWORD MANAGEMENT FOR WINDOWS SERVERS

Using Windows NT Server, User Manager for Domains is a utility for managing users, security, member servers, and workstations. With it, you can select and administer a domain or computer, create and manage user accounts, groups, and security policies.

For managing new user accounts, follow these steps:

Step 1 — From Start → Programs → Administrative Tools → User Manager for Domains, on the User menu click New User.

Step 2 — Type the appropriate information in the dialog box as follows:

✓ In Username, type a user name. A user name cannot be identical to any other user or group name of the domain or computer being administered. It can contain up to 20 uppercase or lowercase characters. However, a user name cannot consist solely of periods (.) and spaces or the following:

■ question mark (?)

■ quotation mark (")

■ slashes in either direction (/ \)

- brackets ([ ])

- ampersand (&)

- asterisk (*)

- pipe symbol (|)

- colon (:)

- semicolon (;)

- equal sign (=)

- comma (,)

- various equation signs (+ < >)

- asterisk (*)

✓ In Full Name, type the user's complete name.

✓ In Description, type a description of the user or the user account.

✓ In both Password and Confirm Password, type a password of up to 14 characters in length. For security, the existing password is represented by a row of asterisks; the number of asterisks displayed differs from the actual number of characters used in the password.

Step 3 — Click to select or clear the check boxes for User Must Change Password at Next Logon, User Cannot Change Password, Password Never Expires, and Account Disabled.

Step 4 — To administer a property associated with a button in the New User dialog box, click the button and complete the dialog box that appears; then click OK.

Step 5 — Click Groups.

Step 6 — To add the user account to one or more groups, select one or more groups in Not Member Of, and then click Add (in the case of a new admin user, add to the Administrators group). To remove the user account from one or more groups, select one or more groups in Member Of, and then click Remove. To change the user-account primary group, select one global group from Member Of, and then click Set.

Step 7 — Click OK

Step 8 — Click Profile to add a user profile path, logon script name, or home directory path to this user account. These settings are optional; therefore, you may jump to Step 13.

Step 9 — To enable the user profile to be roaming or mandatory, create a share on the appropriate server, grant Full Control to Everyone, and type the full path in User Profile Path, such as: `\\profiles\joepublic`

Step 10 — To assign a logon script, type the filename in Logon Script Name, such as `marketing.cmd`. If the logon script is stored in a subdirectory of the logon script path, precede the filename with that relative path, such as `marketing\joepublic.cmd`.

Step 11 — To specify a home directory, click Connect, specify a drive letter, click To, and then type a network path, such as `\\users\joepublic`. If the directory does not exist, User Manager for Domains creates it. Optionally, you can substitute `%USERNAME%` for the last subdirectory in the home directory path, such as `\\users\%username%`.

Step 12 — Click OK

Step 13 — In the User Properties dialog box, click Dial-in. These settings are optional; therefore, you may jump to Step 16.

Step 14 — In the Dial-in Information dialog box, click Grant dial-in permission to user if this user should have such rights. When selected, it grants permission to the selected user. You can revoke the selected user's permission by clicking to clear the checkbox.

Step 15 — Under Call Back, select only one of the following:

To disable callback for a user account, click No Call Back (the default setting).

To cause the server to prompt the user for a telephone number, click Set By Caller.

To cause the server to call the user at a fixed telephone number, click Preset To, and then type in the fixed phone number. The server will call the user back at this number only.

Step 16 — Click Add.

Step 17 — Repeat the previous steps to add another user, or click Close to finish.

For managing logon hours, the default settings allow users to connect at any time, but you can restrict individual users to certain days and hours. These settings affect only connections to the server; they do not affect a user's ability to use a workstation. To manage logon hours:

Step 1 — From Start → Programs → Administrative Tools → User Manager for Domains, click Hours in the New User, Copy Of, or User Properties dialog box.

Step 2 — In the Logon Hours dialog box, select the hours to be administered:

✓ To select one hour, click that hour.

✓ To select a block of time, click the beginning hour and drag through the rows and columns to the ending hour.

✓ To select an entire day, click that day in the left column.

✓ To select one hour for all seven days, click the top of that column.

✓ To select the entire week, click the upper-left box (above Sunday).

Step 3 — To allow connections during the selected hours, click Allow. Or, to deny connections during the selected hours, click Disallow.

Step 4 — Repeat Steps 2 and 3, as necessary.

To manage user account policy information, the Account Policy window is used to configure how passwords must be used by all user accounts of the workstation or member server. Before you start changing Account Policy settings, if you select Allow Changes Immediately under Minimum Password Age, you should also click Do Not Keep Password History under Password Uniqueness. If you enter a value under Password Uniqueness, you should also enter a value for Allow Changes in _ Days under Minimum Password. Maximum values for the various options are as follows:

✓ 1 to 999 days for Maximum Password Age and Minimum Password Age.

✓ 1 to 14 characters for Minimum Password Length.

✓ 1 to 24 passwords for Remember _ Passwords under Password Uniqueness.

Follow these steps to manage the Account policy:

Step 1 — From Start → Program → Administrative Tools → User Manager for Domains, on the Policies menu, click Account.

Step 2 — Enter the values you want under any of these groups: Maximum Password Age, Minimum Password Age, Minimum Password Length, and Password Uniqueness. Or, click Password Never Expires, Allow Changes Immediately, Permit Blank Password, or Do Not Keep Password History.

Step 3 — Click Account lockout, and then enter values in Lockout after, Reset count after, and Lockout duration. Or, click No account lockout.

Step 4 — If necessary, select or click to clear the "Forcibly disconnect remote users from server when logon hours expire" check box.

Step 5 — If necessary, select or click to clear the "Users must log on in order to change password" check box.

Windows 2000 Servers manage users with *Active Directory*. User and computer accounts represent a physical entity, such as a computer or person. Accounts provide security credentials for users or computers, enabling users and computers to log on to the network and access domain resources. An account is used to:

- ✓ Authenticate the identity of the user or computer.

- ✓ Authorize access to domain resources.

- ✓ Audit actions performed using the user or computer account.

User and computer accounts are added, disabled, reset, and deleted using Active Directory Users and Computers. An Active Directory user account enables a user to log on to computers and domains with an identity that can be authenticated and authorized for access to domain resources. Each user who logs on to the network should have his or her own unique user account and password. User accounts can also be used as service accounts for some applications.

Windows 2000 provides predefined user accounts that you can use to log on to a computer running Windows 2000. These predefined accounts are:

- ✓ Administrator account

- ✓ Guest account

Predefined accounts are default user accounts designed to let users log on to a local computer and access resources on that computer. They are designed primarily for initial logon and configuration of a local computer. Each predefined account has a different combination of rights and permissions. The Administrator account has the most extensive rights and permissions, while the Guest account's rights and permissions are limited.

If predefined account rights and permissions are not modified or disabled by a network administrator, they could be used by any user or service to log on to a network using the Administrator or Guest identity. To obtain the security of user authentication and authorization, create an individual user account for each user who will participate on your network by using Active Directory Users and Computers. Each user account (including the Administrator and Guest account) can then be added to Windows 2000 groups to control the rights and permissions assigned to the account. Using accounts and groups that are appropriate for your network ensures that users logging on to a network can be identified and can access only the permitted resources.

Each Active Directory user account has a number of security-related options that determine how someone logging on with that particular user account is authenticated on the network. Several of these options are specific to passwords:

✓ User must change password at next logon

✓ User cannot change password

✓ Password never expires

✓ Save password as encrypted clear text

These options are self-explanatory, except for "Save password as encrypted clear text." If you have users logging on to your Windows 2000 network from Apple computers, select this option for those user accounts.

When creating a new user account, note that a new user account with the same name as a previously deleted user account does not automatically assume the permissions and memberships of the previously deleted account, because the security descriptor for each account is unique. To duplicate a deleted user account, all permissions and memberships must be manually re-created. To add a user account, using the Active Directory admin utility, follow these steps:

Step 1 — In the console tree, double-click the domain node. In the Details pane, right-click the organizational unit where you want to add the user, point to New, and then click User.

✓ In First name, type the user's first name.

✓ In Initials, type the user's initials.

✓ In Last name, type the user's last name.

✓ Modify Full name as desired.

✓ In User logon name, type the name with which the user will log on and, from the drop-down list, click the UPN suffix that must be appended to the user logon name (following the @ symbol). If the user intends to use a different name to log on from computers running Windows NT, Windows 98, or Windows 95, change the user logon name as it appears in User logon name (pre-Windows 2000) to the different name.

✓ In Password and Confirm password, type the user's password.

✓ Select the appropriate password options.

Step 2 — After creating the user account, right-click the New User and click Properties to edit the user account and/or enter additional user account information. You can edit general user information, group memberships, dial-in access, Terminal Server access, and session settings.

User accounts can be disabled as a security measure to prevent a particular user from logging on, rather than deleting the user account. By creating disabled user accounts with common group memberships, disabled user accounts can be used as account templates to simplify user account creation. To disable/enable a user account, using the Active Directory admin utility, follow these steps:

Step 1 — In the console tree, double-click the domain.

Step 2 — In the console tree, click Users or click the folder that contains the desired user account.

Step 3 — In the Details pane, right-click on the user and click Disable or Enable Account.

To copy, delete, rename, or move a user account, using the Active Directory admin utility, follow these steps:

Step 1 — In the console tree, double-click the domain

Step 2 — In the console tree, click Users or click the folder that contains the desired user account.

Step 3 — In the Details pane, right-click on the user and select the appropriate course of action.

## LOGIN AND PASSWORD MANAGEMENT FOR CISCO ROUTERS

Just like most of your internetworking equipment, Cisco routers have several login modes. When you access your router, you have access to the command interpreter referred to as "EXEC", in full privileged mode. In this example, there are really only two operation modes to be concerned with:

✓ User mode — Supports tasks for monitoring basic router status information. The user mode prompt looks like this: 2611>

✓ Privileged mode — Supports tasks for modifying the router configuration and accessing advanced status information, debugging, and troubleshooting. The privileged mode can be entered by typing enable at the user mode prompt: 2611>enable (then press Enter). The privileged prompt looks like this: 2611# To exit back to the user mode, type disable at the privileged mode prompt: 2611#disable (then press Enter).

Other important router EXEC modes to know include the following:

✓ Setup mode — The interactive prompted dialogue at the console that we've just previously executed.

✓ Global configuration mode — One-line command mode to perform simple configuration tasks.

✓ RXBOOT mode — Maintenance mode used to recover lost passwords, and other techniques.

Now let's powercycle the router and view the login process from both the console and remote terminal access via Telnet. Using a direct console, from HyperTerminal, after the initial bootstrap and configuration loading processes, you'll be faced with the EXEC user mode prompt. From there, simply type enable and your secret password, such as ciscosecret, and press Enter to enter back into the privileged mode.

To log in remotely via Telnet, go to Start → Run on your Windows system and type telnet ip_address (i.e., 192.168.0.3). Press Enter. At the first prompt, enter the virtual terminal password vterminal and then press Enter. This will log you once again into the EXEC user mode.

From there, simply type `enable`, then the secret password `ciscosecret` and press Enter to enter into the privileged mode.

Among the most critical router administration functions include password maintenance and identification and banner management. Password management can be performed using the following commands:

Changing the virtual terminal password in a Cisco router:

```
2611#config t
Enter configuration commands, one per line.  End with CNTL/Z.
2611(config)#line vty 0 4
2611(config-line)#login
2611(config-line)#password vterm
2611(config-line)#^Z
2611#
```

Changing the console password in a Cisco router:

```
2611#config t
Enter configuration commands, one per line.  End with CNTL/Z.
2611(config)#line console 0
2611(config-line)#login
2611(config-line)#password ciscocon
2611(config-line)#^Z
2611#
```

Changing the enable password in a Cisco router:

```
2611#config t
Enter configuration commands, one per line.  End with CNTL/Z.
2611(config)#enable password cisco2611
2611(config)#^Z
2611#
```

Changing the secret password in a Cisco router:

```
2611#config t
Enter configuration commands, one per line.  End with CNTL/Z.
2611(config)#enable secret ciscosec
2611(config)#^Z
2611#
```

## ADDING A LOGIN/PASSWORD DIALOG TO PROJECTS

The type of login dialog module shown in Figure 10-4 can easily be implemented in your custom projects. In the first example, the password *Password1* is compiled with the source for added security as opposed to calling the password from a text or hidden file or registry key.

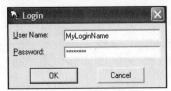

**Figure 10-4:** Adding a login dialog box to your custom projects

**SOURCE (SEE *LOGIN.ZIP*)**    This form of authentication requires case-sensitive input, but only for the password. The username is not required.

```
Public fMainForm As frmMain

Sub Main()
    Dim fLogin As New frmLogin
    fLogin.Show vbModal
    If Not fLogin.OK Then
        'Login Failed so exit app
        End
    End If
    Unload fLogin


    Set fMainForm = New frmMain
    fMainForm.Show
End Sub

Private Declare Function GetUserName Lib "advapi32.dll" Alias "GetUserNameA"
(ByVal lpbuffer As String, nSize As Long) As Long

Public OK As Boolean
Private Sub Form_Load()
    Dim sBuffer As String
    Dim lSize As Long
    sBuffer = Space$(255)
    lSize = Len(sBuffer)
    Call GetUserName(sBuffer, lSize)
    If lSize > 0 Then
        txtUserName.Text = Left$(sBuffer, lSize)
    Else
        txtUserName.Text = vbNullString
    End If
```

```
End Sub

Private Sub cmdCancel_Click()
    OK = False
    Me.Hide
End Sub

Private Sub cmdOK_Click()
    'ToDo: create test for correct password
    'check for correct password
    If txtPassword.Text = "Password1" Then
        OK = True
        Me.Hide
    Else
        MsgBox "Invalid Password, try again!", , "Login"
        txtPassword.SetFocus
        txtPassword.SelStart = 0
        txtPassword.SelLength = Len(txtPassword.Text)
    End If
End Sub
```

**SOURCE (SEE *LOGIN2.ZIP*)**   This form of authentication requires case-sensitive input for the username and password. Data is stored in a hidden Microsoft Access database file. This project uses ActiveX Data Objects (ADOs).

```
Dim CON As Connection
Dim i As Integer
```

'Declaring 'i' for counting the wrong passwords

```
Dim rs As New Recordset

Private Sub cmdCancel_Click()
End
End Sub

Private Sub cmdEnter_Click()
```

'First line of code checks for the value of i being less then 3.  (i.e. it accepts maximum of three wrong passwords)

```
If i > 1 Then
```

```
    rs.Open "Select * from Login where name='" & txtName.Text & "' and pass='"
& txtPass.Text & "'", CON, adOpenKeyset, adLockOptimistic
    If rs.RecordCount = 0 Then
        MsgBox "InValid User & Password", vbCritical, "Failure!"
    Else
        MsgBox "Password Correct", vbInformation, "Success!"
        Unload Me
    End If
    rs.Close
    i = i - 1
Else
    MsgBox "InValid User & Password Unloading", vbCritical, "Failure"
    End
End If
End Sub

Private Sub Form_Initialize()
```

'Initializing the value of 'i' for checking wrong passwords

```
i = 3
```

''Making an instance of the Connection

```
Set CON = New Connection
```

''This is nothing but a connection string for the database
''This string varies for any other database like SQL

```
CON.Open "Provider=Microsoft.jet.oledb.4.0; Data Source=" & App.Path &
"\LoginCheck.mdb"
End Sub

Private Sub Form_Load()
MsgBox "The username & password is 'JOHN'"
End Sub

Private Sub Form_QueryUnload(Cancel As Integer, UnloadMode As Integer)
    End
```

'Ending the program

```
End Sub

Private Sub txtName_KeyPress(KeyAscii As Integer)
```

'First line of code will check whether the user is using Ctrl+C or Ctrl+X or Ctrl+V
'The second line of code will make the value of keyascii to carry nothing

```
If KeyAscii = 3 Or KeyAscii = 22 Or KeyAscii = 24 Then
    KeyAscii = 0
ElseIf KeyAscii = 13 Then 'This is for using the Enter key
    KeyAscii = 0
    SendKeys "{Tab}"
Else
```

This is for changing the lower case alphabets to upper case.

```
    KeyAscii = Asc(UCase(Chr(KeyAscii)))
End If
End Sub

Private Sub txtPass_KeyPress(KeyAscii As Integer)
If KeyAscii = 22 Or KeyAscii = 3 Or KeyAscii = 24 Then
    KeyAscii = 0
ElseIf KeyAscii = 13 Then
    KeyAscii = 0
    SendKeys "{Tab}"
    Call cmdEnter_Click
Else
    KeyAscii = Asc(UCase(Chr(KeyAscii)))
End If
End Sub
```

# Tickets

In regards to Kerberos (web.mit.edu/kerberos/www/) and as explained by TechTarget, tickets are used in the Kerberos authentication system as a secure method for authenticating a request for a service in a computer network. Kerberos was developed in the Athena Project at the Massachusetts Institute of Technology (MIT). The name is taken from Greek mythology; Kerberos was a three-headed dog who guarded the gates of Hades. Kerberos lets a user request an encrypted "ticket" from an authentication process that can then be used to request a particular service from a server. The user's password does not have to pass through the network. A version of Kerberos (client and server) can be downloaded from MIT, or you can buy a commercial version.

Briefly, here's how Kerberos works: Suppose you want to access a server on another computer (which you may get to by sending a Telnet or similar login request). You know that this server requires a Kerberos "ticket" before it will honor your request.

To get your ticket, you first request authentication from the Authentication Server (AS). The Authentication Server creates a "session key" (which is also an encryption key), basing it on your password (which it can get from your username) and a random value that represents the requested service. The session key is effectively a "ticket-granting ticket."

You next send your ticket-granting ticket to a ticket-granting server (TGS). The TGS may be physically the same server as the Authentication Server, but it's now performing a different service. The TGS returns the ticket that can be sent to the server for the requested service.

The service either rejects the ticket or accepts it and performs the service. Because the ticket you received from the TGS is time-stamped, it allows you to make additional requests using the same ticket within a certain time period (typically, eight hours) without having to be reauthenticated. Making the ticket valid for a limited time period makes it less likely that someone else will be able to use it later.

The actual process is much more complicated than just described. The user procedure may vary somewhat according to implementation.

## Tokens

A token is actually a physical security device that knows something of the user, such as a certification, PIN, or password, and enables authorized access to a system or network. An example of a one-time password token mechanism is RSA's SecureID (www.rsasecurity.com).

Security tokens provide an extra level of assurance through a method known as *two-factor authentication*: the user has a personal identification number (PIN), which authorizes him or her as the owner of that particular device; the device then displays a number which uniquely identifies the user to the service, allowing him to log in. The identification number for each user is changed frequently, usually every five minutes or so.

Unlike a password, a security token is a physical object. A key fob (a small hardware device with built-in authentication mechanisms), for example, is practical and easy to carry, and thus easy for the user to protect. Even if the key fob falls into the wrong hands, however, it can't be used to gain access because the PIN (which only the rightful user knows) is also needed.

# Summary

In this chapter, we explored other common two-factor and multibiometric authentication schemes you can implement with some of the systems discussed throughout this book. We reviewed some common development kits you can customize for proprietary system development, and analyzed a complete working kit you can use to create a multifactor biometric system for authenticating users.

For the remainder of the chapter, we reviewed two-factor authentication with passwords, tickets, and tokens, and stepped through login and password management for Windows servers and Cisco routers. In addition, we analyzed working login dialog plug-ins you can add to your projects.

# Chapter 11

# Executive Decision

UNTIL NOW, THE BOOK has covered physical and behavioral biometric technologies, along with multifactor authentication and some data-hiding techniques. This information was combined with real-world sample (standalone) product installations, uses, and tuning in an effort to wet your biometric technology whistle. Although you derive many benefits from the use of standalone biometric products in publicly accessible and physical-access arenas, biometric products must be evaluated much as you would other security products used in similar environments if you decide to use them for shared solutions, such as in data networks.

This chapter combines the knowledge learned up to this point with solid criteria to assist you in selecting the biometric technology to use for your own situation. The information discussed thus far is used to build a solid foundation from which to begin selecting and eliminating potential biometric technology implementations. The criteria discussed in this chapter include the following:

- ✓ Business reasons (usage)
- ✓ Cost
- ✓ Technology strength(s)
- ✓ Security classification categories
- ✓ Ease of use
- ✓ FAR (False Acceptance Rate)
- ✓ FRR (False Reject Rate)
- ✓ CER (Crossover Error Rate)
- ✓ Environment
- ✓ Architectures
- ✓ Management tools
- ✓ Fault tolerance selection
- ✓ Enrollment
- ✓ Planning and designing criteria

# Establish Goals

One of the most important components of any successful project is to establish appropriate goals. Doing so ensures that your focus remains on the task(s) at hand. In this case, your primary goal is to select and implement a biometric solution. Your purpose for implementing such a solution may vary, based on many factors, but should be clearly understood by all appropriate parties within the environment.

To establish such goals, a problem or need must exist.

# Needs Analysis

Before you select a technology (biometric or otherwise), you should have a need for it. To determine whether such a need exists, you can perform a *needs analysis*. The needs analysis may be very simple or very complex, but the end result should be a factual determination that a need (or very reasonable use) does exist for a specific technology. Although many organizations could benefit from the use of biometric devices, implementing them without a valid need or justification is not advisable. After a valid need or use is identified, you can develop your selection criteria. These selection criteria can assist in determining which biometric technology is best or most well-suited in the environment, as well as which manufacturer's device(s) offer the best fit within that environment.

# Selection Criteria

The following section outlines criteria that act as a solid starting point to assist you in the biometric technology selection process. Although we recommend that you at least consider them all for thoroughness, you could conceivably extract certain criteria from this list to form a smaller set of selection criteria. A more likely scenario (in fact, one that we highly encourage) is that you add to these selection criteria to create as encompassing an evaluation as possible.

## Approach

This chapter uses a spreadsheet-style approach to create a baseline from which you can build your overall evaluation and decision-making process. This spreadsheet is designed to help account for—and to assist you in addressing and/or integrating—a network-based biometric solution, while maintaining a focus on the following areas:

- ✓ Access methods to be used
- ✓ Administration
- ✓ Biometric device evaluation criteria
- ✓ Other considerations
- ✓ Cost/cost reduction

- ✓ Data classifications
- ✓ Environment
- ✓ Evaluation criteria
- ✓ Leveraging the investment
- ✓ Multifactor/multibiometric
- ✓ Overcoming objections
- ✓ Problem to be solved
- ✓ Restrictions
- ✓ Security policies, procedures, applications, and transactions
- ✓ Selecting the appropriate device(s)
- ✓ Shared devices or individual
- ✓ Strength needed
- ✓ Strength of template
- ✓ Support staff skill requirements
- ✓ System requirements
- ✓ User acceptance/user convenience
- ✓ Weaknesses/countermeasures

Each of these areas, as well as other, more-specific information within your environment, must be considered to ensure that a sound evaluation is performed and to ultimately enable you to make a sound biometric technology decision.

# Criteria Overview

Before proceeding to the evaluation spreadsheet, you need to understand the components and definitions that make up the spreadsheet. This section briefly outlines each item. If your organization uses a multiphase approach, individual sections from the spreadsheet can be selected and used at different phases of the evaluation to create a set of evaluation criterion for each phase (multiple spreadsheets), or you can use only those initial sections that are necessary for a given phase.

## ACCESS METHODS

*Access methods* are those means by which a user can gain access to network-based resources. This access can include both physical and logical access. The following items (as well as others) need to be included in the evaluation process:

- ✓ Is application authentication required?
- ✓ Is dial-in access to be used?

✓ Is a network login required?

✓ Is password replacement required?

✓ Is remote access required (RAS, Citirx, PCAnywhere, and so on)?

✓ Is Telnet access required?

✓ Is virtual private network (VPN) access to be used?

✓ Are multiple Web site authentications required?

Each access method affected by a biometric technology must be identified and entered as part of the evaluation criteria to ensure that a selected solution addresses all your access needs.

## ADMINISTRATION

Administration of any system is vital, and this holds true for biometric solutions as well. Administering biometric solutions involves such components as the initial installation process, the enrollment process, a centralized or distributed identification/authentication mechanism, special backup process requirements, and protection of the end user's templates. Additionally, depending on the biometric technology that you choose, users may need to periodically re-enroll. This is important because the administration of the enrollment process in large organizations is substantial. The product selected should provide the necessary security while limiting administration requirements wherever possible. The following questions can provide a foundation for the administration portion of your evaluation process:

✓ Are additional administrative measures required to protect end user templates?

✓ Are special backup requirements needed?

✓ Is the primary need for the biometric solution to reduce administration costs?

✓ Must the enrollment process be easy?

✓ Should the biometric template store be distributed?

✓ Should the biometric templates be stored centrally?

✓ Is a periodic re-enrollment process to be required?

## BIOMETRIC DEVICE EVALUATION CRITERIA

Afteryou determine that security benefit(s) can be derived from using biometric identification/ authentication, a formal method leveraging solid evaluation criteria is used during the selection process. This evaluation process is two-fold and is designed primarily to help determine which biometric product(s) best fit your need.

One portion of the evaluation criteria, in conjunction with the entire Biometric Selection Spreadsheet, is designed to assist you in determining which biometric technology best provides the level of protection that you need, based on your data classification and protection needs.

The other portion of the evaluation criteria deals primarily with individual devices. After a general biometric technology is chosen (fingerprint biometric technology, for example), you need to know what evaluation criteria to use to differentiate one product from another? The answer may be as simple as ensuring that the selected product meets all the criteria in the Biometric Selection Spreadsheet, or you may need to take additional parameters into consideration. If fingerprint technology is chosen, for example, what characteristics must the device have, specific to that technology? Maybe the device needs to be integrated with other equipment, such as directly in a PDA, keyboard, or computer, or maybe you'd prefer a standalone device, such as a USB fingerprint sensor. Moreover, you may need to limit your selection to only those devices that attempt to ensure that the biometric presented to the device (a finger, for example) is living. The questions in the following list provide a starting point for this section of the selection criteria:

- ✓ Is reducing the false acceptance rate most important?
- ✓ Is reducing the false reject rate most important?
- ✓ Is a crossover accuracy rate of 1:50 to 1:500 acceptable?
- ✓ Is a crossover accuracy rate of greater than 1:500 required?
- ✓ Must the biometric device be embedded in another device (for example, a keyboard)?
- ✓ Must the biometric device be standalone?
- ✓ Is proof of life required?

## OTHER CONSIDERATIONS

Additional considerations should include items that may not fit cleanly into other categories. Such items could include failover planning designed to provide access in case the biometric solution fails (which could also be included under a heading of Disaster Recovery and Redundancy), biometric solution redundancy, and enabling the use of encryption technology and current technology within the environment. The following list provides some sample considerations:

- ✓ Is there a predetermined failover mechanism for the biometric solution?
- ✓ Must the biometric solution enable redundancy?
- ✓ Is the biometric solution to be used for encryption technology?
- ✓ Can it work with the current technology within the environment?

An example of an additional consideration may include a product that contains replicated biometric template information that can be used in conjunction with e-mail encryption technology. Additionally, a particular environment may already heavily use voice recognition, signature devices, or Web cameras for other business functions. This could present an opportunity to further or better use the existing equipment.

## COST/COST REDUCTION

One of the greatest challenges of password authentication is making sure that passwords are too difficult for someone to guess. To this end, passwords should be totally random and contain upper- and lowercase letters, numbers, and special characters. Unfortunately, this also makes the password difficult for the end user to remember. Furthermore, to reduce the possibility of brute-force attacks, these already difficult-to-remember passwords should be changed regularly. Because of this requirement, end users often write their passwords down and frequently place them somewhere within their workspaces. So a potential wrong doer could search the end users' areas and collect passwords, couple them with the organization's standard user-naming convention, and easily breach the network.

Even if a strong password scheme does not lead users to write down passwords, it most certainly leads to the increased costs associated with password resets. Cost reductions can be realized, however, by using a biometric solution, and these cost savings become even more substantial if the selected technology can reduce the need for multiple passwords across many systems.

Even where multibiometrics are used — as long as the biometric solution is user-friendly — multiple authentications can frequently be performed without much end-user discomfort.

A password can be shared; a biometric trait must be duplicated.

Asking the following questions can aid in determining cost information:

- ✓ Can the biometric solution reduce help desk costs?
- ✓ Can the biometric solution reduce administration costs?
- ✓ Are other cost reductions possible by implementing a biometric solution?
- ✓ Can the costs of other technologies currently in use be reduced (for example, token technology)?

Add to these considerations other cost/accounting questions, as needed.

## DATA CLASSIFICATIONS

One of the most important factors in determining what level of security to apply to a given solution — and as an aid in selecting the appropriate biometric identification/authentication technology — is to understand how your data is classified.

Understanding what you are trying to protect is critical; this is where data classification comes in. Using five primary data categories is recommended. These categories are a combination of public- and military-style data-classification categories. Keep in mind that the application(s) are not being classified, but the data produced and how the application handles the data. For example, you can produce a public document by using a word processor, and you can also produce a private document by using a word processor. Correctly handling such classifications is the goal.

**CORPORATE/COMPANY/MILITARY**    Following are categories for classifying data that you may find in corporate/company and even military environments:

- ✓ **Public** — Public data is data that is available to the general public or data that, if disclosed to the general public, is of little or no consequence to the organization.

- ✓ **Sensitive** — Sensitive data should be protected from disclosure or unauthorized modification. Such data is not for public eyes but is not considered private or confidential.

- ✓ **Private** — The unauthorized disclosure of private data could adversely affect a company, its business, or employees. An example in many organizations would be personnel information containing employee names, home addresses, and phone numbers. If disclosed, this could result in both legal action against the company and loss of confidence in the organization.

- ✓ **Confidential** — Confidential data is generally considered the highest classification within a company. If this information were compromised (disclosed, altered, and so on), extreme damage to an organization could occur, up to and including causing the company to go out of business. Some examples of data in this category include prototypes and designs, new product development information, contract negotiations, and so on.

The preceding examples may fall within different categories in different organizations, depending on their primary business. Within a placement agency, for example, employee information may be considered classified.

**MILITARY**    The military uses the following five classification categories:

- ✓ **Unclassified** — Similar in nature to its public counterpart, unclassified data can be available to the general public or, if disclosed to the general public, is of no consequence to national security.

- ✓ **Sensitive but Unclassified** — Sensitive data should be protected from disclosure or unauthorized modification.

- ✓ **Confidential** — The unauthorized disclosure of confidential information or material could cause damage to U.S. national security.

- ✓ **Secret** — The unauthorized disclosure of secret information or material could cause serious damage to U.S. national security.

- ✓ **Top Secret** — The unauthorized disclosure of top-secret information or material could cause exceptionally grave damage to U.S. national security.

You can find fuller definitions of these categories by searching for "U.S. military security classifications" on your favorite search engine.

**COMBINE DATA CLASSIFICATIONS**    After data is classified, you can combine similar data classifications together. Each data classification should have its own associated security policy. Data should not be put in more than one classification category. If data ends up in two classification categories during your classification process, use the highest classification.

**CATEGORIZE THE DATA**    In addition to classifying data, you should define and separately classify your applications in categories if all the data produced from such an application falls into one category. The key here is to understand the nature of the data and where the data is needed. Some examples follow:

- ✓  Engineering applications used only for prototypes
- ✓  Databases containing only one classification of data
- ✓  Identity management stores
- ✓  E-mail used to communicate both internally and externally

Add additional categories as needed, but make sure that common, understood definitions are consistently used.

**DEFINE LEGAL OBLIGATIONS FOR DATA**    Define both the potential legal repercussions and legal obligations that the company can face involving its data. Knowing what constitutes illegal activities that can be used against the company, as well as what are the company's responsibilities and legal obligations, is important. Do your homework and consult legal council that specializes in this area.

As a minimum, the following data categorization questions should be included in your evaluation criteria:

- ✓  Is the data classified as public?
- ✓  Is the data classified as sensitive?
- ✓  Is the data classified as private?
- ✓  Is the data classified as confidential?
- ✓  Is the data classified as top secret?
- ✓  Is this a military, government, or other national agency?
- ✓  Have the data classifications been combined?
- ✓  Have all data and specific applications been categorized?

## ENVIRONMENT

The environment can be one of the most critical factors in selecting a biometric technology. The environment encompasses such concerns as temperature, weather (indoor or outdoor use), lighting, and general conditions. What environment is the product to be used in? Does the environment affect your selection of product? Some examples follow:

- ✓ Is the temperature controlled?
- ✓ Is the temperature between 60 and 95 degrees Fahrenheit?
- ✓ Is the lighting adequate?
- ✓ Is the environment clean, dust-free, and free of other contaminants (for example, grease)?
- ✓ Is the biometric device(s) to be used indoors?
- ✓ Is the biometric device(s) to be used outdoors?

If the biometric device(s) are to be used in varying conditions, special accommodations may be necessary to ensure accurate identification/authentication. Devices used outside need to be protected from the elements, including extreme heat/cold, rain, snow, sleet, and so on. Additionally, you need to protect the device(s) from tampering, vandalism, and other unauthorized use. In remote locations, using monitoring equipment and devices in conjunction with the biometric device(s) may be necessary. Even if the device(s) are indoors, you should be aware of where they are located, how they are accessed, what mechanism(s) protect them, and whether they need to be monitored.

## LEVERAGING THE INVESTMENT

During the selection process, you need to determine how the biometric technology is best utilized. If the biometric solution can be used for many functions (to achieve greater levels of security) in many areas within an organization, that solution provides much greater flexibility and is likely to be a better investment. Similarly, if the selected biometric solution performs the necessary identification/authentication and can be further integrated into the environment, either innately or by using a software development kit, the product better leverages your investment. Some questions that can lead to a better understanding of how best to leverage your investment include the following:

- ✓ Is a Software Development Kit (SDK) required?
- ✓ Must the biometric technology provide protection for individual e-mails, documents, and so on?
- ✓ Can the biometric be used on multiple operating system platforms?

A product that provides only identification/authentication and an SDK for example, may be used for e-mail, file, folder, or disk encryption by using the biometric as an authentication device.

Misuse of a Software Development Kit (SDK) can lead to vulnerabilities.

## MULTIFACTOR/MULTIBIOMETRIC

Based on your data classification, is single identification/authentication sufficient or is a multifactor and/or multibiometric solution required?

As previously shown, a single biometric solution may not provide the security strength necessary to adequately identify/authenticate an individual for confidential or top-secret information. This becomes very evident in reviewing crossover accuracy, as shown in Table 11-1.

**TABLE 11-1: Crossover Accuracy**

| Biometrics | Crossover Accuracy |
| --- | --- |
| Retinal scan | 1:10,000,000+ |
| Iris scan | 1:131,000 |
| Fingerprints | 1:500 |
| Hand geometry | 1:500 |
| Signature dynamics | 1:50 |
| Voice dynamics | 1:50 |
| Facial recognition | Theoretical |
| Vascular patterns | Theoretical |

If you use a single biometric solution with passwords or token devices, however, or combine two biometric solutions, the result creates a stronger identification/authentication scheme than a single biometric solution can provide. A good example is to combine voice and signature dynamics. Using only one technology provides a crossover accuracy of only 1:50, while both combined produces a theoretical crossover accuracy greater than 1:100 (theoretical unknown).

Some questions that can assist you in determining whether a multifactor and/or a multibiometric solution should be used are as follows:

✓ Are passwords still to be required in addition to the biometric?

✓ Is a multibiometric solution preferable?

✓ Is a multibiometric solution required?

✓ Can devices already in place be used for biometric technologies (for example, microphones or Web cams)?

✓ Are multifactor/multibiometrics required throughout the environment or only in limited areas?

## OVERCOMING OBJECTIONS

Overcoming potential objections can be one of the most difficult factors in determining which biometric technology to use in a given environment. Change is inevitable but not necessarily readily accepted by all users.

Objections can be real or perceived. Many of the book's chapters discuss methods to overcome challenges and objections in sections entitled "Fact/Fiction." These sections deal with many of the issues surroundign objections to this technology. Anticipating such objections (whether real or perceived) enables you to adequately prepare the appropriate responses. Remember that even objections that are only perceived must be addressed. To assist with some of the more common objections, the Biometric Selection Criteria spreadsheet contains some leading questions to help you understand what types of questions can lead to possible objections. Knowing these enables you to formulate other questions, based on your environment. Examples include the following:

✓ Is physical contact with the device required?

✓ Are multiple people to use a single device?

✓ What potential (real or perceived) damage could be caused by using the device?

✓ Can the user's biometric information become compromised?

✓ Can a user's biometric trait be rebuilt from a given template?

These questions are very basic. Based on your environment and users, this section should become very comprehensive and should enable you to address the specific objections that may arise in your environment.

## PROBLEM TO BE SOLVED

What is the primary problem to be solved by your choice of a biometic solution? This question could be the single most important one that you ask, especially in the formative stages of your evaluation. Biometric solutions are most often used to solve and identify management problems — meaning that a genuine need exists to know who is doing something. The "something" may be as simple as accessing a room, or it may be extremely complex, and it is the root of the problem to be solved.

Suppose that you have very stringent change-control processes in place but are currently using username/password protection as the only authentication mechanism. Many support staffers log in as the super user (that is, administrator, admin, root, or supervisor) to perform their duties.

This situation makes determining exactly who made a specific changes difficult. One method of addressing this problem is to set up multiple, individual administrative accounts for each support member by using username/password and enable-logging mechanisms that, in many scenarios, are sufficient. If greater identification is necessary, however, implementing a biometric solution (with logging enabled) helps to ensure that the support staff members making configuration changes are identified and authorized and that their actions are tracked based on their identities.

Or the problem you need to solve may be as simple as reducing help desk password reset calls.

The Biometric Selection Criteria spreadsheet lists a few of the more common problems that biometric solutions can be used to solve, such as the following:

✓ Is the biometric solution to be used for network identification of users only?

✓ Is configuration control identification a problem to be solved?

✓ Is the biometric solution meant to reduce help desk-related password resets?

✓ Is the identification of virtual private network (VPN) users a problem?

✓ Is the biometric solution meant to replace existing technology, such as tokens?

## RESTRICTIONS

Another important component of any successful evaluation or selection process is what items may limit or eliminate specific technologies as valid within the selected environment. Some restrictions may be based on environmental issues, while others may be related to many items, including usage scenarios, type of work performed, and user conditions.

A plant that requires helmets with shields to be worn at all times, for example, may not be the best fit for retina vascular pattern technology. Similarly, a very noisy location would not likely be a candidate for voice recognition technology.

Finally, you could also face physical restrictions, as might be the case if workers use their hands frequently in abrasive environments (for example, brick layers, construction workers, and so on). These types of jobs may require users to enroll and re-enroll too frequently to make the solution viable. Using biometric fingerprint technology, for example, may not work as well in such a situation as signature, voice, or face recognition or combinations thereof.

Sample restrictions to consider include the following:

✓ Do any environmental restrictions need to be considered?

✓ Do any physical restrictions exist that would preclude a specific biometric technology?

✓ Do any handicap considerations exist that could lead to restrictions?

✓ Do any company policies impose restrictions on potential biometric solutions?

✓ Are any restrictions imposed by specific equipment?

## SECURITY POLICIES, GUIDELINES, PROCEDURES, AND PRACTICES

If you're considering biometric solutions, one would hope that security policies and procedures already exist within the environment. Sadly, this is often not the case. In many organizations, technology decisions are often knee-jerk reactions to a specific problem, whether a misconfiguration, unauthorized access, a breach, or countless others. To avoid this scenario in dealing with security technologies, evaluate such technologies in terms of your company's overall security needs. To accomplish this, create and maintain sound security practices. Such practices include the generation and appropriate maintenance of security policies, guidelines, procedures, and practices. In evaluating potential biometric solutions, you should make these policies the gauge by which you measure any biometric technology.

Security policies, guidelines, procedures, and practices encompass many areas, and each should be considered in integrating additional security technologies within the environment. A few such considerations are listed here to get you started:

- ✓ Do security policies exist?
- ✓ Do you have any specifics for biometric technologies?
- ✓ Can a biometric solution strengthen your overall security?
- ✓ Can the biometric technology be used to strengthen application security?
- ✓ Can the biometric technology fill a void in your existing security schema?

The importance of security policies, guidelines, procedures, and practices cannot be over-emphasized. They are critical in creating a truly secure environment.

## SELECTING THE APPROPRIATE DEVICE(S)

If you choose to implement a biometric solution (or multiple solutions/devices), you must be able to differentiate between the different offerings available. You may base your decision on your overall criteria, or you choice may be limited because only one or two manufacturers of a given biometric solution exist. If multiple offerings do exist, however, you need to determine what criteria to use to select among the varying devices available for the different biometric technologies. Where you have many manufacturers, what criteria can you use to select a specific device within a given biometric technology?

Fingerprint technology is emerging as today's biometric leader, largely because of its ease of use and general acceptance. You can, therefore, find many manufacturers of fingerprint devices in the marketplace today, as evidenced by the ubiquity of such devices as laptops and PDAs with built-in fingerprint technology. If multiple options exist, you must devise a method of determining which technology best fits your need. To accomplish this goal, you should establish some solution-specific evaluation criteria.

If multiple fingerprint sensor devices can support a given software product, for example, how do you determine which device is the best? The following questions give you a head start in establishing your criteria:

- ✓ Does the device create the biometric template before any transmittal?
- ✓ Does one acquisition device have a better CER, FRR, and/or FAR than the others?
- ✓ Are durability factors an issue?
- ✓ Does one device/manufacturer offer better service?
- ✓ Is one manufacturer a clear leader in terms of maturity of product?

Again, completely list and evaluate those criteria that seem important to your decision-making process. Cost, of course, is almost always a main factor. Nonetheless, in evaluating security products, try to remove cost from the equation and evaluate only the strengths and weaknesses of each product within a biometric solution family. This process should be performed separately for each type of biometric device, biometric drivers, software, and related product (such as SDK) that you're considering. If a multibiometric solution is required, an evaluation should be performed for each biometric technology acquisition device, driver, and software solution.

## SHARED OR INDIVIDUAL DEVICES

Depending on the solution that you select, you may need a shared device solution (such as a retina vascular pattern scanner), individual devices, or a mixture. You should understand where each type of device is to be used to accurately scope the solution. Individual devices may not require provisions for mounting, cleaning, and so on, whereas shared devices may require such provisions. Ask the following questions:

- ✓ Can acquisition devices be shared?
- ✓ Do you need a mix of standalone devices and shared devices?
- ✓ Are special considerations needed for shared devices (such as cleaning)?
- ✓ Do shared devices require special mounting, device protection, and so on?
- ✓ Do individual devices require special protection, mounting, and so on?

This section may not be neceesary if only individual devices are to be used; however, make sure that you include special requirements, such as cleaning, in other evaluation areas.

## STRENGTH NEEDED

You can't deny that any implemented biometric solution must be strong, but how strong must the biometric security be? What are considered acceptable CER, FAR, and FRR? This section of the evaluation deals with the biometric solution's general strength. Some examples are posed in the following list:

✓ Is the CER within reasonable tolerances?

✓ Is the FAR within reasonable tolerances?

✓ Is the FRR within reasonable tolerances?

✓ Does the software solution enhance CER, FAR, and FRR?

✓ Does the solution implement any countermeasures?

## TEMPLATE STRENGTH

Although template strength greatly affects overall strength, understanding the makeup and strength of the biometric solution is also important. This can be a very important factor in reducing or eliminating many objections that users may have, as well as in understanding how the biometric trait is processed into templates, propriety, encryption, and other protection. Some factors affecting template strength are as follows:

✓ Is the algorithm used to create the template strong?

✓ Is the algorithm used to create the template mature?

✓ Can the template be used with other biometric solutions?

✓ Is the template encrypted?

✓ Is the template store protected?

Factor in the overall strength of the template(s) during the selection process to determine which technology/technologies provide the best template protection.

Many users' fears of biometric technology are predicated on someone obtaining their biometric information and using it elsewhere. Because a biometric trait such as a fingerprint, iris, or retina cannot be changed (at least with today's technology), the fear may be somewhat valid. If the selected technology creates a proprietary template for that system only, however, the affect of unauthorized template capture can be limited.

## SUPPORT STAFF SKILL REQUIREMENTS

Many people have a limited understanding of biometric technologies and, ultimately, their implementations. Much of this limited understanding is due to the overall maturity of biometric solutions, as well as the fact that most people have limited exposure and availability to biometric technologies. For this reason, you need to consider the skill sets of the current staff in relationship to potential biometric technology options. If a wide gap exists between the knowledge and skill set(s) necessary for the implementation and ongoing support of a particular product, this can have a direct effect on how the selected technology is implemented and supported.

The skill set must also include the environment of the associated biometric solution software. If the solution requires much custom programming, many technical personnel may not be adept at the required programming techniques. Outside resources or additional employees must therefore be considered, either short or long term. If the intent is for the current staff to support the biometric solution, training needs must be included in the selection, evaluation, implementation, and maintenance process.

Some of the support staff skill requirements to consider are as follows:

- ✓ Does the current staff have a solid understanding of biometric technology solutions?

- ✓ Is the current staff to be tasked with performing the initial implementation?

- ✓ Is the current staff to be tasked with the continuing maintenance?

- ✓ Has a training method been identified?

- ✓ Do remote support personnel require additional training?

Other skill set-related items should be added to the evaluation criteria as appropriate to your specific environment. Some possible additions may relate to outsourcing skill sets and maintenance options, as well as many others.

## SYSTEM REQUIREMENTS

The system requirements evaluation section is considered by many to be one of the most important factors in the selection process. Many people, however, look at only the published individual system requirements by a given product's manufacturer. Because so many factors affect the overall system, all the system (or often systems) requirements are not accounted for. The system requirements section, therefore, could ultimately become one of the largest sections in your evaluation matrix, depending on the environment. To get a better feel for how extensive this area can be, look at some of the factors that can have a dramatic effect on system(s) requirements.

Suppose that you are reviewing a product for a single building and 100 users, and the potential products can be set up in a distributed or centralized mode. If you're using the product in a centralized mode, the product can be installed on an existing server as long as the server meets the appropriate system specifications (such as ample available processing power, sufficient drive space, appropriate memory requirements, and so on), as defined by the biometric solution's manufacturer.

Suppose, however, that a different scenario involves multiple locations, each of which must be identified and authenticated locally, but that central administration is required. In this scenario, many other factors must be considered, such as whether multiple servers are needed. Other considerations in this scenario include the method that you use to synchronize the authentication, available bandwidth between locations to be synchronized, method of distributing authentication devices, and so on. The environment, biometric technology, designs, and implementation method, therefore, can affect all the system(s) requirements. The following criteria questions can help you begin determining which items to use to identify your system(s) requirements:

- ✓ Is the biometric solution distributed?

- ✓ Are multiple biometric data stores required?

✓ For distributed environments, has the communication method been defined?

✓ In distributed environments, is bandwidth adequate to accommodate synchronization?

✓ Do you use multiple methods of configuring synchronization?

## USER ACCEPTANCE

User acceptance can often determine whether a given biometric technology is successful in a given environment. Many users have their own opinions of and objections to specific types of technologies. You should be aware, however, of which user acceptance factors are the most critical in a given environment. To gain a better understanding of how well specific technologies may be accepted, you can use the following criteria to start the evaluation process:

✓ Does any data exist currently on user acceptance of specific technologies?

✓ Can a survey be used to gain an understanding of which technologies might be better received?

✓ Does the user need to perform additional end-user maintenance functions?

✓ Can the biometric solution be perceived as intrusive?

✓ Can the biometric solution cause technical challenges to the user?

These items and many more can help you achieve a solid understanding of how well (or how poorly) a proposed solution may be received in your environment. Often, if users are minimally affected or can realize some benefit from the proposed solution, the solution is much more palatable to them.

## USER CONVENIENCE/SPECIAL FEATURES

One of the best ways to overcome objections and to create better acceptance by the user community is to offer conveniences or special features. A biometric solution that can reduce the end users' work load, lower frustration levels (as may be associated with multiple passwords), or provide them with other features that they may need is more likely to gain support over one that simply introduces another identification/authentication level. Some of the more common features that often peak the interests of many users are as follows:

✓ Can the number of passwords a user must type be reduced?

✓ Can the device provide other authentications to other applications, such as document password replacement or VPN authentication information?

✓ Can the user use the biometric solution to provide security for his/her own applications (for example, databases)?

✓ Is the biometric device easily transportable?

✓ Can the device be used by multiple users on a single machine to provide automatic identification?

Although some of these items may seem insignificant, these are often key selling points for end users. Remember that, the more convenience that you can provide to end users, the more likely they are to concede on some of or all their objections.

## WEAKNESSES/COUNTERMEASURES

Technology devices have both strengths and weaknesses, and biometric solutions are no different. The method of deployment, environment, and other factors can contribute to or create new weaknesses. If you are considering implementing biometric technology (or any technology, for that matter), keep in mind the weaknesses associated with the solution and other weaknesses that can be imposed or introduced. Weaknesses relating to specific biometric technologies have already been discussed, and they should be included in your evaluation.

You should also include known countermeasures that need to be used within the environment. General countermeasures have already been discussed throughout the text; the following list focuses on other weaknesses/countermeasures that may not necessarily be solution-specific.

- ✓ Is or can the environment be made tamper resistant?
- ✓ Can the general public access any devices?
- ✓ Are personnel or noncompany persons ever unattended in the facility?
- ✓ Are access areas biometrically controlled?
- ✓ Is the software portion of the biometric solution to be evaluated for tamper resistance?

Trying to include every possible weakness in all scenarios for each varying environment is difficult. Your security policies, guidelines, procedures, and practices, therefore, must consistently and continually check for and evaluate the overall security within the environment to reduce weaknesses, implement countermeasures, and ultimately make overall security stronger. Selecting an appropriate methodology for achieving this goal often makes creating a more secure environment more manageable.

Ensure that your evaluation accounts for all affected locations, including those outside the primary country.

## ADDITIONAL INFORMATION

We have included a section on the Selection Criteria spreadsheet within the Biometric Selection Criteria workbook. This area can also be used to provide additional selection criteria or simply for adding information, including items, taking notes, and so on.

Some items that may be added here could include an Access Control Method (Bell-LaPadula or Take Grant), protocols, training requirements, installation requirements, and so on.

# Ripple Security Logic

One of the methods that can be used to assist in creating a more secure environment is Ripple Security Logic (RSL), which stems from an inward-out/outward-in look at securing specific devices.

Ripple Security Logic is predicated on starting from the center and working out. Starting at the lowest security level possible is important. Many people start from the identification/authentication level, for example, can you start from a file, a block, a bit, or even an electron? You get the idea.

Ripple Security Logic can help determine what needs to be protected, what level of protection may be required, and what inside and outside influences may affect the protection, as well as help to create an ongoing testing process. This can help narrow the selection process relating to biometric technology solutions.

For more information on Ripple Security Logic (RSL), see *Storage Security: Protecting SANs, NAS and DAS*, another great Wiley publication, at www.wiley.com/compbooks.

# Completing the Workbook

We have created a Microsoft Excel workbook that can be used as the basis for the Biometric Selection Criteria, which you can find on the accompanying Web site for this book. This spreadsheet is designed to accept Yes or No answers, as indicated by its check boxes. A check in a box indicates a Yes response, and a blank check box indicates a No response. The initial responses are all No. As you go through and check boxes to indicate a true response to a given question, the corresponding Summary worksheet changes based on your selections. The corresponding changes in the Summary worksheet are generally simple responses designed to ensure that the appropriate questions and criteria are used in evaluating products and to serve as a guide for vendors who may be proposing solutions to create a more-level evaluation. After all, your criteria are what are important, not necessarily all the other bells and whistles that manufacturers and vendors try to tout.

After you have completed the Selection Criteria worksheet, click the Summary tab (worksheet in the workbook) to view the results. This summary section can be printed and given to the previously mentioned vendors or manufacturers. Figure 11-1 illustrates a portion of the Selection Criteria spreadsheet that has been completed.

The results of these selections are shown in Figure 11-2, the Summary worksheet in the Biometric Selection Criteria workbook.

**Figure 11-1:** Sample of Selection Criteria

**Figure 11-2:** Sample Summary

# Selection Process

After the Biometric Selection Criteria worksheet is filled out, you can either print the Summary sheet or select the Summary sheet and include it in a selection/product evaluation document containing additional information, as necessary. This document can be used to create a Request for Information (RFI), Request for Pricing (RFP), Request for Quote (RFQ), or other such documents that your company may require in considering a biometric solution.

After this information is provided to prospective vendors, manufacturers, developers, and so on, a compliancy matrix should be generated. One very simple method of creating such a compliancy matrix is to again use the Selection Criteria Summary as a guide. Two possible methods of accomplishing this (although many others exist) follow:

**1.** Cross-reference the responses from the appropriate cell in the Summary worksheet and add titles for the prospective solution providers, manufacturers, vendors, developers, and so on. Figure 11-3 shows an abbreviated example of this method.

| Response | Vendor 1 | Vendor 2 | Vendor 3 | Vendor 4 |
|---|---|---|---|---|
| Access Methods | | | | |
| The selected biometric solution must be able to provide Application Authenticaiton. | | | | |
| The selected biometric solution does not need to accommodate for dial-in access. | | | | |
| Network identification/authentication is required. | | | | |
| Password replacement using the biometric trait is required. | | | | |
| Remote Access solution(s) will be used. Remote access authentication options must be investigated. | | | | |
| No telnet access is required | | | | |
| No VPN access is required | | | | |
| The biometric solution will not be used for WEB authentication. | | | | |
| | | | | |
| Administration | | | | |
| It appears that the end user templates are adequately protected, ensure this is true. | | | | |
| It appears that a standard backup solution will function properly for the proposed biometric solution. | | | | |
| Cost is the primary reason for the biometric solution, adequate strength without using passwords must be achieved. | | | | |
| The biometric solution must provide easy enrollment without jeopardizing enrollment control. | | | | |
| It is not necessary for the template store to be distributed. | | | | |
| The template store must be centralized. | | | | |
| The intent is to periodically have users re-enroll to reduce FRRs and to ensure identity. | | | | |

**Figure 11-3:** Abbreviated cell cross-reference

The response information is printed right on the evaluation form. This is an easy method but may create a spreadsheet that is too large to print on standard-format paper.

**2.** Cross-reference the row numbers associated with the responses in the Summary worksheet to item numbers in the Compliancy worksheet. Again, add the title information for the prospective suppliers of the biometric technology/technologies. Figure 11-4 shows an abbreviated example of this method.

| | Response | Vendor 1 | Vendor 2 | Vendor 3 | Vendor 4 |
|---|---|---|---|---|---|
| | Access Methods | | | | |
| Item 6 | | | | | |
| Item 7 | | | | | |
| Item 8 | | | | | |
| Item 9 | | | | | |
| Item 10 | | | | | |
| Item 11 | | | | | |
| Item 12 | | | | | |
| Item 13 | | | | | |
| | | | | | |
| | Administration | | | | |
| Item 16 | | | | | |
| Item 17 | | | | | |
| Item 18 | | | | | |
| Item 19 | | | | | |
| Item 20 | | | | | |
| Item 21 | | | | | |
| Item 22 | | | | | |

**Figure 11-4:** Abbreviated item reference

Using the second method condenses the format but requires the Summary information to be included separately.

After you have chosen a format, determine your evaluation rankings. Try using a compliancy ranking of at least 1 to 3. (1 to 5 or greater may also be used, as needed.) The 1-to-3 compliancy ranking breaks down as follows:

- ✓  1 = Does not meet any of the criteria
- ✓  2 = Meets the criteria
- ✓  3 = Exceeds the criteria

Whatever ranking method is used, consistency is important.

The compliancy-ranking spreadsheet can be used for evaluating compliancy for individual biometric technologies (for example, fingerprint) or for evaluating different biometric technologies together (for example, iris versus fingerprint).

After the Compliancy spreadsheet is created, you can begin the process of evaluating the prospective biometric technology solutions. Using the cell cross-reference example, an evaluation of prospective biometric vendor technologies would appear similar to the abbreviated evaluation shown in Figure 11-5.

| Response | Vendor 1 | Vendor 2 | Vendor 3 |
|---|---|---|---|
| Access Methods | | | |
| The selected biometric solution must be able to provide Application Authenticaiton. | 2 | 1 | 3 |
| The selected biometric solution does not need to accommodate for dial-in access. | 2 | 2 | 2 |
| Network identification/authentication is required. | 2 | 2 | 2 |
| Password replacement using the biometric trait is required. | 2 | 1 | 3 |
| Remote Access solution(s) will be used. Remote access authentication options must be investigated. | 2 | 2 | 2 |
| No telnet access is required | 2 | 2 | 2 |
| No VPN access is required | 2 | 3 | 2 |
| The biometric solution will not be used for WEB authentication. | 2 | 2 | 1 |
| | | | |
| Administration | | | |
| It appears that the end user templates are adequately protected, ensure this is true. | 2 | 3 | 1 |
| It appears that a standard backup solution will function properly for the proposed biometric solution. | 2 | 3 | 1 |
| Cost is the primary reason for the biometric solution, adequate strength without using passwords must be achieved | 2 | 1 | 2 |
| The biometric solution must provide easy enrollment without jeopardizing enrollment control. | 2 | 3 | 1 |
| It is not necessary for the template store to be distributed. | 2 | 1 | 2 |
| The template store must be centralized. | 2 | 1 | 2 |
| The intent is to periodically have users re-enroll to reduce FRRs and to ensure identity. | 2 | 1 | 2 |
| Composite Score | 2 | 1.86666667 | 1.86666667 |

**Figure 11-5:** Abbreviated compliancy evaluation

In the abbreviated compliancy evaluation, notice that, in some areas, a certain biometric solution from a given vendor exceeds or falls short of the requirement. At first glance, it may appear that you should have only two options (meets or does not meet the criteria). Reviewing an example of how a particular solution may exceed a given criteria, however, could help to clear up any confusion.

In this example, for the very first item ("The selected biometric solution must be able to provide Application Authentication"), Vendor 1 meets the criteria, Vendor 2 falls short, and Vendor 3 exceeds the criteria. This is possible because Vendor 1 can provide application authentication by selecting the appropriate executable file and requiring identification/authentication before the file can run. A password is required, however, and the biometric identification/authentication causes the password to be automatically entered. The solution does not actually integrate and replace the need for a password association in the solution, so the biometric template is not actually tied to the file for the executable. The potential exists for file execution using only a password. Nonetheless, the solution meets the criteria as described, whereas Vendor 2 does not provide built-in application security.

Vendor 3 exceeds the criteria in the sample compliancy evaluation because it not only provides the capability to secure applications, but it also provides two additional protection mechanisms. Vendor 3 requires identification/authentication before a file actually executes by using only a biometric template (no password association is required). And should someone try to copy the executable file in an effort to circumvent the protection, the software has enough intelligence to keep an association with the copied file and prevent execution without identification/authentication.

 Cause and effect must be considered in performing the compliancy evaluation. If a solution meets the selection criteria, how it met that criteria and the method used to meet those criteria could have a differing effect on the overall security.

# Weighting the Selection Process

Certain selection criteria may be more important in the overall evaluation process than others. You can assign a weight to each of the selection criteria. The weighting scale can be designed in similar fashion to the compliancy rating, as the following scale shows:

✓ 1 = Not needed

✓ 2 = Desirable

✓ 3 = Required

These weights become multipliers for the appropriate selection criteria. Figure 11-6 shows how this can be integrated into a sample Compliancy spreadsheet.

| Response | Weight | Vendor 1 | V1Sum | Vendor 2 | v2Sum |
|---|---|---|---|---|---|
| Access Methods | | | | | |
| The selected biometric solution must be able to provide Application Authenticaiton. | 2 | 2 | 4 | 1 | 2 |
| The selected biometric solution does not need to accommodate for dial-in access. | 1 | 2 | 2 | 2 | 2 |
| Network identification/authentication is required. | 3 | 2 | 6 | 3 | 9 |
| Password replacement using the biometric trait is required. | 3 | 2 | 6 | 3 | 9 |
| Remote Access solution(s) will be used. Remote access authentication options must be investigated. | 2 | 2 | 4 | 2 | 4 |
| No telnet access is required | 1 | 2 | 2 | 2 | 2 |
| No VPN access is required | 2 | 2 | 4 | 3 | 6 |
| The biometric solution will not be used for WEB authentication. | 1 | 2 | 2 | 1 | 1 |
| | | | | | |
| Administration | | | | | |
| It appears that the end user templates are adequately protected, ensure this is true. | 3 | 2 | 6 | 3 | 9 |
| It appears that a standard backup solution will function properly for the proposed biometric solution. | 3 | 2 | 6 | 3 | 9 |
| Cost is the primary reason for the biometric solution, adequate strength without using passwords must be achieve | 1 | 2 | 2 | 1 | 1 |
| The biometric solution must provide easy enrollment without jeopardizing enrollment control. | 3 | 2 | 6 | 3 | 9 |
| It is not necessary for the template store to be distributed. | 1 | 2 | 2 | 1 | 1 |
| The template store must be centralized. | 3 | 2 | 6 | 1 | 3 |
| The intent is to periodically have users re-enroll to reduce FRRs and to ensure identity. | 2 | 2 | 4 | 1 | 2 |
| | | | | | |
| Composite Score | | 2 | 4.133333 | 2 | 4.6 |
| Required Categories | | | 36 | | 48 |

Figure 11-6: Compliancy weighting

In the example weighting system, notice that, although both Vendor 1 and Vendor 2 are equal in their initial evaluation of criteria, Vendor 2 is clearly the winner based on the weighting system, because it exceeds the criteria in the critical (#3 weighting) categories. This is an example of where the weighting system can help determine which technology is best suited for a given environment, based on the most important criteria for that environment.

## Completing the Selection Process

Whether or not you use weighted compliancy ratings, after all the selected biometric solutions are rated and tallied, a determination can be made as to which vendor, solution, manufacturer, developer, and so on is best suited for a given environment. In the event of a tie, return to the process and add weightings to the compliancy ratings if weights were not used. If weighting was used and a tie still exists, and all other criteria are equal, consider using cost as the deciding factor.

# Implementation Plan

After establishing goals, performing a needs analysis, and creating and completing the selection process, you must create an implementation plan. Although some of the components of the implementation plan vary depending on the selected technology/technologies, a baseline implementation plan is presented here that can be added to, modified, or have steps removed, based on your needs.

## Step 1: Review the Established Goals

The first step in a successful implementation plan should be to review the goals that were established prior to the needs analysis. This is necessary because, during the course of the needs analysis and selection process, the original intent of the proposed solution is often either forgotten or lost in the evaluation process. After you determine that the original goals are still addressed by the proposed solution, the implementation planning process can continue.

## Step 2: Review Security Policies, Guidelines, Procedures, and Practices

The second step in creating a successful implementation plan is to ensure a solid understanding of the existing security policies, guidelines, procedures, and practices. A review of these not only creates a greater awareness of their importance before the implementation begins, but often generates additional ideas for ensuring that the implementation is performed in a secure fashion and that the end result complies with the intent of the security policies, guidelines, procedures, and practices. Revisiting and revising security policies, practices, and procedures is often necessary. The process for accomplishing revisions should be contained within your current security policies, guidelines, procedures, and practices. If a revision process has not been accounted for, now is an excellent time to add one.

Including and updating the methods and mechanisms that are to be used to enforce the security policies, guidelines, procedures, and practices also is important.

We also recommend reviewing the appropriate sections from Wiley's *CISSP Prep Guide* to ensure thoroughness in covering your security objectives.

## Step 3: Classify the Data

The primary objective relating to network biometric security is often to better protect the data. In this step, determine which specific data within the environment falls into each classification category (as discussed earlier in this chapter).

## Step 4: Combine Data Classifications

After each data type to be protected by the biometric solution is classified, sort these into similar categories. All public data elements, for example, should be listed under the classification of public. Similarly, all confidential data elements should be listed under the classification of confidential. Continue this process for all classifications.

## Step 5: Categorize the Data

You should also categorize data by use. Categories such as development, production, end-user information, and so on can be used to create a better understanding of the data's use. This is important because different components of production data may fit into more than one classification. Production data from one data source (such as a database) may be public, for example, whereas production data from another data source (such as employee information) may be classified.

You can also categorize by application, such as e-mail, word processing, database, spreadsheet, and many others. Whatever categories you use, make sure that you are consistent.

## Step 6: Define Legal Obligations for Data

Ensure that legal obligations have been met based on the legal obligation criteria previously discussed.

## Step 7: Create Implementation Overview

Before actually implementing the biometric solution, create an implementation overview. This overview should include the following components (at least):

- ✓ Access control methodology
- ✓ Branch offices, remote locations, and external entities
- ✓ Current network/infrastructure diagrams
- ✓ Device diagrams or listings
- ✓ Enrollment plan/tracking
- ✓ Equipment upgrades or special equipment

✓  Method of biometric hardware deployment

✓  Method of software deployment (for example, manual or automatic using software distribution)

✓  Biometric solution's proposed installation method

✓  Proposed network/infrastructure diagrams

✓  Training requirements

✓  Operating system(s) that leverage the biometric solution

✓  Wireless connectivity solution integration

✓  Additional implementation plan considerations

A good starting point for creating your implementation overview is to select each of the Biometric Selection Critiria main headings from the Biometric Selection Critieria workbook and add and/or delete as appropriate to create the foundation for your plan.

## ACCESS CONTROL METHODOLOGY

In the military, access is granted on a need-to-know basis and only if the appropriate clearance is met. If both criteria are not met, access is not granted.

In the corporate world, you can apply the same logic. Create a spreadsheet with data classifications, possible access entities, and what conditions access would be granted under. Two such methods are listed within the Common Book of Knowledge (CBK): the take-grant method and the Bell-LaPadula method.

**TAKE-GRANT MODEL**    This method specifies the rights a user/process can transfer to or take from an object. An *object* can be any administered item that falls under this category, but typically it refers to files, disks, printers/print servers, databases, and so on. In the case of a database, several take-grant rules are most likely assigned based on the need for access to specific database functions and data. If a database contains both human resources and payroll information, for example, a payroll clerk may need access only to the employee name, address, phone number, and specific payroll information but not to any associated personnel-related information.

The take-grant model often utilizes a created grid specifying the resource and the associated access needs of users/processes. Table 11-2 illustrates a sample spreadsheet.

**BELL-LAPADULA MODEL**    This model addresses the special needs of the Department of Defense's security policies (unclassified through top secret). This model addresses the issues concerned with ensuring confidentiality but does not address the availability or integrity of the protected material.

In addition to the security model, choosing the right security administration process is also very important. In some instances, distributed security management (with central policy control) is a good practice. This falls into the category of "not putting all your eggs into one basket." If a single failure or breach occurs, it may not affect any other area. Conversely, if central policies are not adhered to, a breach could affect the entire organization.

**TABLE 11-2: Take-Grant Matrix**

| Users | Files/Applications/Processes | | | | |
|---|---|---|---|---|---|
| | *File1* | *File2* | *Payroll* | *HR* | *GL* |
| Billy Bob | Read | Read/Write | Execute | Poll | Admin |
| Jane Doe | Read | Read/Write | Poll | Poll | Poll |
| John Doe | Read/Write | Read/Write | Admin | Admin | None |
| John Smith | Read | Admin | Execute | Execute | Execute |
| Kyra Smith | None | Read | Poll | Execute | Execute |
| Tom Thumb | Admin | Read | None | None | None |

You can accomplish central security policy management and central security control/authentication by using many different tools. Remote Authentication Dial-In User Service (RADIUS) and Terminal Access Controller Access Control System (TACACS) are two methods used to administer security on multiple devices from a central point. Such methods can provide a consistent administration point. If central security policy management and central security control/authentication is the selected method, your biometric solution needs to integrate into this model.

Make sure that you have a backup plan in place in the event that the central security control/authentication fails. You must also ensure, however, that your backup plan does not jeopardize the security measures that are being implemented.

## BRANCH OFFICES, REMOTE LOCATIONS, EXTERNAL ENTITIES

During the selection criteria process, if remote connectivity needs were established and if the selected biometric technology accommodates the remote needs, the implementation method for the branch offices, remote locations, and other external entities should be outlined.

## CURRENT NETWORK/INFRASTRUCTURE DIAGRAMS

Ensure that current network and infrastructure diagrams exist. These diagrams can be an invaluable tool in helping to ensure that all items are accounted for in the implementation plan. Be careful, however, not to solely rely on such diagrams, because they may not be completely accurate or up to date.

## DEVICE DIAGRAMS OR LISTINGS

Device diagrams differ from network and infrastructure diagrams in that they provide more detailed information on specific devices. Examples include (but are not limited to) the following:

✓ Specific rack-mount computer layouts and configurations

✓ Network communication device configurations (switch, router, CSU/DSU, and so on)

✓ Mini- and mainframe configuration

As is true with network and infrastructure diagrams, be careful not to rely solely on these diagrams because they can be incomplete or out of date.

## ENROLLMENT PLAN/TRACKING

Generally, the main reason for implementing biometric technology is to identify someone. To accomplish this, users must enroll by using the biometric technology. Because the potential exists for someone to enroll by using another person's identity (state that he or she is someone other than who he or she is), a solid enrollment plan that verifies identity before allowing enrollment, ensures correct enrollment, and verifies identity post enrollment is key to ensuring security. As previously mentioned in this book, the required enrollment process is often one of the major objections corporations have to biometric solutions. Much of the objection stems from needing to coordinate such an effort. After the enrollment process has taken place, however, password and other user authentication issues are often greatly reduced. The enrollment plan/tracking should, at a minimum, include the following:

- ✓ Scheduling enrollment timeframes
- ✓ Setting up enrollment locations
- ✓ Securing the enrollment locations
- ✓ Tracking access to enrollment locations
- ✓ Initial identity verification, which may include requiring the end user to present multiple forms of identification, among other procedures
- ✓ Setting up sign in/sign out logs that can be used for signature verification
- ✓ Visually monitoring each user enrollment
- ✓ Ensuring the enrollment was successful
- ✓ Accounting for re-enrollments needs
- ✓ Establishing a secondary enrollment process for those who cannot enroll by using the selected technology

## EQUIPMENT UPGRADES OR SPECIAL EQUIPMENT

For some solutions, depending on the environment, equipment upgrades or special equipment may be required. If, for example, a selected biometric technology solution lists minimum server and workstation requirements, some servers and workstations may need to be upgraded. Another example may be a biometric acquisition device that connects to a serial or USB port. If devices in the existing environment already use all the existing ports, you need to make provisions to address the issue(s). Addressing such issues can include implementing additional serial interface cards, adding USB hubs, or other similar solutions.

## METHOD OF BIOMETRIC HARDWARE DEPLOYMENT

Because most biometric solutions require accompanying hardware, you must consider what hardware is to be used and how it is to be deployed. If an iris sensor is to be used for each user, for example, provisions must be made to ensure that the device is deployed, installed, and tested.

## METHOD OF SOFTWARE DEPLOYMENT

Some biometric solutions offer only a centralized implementation, whereas many other biometric solutions offer more than one implementation option. As this is the case, you should account for how the product is to be deployed and implemented. Is a central design sufficient, for example, or is a distributed design more appropriate?

## PROPOSED NETWORK/INFRASTRUCTURE DIAGRAMS

Creating proposed network/infrastructure diagrams is more than just an exercise. This is a proven method for ensuring that you obtain and can demonstrate a complete understanding of the end result (goal). It is also a key step toward identifying potential problems in the selected solution, environment, and implementation plan, as well as in many other areas.

## TRAINING REQUIREMENT

Before beginning the implementation, identify, outline, and address all training requirements, as appropriate. Training requirements are likely to be required before, during, and after the implementation. The before requirements often encompass ensuring that the implementation team is adequately trained and prepared for the implementation. During the implementation, on-the-job training occurs and may consist of the implementation team learning installation tips and tricks, performing and learning additional administration functions, and learning some of the biometric solution's idiosyncrasies. End-user training may also take place during the implementation.

Effective end-user training requires a very coordinated effort. During the implementation, coordinate training for each end user to occur while that end user's equipment is being installed or upgraded. After the end user returns from training, he or she is now using the new technology. This is effective because the information is still fresh in the end user's mind, and the user can immediately apply the knowledge.

Ensure that users within the environment are trained on what is and will be expected of them in relationship to the overall security goals. This should be included as a core component of your security policies, guidelines, procedures, and practices. For more information, see Wiley's publication, *CISSP Prep Guide*.

## DETERMINE WHICH OPERATING SYSTEM(S) LEVERAGE THE BIOMETRIC SOLUTION

The selected biometric solution should achieve a specific goal, and, as such, the implementation plan should be designed to achieve that goal. If that goal is to implement the biometric solution on only one operating system platform, this determination becomes very simple. If the goal is to secure multiple operating systems, however, you must account for the specific requirements of each in the implementation plan.

### ADDITIONAL IMPLEMENTATION PLAN CONSIDERATIONS

Other items that you could include in your implementation overview, in addition to those already listed, include the following:

- ✓ Availability (personnel, locations, equipment, and so on)
- ✓ Backup process, timing, and security
- ✓ Resources required to complete the implementation
- ✓ Schedule
- ✓ Size of the implementation
- ✓ Whether other projects affect the implementation?
- ✓ Wireless connectivity solution integration

# Step 8: Create a Comprehensive Security Checklist

Create and use security checklists for each device, based on the type of device. Many companies use a Windows 2000 security checklist for Windows 2000, for example, and a Unix security checklist for Unix. The same holds true for implementing biometric solutions. We recommend creating a security checklist, based on your environment, by using Ripple Security logic. This includes all devices.

Make a special effort to create a security checklist for the biometric authentication and template data stores and locations.

# Step 9: Enterprise Security Plan

Although you should keep enterprise policies in mind when creating your biometric security plan, after it is completed, you should review it against such policies. In many instances, the enterprise security policies must be updated to accommodate the needs of the biometric security program, and the reverse may also be true. After it's complete, however, the biometric security program should become an integral part of the overall enterprise security plan.

# Step 10: Incident/Response Planning and Escalation

All the features of biometric technology can become severely limited if no plan exists to address issues as they occur. This is where incident response comes into play. You have gone through the process of charting, mapping, plotting, planning, documenting, researching, and so on, but what happens if unplanned activities or outages occur?

An incident response plan should be descriptive, categorized, and formal. This is yet another area where a spreadsheet or grid could be helpful. Because the nature of unplanned activity is that it *is* unplanned, however, make sure that the categories are flexible enough to account for unplanned or unforeseen events.

The following list provides examples:

- ✓ Undefined errors/issues — TOP PRIORITY
- ✓ FARs — TOP PRIORITY
- ✓ FRRs — HIGH PRIORITY
- ✓ Failing individual biometric devices — PRIORITY
- ✓ Authorized access — NORMAL

Define each priority and its associated action. Incident planning should be a complete process unto itself. For now, know that it is an integral part of any successful security plan.

Plan for issues to occur and create an escalation path to enable issues to be quickly and efficiently addressed as they occur. Account for the possibility that the project may need to be put on hold to address difficult-to-resolve issues and create a separate backout plan as appropriate.

## Step 11: Change Control

Implement a change-control process as part of the implementation plan. This process should be formal and provide a mechanism for changes and/or deviations to occur without affecting the implementation's goal.

## Step 12: Design Review

After the design is finished, review it thoroughly to ensure that it is accurate and complete. If a third party created the plan, have the plan reviewed by another competent party. This could be personnel within the company or another third party. Document everything, including the policies, procedures, references, resources, and so on.

## Step 13: Testing

Because testing is such a critical component of a successful implementation plan, and because many potential issues to test for exist, this process could be lengthy and time-consuming, depending on the environment. On the other hand, not performing thorough testing can cause failures and unplanned downtime.

In addition to testing the implementation plan, you should test the overall security of the biometric implementation after it's complete.

For more informationon on security testing, see *Hack Attacks Testing: How to Conduct Your Own Security Audit,* from Wiley, at www.wiley.com/compbooks.

## Step 14: Finalize the Implementation Plan

After you complete Steps 1 through 13, review the implementation plan for any final modifications. Verify and date each documented page of the plan. Ensure that you note the date that the plan was finalized. Ensure that final acceptance by the necessary parties has been granted. Ensuring that management approval has been formally given is vital. Document appropriate information pertaining to management approval and begin the implementation process.

For more information on management approval processes, see the *CISSP Prep Guide* from Wiley at www.wiley.com/compbooks.

## Step 15: Begin the Implementation

During implementation, make sure that the implementation plan is being followed and that any issues, changes, or deviations are addressed as defined in the implementation plan.

As a separate action, consider performing periodic, post-implementation reviews.

# Summary

Choosing and implementing any new technology can be a daunting task. Designing, selecting, and implementing a biometric technology is no different. The key to successful selection and implementation is using sound and proven methods, techniques, and tools.

This chapter discussed many of the components necessary to assist you in deciding which biometric technology to choose and provided baseline implementation methods and tools that reduce the effort and anxiety that can accompany a technology decision-making process.

# Chapter 12

# Biometric Solution Case Study

THROUGHOUT THIS BOOK, WE have outlined and discussed the different biometric technologies, illustrated some sample biometric product installations, and analyzed various uses. We have also provided code from which you can begin to build your own biometric implementations and add to your proprietary applications. This information was coupled with sound criteria from which solid biometric technology selections can be made. Along the way, we also provided the foundation for building a successful biometric solution implementation plan.

This chapter illustrates an example of how a biometric solution can be used to solve an identification/authentication problem, while accommodating different needs within a given work environment. This solution and the environment will be outlined in case study format with an eye on the specific challenges within the environment. Upon completion of the case study, you will learn how to scale the solution to accommodate a larger environment.

## Sample Biometric Solutions Deployments

Biometric technology can be used in many ways to achieve many objectives, all of which center around identifying an individual as to who they claim to be. However, it is projected that biometric technologies will grow substantially in the PC and networking arenas (which may be why you're reading this book). This means that in the near future you will, at the very least, be introduced to biometric technology in some fashion, probably in the workplace. It is also very likely that as a technology professional, you will be asked to model and implement a biometric solution in your environment. This solution might be a test environment (recommended) initially, or an actual design. In either case, it is important to understand the many factors you will need to consider to ensure a successful project.

To that end, this chapter will outline two network-based biometric implementations, along with the associated issues and challenges that may be faced with each. These sample network-based solutions will be outlined in case study format.

For the purpose of outlining the case studies, company names will be used. However, all case studies presented in this material and any associated company names used are fictitious.

353

# Case Study 1: PQR Inc.

PQR Inc. is a small pharmaceutical research company. The company has 25 employees and a single Microsoft Windows 2000 Server with Active Directory implemented. All workstations are Microsoft Windows XP. One of the unique traits of PQR Inc. is that they bring in pharmaceutical consultants for short to long periods of time. They have had at least one incident where a previous consultant gained access using another password. This one incident caused grave damage and cost PQR Inc. one of their major clients.

Although the method in which the consultant obtained the password must be identified to ensure that future incidents do not occur, for our purposes it is only important to know that the password was wrongfully obtained.

Based on this incident, and in an effort to better protect the company assets (research and pharmaceutical data), the CEO has brought you in to design and implement a biometric network identification/authentication solution. Additionally, because some users work in "clean rooms" with latex gloves and in some cases masks on, it is important that the solution be able to accommodate these users as well as other users, while providing some user convenience. All necessary data encryption has already been implemented and leverages Active Directory for authentication/authorization.

The CEO has also requested that fingerprint identification be the primary biometric used because his users have told him they really prefer fingerprint technology over Iris technology. The CEO follows up by mentioning that each system purchased contains a sound card, microphone, and Web camera so the users can Web conference with their clients.

PQR's network is outlined in Figure 12-1.

The Active Directory design is straightforward, and the users are divided up evenly, with five users per department. One server exists in the environment, but the server contains four Pentium III 850MHz processors, 6GB memory, is very redundant, has plenty of storage capacity (500GB), is currently operating at 23 percent utilization, and downtime of up to 24 hours can be tolerated. Therefore, the CEO does not want to purchase an additional server. Rather, he would like to layer the biometric solution on top of the server services. Cost is not the most important factor, but is definitely a consideration. Finally, no other special features (that is, password replacement for Web applications) are required, but if possible, the CEO would like the ability to leverage them in the future.

It is generally and highly recommended that hardware redundancy and at least two Domain Controllers (DCs) be implemented in any environment. We show one for ease of understanding.

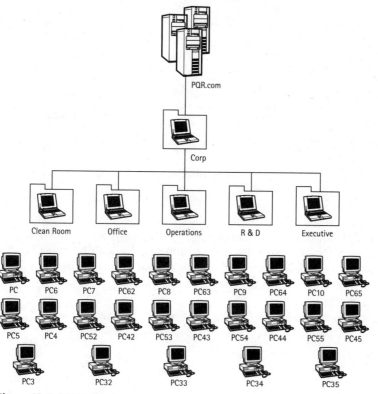

Figure 12-1: PQR Network

## DETERMINING THE SOLUTION

Although the CEO determined the need for the biometric solution based on the incident that occurred, and the loss of one of their customers, it is still important to ensure the decision is sound. We would recommend validating the decision using the Biometric Selection Criteria workbook. This is important, as it can give you additional information that may have been overlooked in the CEO's outline. After completing the Biometric Selection Criteria, the following information is obtained:

✓ No additional special environmental issues exist.

✓ Crossover accuracy must be minimally 1:50.

✓ Different biometric devices will be required in certain areas (that is, a clean room).

✓  No remote access is needed (other than Web conferencing)

✓  Most sensitive data is classified as Confidential.

✓  A software kit is not required, but is preferred for future possibilities.

✓  No passwords will be required.

✓  Server identification/authentication is required.

✓  Fingerprint acquisition devices must check for live fingers.

✓  Web cameras can be leveraged for identification/authentication.

✓  Sound cards with microphones can be leveraged for identification/authentication.

✓  Biometric template store must be encrypted.

With this additional information, you can begin to build a solution and implementation plan based on sound criteria.

## SOLUTION/DESIGN

Based on the information provided, the solution must have fingerprint identification/authentication, and must not use eye biometric technology (Iris, Retina). Additionally, the solution must be able to identify other users without the benefit of fingerprint or hand technology. Because some users do not have to wear masks in addition to the latex gloves, and other users do have to wear masks, a couple of other options are possible.

For users that do not need to wear masks, the following options are available:

✓  Keystroke dynamics

✓  Face scans

✓  Voice biometrics

✓  Signature

Because potential acquisition devices already exist within the environment (keyboard, microphones, cameras) it does not make sound business sense to introduce a signature acquisition device, as other potential devices have similar Crossover Accuracy rates. Likewise, you would prefer not to require users to type lengthy passwords or pass phrases if at all possible. Even with keystroke dynamics, it is still recommended that either strong passwords or long pass phrases be used. As the CEO would like to provide some user convenience if possible, keystroke dynamics can be replaced with one of the other technologies to provide this convenience. This leaves you with the following biometric solution options:

✓  Fingerprint

✓  Face scans

✓  Voice biometrics

After searching for a potential solution, we chose SAF2000 from s_flink corporation as our pilot product because it can accommodate multiple biometric technologies. Additionally we will use s_f fingerprint acquisition devices, while leveraging the current investment in sound cards, microphones, and Web cameras. Furthermore, we chose s_f fingerprint (AuthenTEC Fingerlock) technology with live finger verification.

## IMPLEMENTATION PLAN

The implementation plan is an important (and, in our opinion, critical) component of any successful technology implementation. Before proceeding any further, it is recommended that you perform the steps outlined in the Implementation Plan section of Chapter 11 to create an actual implementation plan.

- ✓ Step 1. Review the established goals — The primary goal is greater security, and the secondary goal is identification/authentication.

- ✓ Step 2. Review security policies, guidelines, procedures and practices — Do they comply with the goal, does the goal comply with them, does the solution comply?

- ✓ Step 3. Classify the data — Maximum data classification is Confidential. Does the solution comply with this data classification?

- ✓ Step 4. Combine data classifications — Where multiple data classifications exist, does the solution address all classifications, as well as accommodate their locations?

- ✓ Step 5. Categorize the data — After categorization, is there any data that can not be protected by the solution? Will it work with all the encryption?

- ✓ Step 6. Define legal obligations for data — Has this been verified with the CEO? Are there any outstanding issues?

- ✓ Step 7. Create an implementation overview — Ensure there are no conflicts with timing, outages, resources, other projects, and product/delivery of product. Ensure that backups have been performed, a back-out plan is defined, a schedule has been created, all equipment and other resources are accounted for, and any purchased products are available. Account for special requirements like backup software, add-ins, and so on.

    - A comprehensive enrollment/monitoring process and checklist should also be created.

    - Determine if other software is already installed such as databases and other applications. Because some biometric solutions leverage SQL, already installed instances of SQL will have to be understood and accounted for. In our case study, SQL is not installed on the file server.

The implementation plan should be the roadmap by which the solution becomes reality. Therefore, be very thorough, descriptive, and calculating when creating it. When it's completed, you should be able to create a timeline from it, based on its contents.

✓ Step 8. Create a comprehensive security checklist — Test every account. Perform breach tests. Perform remote connectivity tests to ensure they are not active.

✓ Step 9. Check the enterprise security plan — Does everything still comply with the enterprise security plan?

✓ Step 10. Incident/response planning and escalation — Has the incident/response plan been created or updated as appropriate? What will happen should an attempted breach occur? What will happen should a breach occur?

✓ Step 11. Change control — How will changes be handled? What is the process to effect a change during the implementation? What can cause a work stoppage?

✓ Step 13. Testing — Perform testing processes, document results, make modifications as necessary and retest.

✓ Step 14. Finalize the implementation plan — After all testing is completed and satisfactory, modify and finalize the implementation plan as appropriate. Ensure that the schedule is correct.

✓ Step 15. Begin the implementation

In this case study, the implementation will take place over a weekend. Details of the requirements follow.

## SAF2000 Implementation

SAF2000 can be installed directly on the existing Windows 2000 server. SQL is also required, and client software is required to run on each PC. Because the environment is small, it is possible to manually install the client portion of the software on each PC without too much time investment.

### REQUIREMENTS

Hardware and software implementation requirements for Case Study 1 are as follows:

### Hardware

✓ Twenty-one fingerprint sensors (one for the server and twenty for the workstations); five not needed for the clean room.

✓ Because Web cams and sound cards with microphones exist, they will be leveraged, but are not required as additional hardware.

Although they are not needed for the clean room, additional fingerprint sensors could be purchased in the event of a sensor failure.

## Software

✓  SAF2000 (included)

✓  Twenty-one additional licenses required (twenty-five, minimum, recommended for growth)

✓  SAF transaction (included but optional for implementation)

✓  Administration tools for enrollment (included, can be distributed)

✓  Client

✓  SQL 7.0 or newer (not included) + SP2 or greater

✓  USB driver software for fingerprint sensors (included)

✓  USB driver for Web cameras

✓  Biometric Solution Provider (BSP) modules for fingerprint, voice, and face (included); other biometric modules (BSPs) can be integrated from other companies that also provide fingerprint, face, and voice.

**SERVER DISK SPACE**    The SAF2000 disk space recommendations are as follows.

✓  2.5 MB required for the program

✓  30 MB for the database

✓  10 MB additional for server software

## PER USER requirements

✓  .5K per workstation

✓  4K for fingerprint templates

✓  25K for voiceprint templates

✓  25K for face templates

✓  If log files are used, .5K per user per day

Therefore, for our 25 users, assuming we will enroll each user with the ability to authenticate using any biometric option, the disk requirements are as follows:

25 × (.5K+4K+25K+25K+.5K) = 25 × 55K = 1.375MB for users + 2.5MB (program) + 30MB+10MB database for a total of 43.875MB server requirement.

note    Disk space requirements assume that all applications, patches, additional drivers (such as Fingerprint USB ) and SQL have alreadybeen loaded.

**RECOMMENDED**   In addition to the SAF2000 recommendations, we recommend ensuring the following:

- ✓ SQL backup agents may be required, depending on the backup solution.

- ✓ Enrollment software is installed on more than just the server PC.

- ✓ Windows service packs are applied.

- ✓ Complete verified backup(s) (preferably two) have been performed.

- ✓ Although 43.875MB is required, we recommend ensuring that at least 250MB or greater is available (after SQL installation) in this scenario to accommodate all additional USB drivers.

## SOLUTION MODEL

Based on the chosen biometric solution and PQR Inc.'s environment, the SAF2000 for the enterprise solution implementation diagram is shown in Figure 12-2.

## INSTALLATION

Once all the steps of the implementation plan are completed, and the pilot is successful, the implementation can be planned. As with many implementations of new technology, our recommendation would be to perform the install and testing process during off-peak periods. For many companies, this means starting the implementation on a Friday night after normal business hours to allow the entire weekend to address issues or roll-back to the original configuration if necessary. After ensuring that all equipment, software, and resources to perform the installation are assembled, and making sure that two (or more) backups have been performed and verified and one copy of the backup is stored off-site but available, the implementation process can begin. The steps are as follows:

- ✓ Ensure that all patches are installed and up-to-date.

- ✓ Verify that all user accounts and groups are created and correct authorization for each.

- ✓ Install SQL in mixed-mode (if not already installed in MIXED-MODE) using the local system account (SA)

- ✓ Install Fingerprint USB drivers

- ✓ Install camera drivers (if not already done)

- ✓ Install SAF2000 software

✓ Install Administration software on server (for enrollment)

✓ Configure SAF2000 software

✓ Perform the enrollment process

✓ Install Administration software on workstations (enrollment workstations)

✓ Install client software on workstations

✓ Test identification/authentication from workstations

✓ Install client software on the server and test

✓ Document results

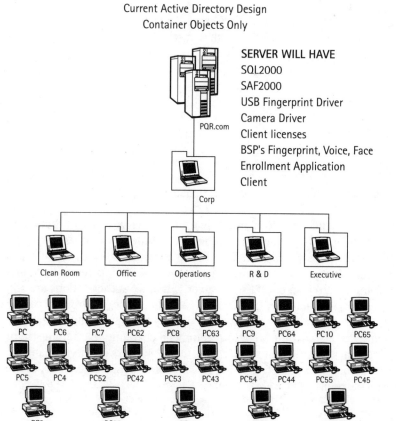

PQR Inc.
Current Active Directory Design
Container Objects Only

**SERVER WILL HAVE**
SQL2000
SAF2000
USB Fingerprint Driver
Camera Driver
Client licenses
BSP's Fingerprint, Voice, Face
Enrollment Application
Client

PQR.com

Corp

Clean Room    Office    Operations    R & D    Executive

PC    PC6    PC7    PC62    PC8    PC63    PC9    PC64    PC10    PC65

PC5    PC4    PC52    PC42    PC53    PC43    PC54    PC44    PC55    PC45

PC3    PC32    PC33    PC34    PC35

\* All user workstations require the SAFLINK client.
\*\* Selected workstations can have the enrollment tools.

**Figure 12-2:** Solution diagram

If additional steps, such as ensuring backup agents (SQL), are required, perform them as well.

## SERVER INSTALLATION

There are two primary installation components for our implementation: the server component and the workstation component. We begin our implementation plan at the Microsoft Windows 2000 server running Active Directory.

**ENSURE ALL PATCHES ARE INSTALLED**   In our example, we are running Windows 2000 with Active Directory. We recommend two methods of ensuring that all patches are installed and up-to-date. The first is by visiting the Microsoft Web site and ensuring that you have downloaded and applied each of the appropriate patches.

The second method can be accomplished using the Microsoft Update feature built within the operating system. For security reasons, we prefer the first method discussed, but either will accomplish the goal of ensuring that patches are up-to-date.

We also recommend ensuring that all other installed software patches and fixes are up-to-date, such as antivirus, backup, applications, and so on.

The Windows 2000 server for PQR in our case study was updated to Service Pack 3.

**VERIFY ALL USER ACCOUNTS AND GROUPS**   It is also important to review all user accounts to ensure that they are only able to access the information they are authorized to access. Our recommendation is to initially perform this verification prior to the implementation and to create a checklist for the implementation. Just prior to implementation, and when user access is no longer available, we recommend using the created checklist to re-verify that all authorizations are still intact prior to installing the biometric solution (SAF2000). If additional user or group accounts need to be created or modified, create and/or modify them, and verify appropriate authorization.

Prior to actually beginning the installation, we also recommend changing the Administrator account name to something other than "Administrator" (if it has not already been changed). Without having an "Administrator" user, someone trying to gain administrative access will have to find another administrator account.

Some implementations change the default Administrator account name, and then add an Administrator account with no rights to throw off would-be attackers.

**INSTALL SQL**    After verifying that everything is in order, and making sure that all licenses are valid, ensure that all running applications are stopped. It may also be necessary to temporarily disable virus protection. You can gain a level of comfort by virus scanning the media prior to implementation.

Once applications have been halted, and you are certain that the media is virus-free, stop the virus protection, and proceed. The first step of the SAF2000 implementation is to install SQL. In our case study, SQL Server 2000 Standard edition is used, and the installation was performed as follows:

Insert the SQL 2000 Server CD. The screen shown in Figure 12-3 should automatically appear, and you can continue.

If the screen shown in Figure 12-3 does not automatically appear, open the appropriate CD drive letter by double-clicking on it. For example, if your CD-ROM drive is the E: drive, double-click on the E: drive and run the appropriate startup file, or double-click on the autorun icon.

**Figure 12-3:** SQL Menu window

Click on the "SQL Server 2000 Components" selection (outlined in a box in Figure 12-3). The Install Components menu should appear, as shown in Figure 12-4.

Click on the Install Database Server option (outlined in a box in Figure 12-4) to begin the SQL database server installation. The installation initially proceeds with the InstallShield Setup window shown in Figure 12-5.

**Figure 12-4:** Install Components menu

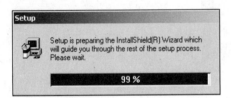

**Figure 12-5:** InstallShield Setup

The installation continues by displaying the Microsoft SQL Server Installation Wizard shown in Figure 12-6.

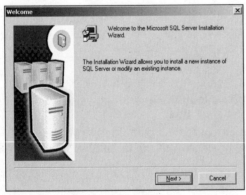

**Figure 12-6:** SQL Install Wizard

Clicking Next to continue the installation causes the Computer Name window shown in Figure 12-7 to be displayed.

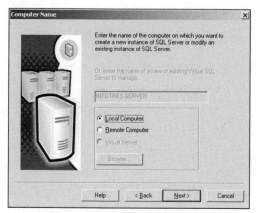

**Figure 12-7:** Computer Name window

Because we are installing SQL on the PQR file server, and the PQR file server will also contain the SAF2000 software, we selected to install SQL Server on the "Local Computer." After making this selection and clicking Next, the Installation Selection window shown in Figure 12-8 appears.

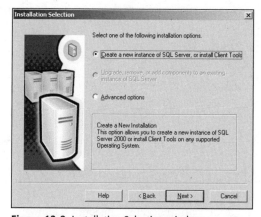

**Figure 12-8:** Installation Selection window

As noted previously, SQL was not installed on the file server, so we have opted to create a new instance of SQL server. Therefore, we ensure the "Create a new instance of SQL Server, or install Client Tools" radio button is selected, and we click Next to continue to the User Information screen shown in Figure 12-9.

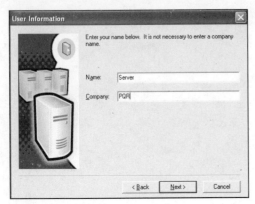

**Figure 12-9:** User Information window

For this case study, we entered a name of Server and the company name of PQR for our SQL User Information. Clicking Next to continue causes the license agreement screen shown in Figure 12-10 to be displayed.

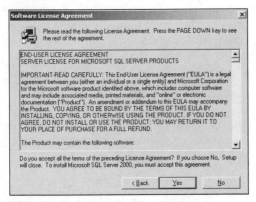

**Figure 12-10:** License Agreement screen

After reviewing the license information, you can continue by selecting the "Yes" button. This causes the installation to continue to the Installation Definition screen shown in Figure 12-11.

In this case study, we selected the Server and Client Tools option because this option allows us to have administration capabilities should they be required. After completing this selection, click Next to continue to the Instance Name screen shown in Figure 12-12.

Because this is the only instance of SQL that is to be installed (at least initially) on the PQR server, we accepted the default option, and ensured that the checkbox next to "Default" was checked (selected). Clicking Next to continue causes the Setup Type screen to be displayed, as shown in Figure 12-13.

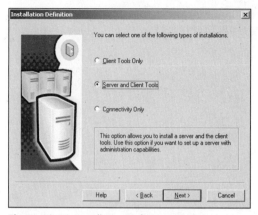

**Figure 12-11:** Installation Definition window

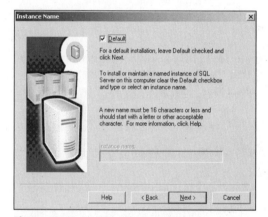

**Figure 12-12:** Instance Name window

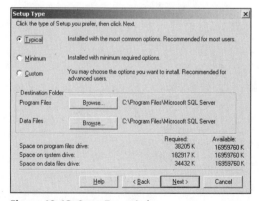

**Figure 12-13:** Setup Type window

We accepted the default to install SQL with the most common options, and clicked Next to continue to the Services Accounts screen shown in Figure 12-14.

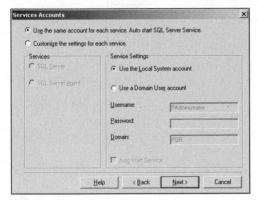

**Figure 12-14:** Services Accounts window

Change the default from "Use a Domain User account" to "Use the Local System account" (local system account is also referred to as "SA") and verify that the "Use the same account for each service. Auto start SQL Server Service" radio button is selected.

If more than one instance of SQL will be run on the server, the configuration parameters should be changed accordingly.

After we have successfully verified the service accounts options, we can click on the Next button to continue to the Authentication Mode selection screen.

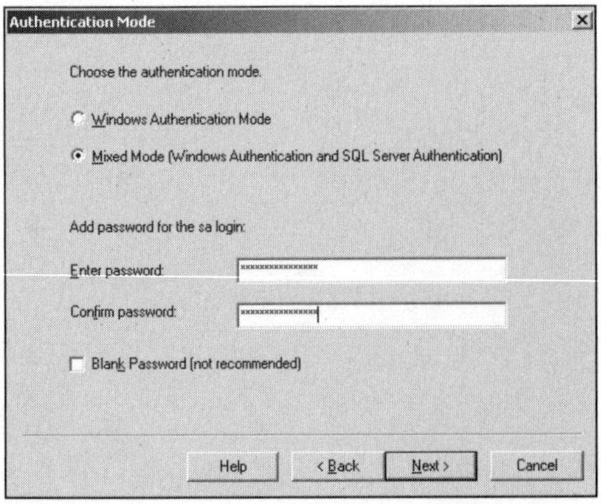

**Figure 12-15:** Authentication Mode window

In order for SAF2000 to operate, SQL must be configured in Mixed Mode. Select the radio button next to the "Mixed Mode (Windows Authentication and SQL Server Authentication)" option. Make sure you enter a strong password in the "Add password for the sa login". Do *not* leave the password blank. We recommend using at least a 16-character password with combinations of upper- and lowercase letters, numbers, and special characters. However, ensure the password will be remembered.

Once the authentication mode has been set to Mixed Mode and a strong password has been entered twice, continue to the Start Copying Files screen shown in Figure 12-16 by clicking Next.

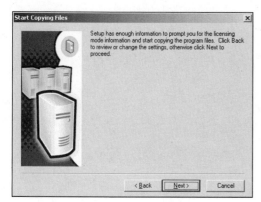

**Figure 12-16:** Start Copying Files window

This screen is somewhat misleading. Before actually beginning to copy files, the license information must be verified. This can be seen by clicking Next to continue to the Choose Licensing Mode screen shown in Figure 12-17.

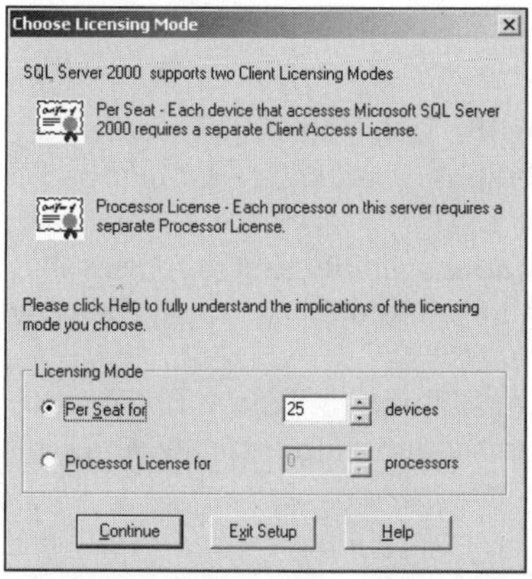

**Figure 12-17:** Choose Licensing Mode window

For PQR, 25 licensed devices will be used. Each device has a valid license; therefore, we have chosen "Per Seat for" licensing and entered 25 devices. It is important to note that once you click Continue, files will begin to copy. If there is any possibility that other applications may still be running, ensure one last time that they are halted. Once the proper licensing information is entered, click Continue to continue to begin copying files as shown in Figure 12-18.

Setup is installing Microsoft Data Access Components (MDAC) ...

**Figure 12-18:** File Copy window

It is possible that some tasks may still be open that can interfere with the SQL installation as shown in Figure 12-19.

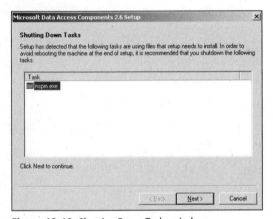

**Figure 12-19:** Shutting Down Tasks window

If any tasks show up in the Shutting Down Tasks window, use the Task Manager to ensure they are stopped or unloaded as appropriate. Once all tasks have been shut down, click Next to proceed to the Installing the Software screen shown in Figure 12-20.

Make one final verification that there will be no tasks, applications, or running processes that should interfere with the installation process, and click Finish to proceed to the initial file copy process shown in Figure 12-21.

Several updates will appear in the center of the screen like those shown in Figure 12-22. Once this portion of the installation successfully completes, the installation automatically proceeds with the file copy process.

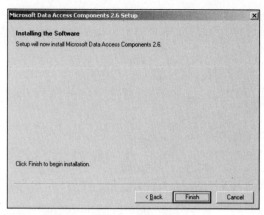

**Figure 12-20:** Installing the Software

**Figure 12-21:** Initial file copy process

**Figure 12-22:** File copy process

The status bar indicates the percentage of completion. Once all files have been copied, the installation automatically proceeds to the "Setup is starting the server and installing your chosen configuration" screen shown in Figure 12-23.

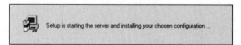

**Figure 12-23:** Starting the server

After this process completes, the installation automatically proceeds to the "Setup Complete" screen shown in Figure 12-24.

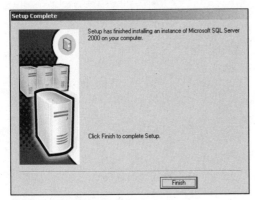

**Figure 12-24:** Setup complete

Press the Finish button to complete the installation. You may be prompted to reboot the server. Even if you are not, we recommend rebooting the server manually. Often, this will identify issues that may not otherwise be apparent if the server is not rebooted.

If there are any issues upon reboot, ensure they are addressed. This may require consulting your service provider, Microsoft, s_flink, or other such resources.

After a successful reboot, log in and continue the installation process.

**INSTALL BIOMETRIC ACQUISITION DEVICE DRIVERS**   After SQL has been successfully installed, we recommend installing the appropriate biometric drivers to prepare for the biometric identification software (SAF2000) installation.

**VOICE**   Because voice, face, and fingerprint biometric acquisition devices will be used, the first step is to ensure that the sound card (if one exists in the server) is installed and functioning properly. Often, this can be easily accomplished by using Microsoft Sound Recorder, typically located in Start → Programs → Accessories → Entertainment on Windows 2000. If you can record and play back your voice, chances are the biometric voice solution will work (as long as the quality is also good). However, some adjustments may be required. Once the sound card functionality has been verified, proceed to the camera acquisition device.

***CAMERA***    In our case study example, the Web camera drivers were previously installed. However, to review how this may be accomplished, you can refer to the chapter on Iris technology (Chapter 4), where we showed how to install the Panasonic Authenticam Private ID drivers. This also enables the camera portion of the Authenticam. We used this exact same method (minus the Secure Suite installation) to install the drivers for our PQR case study. The added benefit here is that PQR could leverage the Authenticam's Iris authentication with the addition of the appropriate BSP. However, the CEO stated that users were not receptive to this.

***FINGERPRINT***    The selected fingerprint acquisition device for PQR was the Authentec fingerprint sensor from s_flink corporation. In order to enable this device, the appropriate USB drivers must be installed. This is accomplished using the following process.

Make sure the USB device is *not* plugged in until the USB driver installation is completed and you have rebooted the PC/server.

Insert the SAF2000 disk. The menu shown in Figure 12-25 should automatically appear. If the menu does not appear, double-click on the associated drive letter for your CD-ROM. This may also cause the program to automatically start (auto play). If this does not start the program, the files on the CD should be visible. Double-click on the SAF2000.exe icon.

Once the menu appears, select the Browse CD option shown in Figure 12-25.

**Figure 12-25:** SAF2000 menu

Browse to the BSP directory shown in Figure 12-26.

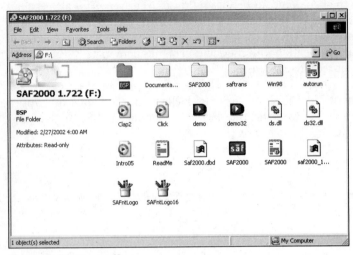

**Figure 12-26:** Browse CD

Double-click on the BSP folder to open its contents, as shown in Figure 12-27.

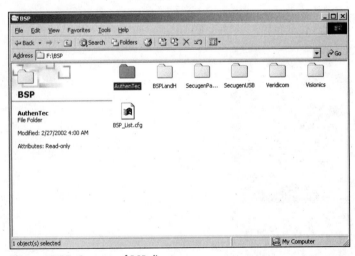

**Figure 12-27:** Contents of BSP directory

Double-click on the AuthenTec folder to open its contents, as shown in Figure 12-28.

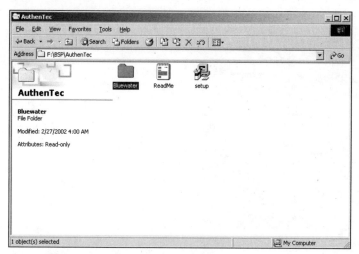

**Figure 12-28:** Contents of AuthenTec directory

Double-click on the Bluewater folder to open its contents, as shown in Figure 12-29.

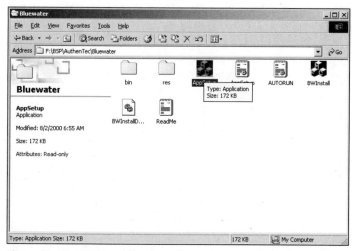

**Figure 12-29:** Contents of Bluewater directory

Once in the Bluewater directory, double-click on the AppSetup.exe file to begin the USB driver installation, as shown in Figure 12-30.

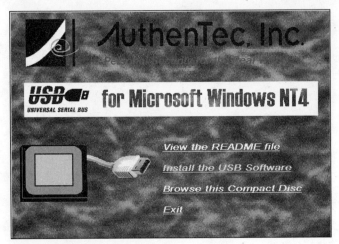

**Figure 12-30:** AuthenTec Inc. menu

Although the menu shows that the USB drivers are for Microsoft Windows NT4, we have tested them on Windows 2000 and Windows XP systems without issue. However, this does not mean that they will not cause issues in your environment. Therefore, we recommend testing them specifically in your environment with your install base and applications before deployment.

Proceed with the USB driver install by clicking on the Install the USB Software option on the menu. This starts the installation process, as shown in Figure 12-31.

Leave the "Install NT4 USB Stack" radio button selected, and click the OK button to continue the installation. A successful installation will display the screen shown in Figure 12-32.

Click the OK button to complete the install and reboot if prompted. If you are not prompted to reboot, we recommend doing so.

**Figure 12-31:** Starting the USB driver install

**Figure 12-32:** A successful install

After the machine successfully reboots (without errors relating to the USB or SQL installs), plug in the biometric fingerprint acquisition device (AuthenTec). The device should be automatically recognized. If you view Control Panel, you should see an ATSC Settings option. Here, you can calibrate the fingerprint sensor, change the orientation of the sensor, force detection, and adjust performance log settings. These are shown in Figure 12-33.

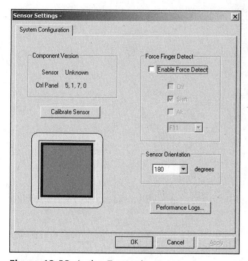

**Figure 12-33:** AuthenTec settings

Ensure that the fingerprint sensor is recognized, set the appropriate orientation (180 degrees is with the cable end up), and continue to the SAF2000 software installation.

**INSTALL SAF2000 SOFTWARE**    After installing SQL and any necessary device drivers for acquisition devices, and testing each device to ensure it is recognized and can function, you can begin the installation of the SAF2000 software. There are multiple components to SAF2000, including clients, servers, utilities, extensions, OEM biometrics and SAFtransactions. There is also a stepped installation and a custom install. Because there is only one server in use at PQR, we will install SAF2000 using the stepped installation method. To begin the installation, insert the SAF2000 CD in the CD-ROM drive of the server. The menu screen shown in Figure 12-34 should appear.

If the installation CD was still in the CD-ROM drive from the USB device driver install, the SAF menu screen can be started by double-clicking the drive letter in which SAF2000 is installed. If this only displays the contents of the SAF2000 CD, double-click on the SAF2000 executable file to start the menu.

**Figure 12-34:** Install a SAF2000 component

Select the Install Products option to proceed to the SAF2000 and SAFtransactions menu screen shown in Figure 12-35.

**Figure 12-35:** Install SAF2000

Click the SAF2000 option to continue to the setup welcome screen shown in Figure 12-36.

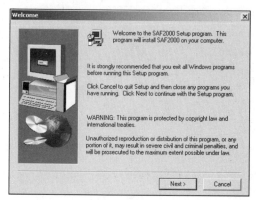

**Figure 12-36:** Setup welcome screen

Click Next to continue to the software license screen shown in Figure 12-37.

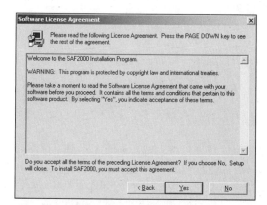

**Figure 12-37:** Software license screen

After reading the license agreement, select the Yes button to continue to the SAF2000 Installation Location screen shown in Figure 12-38.

If SAF2000 will be installed in the default directory, select Next to continue to the SAF2000 Installation screen shown in Figure 12-39. If you elect to change the default directory here, browse to the appropriate directory, ensure it gets created, and continue with the installation.

The first time you install SAF2000, you should be in a test environment, and we recommend performing a step-by-step installation. Once you are comfortable with SAF2000 operation, we recommend removing SAF2000 and re-installing it using the custom installation option to become familiar with its operation.

**Figure 12-38:** Installation Location screen

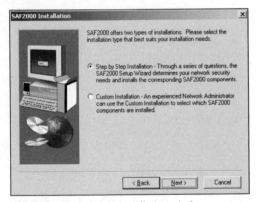

**Figure 12-39:** SAF2000 Installation window

Because we are installing SAF2000 on the PQR server, and because it is the only server, we will also use the step-by-step installation method. After ensuring that the "Step by Step Installation" radio button is selected, click Next to continue to the Network Operating System Type screen shown in Figure 12-40.

Because we are installing SAF2000 on a Windows 2000 Server platform, and no Novell Netware exists in the environment, we can select the "I use Windows NT as my Network Operating System" radio button.

If both Novell Netware and Microsoft Windows are in an environment, use the Custom installation.

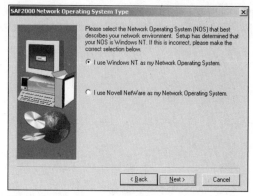

**Figure 12-40:** Operating System Type selection screen

After verifying the selection, click Next to continue to the Component Type Selection window shown in Figure 12-41.

**Figure 12-41:** Component Type Selection window

The three selections here are as follows:

- ✓ SAFserver will install the SAF server components, and will later ask to install the Administrative Utilities that are used for management and enrollment.

- ✓ SAF2000 Administrative Utilities will install the administrative utilities.

- ✓ SAF2000 Client will install the workstation client required for biometric identification/authentication to function.

We will install to the PQR server using the SAFserver option. Verify that the radio button next to the SAFserver option has been selected and click Next to continue to the SAFserver installation verification window shown in Figure 12-42.

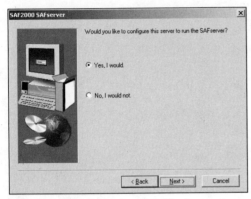

**Figure 12-42:** SAFserver install verification

Verify that the software will in fact be installed to the PQR server by ensuring that the "Yes, I would" ration button is selected. Click Next to continue to the SAF License Certificate entry screen shown in Figure 12-43.

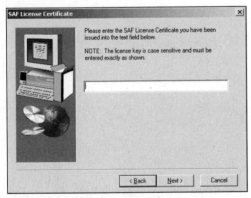

**Figure 12-43:** SAF License Certificate entry screen

Accompanying the SAF2000 kit is an End-User License Agreement sheet with the license key listed on it. Enter the license key exactly as it is typed on this sheet into the field provided. When the license has been properly entered, click Next to continue to the Installation Overview screen shown in Figure 12-44.

note

An error window will be displayed if the license key is entered incorrectly.

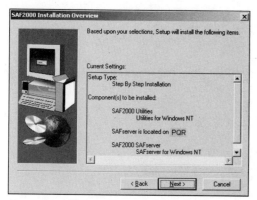

**Figure 12-44:** Installation Overview screen

Review the installation overview, and ensure that it is correct. Once you have determined that it is, click Next to begin the file copy process shown in Figure 12-45.

 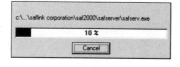

**Figure 12-45:** Starting the file copy process

The file copy continues automatically until completed. If any errors are displayed, note them and take appropriate action(s). If no errors occur, the installation automatically continues by displaying the SAF Database Configuration SA password entry window shown in Figure 12-46.

Enter the same password used in the SQL configuration (see Figure 12-15). Because there is only one entry here, and no password confirm field, be especially careful to enter the password exactly. If an invalid password is entered, a "SA Password is not typed correctly, Please try again" window will appear. Once the password is entered correctly and, Next> is clicked, the installation proceeds to the database location, and database sizing screen shown in Figure 12-47.

In the calculations for the template storage, it was identified that PQR would register/enroll all biometric traits for each user plus logging. This requires 55K per user times 25 users, which equals 1.375MB. The default is 5MB, and will therefore accommodate the needs of PQR.

**Figure 12-46:** Database Configuration screen

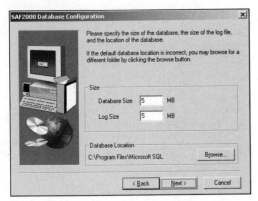

**Figure 12-47:** Database location and sizing

Plenty of space exists on the C: drive for PQR as well, and SQL is installed on the C: drive. Therefore, the default database location is sufficient.

Click Next to create the database, as shown in Figure 12-48.

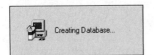

**Figure 12-48:** Database creation

Once the database has been successfully created, the installation automatically continues to the Core Component Setup Complete window shown in Figure 12-49.

Clicking the Finish button starts the OEM BSP installation. The BSP installation is where we will select the biometric acquisition components that will be used for PQR Corp. Click Finish to proceed to the OEM BSP selection window shown in Figure 12-50.

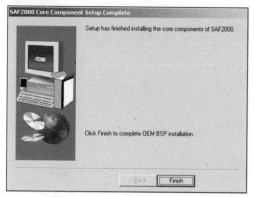

**Figure 12-49:** Core Component Setup Complete window

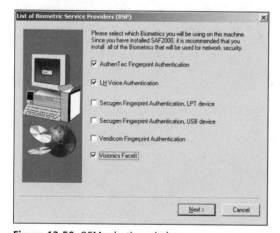

**Figure 12-50:** OEM selection window

As PQR will be using the SAF AuthenTec fingerprint acquisition device, voice verification and face verification, you will need to select these components by clicking the checkboxes next to each as shown above. Once all the appropriate devices have been selected, click Next to continue to the individual installations for each BSP. The first screen that appears is a question window asking for verification to install the AuthenTec components as shown in Figure 12-51.

**Figure 12-51:** AuthenTec verification question

To proceed, select Yes to begin the AuthenTec BSP installation. A welcome screen is displayed, as shown in Figure 12-52.

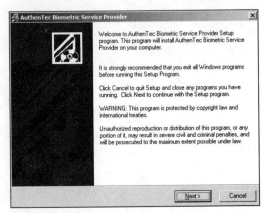

**Figure 12-52:** AuthenTec welcome screen

After reviewing the welcome screen, click Next to display the destination file location screen illustrated in Figure 12-53.

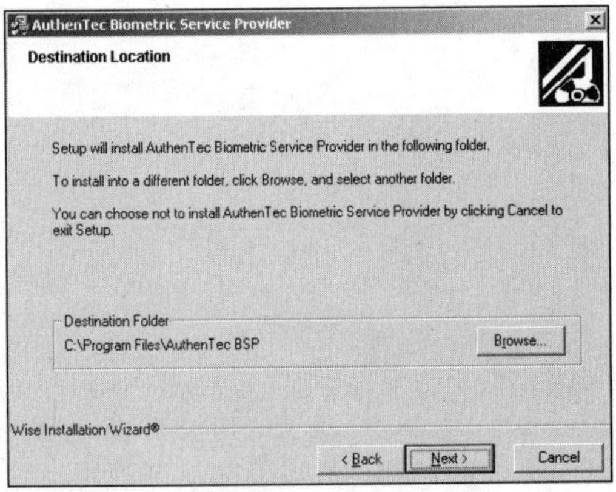

**Figure 12-53:** Destination Location screen

Choose a destination or accept the default of C:\Program Files\AuthenTec BSP, and click Next to display the Start installation screen shown in Figure 12-54. For PQR, the default destination folder was selected.

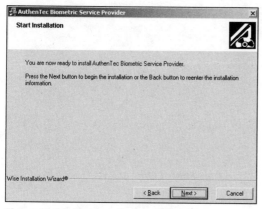

**Figure 12-54:** Start Installation window

Click the Next button to begin the file copy process shown in Figure 12-55.

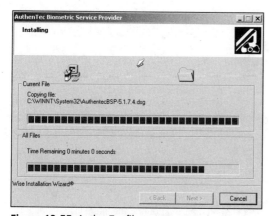

**Figure 12-55:** AuthenTec file copy process

After all the files have been successfully copied, the AuthenTec BSP installation continues automatically to the Finish window displayed in Figure 12-56.

Clicking the Finish button causes the next BSP install to begin. For PQR, the remaining two BSP installations were completed. Clicking Finish displayed the SAF2000 installation complete screen shown in Figure 12-57.

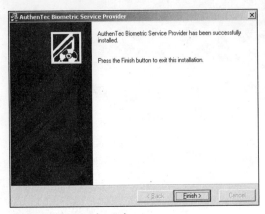

**Figure 12-56:** Finish window

**Figure 12-57:** SAF2000 install complete screen

The SAF2000 installation has been completed. Click OK. You may now be prompted to reboot. If you are not, we recommend that you reboot anyway. Oftentimes, this may illustrate a potential problem earlier than may otherwise be seen. After rebooting the PQR server, we proceeded to the client install.

If the Administration utilities had not been installed on the server during the initial PQR installation, we would have installed them next.

**INSTALL ADMINISTRATION SOFTWARE ON SERVER (FOR ENROLLMENT)**   This step was completed during the Server installation; proceed to the SAF2000 software configuration step.

**CONFIGURE SAF2000 SOFTWARE**   Before actually trying to authenticate using any devices, the SAF2000 software must be configured. This is accomplished using the Administration tools. To begin this process for the PQR case study, we went to Start menu → Programs → SAF2000 → SAFELINK Server Manager. This displays the SAFLink Biometric Server Manager window shown in Figure 12-58.

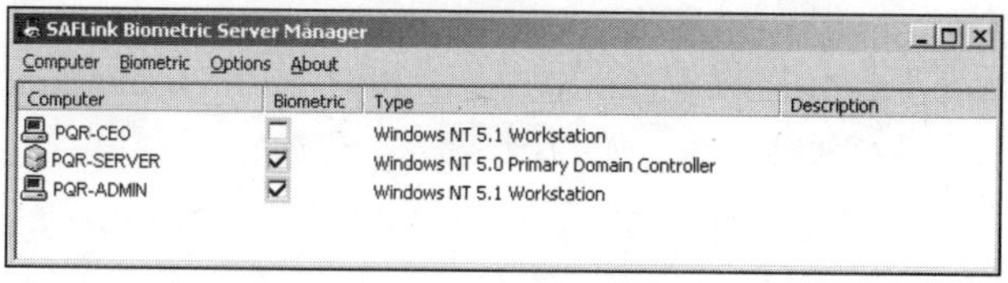

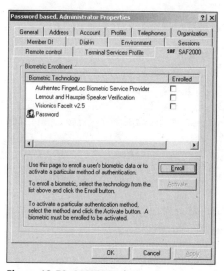

**Figure 12-58:** SAFLink Server Manager window

Select the systems that will participate in the biometric authentication process by ensuring that the associated checkbox in the "Biometric" column contains a check. Once all the appropriate systems have been selected, close SAFLink Biometric Server Manager, and proceed to Active Directory Users and Computers.

Earlier in this case study, we recommended changing the default Administrator. We used PAdministrator in place of Administrator, and a strong password (16 random characters). Select the PAdministrator user. Select the SAF2000 tab that now appears because SAF2000 is installed. This is illustrated in Figure 12-59.

**Figure 12-59:** SAF2000 tab

Also notice that there are four options under the SAF2000 tab: -AuthenTEC FingerLoc Biometric Service Provider, Learnout and Hauspie Speaker Verification, Visionics FaceIt V2.5, and Password. Password is the default authentication method. To enroll users, select one of the biometric options and click the Enroll button. We will illustrate an enrollment using the fingerprint sensor.

**PERFORM ENROLLMENT PROCESS**    The enrollment process is very straightforward. Click once on the AuthenTEC FingerLoc Biometric Service Provider option shown in Figure 12-59, and then click the Enroll button. This displays the window shown in Figure 12-60.

**Figure 12-60:** AuthenTec enrollment wizard

Click Next to continue to the enrollment screen shown in Figure 12-61.

**Figure 12-61:** Placing a finger on the sensor

A prompt appears, requesting the user to place their finger on the sensor. This will occur three times for the first finger. Once three successful fingerprint acquisitions have occurred, the currently grayed out Finish button changes to a Next button. Click on the Next button to continue.

The user is then prompted to enroll another fingerprint. Repeat the process for the second finger-print. Once the fingerprints of two fingers have been successfully acquired, the Finish button appears. Clicking on Finish (if the defaults of SAF2000 were used) displays the warning message shown in Figure 12-62.

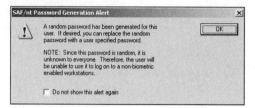

**Figure 12-62:** Password Generation Alert

In essence, this alert warns the enrollee that the current password will be replaced with a ran-domly generated password (the default is 14 characters). This makes it very difficult for anyone to share the password, as it is not shared even with the enrollee.

After at least one successful enrollment (we recommend several), proceed to an enrollment PC.

We do not recommend initially enrolling all administration accounts until verification of the installation and enrollment process has occurred. Upon successful verification of the enrollment and identification/authentication process using client access, complete the enrollment process for all users. Ensure that one of the passwords for one administrator is changed to a known (16-character password recommended) password for recovery purposes.

**INSTALL ADMINISTRATION SOFTWARE ON WORKSTATIONS (ENROLLMENT WORKSTATIONS)**
Enrollments can be performed at designated workstations rather than at the server. Although this provides convenience, it can create additional security challenges. Therefore, it is extremely important to ensure machines that can perform enrollments are secure both physically and logi-cally, and that any enrollments are planned, scheduled, supervised, monitored, documented, and witnessed.

Do not allow the enrollment process to be compromised. If the enrollment process has been com-promised, we recommend at the very minimum that all accounts be re-verified for appropriate access policies, and that a complete re-enrollment be performed.

To begin the utilities installation, go into the enrollment PC as an administrator. Install the Microsoft Administrative Tools for the appropriate operating system running on the PC. These tools provide administrative tools for the 2000 server environment, including Active Directory Users and Computers.

If appropriate, the SAF2000 utilities (SAFLINK Server Manager) can also be installed on the PC. This can be done by using the step process defined earlier and selecting only the SAF2000 Administrative Utilities radio button. Once the utilities have been installed, install the SAF2000 client software.

**INSTALL CLIENT SOFTWARE ON WORKSTATIONS**    The minimum recommended system requirements for the client installation are:

- ✓ Pentium I 120 MHz
- ✓ 64MB RAM
- ✓ 80MB hard disk space
- ✓ Windows NT 4, 2000 or XP Professional

**INSTALL CLIENT SOFTWARE ON SERVER AND TEST**    The client is the software component that enables the workstations (or server) to leverage the biometric (SAF2000) identification/authentication installed on the server. Without the client, a workstation could still authenticate to the server using password-only authentication. However, if all users have enrolled and all passwords have been randomly generated, this would be extremely difficult. So, the client must be installed on each workstation and the server if each will use biometric identification.

Before actually installing the client software, however, it is recommended that all appropriate biometric acquisition device drivers be installed, as was the case with the server install. Install or verify that the following have been completed:

- ✓ Sound card drivers have been installed and the sound card is functional.
- ✓ Microphone is functional (this can be accomplished using Microsoft Sound Recorder).
- ✓ Web camera drivers are installed and the Web camera is functional.
- ✓ AuthenTec Fingerprint Sensor USB drivers have been installed and are recognized (outlined in the server section of this chapter).

After successfully verifying the above, reboot as appropriate, and begin the client install. To install the client software, insert the SAF2000 CD and proceed through the stepped process outlined earlier in the SAF2000 installation section of this chapter. Upon reaching the SAF2000 Component Type Selection window, select the radio button next to "SAF2000 Client." This is shown in Figure 12-63.

The client installation continues using the default options for the PQR install. The installation continues in much the same manner as the server installation process in that once the appropriate files have been copied, the Biometric Solution Provider selection screen appears. Select the same options as illustrated in the server section of this chapter (AuthenTec Fingerprint, LH Voice, and Visionics FaceIt). Continue the installation until each BSP has completed. At the end of the installation, a reboot prompt appears. By default, No is selected, so the machine will not reboot. We recommend performing the reboot (if the enrollment process has already been completed for a user that can log in to this machine).

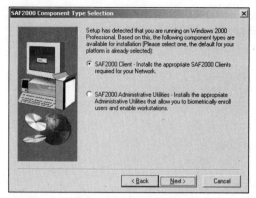

**Figure 12-63:** SAF2000 Component Type Selection window

After the reboot, the following changed login screen appears, as shown in Figure 12-64.

**Figure 12-64:** Begin Logon screen

Pressing Ctrl+Alt+Del initiates the logon process. The Logon Information window appears, as shown in Figure 12-65.

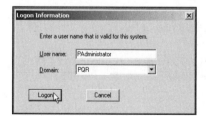

**Figure 12-65:** Logon Information window

Select the appropriate user name and domain (PAdministrator and PQR for this case study) and click Logon. Because the user PAdministrator has previously been enrolled, fingerprint authentication can occur. Clicking Logon causes the fingerprint authentication window to appear, as shown in Figure 12-66.

**Figure 12-66:** Fingerprint authentication window

To be identified, PAdministrator must authenticate using one of the fingers that PAdministrator enrolled with by simply placing their finger on the sensor. When the fingerprint acquisition occurs and the acquired fingerprint matches that of one enrolled for PAdministrator, the user is identified, authentication occurs and access is granted.

Subsequent to ensuring that identification can occur using the biometric identification system, return to the enrollment process and complete enrollment for the remaining users. This does not have to be completed all at once, but a schedule should be defined to ensure that all users ultimately get enrolled.

**DOCUMENT RESULTS**    All successful implementations are based on sound planning. A large portion of such a success hinges on proper documentation — not just for the installation, but for each step, roadblock, hurdle, and problem encountered. By documenting along the way, with proper timelines, a map of sorts begins to appear. This map can be used to limit the scope and time that may be involved in completing the implementation and/or resolving issues in a timely fashion.

It is also likely that certain users may have difficulties that prevent them from enrolling. These issues should be documented, and their alternative method of identification should also be documented.

Finally, documenting the process along the way allows an installation summary to be generated. This summary can be used to quickly recover/re-install in the event of a failure should a restore also fail.

## CONSIDERATIONS

So now PQR has a working biometric solution. In the case study for PQR Corporation, no remote identification/access was needed. However, in many organizations this is a requirement. When these requirements exist, there are some key considerations.

✓ Remote access — Will biometric authentication be needed for remote access? If so, how will the biometric template be transmitted? Does the remote access solution support such authentication? If the remote access solution does not support biometric templates being transmitted, an alternative might be to use local biometric identification and also use the biometric identification for VPN identification. This can help ensure that the person accessing the VPN was at least originally who they said they were.

✓ Remote administration — If remote administration is a requirement, consider the same identification issues outline in remote access. Also consider that remote administration by default insinuates Administrator privileges (although this does not have to be true). Therefore, additional layers of security may be needed. One possible solution might be to use voice authentication over phone lines.

✓ Periodic enrollment — Although biometric solutions can pretty much eliminate password resets and password-related help desk calls, it is still wise to re-enroll users periodically. This achieves two goals.

✓ First, users must re-identify using the predefined enrollment process. This means that they will have to produce proof of who they are, and the enrollment process will be re-documented.

✓ Second, biometric templates and the user's traits can change slightly. Re-enrollment often reduces false rejects.

## OUTSIDE OF SCOPE KEY SECURITY NOTES

SAF2000 can automatically change passwords to unknown passwords. The default is 14 characters, but can be modified. We recommend at least 16 characters and using random passwords.

If remote Administration was needed, we recommend using VPN and authentication from the workstation that leverages the biometric (although in our case study, this is not needed).

Any remote control programs such as Terminal Services or Citrix should be installed on separate devices.

Leave at least one password-only account with a very strong (16 or more mixed characters, numbers, and special characters) password.

# Expanding the Case Study

In the previous case study, we discussed how to implement a biometric solution when one server is involved. However, if more servers and hundreds of users are involved, it is relatively easy to expand this scenario to include each server to incorporate the additional users. The solution can also be implemented to allow for distributing the biometric identification/authentication load.

One example would be to install SAF2000 on multiple servers and choose which users each SAF2000 server will handle. In this fashion, the load can be manually distributed. Likewise, for branch offices, SAF2000 can be installed on the local authentication servers and these servers can provide biometric authentication for the branch users while maintaining the Active Directory schema.

Finally, SAF2000 can handle a mixed Novell and Microsoft environment, allowing identification and authentication to both platforms.

## Final Notes

Although our case study displays implementing SAF2000 as a potential solution, it is definitely not the only possible biometric solution. It is important to work with savvy consultants and biometric solution providers. Like doctors, we recommend getting at least a second opinion.

# Summary

A lot of ground was covered in this chapter. PQR Corporation defined a need or user identification based on issues previously incurred. There were some specific and unique issues to be dealt with in the PQR environment. The users were not very open to Iris scan technology, the clean room precluded using fingerprint technology and, in some cases, face recognition technology. To overcome these, the solution incorporated fingerprint biometric technology for those that could use it, face technology for those that could not use fingerprint technology, and voice technology for those that could not use either fingerprint or face technology. Keystroke dynamics was ruled out because the CEO preferred to eliminate passwords if possible. Additionally, no other features were required (such as Web page password replacement), but development options were included as part of the evaluation to allow future uses of the biometric technologies in the environment.

After determining which technologies could be used in the environment and ensuring that future development could be accommodated, we selected SAF2000 for its ability to integrate multiple biometric acquisition technologies and because it contained a SDK (SAFtransactions) to allow future development.

After verifying that all the appropriate steps were taken, we proceeded with the installation of the necessary components, including SQL, biometric acquisition device drivers, SAF2000, administration tools. Once SAF2000 was installed, we verified that users could enroll using fingerprint technology.

Upon successful enrollment of a user, the administration software was installed on a workstation to allow enrollments to occur on PCs other than the server. The client software was also installed on the workstation, and identification began using the PAdministrator account, which was previously set up for fingerprint authentication.

Finally, we outlined how this style of biometric implementation could be expanded on to incorporate many more users and file servers.

In conclusion, we hope the information contained in this chapter, as well as the previous chapters, helps you make sound choices and decisions relating to biometric technologies and provides a solid foundation from which to begin the planning and implementation process.

# Appendix A

# What's on the Web Site

THE COMPANION WEB SITE to this book contains links to the additional material, tools, source code, and matrix spreadsheets mentioned in this book. You find it at www.wiley.com/compbooks/chirillo.

For more information, independent studies, advisories, and biometric solutions, visit www.TigerTools.net.

## TigerSign

Depending on your requirements, implementing a biometric signature system can be an onerous task; if you use the products discussed in the book, however, the process can be quite simplistic. The source is available as a kernel module for you to customize for your own proprietary implementations. TigerSign is the first on-screen mouse-signing behavioral biometric system that also supports tablets and touch-screens. With TigerSign, you can implement signature recognition into any application, adjust the error-acceptance level, and add two-factor or strong authentication by adding a logon password, passphrase, or PIN.

## TigerHandPrint and HandPrintCompare

The book contains topics on configuring TigerHandprint Analysis for custom handprint authentication. The handprint scanner kernel adheres to a layered approach for interoperability with different vendor devices that support the Technology Without An Interesting Name (TWAIN) standard. This scanning control is easy to use and can acquire images from most TWAIN-compliant devices. The TWAIN scanner interface is an industry standard interface used by Windows for the transfer of data — usually graphical in nature — from scanning devices (flatbed scanners, digital cameras, hand scanners, and so on) directly into applications that can use this data.

# Voice

As mentioned throughout the book, voice-scan authenticates a user based on his or her voice characteristics, while speech recognition is used for the technological comprehension of spoken words. The latter can be used with an authentication system to add additional security for command execution, such as in opening files and performing system functions. With that said, the Web site contains a voice recognition developing kit that can be customized for proprietary development. The kit contains three main modules for the framework: recognizing, enrolling, and administering speech patterns and templates.

# FacePrint and TigerHide

The first piece of the steganography puzzle — in regard to discussions in the book — is to acquire a biometric faceprint. The module source provided on the Web site (and in Chapter 9) can be used as a generic foundation for snapping an image with a digital camera or Web cam that's already configured to work with your system. The code utilizes the Wang Laboratories and Kodak Imaging Controls from IMGSCAN.OCX — which comes as part of MS Imaging and can be used to capture input from any TWAIN-compatible device (such as cameras).

TigerHide is simply a source software development kit (SDK) of kernel modules that you can freely modify to use in your own development. Other precompiled steganography programs and trial software can be downloaded from the Internet, such as the well-liked S-Tools from `www.pcworld.com/downloads/file_download/0,fid,4699,fileidx,1,00.asp`.

# Login and Login2

Use Login and Login2 for adding a login/password dialog to projects. The types of login dialog box modules referred to in the book can easily be implemented into your custom projects. In the first example, Login, the password, *Password1*, is compiled with the source for added security — this form of authentication requires case-sensitive input but only for the password. The username is not required.

In Login2, the form of authentication requires case-sensitive input for the username and password. Data is stored in a hidden Microsoft Access database file. This project uses ActiveX Data Objects (ADO).

# DevKit

As an example of a complete working development kit with source, the book presented the Anveshak system by Vikrant Thakker. You can use this kit to develop a single or multifactor biometric system, and you can even add a two-factor login dialog box. The Anveshak project is an open system that can be used to analyze and classify hand-written characters and input patterns.

It analyzes the input pattern in terms of mouse movement information as well as the speed with which it was entered.

# Matrices

A technology security matrix can be used to evaluate each biometric technology. You can download compilation matrices from the companion Web site and modify them to suit your environment. We recommend using this type of logic outside the performance evaluation criteria to gain a good understanding of which technology makes the most sense from a security perspective. In using a technology security matrix, a good idea is to limit the scope of the matrix to be pertinent to the type of technology being evaluated. The reason is that components of the technology may not apply across technology boundaries.

A selection matrix is also provided and can be downloaded from the Web site to assist in determining which type of solution or solutions best fit your requirements, as entered into the matrix. This matrix is not meant to be an all-encompassing tool that includes every possible scenario but rather a solid foundation on which to build your own evaluation criteria.

## Take-Grant Matrix

In addition to the matrices that can be used to assist in the biometric selection process, we have also included a take-grant matrix that you can use as a template. This template can be modified based on your specific environment and provide a baseline from which you can build your security methodology.

The matrix spreadsheets require Microsoft Excel with macros enabled. For more information on macros and safety measures, visit `http://search.office.microsoft.com/result.aspx?qu=macro`.

# Index

*continued*

*continued*

continued